List p. 296

C Hede p. 174
D. Heate p174

Import
Competition
and Response

A Conference Report
National Bureau of
Economic Research

Import
Competition
and Response

Edited by   Jagdish N. Bhagwati

The University of Chicago Press

Chicago and London

JAGDISH N. BHAGWATI is the Arthur Lehman Professor of
Economics and director of the International Economic Research
Center at Columbia University. He is the editor of the *Journal of
International Economics*.

The University of Chicago Press, Chicago 60637
The University of Chicago Press, Ltd., London
© 1982 by The National Bureau of Economic Research
All rights reserved. Published 1982
Printed in the United States of America
89 88 87 86 85 84 83 82   5 4 3 2 1

Library of Congress Cataloging in Publication Data
Main entry under title:

Import competition and response.

(A conference report/National Bureau of Economic Research)
Papers presented at the National Bureau of
Economic Research Conference on Import Competition
and Adjustment: Theory and Policy held in Cambridge,
Mass., May 8–11, 1980.
Bibliography: p.
Includes indexes.
1. Trade adjustment assistance—Congresses.
I. Bhagwati, Jagdish N.   II. National Bureau of
Economic Research Conference on Import Competition
and Adjustment: Theory and Policy (1980: Cambridge,
Mass.)   III. Series: National Bureau of Economic
Research conference report.
HF1421.I47   382.5   81-21831
ISBN 0-226-04538-2   AACR2
ISBN 0-226-04539-0 (pbk.)

Since this volume is a record of conference proceedings, it has been exempted from the rules governing critical review of manuscripts by the Board of Directors of the National Bureau (resolution adopted 6 July 1948, as revised 21 November 1949 and 20 April 1968).

Contents

Preface

The present volume is the result of the National Bureau of Economic Research Conference on Import Competition and Adjustment: Theory and Policy, which was held in Cambridge, Massachusetts, 8–11 May 1980.

Supported financially by the Ford Foundation, the conference was aimed at developing theoretical concepts and ideas concerning the topic of import competition, defined broadly to include different types of economic responses to the fact of import competition. Thus, international economic theorists of distinction were invited to model processes such as lobbying relative to import competition, for instance. The volume therefore addresses a number of theoretical issues that are fairly novel and which also bear on policy questions, in many cases fairly directly.

For making the conference highly successful and a pleasant experience, Kirsten Foss of the NBER and Maureen Ryan of MIT deserve special thanks. Maureen Kay of the NBER provided cheerful and prompt help through the year that preceded the conference. Won Chun of Columbia helped ably with the finalization of the volume for the University of Chicago Press. Anne Spillane assisted cheerfully with the publication of the volume. Peter Ruof of the Ford Foundation was, as always, extremely generous with his ideas and deserves special thanks.

Finally, Robert Feenstra worked through all the papers and spotted numerous errors in spelling, algebra, and economics. His conscientious and acute reading of the papers has improved the quality of the volume immeasurably.

Jagdish N. Bhagwati

1   Introduction

Jagdish N. Bhagwati

As the threat of "new protectionism" has grown during the 1970s and the governments of most developed countries are struggling to keep intact the "liberal international economic order" of the three postwar decades, the question of import competition has risen to the forefront of policy discussions. A great body of literature has developed in response to this reality, most of which is empirical and often consists of case studies. What has been missing is the development of a corpus of respectable theoretical work that conceptualizes the issues raised by import competition and enables the empirical analyst to examine the phenomenon of import competition insightfully. It is this task that the bulk of the papers in this volume aim to fulfill.

There are, indeed, three major empirical papers at the end of the volume. They provide important insights into the adjustment processes set into motion by import competition, as in Dore's simply splendid account of the Lancashire town of Blackburn, in decline since the beginning of the century (chapter 11); into the complex mosaic of reality that constrains and determines the impact of real-life adjustment assistance programs, as in Richardson's masterly analysis of the working of trade adjustment assistance under the United States Trade Act of 1974 (chapter 12); and into the political economy of protectionist demands in response to imports, as in the informed account by Verreydt and Waelbroeck of the European Community situation vis-à-vis imports of manufactures from the developing countries (chapter 13). These papers can be read with great pleasure and profit.

Jagdish N. Bhagwati is the Arthur Lehman Professor of Economics at Columbia University. He has written on trade theory, developmental theory and policy, internal and international migration, and education models. He is editor of the *Journal of International Economics* and author (with T. N. Srinivasan) of *Lectures on the Theory of International Trade*, to be published by MIT Press.

But the central thrust of the volume is provided by the theoretical contributions. How do these relate to one another? In what follows, therefore, these theories are brought into a coherent whole, so that the reader is not baffled by the different approaches that many of them take to the problem at hand but rather sees them within a common framework. To do this, we begin by first reviewing the "traditional" textbook approach to import competition and then contrasting the contributions in this volume to that.

1.1   The Traditional Perspective

The "pure," traditional core of international trade theory on the subject of import competition is set out readily as follows. In figure 1.1, a shift in the external terms of trade, lowering the relative price of the importable good, leads to a shift in production along the long-run production possibility curve AB from P_1 to P_2. This shift furthermore represents a welfare-improving move in the Pareto sense. A system of lump-sum transfers could improve someone's welfare without reducing that of others; the standard procedure is to use a well-behaved social utility function to demonstrate the welfare gain.

The theory of trade and welfare, as exemplified in the work of Bhagwati, Ramaswami, Srinivasan, Johnson, etc., can then be used to consider different market imperfections that require policy intervention such that the terms of trade improvement indeed translate into a welfare-improving move. For example, in such an analysis of a generalized sticky wage à la Brecher, different policy interventions can be rank-ordered according to their impact on welfare.

1.2   Alternative Extensions of Traditional Analysis

The papers in this volume make important departures from this traditional perspective, modifying the theory in several realistic and policy-oriented ways.

1.2.1   Adjustment Paths

The papers by Neary (chapter 3) and Mussa (chapter 4) essentially model the *path* that the economy would take in going from P_1 to P_2 in figure 1.1 and discuss the issue of "adjustment costs" and the rationale for governmental policy intervention by reference thereto. "Adjustment costs" are to be distinguished in their work as being *either* costs that arise from the socially necessary utilization of resources to make the transition (as in Mussa) such that, *over* the time path, the net production of goods is inferior to the long-run possibility curve AB and unavoidably so, *or* those that arise from the inescapable constraints on the rate at which capital at

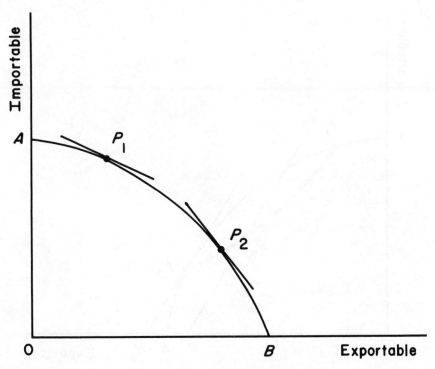

Fig. 1.1

P_1 can be shifted (via depreciation in one sector and net investment in the other) to P_2 (as in Neary's basic model), *or* those that arise from *market imperfections* of the kind additionally modeled in Mussa and alternatively in Neary. The former two kinds of adjustment costs are socially necessary, and they may be estimated, as Neary suggests, as the present discounted value of the equivalent-variational measure of the loss along the path vis-à-vis the optimal, long-run shift to P_2. (E.g., in figure 1.2, at P_3 on the adjustment path from P_1 to P_2, the loss at the new terms of trade is QR; this cost, and others corresponding to each point at different moments of time on the path $P_1 P_3 P_2$, would be discounted back to their current value to get the measure of the adjustment cost.) On the other hand, the market imperfections add an avoidable loss to this measure of the adjustment cost and equally entail a set of policy measures that should, in principle, eliminate this loss, as indeed discussed by both Mussa and Neary for their respective market imperfections. In devising these policy measures, both authors of course continue assuming implicitly or explicitly the possibility of lump-sum transfers, thus holding on to this critical element of traditional argumentation, which is instead what is relaxed in the work of some of the other papers in the volume.

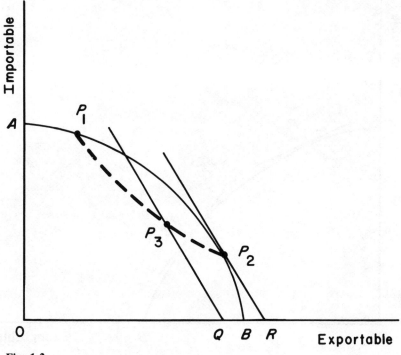

Fig. 1.2

The important paper of Bruno (chapter 2), in contrast, does not consider policy questions explicitly but addresses itself to the response of an economy to import competition, modeling the economy in the framework of macrodisequilibrium along the lines pioneered by Barro and Grossman and developed further by the so-called French school. Hence, conceptually, the economy is working in a "fix-price" system, i.e., subject to *market imperfections*, so that the adjustment costs in Bruno's analysis must reflect this set of assumptions rather than the Mussa-Neary type of socially necessary utilization of resources underlying the transition between two situations, before and after the goods price change implied by import competition.

1.2.2 Lobbying Responses

Other papers in this volume approach the problem at hand by formally introducing into the analysis of import competition not the distinction between the time path of adjustment and the instantaneous shift to the long-run equilibrium, but rather the possibility of lobbying that is triggered off by the income distributional and related implications of the shift in import competition (construed formally as an exogenous shift in the external terms of trade). Such lobbying itself uses real resources—and this resource diversion may be on a steady-state basis since lobbying is likely to be needed on a continuous basis to keep certain policy interventions in place—and will frequently be successful in getting its sought-after policy interventions implemented. Therefore an alternative concept of adjustment costs follows: namely, the social waste that accrues vis-à-vis the optimal long-run equilibrium without such lobbying and the policy distortions that probably result from such lobbying.

Two papers that formally model the lobbying response to import competition, as well as its welfare implications, are by Feenstra-Bhagwati (chapter 9) and Findlay-Wellisz (chapter 8). Whether lobbying will actually materialize, and in what likely form, is discussed in the papers by Bhagwati (chapter 6) and Krugman (chapter 7) from different angles and utilizing very different implicit and explicit models of the economy. (The Dore paper, on the other hand, gives a beautiful account of the process of adjustment, and hence also of the different lobbying groups, in the Lancashire town of Blackburn.) The Baldwin paper (chapter 10) again, in its elegant synthesis of the existing work on the political economy of protectionism, offers much that is useful in explaining the existence of different kinds of lobbying responses to import competition.

While the Findlay-Wellisz paper formally considers a Madisonian problem in a Jones-Neary model where the landed interests and the capitalists in the manufacturing sector are locked in lobbying combat, with one seeking protection and the other resisting it, it is easy to recast the analysis such that, in response to import competition, the class that is damaged by the terms of trade improvement seeks to lobby for a tariff so as to restore its real wages whereas the other seeks to maintain its improved earnings. The Findlay-Wellisz analysis leads to a tariff-equilibrium, with the government "acquiescing" in the outcome, whose welfare implications are then examined in the customary fashion: with the aid of a well-behaved social utility function. The "adjustment costs" in this model can then be defined, simply and meaningfully, as the equivalent-variational difference between the nonlobbying long-run equilibrium after the postulated terms of trade shift and the actual outcome with the lobbying process and its distortionary outcome both in place. By contrast, the Feenstra-Bhagwati paper analyzes the traditional 2×2 model and assumes that the factor damaged by the terms of trade change will be able to lobby for a tariff (up to the point of restoring it but not beyond), and then works out the lobbying-inclusive tariff equilibrium that will emerge. However, while the "adjustment cost" as just defined in the context of the Findlay-Wellisz model can also be deduced from this lobbying-inclusive equilibrium vis-à-vis the nonlobbying equilibrium at the new terms of trade, Feenstra-Bhagwati develop the analysis in a very different direction, examining whether the government can improve on the lobbying equilibrium by utilizing the tariff revenues (generated by the successful lobbying itself) to bribe labor into accepting a lower-cost tariff that, with the bribe, will yield a payoff identical to that yielded by the pure lobbying equilibrium (in the absence of such a bribe); an exercise that represents yet a different class of innovation (to be discussed below).

While the lobbying in the Feenstra-Bhagwati and Findlay-Wellisz papers is for tariffs, the lobbying response to a situation of import competition is by no means confined to this. The Bhagwati paper, for instance, opens up the possibility that, in labor-intensive industries in particular, given the fact that it is governmental policy to control immigration, a response by entrepreneurial lobbies to increasing competition from abroad may well be to ask the government to relax the immigration quotas and to let in more *gastarbeiters*, for instance. Bhagwati formally analyzes the welfare consequences when this lobbying response is successful, contrasting the outcome with that under a successful tariff-seeking response; and, in each case, the "adjustment cost" of the chosen response can be defined vis-à-vis the case where the economy is allowed to shift without lobbying to the traditional long-run equilibrium at the improved terms of trade. Bhagwati, like Findlay-Wellisz, formally assesses the welfare impact again by reference to a well-behaved social utility function.

1.2.3   Policy Intervention in the Absence of Lump-sum Taxation

It is fair to say that the theoretical papers reviewed above generally assume (1) either (as in Mussa and Neary, following the traditional analysis in Bhagwati, Johnson, et al.) that the government will be able to intervene with suitable policy requiring subventions from the budget, if necessary, without there being a revenue constraint or any constraint on the ability to raise lump-sum revenues; (2) or (as in Findlay-Wellisz and Feenstra-Bhagwati) that the government will *not* intervene, using lump-sum transfers, to "bribe" the offending lobby into accepting the Pareto-better, long-run improvement from the terms of trade.

But two theoretical papers depart from this extreme set of assumptions and consider whether the government can improve the situation without utilizing lump-sum transfers. The Feenstra-Bhagwati paper does this in the context of the lobbying activities, arguing that the tariff revenue in the lobbying equilibrium can itself be utilized, in an earmarked fashion, to "bribe" (in a Stackelberg fashion) the lobby into accepting a welfare-improving tariff outcome. On the other hand, the Diamond paper (chapter 5) takes a model with no role for lobbying but takes the modern public-finance-theoretic approach to ask: If the shift to the new long-run equilibrium results in an income distribution that cannot be fixed by lump-sum transfers to achieve a Pareto-superior outcome where someone is actually better off and others are not actually worse off, is there a suitable mix of policy instruments that can achieve a second-best outcome? His model thus explores a mix of two policy instruments: a production subsidy to improve the incomes of those remaining in an industry whose relative prices have fallen due to import competition, and a subsidy on moving out that serves principally to offset the deleterious effect of the production subsidy on the incentive to move to an industry whose prices have increased; the revenue cost of the two subsidy instruments being financed by a poll tax that is nondistortionary. Note two differences from the Feenstra-Bhagwati approach. (i) The poll tax does away with the revenue constraint in the Diamond model; of greater empirical relevance could be an analysis of the combined effects of a tariff on the import-competing industry (in lieu of the production subsidy) and the outward-movement subsidy, with the revenue from the tariff financing the subsidy on mobility so that no poll tax would have to be relied upon to raise the revenues, as is in fact done in the Feenstra-Bhagwati analysis. (ii) In Feenstra-Bhagwati the revenue is used as a "bribe" to secure a lower-cost outcome by inducing the lobby into modifying their wasteful lobbying activities, whereas in the Diamond model the subsidies (as in analyses like that of Mussa-Neary) are simply used to induce economic agents into taking decisions that are in the welfare-improving direction in accordance with the specified social welfare function.

1.3 Concluding Remarks

This volume offers a rich and variegated menu for those who wish to think seriously about the various responses to import competition. In addition, the volume contains analyses of important recent developments in the theory of international trade, albeit in discussing the topic of import competition. Thus, for example, the Krugman paper and the Comments to it by Lancaster, Mussa, and Chipman (chapter 7) offer a comprehensive and penetrating analysis of the recent theories of trade in "similar products." Again, the papers of Findlay-Wellisz (chapter 8) and Feenstra-Bhagwati (chapter 9) offer analyses that bear directly on the recent developments in the theory of trade and welfare which relate to lobbying and other directly unproductive, profit-seeking (DUP) activities (Bhagwati 1980, 1982).

References

Bhagwati, J. N. 1980. Lobbying and welfare. *Journal of Public Economics* 14: 355–63.
_____. 1982. Directly-unproductive profit-seeking activities: A welfare-theoretic synthesis and generalization. *Journal of Political Economy* (forthcoming).

I. Adjustment Processes and Policies: Theoretical Issues

2   Import Competition and Macroeconomic Adjustment under Wage-Price Rigidity

Michael Bruno

A fall in import prices constitutes an improvement in the terms of trade and is welfare increasing when wages and prices are fully flexible. Problems of internal adjustment arise when they are downward sticky and the system is not otherwise in a process of rapid change. Two kinds of short-run unemployment may occur. (1) Workers may be thrown out of jobs in the directly competing domestic industry because of a rise in the product wage. (2) Unemployment may arise as a result of contraction in a home industry which is an imperfect substitute on the demand side. The second kind of unemployment can in principle be remedied by macroeconomic expansion. Since it comes from the production side, the first type of unemployment requires a transfer of workers from the import-competing industry to the home-goods sector. In the short run this means reducing the real product wage in that sector. If the nominal wage is downward sticky but prices are upward flexible, this could, in principle, be brought about by expansionary fiscal policy (coupled with a devaluation). Under certain conditions, however, even that may not be possible if it also entails a reduction in the real consumption wage. In this as well as the other case intervention on the supply side may be required.

In practice, the employment replacement effects of the exports of NICs (newly industrialized countries) seem to have been relatively small. Since import competition is nothing new, one may ask why it has received so much more attention in recent years. A possible answer is that its effects

Michael Bruno is professor of economics at the Hebrew University, Jerusalem. His major writings are in development theory, international trade, and capital theory. He is a Fellow of the Econometric Society.

The author is indebted to Jeffrey Sachs for very helpful discussions and comments on a rough draft. Except for a few minor changes of wording the version printed here replicates the paper read at the conference. Thanks are due to Peter Neary and Pentti Kouri for illuminating discussion.

depend on the general economic environment. The supply shocks that affected industrial countries in the 1970s introduced structural adjustment problems of a kind that turn out to resemble those caused by import competition. At times of rapid growth and excess demand in both the goods and labor markets, such as the late 1960s and early 1970s, import competition could alleviate shortages and reduce inflationary pressure. By contrast, during a period of persistent slack, as after 1973, it may compound existing adjustment problems.

The aim of this paper is to clarify these issues in the context of a two-sector open economy macromodel which is analyzed in terms of the recent disequilibrium approach. Section 2.1 lays out a two sector model which incorporates a domestically producible import good and an exportable home good. The effect of a fall in import prices under nominal or real wage stickiness is analyzed within the main markets (goods, labor, and foreign exchange). We consider the differential response to import competition under the main disequilibrium regimes. We also discuss the extent to which demand management and exchange-rate (or tariff) policy can be applied. Wage subsidies and capital accumulation are discussed in section 2.3. Section 2.4 relates the theory to the environment of the 1970s and briefly considers the problem of import competition in final goods within a modified framework in which the price of key imported raw materials has risen. This helps to bring out the point that the adjustment problem depends crucially on the nature of the underlying macroeconomic environment.

2.1 Analytical Framework

The effect of import competition will here be analyzed within a conventional two-sector framework adapted to our specific purpose.[1] The import good can be produced by a perfectly competitive domestic industry whose output is denoted by X_1. With domestic consumption C_1, the excess $(C_1 - X_1)$ is imported. Producers and consumers will face a domestic price $p_1 = p_1^* e\tau$, where p_1^* is the international c.i.f. price, e is the exchange rate, and τ is a tariff factor (1 + rate of tariff).

The other sector produces a home good X_0 at price p_0. This can be used for private consumption (C_0), public consumption (G_0), or investment (I_0).[2] Unlike in the simplest two-sector model, we shall assume that this good is semitradable. It can be exported as an imperfect substitute (E_0) for a world export good whose price is p_0^*. This modification of the basic model is helpful in that it allows for a distinction between imports and exports and at the same time maintains the simplicity of a two-sector macromodel for the home economy. We now consider the main building blocks.

2.1.1 Production and Employment

We adopt the conventional short-run two-factor production framework: $X_i = X_i(L_i, K_i)$, $i = 0, 1$. Labor (L_i) is a variable factor whose total supply L is assumed to be fixed exogenously. Capital stock (K_i) in both sectors is fixed in the short run (capital accumulation is discussed in section 2.3). Labor and capital are gross complements. Denoting the nominal wage by w and allowing for a tax (subsidy) on wages ($\theta_i = 1 +$ tax rate or $1 -$ subsidy rate), we obtain the two notional labor-demand functions $L_i^d(\theta_i w/p_i, K_i)$ and the full-employment constraint

$$(1) \qquad D_L = L_0^d(\theta_0 w/p_0, K_0) + L_1^d(\theta_1 w/p_1, K_1) - L \leq 0.$$
$$ {-} {+} {-} {+}$$

For simplicity, it is assumed that when there is excess demand for labor $(D_L > 0)$, only home-good producers are rationed in the labor market, i.e., $L_0 = L - L_1^d(\theta_1 w/p_1) < L_0^d(\theta_0 w/p_0)$; in that case $\partial X_0/\partial L_0 > w/p_0$.

Figure 2.1 shows the two labor-demand curves in a box diagram whose length L marks the total labor supply. For given p_i, θ_i, K_i, the intersection

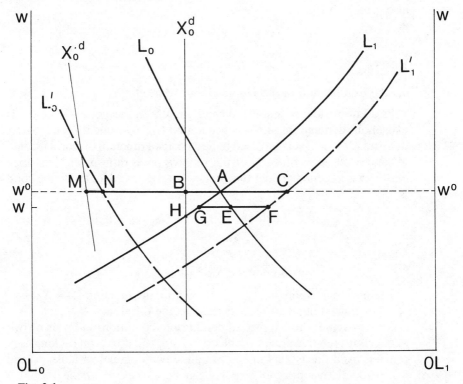

Fig. 2.1

of the two curves at A $(w = w^0)$ gives the equilibrium allocation of labor between sectors. For example, a fall in the price P_1 will shift L_1 to L'_1 and at the given wage w^0, unemployment of AC will emerge.[3] If the nominal wage were set at $w' < w^0$, there would be excess demand for labor of GE in the original position. By assumption, labor allocation would be represented by the point G, below the curve L_0, illustrating the case where $w/p_0 < \partial X_0 / \partial L_0$ (and $w/p_1 = \partial X_1 / \partial L_1$).

2.1.2 Product, Income, and Household Behavior

Nominal GNP is given by $p_0 X_0 + p_1 X_1$; real GNP in home-good units is $Y = X_0 + X_1/\pi$, where $\pi = p_0/p_1$ denotes the internal terms of trade between the two sectors. Disposable household income is $Y - T$, where T is total (direct and indirect) net taxes in the system measured in units of X_0.

Assume next that a given share c of disposable income is consumed (or $s = 1 - c$ is saved), while total consumption expenditure C is broken down into its components according to a standard consumption function $C_i^d = C_i(C, \pi)$, where $C = C_0 + C_1/\pi$. If both goods are normal and are also gross substitutes,[4] we have

(2)
$$0 < C_{ic} < 1 \qquad\qquad C_{0c} + C_{1c}/\pi = 1$$
$$C_{0\pi} < 0, \; C_{1\pi} > 0 \qquad C_{0\pi} + C_{1\pi} = C_1/\pi$$
$$C = C_0 + C_1/\pi = c(Y - T) = c(X_0 + X_1/\pi - T).$$

2.1.3 Equilibrium in the Home-Goods Market

In addition to household demand for the home good C_0, there is exogenous demand for public consumption G_0, investment I_0 and export demand E_0. The last is assumed to be a positive function of world income Y^* and a negative function of the relative price ratio p_0/ep_0^*; its price elasticity is assumed greater than unity. Total demand for the home good is

(3)
$$X_0^d = C_0[c(Y - T), \pi \,] + G_0 + I_0 + E_0(Y^*, p_0/ep_0^*),$$
$$\qquad\qquad\quad + \qquad - \qquad\qquad\qquad\qquad + \qquad -$$

where
$$Y = X_0 + X_1^s/\pi, \; X_1^s = X_1(\theta_1 w/p_1, K_1),$$
$$\text{and } X_0 = \min(X_0^d, X_0^s).$$

The notional supply of X_0 is given by a supply function $X_0^s = X_0(\theta_0 w/p_0, K_0)$. Excess demand D_0 is defined as the difference $X_0^d - X_0^s$.

It is convenient to express all equilibrium conditions in terms of two endogenous relative price variables $\pi = p_0/p_1$ and $w_1 = w/p_1$ (as long as p_1 remains fixed this is the same as using the two nominal variables p_0 and w). The relative price of exports can be expressed in the form $p_0/ep_0^* = \tau\pi/\pi^*$, where $\pi^* = p_0^*/p_1^*$ is the given international relative price ratio and τ is the import tariff factor. Similarly, the real wage in home-good units w/p_0 can be written as the ratio w_1/π. Equilibrium in the home-goods market can thus be defined as

(4) $$D_0 = X_0^d - X_0^s = D_0(\pi, w_1; z) = 0,$$

where z is the set of exogenous variables $(\pi^*, Y^*, \theta_i, K_i,$ etc.$)$.

As shown in the appendix, the assumptions made so far guarantee that excess demand will be a negative function of π $(\partial D_0/\partial \pi < 0)$, as is required by stability.

The sign of $\partial D_0/\partial w_1$ is ambiguous. While an increase in the wage rate reduces the supply of X_0, it also reduces disposable income and consumption through its effect on output in both sectors. There is no ambiguity when only wages are consumed (see Neary 1980). As shown in the appendix, $\partial D_0/\partial w_1 > 0$ iff $cC_{0c} < \beta$, where $\beta = L_0\eta_0/(L_0\eta_0 + L_1\eta_1)$ and η_i are the labor-demand elasticities. This means that the marginal propensity to consume home goods out of income is smaller than the weighted share of employment in the home-goods sector, a condition that will probably hold.[5] For convenience we shall indeed use the assumption $\partial D/\partial w > 0$, and, in the absence of a full-employment constraint, the elasticity of the D_0 curve will in that case be greater than unity.[6]

The relevant curve, marked D_0 in figure 2.2 (expressed in logarithms of π and w_1), divides the π–w_1 space into a region of excess supply (to the right of D_0) and an excess demand region (to the left of d_0). An increase in G_0, Y^*, π^*, τ, θ_0, or K_1 increases D_0, thus shifting the D_0 curve to the right, while an increase in T, θ_1, or K_0 shifts it to the left.

2.1.4 The Three Main Regimes

To give a fuller picture of the main disequilibrium regimes, the labor-market equilibrium condition is also drawn in figure 2.2, now expressed in terms of the transformed variables π and w_1:

(1′) $$D_L(\pi, w_1) = L_0^d(\theta_0 w_1/\pi, K_0) + L_1^d(\theta_1 w_1, K_1) - L \leq 0.$$
$$\quad\quad\quad\quad\quad\quad\quad - \quad + \quad\quad\quad - \quad +$$

As can easily be shown, the equilibrium D_L curve in the figure is upward sloping with elasticity $\beta = (L_0\eta_0 + L_1\eta_1)^{-1}L_0\eta_0$, which is less than unity. Below D_L there is excess demand for labor; above it there is excess supply. The curve will be pushed up by an increase in K_i or a decrease in θ_i (the case of wage subsidies).

We can now combine the information about the markets for labor and home goods in order to consider the labor market under excess supply of home goods.

When producers are constrained by the home-goods market, employment L_0 will be a positive function of X_0^d, which in turn is a negative function of the domestic (relative) price π. To maintain equilibrium in the labor market, the wage w_1 will now have to fall, rather than rise, with

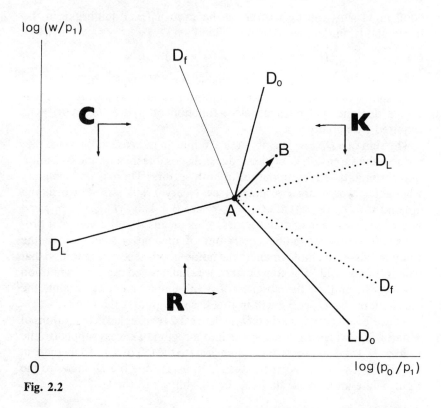

Fig. 2.2

an increase in the price π.[7] This leads to a downward sloping labor-equilibrium curve LD_0 when there is excess supply in the home-goods market. The whole of the region K, bordered by D_0ALD_0, is one of generalized excess supply in both the labor and home-goods markets (but only the part under D_L constitutes Keynesian unemployment).

Any exogenous change such as fiscal policy, shifting the D_0 curve to the right, will shift the curve LD_0 with it so that their intersection always moves along the notional full-employment line D_L (see, for example, the shift from D_0ALD_0 to $D_0'A'LD_0'$ in figure 2.3).

Next, note that by our assumption about labor allocation under rationing there will be no region in which excess supply of goods coincides with excess demand for labor.[8] The same downward sloping curve (LD_0) must thus also be the continuation of the commodity-equilibrium curve D_0 in the labor-rationing region. This leaves the whole of region R as that of generalized excess demand (Malinvaud's "repressed inflation" case).[9]

The third region C, is the familiar case of classical unemployment, combining excess demand for home goods with excess supply of labor. Since in this model the notional supply of labor is taken as fixed, demand

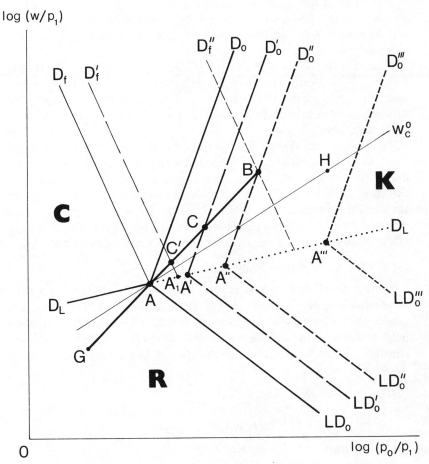

Fig. 2.3

for home goods will not depend on labor-market restrictions. The difference between actual output $X_0 = X_0^s(w_1/\pi)$ and the higher output demand X_0^d takes the form of forced private savings (i.e., $G_0 + E_0 + I_0$ will always be supplied).

2.1.5 The Current Balance of Payments

The current-account deficit is $p_1^*(C_1 - X_1) - (p_0/e)E_0$ in foreign currency terms. For convenience, we divide this by p_1^* and refer to excess demand for tradable goods D_f in real terms,

$$(5) \qquad D_f = C_1(C, \pi) - X_1(\theta_1 w_1, K_1) - \tau\pi E_0(Y^*, \pi/\pi^*)$$
$$\qquad\qquad {\scriptstyle +\ \ +} \qquad\qquad {\scriptstyle -\ \ \ +} \qquad\qquad\quad {\scriptstyle +\ \ -}$$
$$\qquad\quad = D_f(\pi, w_1; z).$$

The signs of the derivatives of this excess demand function will, in general, be ambiguous with respect to the endogenous price ratios π and w_1. As shown in the appendix, under reasonable assumptions we have $-\partial D_0/\partial \pi > \partial D_f/\partial \pi > 0$.

Next, we have $\partial D_f/\partial w_1 \gtreqless 0$ iff $1 - cC_{1c}/\pi = (1 - c) + cC_{0c} \lesseqgtr \beta$. If $\partial D_f/\partial w_1 > 0$, D_f is negatively sloped.[10] If $\partial D_f/\partial w_1 < 0$, D_f is positively sloped and its slope is greater than that of D_0. The sign of the slope makes no difference to our subsequent analysis. In the K (or the R) region the slope of D_f is definitely negative.

The line D_f in figure 2.2 relating to the equilibrium condition $D_f(\pi, w_1) = 0$ is drawn negatively sloped with deficits $(D_f > 0)$ on the right and surpluses $(D_f < 0)$ on the left. This curve will shift in the same direction as D_0 for changes in the relevant exogenous variables (z), with the exception of the sector-specific G_0 and I_0. By assumption, X_1 is never rationed and the tradable-goods market need not clear.[11] The monetary effect of changes in foreign exchange reserves will be mentioned later.

2.1.6 The Government Budget

Two types of indirect taxes, a tax (subsidy) on wages (θ_i) and tariffs (τ), have already appeared in the system. Next, assume that the government can levy a direct tax T_d which forms part of total net tax receipts (T). (This helps to allow for the net effect of an indirect tax $[\theta_i$ or $\tau]$ with total T held constant.) Denoting the government deficit by D_g (measured in X_0 units), we have

(6) $\qquad D_g = G_0 - T,$

where $T = \qquad T_d + (w/p_0)[(\theta_0 - 1)L_0 + (\theta_1 - 1)L_1]$
$\qquad\qquad + (\tau - 1)(p_1^* e/p_0)(C_1 - X_1).$

2.1.7 Savings, Investment, and Money

Full-fledged treatment of wealth formation requires detailed specification of supply and demand for physical as well as financial assets. This will not be attempted here. It is nonetheless of some help to mention the simplest links that might close the system in this respect. The savings-investment identity can be put in the form $I = S - D_g + D_f/\pi$, where $I = I_0$, $S =$ private savings, and all magnitudes are expressed in home-goods units (assume here that $\tau = 1$).

Suppose now that the current-account deficit is financed by running down reserves and the government deficit is financed by central bank credit, the sum of these assets forming the money base H. The total quantity of money M can be controlled through the money multiplier m. One can thus write

(7) $\qquad M = mH = m[H_{-1} + p_0(D_g - D_f)_{-1}]$
$\qquad\qquad = m[H + p_0(S - I)]_{-1},$

where subscript -1 indicates one-period lag.

Total investment I equals gross capital accumulation in the two sectors. For simplicity one may assume that $\Delta K_i = I^i(R_{i-1}, M/p_0) - \delta_i K_i (i = 0, 1)$ and $I = I^0 + I_1$, where R_i are profits in sector i, δ_i is the depreciation rate, and M/p_0 is a proxy for the negative effect of the rate of interest (on investment). In this way one can incorporate the effect of endogenous or planned changes in real balances in the short run as well as changes in profits on capital accumulation in the long run. Changes in K_i will only be mentioned very briefly (see section 2.3).

2.2 Analysis of Import Price Competition

Let us now consider the impact effect of a reduction in foreign prices. We begin with the case in which p_1^* and p_0^* both drop, leaving the relative price ratio π^* unaffected. The advantage of considering this case first is that such a change does not alter the general equilibrium curves in figure 2.2.[12] At given price p_0 and nominal wage level w; the effect of a fall in p_0^* is to increase the relative prices π and w by the same amount, thus moving the economy from an initial equilibrium point A along a 45° vector to, say, the point B. This point is in the Keynesian unemployment region K, with excess supply in the commodity and labor markets as well as excess demand for traded goods.

The intuitive explanation is straightforward. A fall in the import price raises the product wage in the X_1 industry, thus reducing employment and output in that sector. At given w/p_0 the potential output supply in the home-goods industry stays constant. However, the increase in the relative price of home goods reduces the demand for C_0 at a given income and the fall in product and income further reduces C_0. Also, exports must fall since p_0^* has dropped. Producers of X_0 are thus rationed in the home-goods market; employment and output drop.

Suppose the Walrasian general equilibrium point remains at A. If prices and nominal wages were fully flexible, a reduction in both of them by the rate of the decrease in foreign prices would return the economy to equilibrium. If nominal wages and prices are downward sticky, there is a policy tool that would have the same effect, namely, a devaluation (increase in e) by the amount required to bring the domestic price p_1, as well as π and w_1, back to its original value, in which case all markets return to equilibrium and all real magnitudes stay the same (the only difference now being that the foreign currency value of both imports and exports has been reduced).

Next, let us consider the more relevant case in which only the price of imports (p_1^*) falls while the price of exports (p_0^*) stays constant. This implies that the relative price π^* rises. In this case import substitutes but not exports are hurt. In terms of the general equilibrium system (see figure 2.3) the implication is that D_0 and D_f both shift to the right, to D_0' and D_f', respectively. As can be seen in the appendix, the relative shift is as shown; namely, D_f shifts to the right by less that D_0 and both shift by less than the initial change in $\log p_1^*$. The intersection of D_f' and D_L is at A_1 and that of D_0' and D_L is at A'. If wages and prices were fully downward flexible, the new short-run Walrasian equilibrium would be at A', if the economy actively borrows to cover the remaining current-account deficit, or at A_1, if foreign currency reserves are allowed to drop and the money supply is allowed to contract correspondingly (shifting D_0' and LD_0' back to the left). At any rate the point B lies in the K region with respect to either A_1 or A' just as in the previous case. But to reach an equilibrium, prices must now fall by less than wages. If wages and prices are downward rigid, a devaluation cannot by itself return the system to equilibrium. A devaluation moving the system back from B to C will get only the home-goods market into equilibrium. A further move to C' will achieve current-account balance, but an inflationary gap emerges. A devaluation all the way to A will achieve full employment with excess demand in the home-goods market and a surplus in the current account. In theory both these gaps in the home-goods and foreign exchange markets can be closed by a suitable combination of fiscal (T_d, G_0) and monetary (m) policy so that full-employment equilibrium can be achieved at A. However, this is obviously a wrong policy from the point of view of optimum resource allocation since at A the original sectoral allocation of labor would only be artificially preserved.

What if wages and prices are flexible upward and are allowed to increase from A to A' (or A_1)? The resulting reduction in the real product wage in the home-goods industry may then bring about the required transfer of workers from L_1 to L_0. There are two qualifications to this solution. One is that the economy must be willing to pay the price of some inflation for this transfer (on the assumption that it would be enough to induce workers to move from the depressed industry into the more profitable one). The other qualification has to do with the possibility of *real*, rather than nominal, wage rigidity which may prevent such a reduction in the product wage.

Suppose the consumption basket of wage earners consists of proportions α and $1 - \alpha$ of home and importable goods, respectively, so that the relevant consumption price index can be written in the form $A p_0^\alpha p_1^{1-\alpha}$, and assume that $w \geq A p_0^\alpha p_1^{1-\alpha}$. A minimum real wage line w_c^0 can thus be defined by

$$(8) \qquad \log w_1 = \log A + \alpha \log \pi.$$

This may provide an effective constraint on adjustment to full employment iff $\alpha > \beta$ where $\beta = L_0 \eta_0 / (L_0 \eta_0 + L_1 \eta_1)$, the elasticity of the full-employment line D_L. In figure 2.3 it is represented by the line w_c^0 which lies between the 45° line (AB) and D_L.[13] The higher the share α of home goods in the wage earners' consumption basket and the higher the ratio

$L_1\eta_1/L_0\eta_0$, the less likely they will be to accept the real product wage cut, in home-good units, that is required to draw more employment into the X_0 sector so as to compensate for the employment loss in the X_1 sector. If, however, $\alpha < \beta$, this problem does not arise.[14]

What is to happen in practice depends on the particular context or phase in which import competition occurs. If only a small share of C_1 is initially imported and if X_1 is a relatively labor-intensive activity or $\eta_1 > \eta_0$, we may get $\alpha > \beta$. In that case, the real wage constraint will be effective in preventing the achievement of full employment by means of exchange-rate policy and demand management alone. If, however, a relatively large share of C_1 is already imported and if labor intensities are about the same, then the share of C_1 in the consumption basket will be higher than the share of L_1 in employment, and we get $\alpha > \beta$. In that case workers may be induced to move into the home-goods industry by an increase in prices and wages due to an expansionary policy while the real consumption wage (w_c) also rises. The welfare gain of import competition will not be wasted.

How would the analysis change if the import price fall went together with expansion of the external market? What it means is that the D_f and D_0 curves both shift further to the right. An extreme case would be one in which export expansion compensated fully for the rise in imports. In figure 2.3 this is shown by curve D_f'' which passes through point B. The current account will now balance at B. If there is no intervention in the commodity market, the corresponding equilibrium curve for home goods (D_0'') must lie to the right of B so that point B will be in the classical unemployment (C) region from the start. However, with excess demand in the commodity market, prices may be free to adjust upward, while the nominal wage remains downward rigid. Whether full employment can or cannot be reached will again depend on whether a real wage constraint has to be violated. In terms of figure 2.3 the question is whether prices must go through a point such as H on the w_c^0 line (in the case $\alpha > \beta$) on the way to equilibrium.

The same consideration applies to the question whether in the absence of exchange-rate adjustments demand management alone could return the system to equilibrium. The curve D_0 can always be pushed far enough to the right from B so that at given nominal wage inflation will reduce w/p_0 sufficiently to reach full employment on the D_L line. In addition to the problem of the current account, which requires suitable fiscal treatment, the feasibility of such a policy will depend on whether a real wage constraint is or is not violated.

2.2.1 Response under Different Regimes

So far we have analyzed the effect of an import price reduction starting from an equilibrium. If the economy is initially in the K region, the adjustment difficulties are more pronounced *a fortiori*. The import price change would then increase excess supply in both the home-goods and the labor market. Things look slightly different if the initial point happens to be in the C region. Say the equilibrium set of curves is given by D_L, D_0'', and LD_0'' while the economy, initially at point C, moves to point B. Here, an import price fall removes the need for the upward adjustment in the domestic price level that would be required to eliminate excess demand in the home-goods market. However, in moving from point C to B unemployment increases just the same.

One would get the best of both worlds if the initial point happened to be in the R region, that is, if the economy started from an inflationary, generalized excess demand, situation. An import price drop, for example, a move from G to A, might serve to eliminate excess demand in both the commodity and labor markets, thus automatically producing an anti-inflationary result!

The effect of an import price change on excess demand under the various regimes is of some interest in itself. Consider first the effect on excess demand (supply) in the home-goods market. We have $\partial D_0 / \partial p_1^* = cC_{0c}(\partial Y / \partial p_1^*) - (\pi / p_1^*) C_{0\pi} - \partial X_0^s / \partial p_1^*$. Calculating $\partial Y / \partial p_1^*$ for each of the regions C, K, R and denoting the labor share in X_1 by ϕ_1, we get

$$\frac{\partial Y^C}{\partial p_1^*} = (\pi p_1^*)^{-1} X_1 (1 + \phi_1 \eta_1) \; > \; 0,$$

(9)
$$\frac{\partial Y^K}{\partial p_1^*} = (1 - cC_{0c})^{-1} \frac{\partial Y^C}{\partial p_1^*} \; > \; \frac{\partial Y^C}{\partial p_1^*},$$

$$\frac{\partial Y^R}{\partial p_1^*} = \frac{\partial Y^C}{\partial p_1^*} - \frac{1}{p_1^*} \frac{\partial X_0}{\partial L_0} \eta_1 L_1 \; < \; \frac{\partial Y^C}{\partial p_1^*}.$$

Now $\partial X_0 / \partial p_1^* = 0$ for the C and K regions but $\partial X_0^s / \partial p_1^* = -(\partial X_0 / \partial L_0)$ $\eta_1 L_1 / p_1^* < 0$ in the R region since in this case $X_0^s = X_0 (L - L_1)$.

A reduction in p_1^* thus causes income to fall and excess supply to increase more in the K than in the C region. In the R region, income either falls by less or even increases, while the increase in X_0^s (which is due to relaxation of labor rationing) helps to reduce excess demand in the R region by more than in the C region ($\partial D_0^R / \partial p_1^* < \partial D_0^C / \partial p_1^*$ by [9]) thus bringing out the potential anti-inflationary role of import price reduction under generalized excess demand.

Next, consider the current account under alternative regimes. Differentiating $(p_1^* D_f)$ with respect to p_1^*, one gets, after some manipulation,

(10)
$$\frac{\partial (p_1^* D_f)}{\partial p_1^*} = c p_1^* C_{1c} \frac{\partial Y}{\partial p_1^*} - X_1 (1 + \phi_1 \eta_1) + \pi^2 C_{0\pi}.$$

Applying the value of $\partial Y/\partial p_1^*$ given in (9) to each of the three regimes, we can conclude that (a) a fall in p_1^* increases the current-account deficit under all three regimes (the derivative in [10] is always negative); and (b) the ordering of the regimes by the size of the deficit increment is $R > C > K$.[15]

The stronger anti-inflationary effect of an import price reduction under the R regime is thus obtained at the cost of a greater deterioration in the current-account deficit, a trade-off which makes intuitive sense. The effect on excess supply of labor coming from an import price drop is the same under all three regimes ($\partial D_L/\partial p_1^* = L_1\eta_1/p_1^*$) since, by assumption, producers in the X_1 sector are always on their notional demand curve for labor.

2.2.2 Tariff Changes

The discussion of import price changes as an anti-inflationary device seems somewhat artificial since a change in p_1^* is an exogenous change over which the economy usually has no control. Suppose, however, that one applies the same argument to a planned change in the domestic price p_1 through a reduction in an existing tariff. Inspection of the underlying model shows that a change in τ works in almost exactly the same way as a change in p_1^* except for its different quantitative effect on the current account. (A 1 percent drop in τ worsens the current account by more than a 1 percent drop in p_1^*. The same applies in reverse, to the imposition of a tariff.) However, the geometrical analysis (movement along a 45° line plus rightward shift of D_0 and D_f curves) for the home-goods and labor markets works in the same way.[16]

In a similar way one can analyze the effect of a tariff imposed in order to counteract the effect of a fall in p_1^*. This is analogous to a devaluation (a move back from B along a 45° line) except that a simultaneous upward shift takes place in curves D_f and D_0. The distortionary effects of a tariff are well known and need not be repeated here.

The upshot of this section is that the effect of import competition and the problems of adjustment cannot be treated without considering the regime in which the economy happens to be when this change takes place. It will help to alleviate an inflationary situation (in both markets in an R regime and in the commodity market in a C regime). It may aggravate an existing unemployment situation (in the K or C regime) if the wage rate or the real consumption wage is downward sticky. The additional unemployment originating in the import-competing sector cannot always be removed by Keynesian demand management policies. In principle, a change in the exchange rate can be used, in conjunction with demand management, to cure unemployment, but there is always a price to be paid in terms of inflation. If the real wage constraint is effective ($\alpha > \beta$), a return to full employment would also involve resource misallocation since the adjustment to a new efficient labor allocation would then be prevented.

2.3 Supply Management and Capital Accumulation

How should the previous analysis be modified if the response of investment to changes in profits is taken into account?[17] Consider the initial experiment in which the import price falls, starting from equilibrium at A. The same forces that reduced employment in both sectors will also reduce profits and investment. This has two effects. One is a further downward pressure on aggregate demand (pushing the D_0 curve to the left), thus increasing excess supply in the home-goods and labor markets.[18] The other, long-run, effect is a fall in K_i, which reduces the optimum level of employment in both sectors. In terms of the general equilibrium picture this expresses itself in a downward pull on the D_L curve, thus exacerbating or creating unemployment. A similar analysis will hold if the economy is initially in the C region. Only in the R region could a fall in p_1^* bring about an *increase* in profits, just as it could lead to an increase in total income.

The effect on capital accumulation can be discussed in the wider context of supply management policy. As we have seen, import competition under wage (and price) rigidity leads to unemployment (except in the R region) which demand management and exchange-rate policy may not be able to solve effectively; or else it might lead to inflation. Policy measures which push up the full-employment line D_L may thus be called for. The simplest tool, in the short run, is a wage subsidy (or a reduction in employment tax) in the X_1 sector. This introduces a wedge between the product wage and the consumption wage and may enable producers to continue production of X_1 without loss. In terms of our model this implies a reduction in θ_1 and a corresponding upward shift in the D_L curve (as well as a rightward shift in the D_0 and D_f curves).[19] In principle, employment L_1 can be kept at its original level (with equilibrium at point B) if θ_1 is determined so that θ_1/p_1^* stays constant. This wage subsidy would be superior to a tariff because it avoids the distortionary tax on consumption of C_1 (see Johnson 1962; Bhagwati and Ramaswami 1963). However, it shares with the tariff the distortionary feature of freezing the productive structure (together with profits and the composition of investment).

Any measure that would help workers move out of sector X_1 into sector X_0 would be better. One candidate in the present context is a wage subsidy (or reduced employment tax) in the home-goods industry. This would decrease the product wage $\theta_0 w/p_0$ (without having to raise p_0) and thus increase X_0^s. In order to be effective, however, it must be coupled with expansionary measures or a devaluation.[20]

Another choice might be investment promotion measures to increase K_0 (e.g., investment credits). Some combination of supply management on $X_0^s(\theta_0, K_0)$, with devaluation cum fiscal policy, might be superior. To make this statement more precise involves a more extensive analysis of intertemporal choice, which is beyond the scope of this paper. (For an analysis centered on long-run adjustment, see chapters 3 and 4 of this volume).

2.4 Structural Problems of the 1970s: An Interpretation

When one leaves the theoretical framework for a moment and considers the world developments of the 1960s and 1970s, two riddles present themselves. One has to do with empirical estimates of the effect of NIC exports on employment in industrial countries. Empirical studies have invariably shown that employment-replacement effects of NIC exports are minute.[21] If they are so small, what is all the fuss about? The second riddle, which may be connected with the first, has to do with the timing of the debate. It would seem that in the 1960s, when NIC export penetration was at its most rapid, the issue of internal adjustment was not a major policy concern in OECD countries; more recently, however, it has become a major issue—at a time when the rate of penetration appears to have slowed down.[22]

A partial answer to the first question lies in the distinction between net and gross employment effects. A specific sector may be very badly affected while the net employment effect on the economy as a whole may be small or even positive (in terms of our model, consider a combination of a fall in p_1^* and a substantial increase in Y^* and K_0).

Another answer, which also relates to the second question, is the crucial role played by the general economic environment in which import competition takes place. During much of the 1960s and until 1973 industrial economies enjoyed rapid expansion of both productive capacity and external trade opportunities. More often than not, industrial economies found themselves in the R regime. Even if the business cycle would now and then throw an economy into a K regime, unemployment was never very prolonged and it was Keynesian—it could be eliminated by pure demand expansion[23] Moreover, it may be that investment behavior anticipated the need to adjust to changes in relative prices; in any event, such adjustments are easier to make when the system is expanding. The events of 1973–74 came as an unexpected shock to the system and started a period of prolonged unemployment, a good part of it classical. Under such conditions import competition imposes an extra strain on a system which is already stuck with a structural adjustment problem.

Our model can be modified so as to illustrate this point. Let us introduce an imported intermediate input N into the production of the home good; its international price is p_n^* and its relative price $\pi_n = p_n^*/p_1^* = p_n/p_1$ (with $\tau = 1$). Suppose the intermediate input and labor are cooperant factors.[24] In the labor market an increase in p_n^* will work like an increase in θ_0: it will shift the D_L curve downward (see D_L' in figure 2.4). In the commodity market the increase in p_n^* will show as a shift to the right of the D_0 curve (see the move from D_0 to D_0' in figure 2.4).[25] Both these changes shift the economy from an initial equilibrium at A into the C region (relative to the new Walrasian equilibrium at E in figure 2.4). If at the same time world demand contracts and investment demand falls (in response to lower profitability in the X_0 industry), or if demand policy is contractionary, the D_0 curve may shift to the left by more than the impact effect of p_n (move to D_0'' in figure 2.4). In that case the economy may find itself in the K region (see A relative to F), but it is important to stress that the resulting unemployment is only partly Keynesian; i.e., given real wage rigidity, pure expansionary policy may fail to restore full employment.

If import competition in X_1 is superimposed on this situation, it only magnifies the existing structural problem. In terms of the analysis of the labor market (figure 2.1), this can be shown as follows: output in the X_0 sector is now constrained along the curve $X_0'^d$, with employment L_0 at point M.[26] The notional labor demand curve has shifted to the left (L_0'). Total unemployment (MC) at the nominal wage level w^0 now consists of some purely Keynesian unemployment (MN), classical unemployment originating in the home-goods industry (NA), and some unemployment from the X_1 industry (AC). In both types of external shock it is supply management policy that may be called for.

This brief discussion may help to show why import competition has played a leading role in policy discussions in the industrial countries in recent years, a role quite out of proportion to its real long-run relative importance.

One final qualification—we have assumed all along that import competition takes place in final goods while the rise in import prices was confined to intermediate goods. This seems, by and large, an empirically reasonable assumption to make, since the bulk of export penetration is in final goods. However, where there is also import competition in intermediate goods (e.g., steel or paper), the same framework can be turned round to show that a price drop may in fact increase total employment.[27]

Appendix

Slope of the D_0 Curve

Differentiating $D_0 = X_0^d - X_0^s$ (as defined in [3] and [4]) by π, we have

$$(A1) \qquad \partial D_0/\partial \pi = cC_{0c} \frac{\partial Y}{\partial \pi} + C_{0\pi} + E_{0\pi} - X_{0\pi}.$$

log (w/p₁)

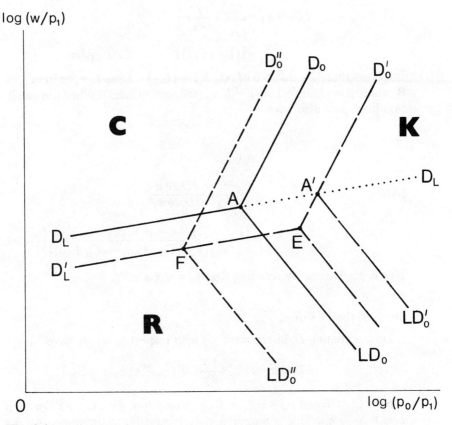

Fig. 2.4

Now $X_{0\pi} = X_0 \phi_0 \eta_0 / \pi$, and since, in the unconstrained case, $Y = X_0[L_0(w_1/\pi)] + X_1(w_1)/\pi_1$, we have

(A2) $$\partial Y/\partial \pi = X_{0\pi} - X_1/\pi^2 = (X_0 \phi_0 \eta_0 - X_1/\pi)/\pi,$$

where ϕ_0 is the elasticity of X_0 with respect to L_0 and η_0 is the demand elasticity of L_0 with respect to w/p_0. Also, $E_{0\pi} < 0$, $C_{0\pi} < 0$, by assumption, and thus

(A3) $$\partial D_0/\partial \pi = -\pi^{-1}[cC_{0c}X_1/\pi + (1 - cC_{0c})X_0 \phi_0 \eta_0]$$
$$+ C_{0\pi} + E_{0\pi} < 0.$$

Similarly, since $X_{0w_1} = -L_0 \eta_0 / \pi$ and $X_{1w_1} = -L_1 \eta_1$,

(A4) $$\partial Y/\partial w_1 = -(L_0 \eta_0 + L_1 \eta_1)/\pi < 0$$

and thus

(A5)
$$\partial D_0/\partial w_1 = cC_{0c}\left(\frac{\partial Y}{\partial w_1}\right) - X_{0w_1}$$

$$= [(1 - cC_{0c})L_0\eta_0 - cC_{0c}L_1\eta_1]/\pi.$$

It follows that $\partial D_0/\partial w_0 > 0$ iff $cC_{0c}/(1 - cC_{0c}) < L_0\eta_0/L_1\eta_1$ or iff $cC_{0c} < \beta$, where $\beta = (L_0\eta_0 + L_1\eta_1)^{-1}L_0\eta_0$ (see section 2.1.3). When this condition holds, we also have

(A6)
$$\left.\frac{\partial \log w_1}{\partial \log \pi}\right|_{D_0}$$

$$= -\frac{\pi}{w_1}\frac{\partial D_0/\partial \pi}{\partial D_0/\partial w_1}$$

$$= \frac{(1 - cC_{0c})X_0\phi_0\eta_0\pi + cC_{0c} - C_{0\pi} - E_{0\pi}}{w_1[(1 - cC_{0c})L_0\eta_0 - cC_{0c}L_1\eta_1]} > 1.$$

This is easily seen by recalling that $\phi_0 = w_1L_0/\pi X_0$.

Slope of the D_f Curve

Differentiating D_f in equation (5) with respect to π, we have

(A7)
$$\partial D_f/\partial \pi = cC_{1c}\left(\frac{\partial Y}{\partial \pi}\right) + C_{1\pi} - \tau(E_0 + \pi E_{0\pi}).$$

Now $C_{1\pi} > 0$ and $E_0 + \pi E_{0\pi} < 0$ by assumption. By (A2), $\partial Y/\partial \pi > 0$ if $\phi_0\eta_0 > X_1/\pi X_0$. This is an empirically reasonable assumption. At any rate, it is a sufficient (but by no means necessary) condition for $\partial D_f/\partial \pi > 0$.

Next,

(A8)
$$\partial D_f/\partial w_1 = cC_{1c}\frac{\partial Y}{\partial w_1} - X_{1w_1}$$

$$= (1 - cC_{1c}/\pi)L_1\eta_1 - (cC_{1c}/\pi)L_0\eta_0.$$

Thus $\partial D_f/\partial w_1 > 0$ iff $(1 - cC_{1c}/\pi)/(cC_{1c}/\pi) > L_0\eta_0/L_1\eta_1$ or iff $(1 - c) + cC_{0c} < \beta$ (see section 2.1.5). If both derivatives are positive, we get

$$\left.\frac{\partial (\log w_1)}{\partial (\log \pi)}\right|_{D_f} < 0.$$

The sign of the slope of D_f outside the C region is unambiguously negative. In the K region, we have $Y = X_0^d + X_1/\pi$ and thus $\partial Y^K/\partial w_1 = -L_1\eta_1/\pi(1 - cC_{0c}) < 0$ and $\partial Y^K/\partial \pi = (-X_1/\pi^2 + C_{0\pi} + E_{0\pi})/$

$(1 - cC_{0c}) < 0$. Then $\partial D_f/\partial w_1 = (1 - c)\eta_1 L_1/(1 - cC_{0c}) > 0$ and
$\partial D_f/\partial \pi = [C_{1\pi} - (\tau E_0 + \pi E_{0\pi})](1 - \lambda) - (\tau - 1)\pi E_{0\pi}$, where $\lambda = (cC_{1c}/\pi)/[(1 - c) + cC_{1c}/\pi] < 1$. Thus $\partial D_f/\partial \pi > 0$ unambiguously in the K region and the slope of D_f must be negative. If D_f happens to pass through the R region (e.g., if D_f is shifted to the left in figure 2.2), a similar analysis shows that its slope is negative in that region too.

Relative Shifts of D_0 and D_f When p_1^* Changes

Let us denote by $(\partial \pi^{D_0}/\partial p_1^*)$ the shift of D_0 along the π axis due to a change in p_1^*. We get

(A9) $$\frac{\partial D_0}{\partial \pi} \frac{\partial \pi^{D_0}}{\partial p_1^*} + \frac{\pi E_{0\pi}}{p_1^*} = 0.$$

Similarly,

(A10) $$\frac{\partial D_f}{\partial \pi} \frac{\partial \pi^{D_f}}{\partial p_1^*} - \pi\tau \left(\frac{\pi E_{0\pi}}{p_1^*}\right) = 0.$$

Multiply (A9) by $\pi\tau$ and add to (A10) to get

$$\pi\tau \frac{\partial D_0}{\partial \pi} \frac{\partial \pi^{D_0}}{\partial p_1^*} + \frac{\partial D_f}{\partial \pi} \frac{\partial \pi^{D_f}}{\partial p_1^*} = 0,$$

and therefore

(A11) $$\frac{\partial \pi^{D_0}}{\partial p_1^*} = -\frac{1}{\pi\tau} \left(\frac{\partial D_f/\partial \pi}{\partial D_0/\partial \pi}\right) \frac{\partial \pi^{D_f}}{\partial p_1^*}.$$

Now, from (A1) and (A7) we find $\partial D_0/\partial \pi + \pi^{-1}(\partial D_f/\partial \pi) = \pi^{-2}[(1 - c)(X_1 - \pi X_0\phi_0\eta_0) + E_{0\pi}(1 - \tau)] < 0$ for τ sufficiently close to 1, and assuming $\partial Y/\partial \pi > 0$ as before. Thus $-\partial D_0/\partial \pi > \pi^{-1}(\partial D_f/\partial \pi) \geq (\pi\tau)^{-1}(\partial D_f/\partial \pi)$. Therefore in (A11) $\partial \pi^{D_0}/\partial(p_1^*) > \partial \pi^{D_f}/\partial(p_1^*)$. Q.E.D.

Notes

1. See Helpman (1976), Bruno (1976), Brecher (1978), and Rødseth (1979) for applications of such a model in a Walrasian general-equilibrium setup. Neary (1980) has recently given a disequilibrium formulation of such a model along the lines of Malinvaud (1977). A similar approach also underlies Bruno and Sachs (1979). See also Liviatan (1979).

2. For simplicity we here assume there is no G_1 and I_1 in the X_1 sector, although these could easily be incorporated.

3. We shall show later that this is augmented by an additional contractionary effect on the demand for home goods (AB in figure 2.1).

4. This assumption could be relaxed; see Hanoch and Fraenkel (1979).

5. E.g., if $c = 0.8$, $C_{0c} = 0.9$, $C_{1c}/\pi = 0.1$, it will hold so long as $L_1\eta_1/(L_0\eta_0) < 0.39$, i.e., even if X_1 is very labor-intensive relative to X_0.

6. The alternative, with the above inequalities reversed, leads to a negatively sloped D_0 curve. This causes no particular problem, but will not be dealt with here.

7. This can be seen as follows from figure 2.1: a fall in X_0^d can be represented as a leftward shift of the vertical line X_0^d from the previous equilibrium point A to B (at given nominal wage w^0). Effective labor demand for L_0 is no longer represented by the demand curve L_0 (which will anyway shift up with a rise in p_0). Equilibrium in the labor market can take place only at the point H, where the nominal wage is below the marginal value product in the X_0 industry.

8. This would be the underconsumption (U) region in the terminology of Muellbauer and Portes (1978). The notation K, C, and R is taken from their paper.

9. If part of L_1 were also rationed, the continuation of the D_0 curve would lie to the left of LD_0 with the R region correspondingly truncated.

10. When c is close to 1, this is the same condition as in section 2.1.3, but there is no presumption that it is so here.

11. The only way in which rationing does come in is through the effect of various regimes on the income response, and thus on the demand for C_1 (see section 2.2).

12. For the moment we also assume that the external market (Y^*) remains unchanged.

13. In the labor market (figure 2.1) a fall in p_1 to p_1' will reduce the minimum nominal wage, which is consistent with a fixed real consumption wage, from $w^0 = Ap_0^\alpha p_1^{1-\alpha}$ to $w' = Ap_0^\alpha (p_1')^{1-\alpha} < w^0$. At given p_0 and w' and with equilibrium in the home-goods market, unemployment would be EF (this corresponds to the intersection of D_0^n and w_c^0 in figure 2.3).

14. When the expenditure elasticity for home goods is close to unitary and wage earners' consumption is representative of total household consumption, we have $\alpha \simeq C_{0c}$. The difference between the condition on the slope of w_c^0 and that on the slope of D_0 (see section 2.1.3) will thus depend mainly on how far c falls short of unity. The assumption $cC_{0c} < \beta$ and the case $\alpha > \beta$ are not mutually exclusive.

15. E.g., for the K regime we find, after substitution from (9), that $\partial (p_1^* D_f)/\partial p_1^* = \pi^2 C_{0\pi} - (1 - cC_{0c})^{-1}(1 - c)(1 + \phi_1\eta_1) < 0$ (since $C_{0\pi} < 0$). The rest follows from the fact that $\partial Y^R < \partial Y^C < \partial Y^K$.

16. In this case one has to assume a compensatory adjustment in direct taxes T_d so as to keep total tax receipts T constant.

17. We again ignore changes in real money balances.

18. We here ignore the reverse pull of new investment directed toward NICs.

19. Again it is assumed that T stays constant; thus T_d must be increased so as to finance the subsidies (or the reduction in employment tax). In terms of figure 2.1 curve L_1' will shift back.

20. The expansion must not only compensate for the fall in demand (X_0^d), but also take up the extra slack entailed by an increase in X_0^s. In terms of figure 2.3, D_L may be pushed up to pass through point B while demand management shifts D_0 to D_0''. Alternatively, one can devalue from B to C or C' and use wage subsidies to push the D_L curve up to pass through one of these points.

21. This literature is summarized in a recent OECD report (1979). See also Baldwin, Mutti, and Richardson (1978) and Krueger (1979).

22. Between 1963 and 1973 the share of NICs in OECD imports of manufactures increased from 2.6 to 6.8 percent. The figures for the following years, 1974–77, are, respectively 7.1, 6.8, 7.9, and 8.1 percent (see OECD 1979, p. 23, table 4).

23. In figure 2.4 the point A' relative to equilibrium at A is in the K region, but a shift from D_0 to D_0' returns the system to full employment. This would not be so if Walrasian equilibrium were, for example, at point E.

24. For a fuller discussion of such a model, see Bruno and Sachs (1979). The disequilibrium formulation of that model is analyzed in an unpublished working paper by the present author.

25. An increase in p_n^* shifts X_0^s supply downward. Similarly, real income will now fall [it is now measured as $Y = X_0 (1 - \mu\pi_n/\pi) + X_1/\pi$, where μ is the intermediate import ratio]. With a sufficiently strong supply effect, D_0 shifts to the right, as with an increase in θ_0.

26. There are now two variable inputs in the X_0 sector, and it can be shown that cost minimization at a given output level gives a downward sloping output-constrained labor-demand curve which is steeper than the notional L_0 demand curve but is not vertical unless intermediate inputs are used in fixed proportions.

27. In this case the fall in L_1 must be weighed against an increase in L_0 coming from gross complementarity of a variable input whose price has dropped. The net effect on total employment is an empirical matter.

References

Baldwin, R. E., J. H. Mutti, and J. D. Richardson. 1978. Welfare effects on the United States of a significant multilateral tariff reduction. Unpublished draft.

Bhagwati, J., and V. K. Ramaswami. 1963. Domestic distortions, tariffs, and the theory of optimum subsidy. *Journal of Political Economy* 71 (February): 44–50.

Brecher, R. A. 1978. Money, employment, and trade-balance adjustment with rigid wages. *Oxford Economic Papers* 30 (March): 1–15.

Bruno, M. 1976. The two-sector open economy and the real exchange rate. *American Economic Review* 66 (September): 566–77.

Bruno, M., and J. Sachs. 1979. *Supply versus demand approaches to the problem of stagflation.* Discussion Paper no. 796. Jerusalem: Falk Institute.

Hanoch, G., and M. Fraenkel. 1979. Income and substitution effects in the two-sector open economy. *American Economic Review* 69 (June): 455–58.

Helpman, E. 1976. Macroeconomic policy in a model of international trade with a wage restriction. *International Economic Review* 17 (June): 262–77.

Johnson, H. G. 1962. *Money, trade, and economic growth.* London: George Allen & Unwin.

Krueger, A. O. 1979. Protectionist pressures, imports, and employment in the United States. Unpublished typescript.

Liviatan, N. 1979. A disequilibrium analysis of the monetary trade model. *Journal of International Economics* 9 (August): 355–77.

Malinvaud, E. 1977. *The theory of unemployment reconsidered.* Oxford: Blackwell.

Muellbauer, J., and R. Portes. 1978. Macroeconomic models with quantity rationing. *Economic Journal* 88 (December): 788–821.

Neary, J. P. 1980. Non-traded goods and the balance of trade in a neo-Keynesian temporary eqilibrium. *Quarterly Journal of Economics* 95:403–29.

OCED. 1979. *The impact of the newly industrialising countries on production and trade in manufactures.* Report by the Secretary-General. Paris: OECD.

Rødseth, A. 1979. Macroeconomic policy in a small open economy. *Scandinavian Journal of Economics* 81, no. 1: 48–59.

Comment   J. Peter Neary

Anyone interested in macroeconomic theory who crosses the Atlantic these days suffers not merely from jet lag but from a strong sense of intellectual dislocation, such are the differences between the two continents in the accepted ground rules for macroeconomic debate. Michael Bruno's extremely rich and interesting paper has spared me some of this sense of dislocation, but since the "disequilibrium" (or, more accurately, "temporary equilibrium with rationing") approach which he pursues is much less acceptable to North American audiences, I want to begin by making some general comments on this class of models.

The main target for criticism of these models is of course their assumption of fixed prices. Whenever I am asked, "Who sets prices?" in such a model, I am tempted to reply facetiously that prices are set by—a little green man! This is no ordinary little green man, however, but the same one who in many other models moves prices costlessly and instantaneously to their Walrasian or market-clearing levels, except that he is on an off day! In other words, I know of no macromodel which provides a satisfactory choice-theoretic basis for its assumptions about price determination. Devotees of an efficient Walrasian auctioneer do not have a monopoly of virtue in this field and tend to forget that "tâtonnement" literally means "groping," which may be many things but is certainly not instantaneous.

J. Peter Neary is professor of political economy at University College Dublin. Since obtaining his D.Phil. from Oxford University in 1978, he has taught at Trinity College Dublin and Princeton, and has been a Visiting Scholar at MIT and at the Institute for International Economic Studies, University of Stockholm. He has published on international economics, macroeconomics, and consumer theory in *American Economic Review, Economica, Economic Journal, European Economic Review, Oxford Economic Papers,* and *Quarterly Journal of Economics.*

The research reported here was suported by the Arts and Social Studies Research Benefaction Fund of Trinity College Dublin.

The same point may be made differently using a parallel which should appeal to specialists in international economics. In the literature on devaluation theory a great many papers assume that external payments are initially balanced. Naive commentators sometimes suggest that these models are fatally flawed, for why would an economy which starts off in external balance ever have recourse to devaluation? But this criticism is of course misplaced, since the same analysis applies whatever the initial situation. Starting in a situation of payments imbalance may introduce some additional complications (as pointed out, for example, in the note by Hanoch and Fraenkel 1979 cited by Bruno), but the gain in analytic clarity of assuming initial balance more than outweighs the loss in realism. In the same way, although the fixed-prices models do in fact pick prices out of the air, it is unfair to interpret this literally. Rather, they should be seen as examining a snapshot of a dynamic economy in which the current wage-price vector is inherited from the past, perhaps from an earlier Walrasian equilibrium which was disturbed by exogenous forces. Although wages and prices do not respond immediately, pressures to change them will build up over time, and in the medium run they are likely to converge toward a new Walrasian equilibrium. However, before this happens (and there is as yet virtually no basis in economic theory for asserting how long the process will take) there is plenty of time for the short-run phenomena emphasized by Michael Bruno to take their course.

In opposition to these arguments there is, especially in North America, a widely held view that rapid, if not instantaneous, price adjustment is an almost inevitable concomitant of rationality and, in particular, of rational expectations. However, I would argue that these are two quite distinct issues. For example, in a paper by Joe Stiglitz and myself it is shown that, if prices are fixed and expected to remain so, not only will agents face quantity constraints today but rational agents will foresee constraints in the future, and such perfect foresight—or "rational constraint expectations" as we call it—enhances rather than emasculates the effectiveness of perfectly anticipated government policy. (Of course, not everyone is convinced by the model in that paper—indeed, since it assumes that prices are fixed both now and for the rest of time, a monetarist colleague of mine, Colm McCarthy, has dubbed it a model of Albania!)

As for the argument that rational expectations in themselves will lead either to instantaneous price flexibility or, more subtly, to rational fix-price contracts which fully embody all available *ex ante* information leaving no role for discretionary policy, this appears to me to reflect an unconvincing jump from one level of reasoning to another. Rationality of expectations or its absence is an assumption about individuals and their perceptions, whereas the process of price formation reflects a much wider range of institutional features, including the rate at which information is disseminated between, and the incentives for coordinating the actions of, atomistic agents. In an infinitely repeated steady state it is conceivable that market institutions which come to reflect rational expectations will embody price flexibility, and the conditions under which this will occur are an important topic for research; however, in the moving temporary equilibria with which macroeconomics must be concerned there is no logical reason why one should imply the other.

Turning at last to Michael Bruno's paper itself, it is one of a growing number which apply the Barro-Grossman-Malinvaud approach to an open economy. In trying to compare it with other contributions, I found it helpful to ask the question, Does Bruno's model describe a small open economy? At one level the answer is trivially no, for Bruno explicitly assumes that the "home" good X_0 is an imperfect substitute for a foreign good and that the level of exports of X_0 is a decreasing function of their relative price. Bruno's economy can thus in principle influence its terms of trade, which distinguishes it from the disequilibrium models of Dixit (1978), Liviatan (1979), Kennally (1979), Neary (1980), and Steigum (1980), in which the world prices of all traded goods are assumed to be parametric. However, while Bruno's assumption of some monopoly power in export markets may well be more appropriate, even for relatively small economies such as Ireland or Israel, I do not believe that this is a crucial feature of his model. In the first place all prices in his model are fixed over the short-run horizon which he considers, so that the terms of trade do not in fact change endogenously, even in response to substantial excess supply of exports. Second, the implications of his model would be unaffected if he assumed that the world price of X_0 was exogenously given, but replaced the export demand function in equation (3) by an exogenous export sales constraint $\bar{E}_0$. This draws attention to the fact (which also emerges from Steigum's model) that there are two distinct dimensions to the usual assumption of a small open economy: first, world prices of traded goods are fixed, and second, it is possible to buy or sell an infinite amount at these prices (i.e., there are no export sales or import supply constraints). Putting this another way, the familiar device of aggregating exportables and importables into a composite traded good requires that their *shadow* prices to domestic agents rather than their market prices stand in fixed proportions to one another, and this will not be the case if agents face quantity constraints. Thus it is the presence or absence of quantity constraints, rather than the fixity or variability of prices, which determines whether disequilibrium phenomena will emerge in traded goods markets. Of course, it is possible to retain both components of the small-open-economy assumption and still generate goods-market disequilibrium by postulating a purely nontraded good whose price is sticky. This is the approach adopted in my own paper, and except for this difference in interpretation and some relatively minor differences in specification (for example, I assume that profits are not redistributed instantaneously, that labor supply is endogenous, and that savings are not separable from commodity expenditures), the two models are extremely similar.

Another way of putting Bruno's paper in perspective is to compare it with similar models of a broadly "neoclassical" kind. Doing this makes it clear that many models share the same basic structure, however we may label them: for example, the condition derived by Bruno in his appendix for the effect of an increase in wages on the excess demand for home goods has also been derived by Helpman (1977) and Noman and Jones (1979) in two papers which ignore explicit disequilibrium considerations such as Clower's dual decision hypothesis and simply append a rigid wage to an otherwise orthodox neoclassical model. Moreover, these models are actually more similar than Bruno's to that of Dixit, which, though it pays careful attention to the consequences of quantity constraints, exhibits extremely "classical" properties, since all goods can be freely traded at fixed world prices. Indeed, there seems to be a general principle operating here, reminiscent of the general theory of the second best: the failure of one market to clear by price adjustment in an otherwise neoclassical environment (as in the models of Dixit, Liviatan, and Kennally) does not of itself give rise to distinctively disequilibrium properties. Rather, it takes at least two sets of quantity constraints to produce these, and it is the simultaneous relaxation of quantity constraints on two sets of agents which gives rise to such quintessentially disequilibrium phenomena as the Keynesian (or perhaps I should say "neo-Keynesian") demand multiplier.

While I am extremely sympathetic to Michael Bruno's model in general, I have some reservations about his treatment of investment. Like Pentti Kouri I found the inclusion of real balances in the investment function as "a proxy for the negative effect of the rate of interest" somewhat unconvincing. More satisfactory methods of endogenizing investment would be either to include a bond market with an explicit interest rate or to try to model the firm's intertemporal decision problem (the approach explored in Neary and Stiglitz 1982). The latter method would also avoid an implication of Bruno's model that investment decisions are unrelated to firms' production decisions and in particular are independent of the regime which prevails in the current period. Dropping this feature of the model would permit a regime of "underconsumption" in which firms were rationed on both labor and goods markets. (Of course, proliferation of regimes is not desirable in itself, but the failure to allow for an underconsumption regime can lead to problems in studying price dynamics, problems which I believe to be of more mathematical than economic interest.) Allowing investment to be regime-dependent would also avoid the implication that it is always profit-constrained. With persistent Keynesian unemployment, or when firms have pessimistic expectations, we would expect desired investment to fall below the profit-constrained level, which would eliminate the additional depressive effect of a fall in import prices mentioned in section 2.3.

Finally, the policy implications of Bruno's model, as with many other disequilibrium models, are very similar to those of traditional Keynesian analysis, though with more satisfactory microfoundations and more careful consideration of the circumstances in which particular policy measures are or are not appropriate. Thus one of his main conclusions, that adjustment is easier when labor and commodity markets are tight, is hardly novel; however, it derives new force from being expressed in terms of a contrast between an economy alternating between states of Keynesian unemployment and repressed inflation, and one pushed deeply into classical unemployment by large exogenous rises in input prices. As far as the specific topic of this conference is concerned, Bruno adds a third justification for adjustment assistance to the allocative and distributional arguments which have been put forward in other papers—namely, the use of adjustment assistance as a supplement to macroeconomic policies in the presence of wage and price rigidities. This may well come closest to a positive economic explanation of why adjustment assistance has been provided in practice, but any attempt to base a welfare-theoretic case for adjustment assistance on it brings us back to the question of how wages and prices are set in the first place, which has been extensively discussed in earlier sessions. As with so many other things, it all depends on what you believe about the little green man!

References

Dixit, A. K. 1978. The balance of trade in a model of temporary equilibrium with rationing. *Review of Economic Studies* 45: 393–404.

Hanoch, G., and M. Fraenkel. 1979. Income and substitution effects in the two-sector open economy. *American Economic Review* 69: 455–58.

Helpman, E. 1977. Nontraded goods and macroeconomic policy under a fixed exchange rate. *Quarterly Journal of Economics* 91: 469–80.

Kennally, G. 1979. Some consequences of opening the Keynesian model. Paper presented to Econometric Society European Meetings, Athens, September.

Liviatan, N. 1979. A disequilibrium analysis of the monetary trade model. *Journal of International Economics* 9: 355–77.

Neary, J. P. 1980. Non-traded goods and the balance of trade in a neo-Keynesian temporary equilibrium. *Quarterly Journal of Economics* 95: 403–29.

Neary, J. P., and J. E. Stiglitz. 1982. Towards a reconstruction of Keynesian economics: Expectations and constrained equilibria. *Quarterly Journal of Economics* (forthcoming).

Noman, K., and R. W. Jones. 1979. A model of trade and unemployment. In J. R. Green and J. A. Scheinkman, eds., *General equilibrium, growth, and trade: Essays in honor of Lionel McKenzie*, pp. 297–322. New York: Academic Press.

Steigum, E. 1980. Keynesian and Classical unemployment in an open economy. *Scandinavian Journal of Economics* (forthcoming).

3 Intersectoral Capital Mobility, Wage Stickiness, and the Case for Adjustment Assistance

J. Peter Neary

This paper extends the two-sector Heckscher-Ohlin model of a small open economy in which capital is sector-specific in the short run to allow for labor-market disequilibrium caused by transitional wage stickiness. The implications for the stability and speed of convergence toward a new long-run equilibrium following an exogenous change in the terms of trade are examined, and conditions are derived under which "immiserizing reallocation" can occur during the adjustment period. The framework presented is used to suggest appropriate measures of adjustment costs and to reconcile recent discussions of the welfare-theoretic case for adjustment assistance.

3.1 Introduction

There seems to be little doubt that many of the most vocal pleas for adjustment assistance are nothing more than old protectionism in new bottles: the prospect of increased low-cost imports from newly industrialized countries is frequently a convenient excuse for providing declining industries with assistance which has little justification from the viewpoint

J. Peter Neary is professor of political economy at University College Dublin. Since obtaining his D.Phil. from Oxford University in 1978, he has taught at Trinity College Dublin and Princeton, and has been a Visiting Scholar at MIT and at the Institute for International Economic Studies, University of Stockholm. He has published on international economics, macroeconomics, and consumer theory in *American Economic Review, Economica, Economic Journal, European Economic Review, Oxford Economic Papers,* and *Quarterly Journal of Economics.*

This paper was begun while the author was a Visiting Scholar at the Institute for International Economic Studies, University of Stockholm. Valuable discussions with Koichi Hamada and Ronald Jones, as well as helpful comments from participants at this conference, especially Avinash Dixit and Michael Mussa, and support from the Committee for Social Science Research in Ireland are gratefully acknowledged.

of comparative advantage. At the same time the liberal economist's instinctive suspicion of such intervention should not be allowed to rule out the possibility that it may on occasions be given some theoretical justification over and above its undoubted tactical value in sugaring the pill of tariff reductions.

The object of the present paper is to attempt to examine some of the issues raised by the adjustment-assistance debate in the light of the positive and normative theory of international trade. As we shall see, the normative prescriptions of this body of theory are, in principle, relatively straightforward, but their application in any individual case depends crucially on the assumptions made about the behavior and institutional environment of the private sector. Section 3.2 of the paper therefore begins by reviewing the implications of one set of assumptions regarding the medium-run adjustment of the standard two-sector Heckscher-Ohlin model of a small open economy. This approach, which assumes that capital is a fixed factor in the short run, but moves between sectors in the medium run in response to intersectoral differences in rentals, has been extensively examined in recent work by Mayer (1974), Mussa (1974, 1978), Jones (1975), Kemp, Kimura, and Okuguchi (1977), and the author (1978a, b) among others. Section 3.3 proceeds to extend this literature by relaxing the assumption made in earlier papers that full employment of labor is maintained throughout the adjustment period by instantaneous wage flexibility. When this assumption is dropped, the labor market as well as the capital market is out of equilibrium during the adjustment period, and the consequences of this for the path followed by the economy are examined.

The model of section 3.3 is then applied in section 3.4 to the question of the appropriate measure of adjustment costs, both private and social, and it is shown that national income can fall temporarily during the adjustment process, a phenomenon which is labeled "immiserizing reallocation." Finally section 3.5 takes up the normative issue of the appropriate form of public assistance to the adjustment process, an issue recently examined by Lapan (1976) and Mussa (1978). The principal conclusion, which is no doubt obvious but still deserves to be stressed, is that the case for adjustment assistance is essentially a second-best one. In an otherwise undistorted economy where the government is no better informed about the future course of the economy than the private sector, there is no case on grounds of allocative efficiency for public intervention to supplement or counteract private decisions. However, intervention may be justified in the presence of domestic distortions, even if the private sector has perfect foresight of future returns to capital. Of course, even when a theoretical case for adjustment assistance can be made, its practical implementation raises some difficult questions of political economy, which are briefly discussed in the concluding section.

3.2 Short-Run Capital Specificity in the Heckscher-Ohlin Model

We begin by reviewing the short-run capital specificity adjustment process assuming continual full employment, using a diagrammatic technique presented in Neary (1978a) and reproduced in panels (i) and (iv) of figure 3.1. We assume an economy producing two goods, X and Y, under conditions of perfect competition and constant returns to scale, using two inelastically supplied primary factors of production, capital (K) and labor (L). Assuming for the present that product and factor markets are undistorted, initial equilibrium in the labor market is determined by the intersection of the labor-demand schedules for the two sectors at point A in panel (i). This equilibrium is contingent on a particular commodity price ratio, given exogenously to the economy, and on a particular allocation of the capital stock between the sectors. This allocation corresponds to the solid horizontal line in the Edgeworth-Bowley box, panel (iv), and since point a, which is vertically below point A, lies on the efficiency locus of the box, it follows that these two points represent a full, or long-run, equilibrium, at which each factor is allocated such that it receives the same return in both sectors.

This initial long-run equilibrium is also represented by point A' in panel (ii) of figure 3.1, at the intersection of the isocost curves c_x^0 and c_y. Each of these curves shows combinations of the wage rate w and the rental rate r which imply a unit cost of production for the sector in question equal to its world price.[1] Hence only the factor prices corresponding to A' ensure zero profits for both sectors. The slope of each isocost curve at a given point equals the capital-labor ratio in the sector in question, so at A' sector X is relatively labor-intensive; this is also indicated, of course, in panel (iv) by the fact that the efficiency locus lies below the diagonal of the Edgeworth-Bowley box.

Consider now the effects of an exogenous once-and-for-all fall in the world price of X. This shifts that sector's labor-demand schedule downward in panel (i) from L_x^0 to L_x^1, and shifts its isocost curve inward toward the origin in panel (ii) from c_x^0 to c_x^1. (These two shifts are by the same proportionate amount as the price fall, so that point S, which lies vertically below A in panel [i], corresponds to the same wage rate as point S', which lies on the ray from the origin to A' in panel [ii].) Assuming that capital is sector-specific in the short run and that the wage rate is perfectly flexible, the fall in the price of X determines a new short-run equilibrium at point B at which the wage rate is lower, and sector Y has expanded, availing itself of some of the now-cheaper labor released by the contracting sector X. Moreover, it is clear from panel (ii) that the return on capital has fallen in sector X and risen in sector Y (to levels represented by the points B_x' and B_y', respectively). Over time, this increased relative attractiveness of renting capital goods to sector Y rather than to sector X may

Fig. 3.1

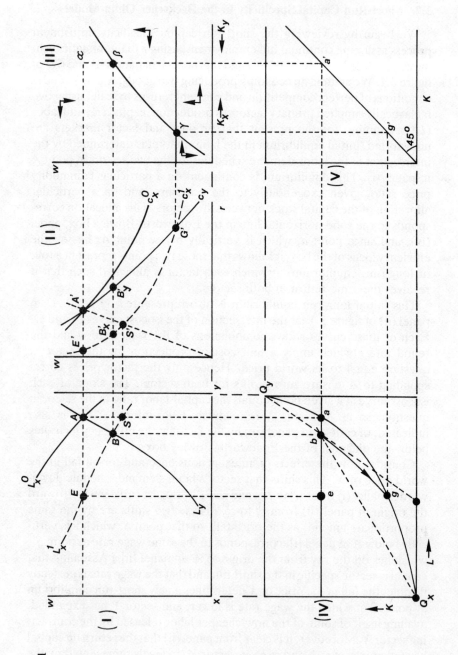

be expected to induce an intersectoral reallocation of the capital stock, and for the remainder of this section we assume that this reallocation takes place at a rate determined by the differential equation:

(1) $DK_x = \phi\{\dfrac{r_x}{r_y} - 1\}$ $\phi' > 0, \phi(0) = 0,$

where D represents the time derivative operator and the capital stock is assumed to be always fully employed:

(2) $K_x + K_y = \bar{K}$.

The adjustment mechanism embodied in equation (1) is ad hoc in at least two respects. In the first place it considers only the return to reallocating capital, thus implicitly assuming constant costs in the "capital-reallocation" industry. Second, the return is measured by the difference between the current rentals on capital in the two sectors rather than by the difference between the present value of the stream of future rentals accruing to a unit of capital in each sector; this implicitly assumes that capital owners have static expectations of future rental rates. Both of these deficiencies are avoided in a recent paper by Mussa (1978) which specifies an explicit microeconomic model of the reallocation decision, and also allows for the general-equilibrium feedback onto wages arising from the direct use of labor by the capital-reallocation industry. However, the richness of Mussa's analysis of the capital market precludes his examining the consequences of sluggish adjustment in the labor market, with which the present paper (as well as much of the applied literature on adjustment assistance) is primarily concerned. Moreover, his own analysis is ad hoc in some respects: in particular, it assumes of necessity that the marginal cost of reallocating capital is a nondecreasing function of the rate of reallocation, since otherwise the optimal adjustment policy is of the "bang-bang" type, and the economy moves instantaneously to the new long-run equilibrium.[2] For these reasons it seems worthwhile to explore the implications of the simple adjustment mechanism (1).

As capital moves out of the labor-intensive sector X into sector Y, the resulting fall in the aggregate demand for labor puts downward pressure on the wage rate, thus inducing a substitution toward more labor-intensive techniques in both sectors. Hence in panel (iv) of figure 3.1 the capital reallocation drives the economy away from point b (which lies directly below B) along a path on which the capital-labor ratios in both sectors are continually falling. Such a path (which must lie in the triangle $Q_x bh$) is shown by the solid line bg. The new long-run equilibrium at g is also illustrated by point G' in panel (ii), where the equality of rental rates in the two sectors is restored.

Since our main objective is to investigate the consequences of sluggish wage adjustment, it is desirable to illustrate the adjustment process in yet another manner, which explicitly relates the wage rate to the intersectoral allocation of capital. This is done in panels (iii) and (v) of figure 3.1 (where panel [v] simply translates the vertical axis of panel [iv] into the horizontal axis of panel [iii]). Point α in panel (iii) represents the initial equilibrium, and the fall in the price of X causes an immediate fall in the wage rate, moving the equilibrium to point β. Over time the reallocation of capital causes a southwesterly movement of the equilibrium point in panel (iii), as the wage rate drifts downward and the proportion of the capital stock employed in sector X steadily falls. The economy therefore follows the path βγ, which corresponds exactly to the path bg in panel (iv), until eventually the new long-run equilibrium at γ is attained.

The different panels of figure 3.1 thus illustrate from a number of perspectives the short-run capital specificity adjustment hypothesis with continual full employment, whose properties are familiar from earlier writings: the initial fall in the price of X lowers the wage rate and brings about a rental differential in favor of sector Y. Over time this induces an intersectoral capital flow, and both factor prices and factor allocations move monotonically toward their new long-run equilibrium levels which, as predicted by the Stolper-Samuelson theorem, exhibit a fall in the wage rate and a rise in the rental rate (now equalized between the two sectors) relative to both commodity prices. We turn therefore in the next section to examine how this picture is affected when we abandon the assumption of rapid adjustment of wages.

3.3 Short-Run Capital Specificity with Sticky Wages

Strictly speaking, the model outlined in the previous section assumed not that the wage adjusts instantaneously, but merely that it moves sufficiently rapidly to restore labor-market equilibrium before capital begins to move between sectors. Previous writers have not made explicit the mechanism by which this equilibrium is brought about, but it seems natural to assume that it involves a positive relationship between wage changes and the level of excess demand for labor:

(3) $$Dw = \psi \{ \frac{L^d}{L} - 1 \} \qquad \psi' > 0, \psi(0) = 0,$$

where L_d is the demand for labor by both sectors and $\bar{L}$ is the fixed aggregate labor supply. Note that, according to equation (3), excess demand for and excess supply of labor affect the wage rate in a symmetric fashion. Without specifying the microeconomic underpinnings of (3) in greater detail, this seems a reasonable simplification, especially since we are primarily interested in the qualitative general-equilibrium consequences of labor-market disequilibrium.

Suppose now that the speed of adjustment implied by the $\psi(\cdot)$ function in equation (3) is *not* instantaneous relative to that embodied in the $\phi(\cdot)$ function in equation (1). This means that both labor and capital markets may be simultaneously out of long-run equilibrium. Assuming that the wage rate is fixed in the short run in terms of good Y, the impact effect of the fall in the price of X is therefore that sector X lays off EA workers (in panel [i] of figure 3.1) which sector Y has no incentive to hire. The resulting unemployment of EA causes the wage rate to drift downward over time while at the same time capital begins to reallocate out of sector X in response to the induced rental differential (represented in panel [ii] by the gap between the rental in X at E' and that in Y at A'). Hence the economy moves away from point α in panel (iii) in a southwesterly direction. But now, by contrast with the full-employment case of the previous section, the time paths of factor prices and factor allocations need not be monotonic. The economy may overshoot the long-run equilibrium point γ, in which case, when the wage falls below its long-run equilibrium level, the rental differential moves in favor of sector X and so the direction of intersectoral capital movement is reversed. The path followed by the economy is thus a counterclockwise spiral in panel (iii), which must bring it into the region of excess demand for labor below the labor-market equilibrium locus $\gamma\beta$. Within this region firms are frustrated in their efforts to hire labor, and so their output levels are determined by their "effective" demand for labor $\bar{L}$ rather than their "notional" demand L^d. As we shall see below, this has a number of implications for the behavior of the economy when excess demand for labor prevails. However, it does not affect the qualitative nature of the adjustment path, and so the dynamic evolution of the economy is governed by the arrows in panel (iii).

Is there any guarantee that the economy will converge toward the new long-run equilibrium at γ? In order to investigate this we examine the local stability of the model, for which it is necessary to derive algebraic expressions for the two stationary loci in the neighborhood of γ. Consider first the capital-market equilibrium locus, the stationary locus of (1). An expression for this in differential form may be derived by manipulating the price-equal-to-unit-cost equations, which reflect the fact that under competition the proportional change in the price of each sector's output must be a weighted average of changes in the returns to the factors employed there, where the relevant weights (the θ_{ij}) are the shares of each factor in the value of the sector's output:

(4) $$\hat{p} = \theta_{lx}\hat{w} + \theta_{kx}\hat{r}_x,$$

(5) $$0 = \theta_{ly}\hat{w} + \theta_{ky}\hat{r}_y.$$

(A circumflex over a variable indicates a proportional rate of change: $\hat{w} = d \log w$.) Manipulating (4) and (5) yields

(6) $$\hat{r}_x - \hat{r}_y = -\frac{|\theta|}{\theta_{kx}\theta_{ky}} \hat{w} + \frac{1}{\theta_{kx}} \hat{p},$$

where $|\theta|$, which equals $\theta_{lx} - \theta_{ly}$, is the determinant of the matrix of value shares, and is positive if and only if sector X is relatively labor-intensive in value terms. Note that from equation (6) the intersectoral rental differential does not depend on K_x: with a fixed wage the capital market is not self-equilibrating. Hence with a fixed wage rate and fixed commodity prices the allocation of capital between sectors is either indeterminate (in the knife-edge case where the wage happens to equal its long-run equilibrium value) or else the economy is driven to specialize.[3]

In the present model, however, the wage is sticky rather than fixed and its dynamic evolution is governed by equation (3). To analyze this case, we note that the aggregate demand for labor equals the sum of the labor demands from each sector, each of which in turn equals the sector's unit labor requirement a_{lj} times its output level:

(7) $$L^d = a_{lx}X + a_{ly}Y.$$

The levels of output themselves equal the available stock of capital in each sector divided by the sector's unit capital requirement a_{kj}:

(8) $$X = K_x/a_{kx}, \quad Y = K_y/a_{ky}.$$

Totally differentiating (7) and (8) yields

(9) $$\hat{L}^d = \lambda_{lx}(\hat{a}_{lx} - \hat{a}_{kx} + \hat{K}_x) + \lambda_{ly}(\hat{a}_{ly} - \hat{a}_{ky} + \hat{K}_y),$$

where λ_{lj} is the proportion of the demand for labor which emanates from sector j. Assuming that neither sector is rationed in the labor market, equation (9) may be expressed in terms of factor prices by invoking the definition of the elasticity of factor substitution:

(10) $$\hat{a}_{lj} - \hat{a}_{kj} = \hat{L}_j - \hat{K}_j = -\sigma_j(\hat{w} - \hat{r}_j) \qquad (j = x, y)$$

(11) $$= -\frac{\sigma_j}{\theta_{kj}} (\hat{w} - \hat{p}_j).$$

(The step from [10] to [11] makes use of equations [4] and [5].) Moreover the changes in sectoral capital stocks in (9) may be related by recalling that they must satisfy the full-employment constraint for capital, (2), which may be written in differential form as

(12) $$\lambda_{kx}\hat{K}_x + \lambda_{ky}\hat{K}_y = 0.$$

Substituting from (11) and (12) into (9) yields an expression in differential form for the aggregate demand for labor as a function of changes in state and exogenous variables only:

$$(13) \qquad \hat{L}^d = -\Delta \hat{w} + \frac{|\lambda|}{\lambda_{ky}} \, \hat{K}_x + \lambda_{lx} \frac{\sigma_x}{\theta_{kx}} \, \hat{p},$$

where Δ, the wage elasticity of the aggregate labor-demand schedule, is a weighted average of the corresponding elasticities in each sector:

$$(14) \qquad \Delta \equiv \lambda_{lx} \frac{\sigma_x}{\theta_{kx}} + \lambda_{ly} \frac{\sigma_y}{\theta_{ky}}$$

and where $|\lambda|$, which equals $\lambda_{lx}\lambda_{ky} - \lambda_{ly}\lambda_{kx}$, the determinant of the matrix of factor-to-sector allocations, is positive if and only if sector X is relatively labor-intensive in physical terms. Equation (13) shows that the aggregate demand for labor falls with a rise in the wage rate (so that the labor market is stable in isolation) and rises with a rise in the relative price of X (the good in terms of which the wage rate is *not* pegged) or with an increase in the proportion of the capital stock employed in the labor-intensive sector.

We are now in a position to examine the local stability of the model. Linearizing equations (1) and (3) around a long-run equilibrium point (K_x^*, w^*), and substituting from (6) and (13) with p fixed, yields the matrix differential equation

$$(15) \qquad \begin{bmatrix} DK_x \\[2ex] Dw \end{bmatrix} = \begin{bmatrix} 0 & -E_\phi \dfrac{|\theta|}{\theta_{kx}\theta_{ky}} \\[2ex] E_\psi \dfrac{|\lambda|}{\lambda_{ky}} & -E_\psi \Delta \end{bmatrix} \begin{bmatrix} (K_x - K_x^*)/K_x \\[2ex] (w - w^*)/w \end{bmatrix},$$

where E_ϕ and E_ψ are multiples of the slopes of the adjustment functions (1) and (3) (e.g., $E_\phi = \phi' r_x/r_y$) and so are measures of the speed of adjustment of the capital and labor markets, respectively. It is clear that the trace of the matrix is negative provided techniques are variable in at least one sector (so that Δ is nonzero). Therefore a necessary and sufficient condition for local stability of the system (15) is that the determinant of the coefficient matrix be positive. This is equivalent to the condition

$$(16) \qquad |\lambda| \, |\theta| > 0,$$

i.e., that the value and physical rankings of the relative factor intensities of the two sectors coincide at a point of long-run equilibrium.[4]

This condition, which is the same as that derived in Neary (1978*b*) under the assumption of continual full employment, is automatically fulfilled if there are no permanent factor-market distortions. Hence we may conclude that, at least for small displacements of the initial equilibrium, the model converges in a stable fashion toward the new long-run

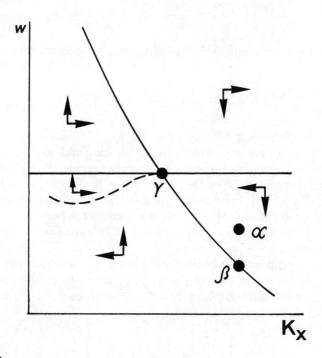

Fig. 3.2

equilibrium point γ in panel (iii) of figure 3.1. A similar phase diagram may be devised for the case where sector X is relatively capital-intensive, and it is illustrated in figure 3.2. The path followed by the economy is now a clockwise loop in (K_x, w) space, and since the price of the capital-intensive good has fallen, the wage rate must rise in the long run. (Compare points α and γ.) But in other respects the medium-run adjustment of the economy is qualitatively similar to that in figure 3.1. Only if there are permanent factor-market distortions can any problem of instability arise. Such a case is illustrated in figure 3.3, where sector X is relatively capital-intensive in the physical sense but has to pay relatively more for labor than for capital by comparison with sector Y, with the result that at the long-run equilibrium point γ sector X is relatively labor-intensive in the value sense. Hence that equilibrium is a saddle point: unless the economy lies initially on the dashed line through γ it is driven to specialize in one of the two goods. This finding reinforces the conclusions of Neary (1978b), where it was argued that stability considerations render implausible the many comparative-statics paradoxes associated with the nonfulfillment of condition (16).

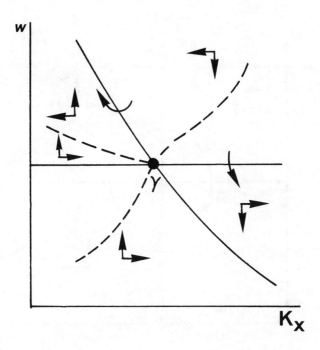

Fig. 3.3

Returning to the stable case, an explicit calculation of the characteristic roots of the coefficient matrix in (15) yields

$$(17) \qquad \mu_1, \mu_2 = -E_\psi \Delta \pm \left(E_\psi^2 \Delta^2 - 4 E_\phi E_\psi \, \frac{|\lambda| \, |\theta|}{\lambda_{ky} \theta_{kx} \theta_{ky}} \right)^{1/2}.$$

It is clear that convergence is more rapid, and cycles are less likely, the greater the potential for factor substitution in either sector, and so the greater the aggregate elasticity of demand for labor. In the extreme case of fixed coefficients in both sectors, the demand for labor is independent of the wage rate. The characteristic roots (17) now have no real parts, and so if both adjustment mechanisms (1) and (3) continue to operate, the economy remains in a limit cycle, as shown in figure 3.4. By contrast, if Δ is relatively large, the value of the wage rate which equilibrates the labor market is sensitive to the allocation of the capital stock, and so convergence is likely to be rapid and monotonic, as figure 3.5 illustrates.

The preceding analysis is strictly applicable only when there is unemployment or when the economy is in the neighborhood of a long-run equilibrium point. When a finite degree of excess demand for labor

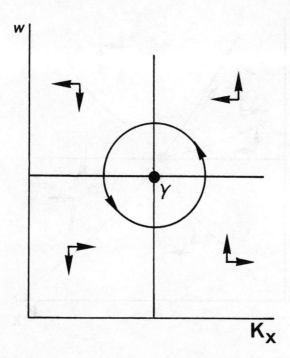

Fig. 3.4

prevails, equations (4), (5), and (10) do not necessarily hold, because if the aggregate demand for labor exceeds the supply, some firms must be rationed in the labor market, which leads them to produce at a point where the marginal product of labor is not equated to the real wage. Hence in the preceding derivations the "notional" factor demand schedules and equilibrium loci, which implicitly assume that no rationing takes place, must be replaced by their "effective" counterparts, in the manner which is becoming familiar from the literature on "disequilibrium" macroeconomics.[5] The details of this procedure are set out in appendix B, where it is shown that, when excess demand for labor prevails, the notional capital-market equilibrium locus (6) is displaced to an extent which depends on the rationing rule for allocating labor between the two sectors. The resulting effective loci are shown as dashed lines in figures 3.2, 3.3, 3.5, and 3.7, and it is clear that they do not affect the qualitative conclusions about the behavior of the economy drawn above.

Before concluding this section, we may note that it has been assumed throughout that it is the wage rate expressed in terms of good Y which is sticky in response to excess demand or supply in the labor market. This asymmetric assumption is not inappropriate when we are concerned with

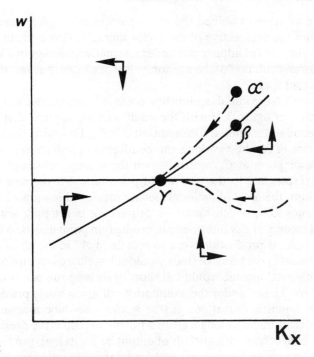

Fig. 3.5

the consequences of a fall in the price of X, and in any case the analysis is not substantially dependent on it. More generally, we may assume that it is the real wage in the sense of the utility level of wage earners which is fixed in the short run and which responds sluggishly to labor-market disequilibrium. Formally, this may be expressed by equating the nominal wage w to the nominal expenditure of the representative wage earner, which is a function of both commodity prices and the wage earner's utility level u:

(18) $$w = E(p_x, p_y, u).$$

Totally differentiating (18) yields

(19) $$\rho\hat{u} = \hat{w} - \xi\hat{p}_x - (1 - \xi)\hat{p}_y,$$

where ρ is the utility elasticity of expenditure and ξ is the budget share of good X. The analysis of this section now goes through almost unchanged provided u is substituted for w in equations (3) to (15); the only qualification is that if real wages are sticky in terms of good X (i.e., $\xi = 1$), a fall in the price of X does not give rise to unemployment in the short run.

3.4 Measuring the Costs of Adjustment

So far we have examined the consequences of sluggish wage adjustment from the perspective of the factor markets. However, in order to quantify the costs of adjustment under alternative assumptions about the medium-run evolution of the economy, it is desirable to recast the analysis in output space.

In figure 3.6 the initial equilibrium point A'' corresponds to the initial equilibrium in figure 3.1, with the additional assumption that X is the import good so that initial consumption is at C_a. Following the fall in the world price of X, the new long-run equilibrium production point is G'' with consumption at C_g, which lies on the income-consumption curve ICC corresponding to the new world price ratio. At the new long-run equilibrium, the level of national income measured in units of Y equals the distance ON, which therefore provides a benchmark with which national income at any intermediate production point may be compared. For example, if production were to remain at A'' in the short run,[6] the improvement in the terms of trade would still yield a consumption gain of HJ but national income would fall short of its long-run potential by the amount JN. Hence under the assumptions of given world prices and no long-run domestic distortions, a true welfare-theoretic measure of the "costs of adjustment" along a given adjustment path is the present value of the stream of all such shortfalls of output below its long-run level ON.[7]

Consider now the adjustment path under the short-run capital specificity hypothesis with continual full employment. As noted by Mayer (1974) the economy is initially constrained by a short-run transformation curve such as $T'T'$ which lies inside the long-run curve TT, and so production moves following the price change from A'' to B''. Over time the capital reallocation shifts the short-run transformation curve progressively to the left and the economy moves along the path indicated by the dashed line toward the new long-run equilibrium point G''. Since the only departure from a full optimum during the adjustment period is the intersectoral rental differential and since this falls steadily as capital reallocates (as shown in panel [ii] of figure 3.1), it is intuitively obvious that the shortfall of national income below its long-run level declines monotonically during the adjustment period. (An algebraic proof of this is provided in appendix A.)

The situation is very different when the wage rate is sticky, however. To begin with, the level of output of good Y remains unchanged in the short run and the output of X falls by more than it does when the wage is flexible. Hence the new short-run equilibrium point E'' lies on the same horizontal line as A'' and to the left of B''. Evaluated at the new world prices, the value of national output must fall, but the change in real national income is ambiguous. Figure 3.6 illustrates the borderline case

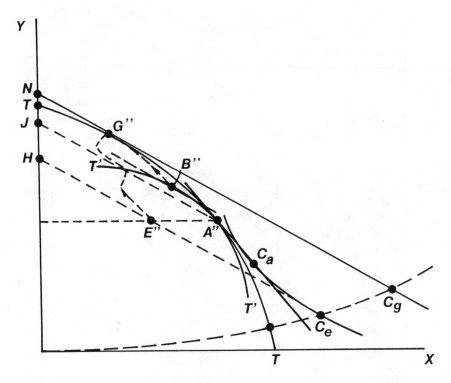

Fig. 3.6

where real national income is unchanged—with production at E'' consumers can just attain, at C_e, the same social indifference curve they enjoyed, at C_a, before the price change. Hence the level of real income remains at OH. But this is just a fortuitous occurrence, and, as noted by Haberler (1950), real income may either rise or fall due to the short-run wage rigidity.

Over time, movements of capital between sectors and adjustments of the wage rate lead the economy along the path $E''G''$, but, unlike the full-employment case, this path need not exhibit any regular properties. Since, as seen in the last section, factor allocations and factor prices may follow cyclical paths, the same is true of output levels. Moreover, there is no guarantee that real income will rise monotonically during the adjustment period, which introduces the possibility of "*immiserizing reallocation*," by analogy with the phenomenon of immiserizing growth, familiar from comparative-statics models.

To see how immiserizing reallocation may occur, consider figure 3.7, which repeats the essential features of figure 3.1, panel (iii). In regions 1

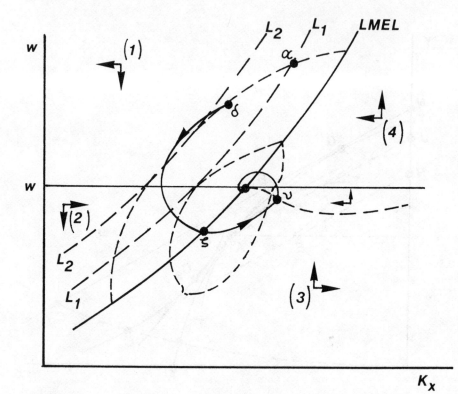

Fig. 3.7

and 2 of figure 3.7, where excess supply of labor prevails, the dashed lines
L_1L_1 and L_2L_2 parallel to the labor-market equilibrium locus represent
given levels of employment, while the dotted lines represent given levels
of national income: these two sets of loci differ since, except at the
long-run equilibrium wage w^*, the failure to equalize rentals between
sectors lowers national income below the maximum attainable with a
given level of employment. Hence along the solid line, which represents
one possible path that the economy may follow starting at point α, the
level of employment falls between α and δ, and to the left of δ the level of
income also falls. Thus immiserizing reallocation takes place even though
the direct consequences of each market's adjusting in isolation—the
reallocation of capital toward the high-rental sector and the fall in the
wage rate which tends to encourage a higher level of employment—tend
to raise national income. These favorable effects are more than offset by
the change in industry mix, whereby the declining labor-intensive sector
(X) releases more labor than the expanding sector is willing to absorb.
    Immiserizing reallocation cannot occur in region 2, since here the
labor-intensive sector is expanding, which reduces the level of unemploy-

ment, and so all three effects tend to raise national income. However, it can occur in region 3, where national income is below its potential not because of unemployment but because marginal products of labor are not necessarily equalized between sectors due to the fact that one or both sectors are unable to realize their notional labor demands. Note that as a result it is not possible to determine the value of national income corresponding to a point in regions 3 and 4 from a knowledge of that point's (K_x, w) coordinates alone, for in addition it is necessary to specify what rationing rule is being used to allocate the scarce labor supply between the two sectors. One plausible assumption is that labor is allocated on a "first come, first served" basis, which implies that along the path segment $\zeta\upsilon$ only sector X is constrained, since at point ζ sector Y is unconstrained and its notional demand for labor falls steadily as its capital stock falls and the wage rate rises. In region 4, however, it is not possible to be so definite, since at some point the return flow of capital into sector Y must lead it to seek to expand its employment level. Hence along the segment of the path above υ in region 4 either or both sectors may face ration constraints on their labor demands. Moreover, as noted in section 3.3, the location of the boundary between regions 3 and 4 and so of the point υ itself also depends on the rationing rule assumed. Fortunately these considerations do not prevent us from reaching definite conclusions about the qualitative behavior of national income along the portions of the adjustment path in regions 3 and 4. In both regions when only one sector is constrained a reallocation of capital toward the high-rental sector and a *rise* in the wage rate tend to raise national income, the latter because it induces the unconstrained sector to shed labor which can be absorbed by the rationed sector where its marginal product is higher. In region 3, however, the inflow of capital into the labor-intensive sector increases the aggregate excess demand for labor, and so increases the gap between the marginal product of labor and the wage rate thus tending to lower national income. It is quite possible for this effect to dominate (as illustrated in figure 3.7 by the fact that the path $\zeta\upsilon$ crosses the dotted iso-income locus), so leading once again to immiserizing reallocation. This cannot happen in region 4, since capital is now moving into the capital-intensive sector and so national income unambiguously rises. However, immiserizing reallocation can still take place in region 4, if substantial excess demand for labor exists and if the labor-rationing rule is such that both sectors are constrained. (These results are proved algebraically in appendix A.)

In conclusion, therefore, the combination of sticky wages and sluggish intersectoral reallocation of capital can lead to phases of immiserizing reallocation, where, because of the combination of two sources of allocative inefficiency, private decisions actually lower real national income. This is most likely to occur in regions 1 and 3, that is, when the wage rate and the proportion of the capital stock in use in the labor-intensive sector move in the same direction; however, it can also happen in region 4 if both sectors are rationed in their demands for labor. Notice finally that this has taken place in an environment with no permanent distortions in factor or commodity markets. Adding such distortions to the model would provide an additional, albeit well-known, source of immiserizing reallocation.

3.5   Policies toward the Adjustment Process

Having examined the positive consequences of our assumptions about dynamic adjustment, we are now in a position to consider their implications for public intervention in the adjustment process.

Within the framework of the present model, adjustment assistance could take many forms, which can be divided into two broad categories, static and dynamic subsidies. By static subsidies we mean subsidies which persist indefinitely at a constant rate, such as a permanent subsidy to capital in sector X. Such a policy can clearly never be first-best provided the social discount rate is less than infinite, since it distorts the long-run equilibrium and thus ensures that maximum national income is never attained (although it is conceivable that if this were the only form of intervention available, the short-term gains which it could make possible might outweigh its long-term costs).

In any case, it is probably more appropriate to reserve the term "adjustment assistance" for dynamic subsidies only. An explicit calculation of the optimal time paths of such subsidies in the model presented in earlier sections would require the solution of an optimal control problem with two state variables (K_x and w) and at least one control variable (the level of tax or subsidy), and such an analysis is unlikely to be very illuminating.[8] However, a number of observations about the optimal form of dynamic intervention can be made on the basis of direct inspection of the competitive time path given in (15). First, given the formal structure of the model, if the government has sufficient instruments at its disposal to simultaneously control the speeds of adjustment in both markets (i.e., E_ϕ and E_ψ) and if there are no constraints on its ability to finance these subsidies in a nondistorting way, then in principle it can bring the economy arbitrarily close to the first-best equilibrium instantaneously and so can reduce adjustment costs arbitrarily close to zero.

The optimal policy to support this first-best plan would imply a subsidy to capital movement in order to raise E_ϕ and thus would speed up the process of capital reallocation. However, if E_ψ, the speed of adjustment of wages, cannot be affected by government policy, then the optimal second-best policy will in many cases imply a *reduction* in E_ϕ, in other words, a slowing down of the capital reallocation process. For, from (17), if the competitive path implies a cyclical movement in factor prices and allocations, then some reduction in E_ϕ will be sufficient to eliminate the cycles and so to lower the present value of the transitional costs of adjustment. The second-best optimal dynamic subsidy is more likely to take this form the slower the speed of adjustment of wages (i.e., the smaller is E_ψ) and the smaller the potential for factor substitution in either sector (i.e., the smaller is Δ).

These considerations illustrate the importance of simultaneously considering the adjustment process in both labor and capital markets in devising the appropriate form of adjustment assistance. At the same time the present model does not provide any microfoundations for the adjustment functions $\phi(\cdot)$ or $\psi(\cdot)$, and so implicitly assumes that these functions represent dynamic distortions rather than true social costs of adjustment. It is of interest therefore to compare our conclusions with those of two recent papers, by Lapan (1976) and Mussa (1978), which provide more complete analyses of the sources of sluggish adjustment in the labor and capital markets, respectively.[9]

Mussa's model, which assumes continual full employment but provides an explicit microeconomic analysis of the capital reallocation decision, has already been summarized in section 3.2. One of his major conclusions is that if capital owners' expectations of the future course of factor prices are rational, then private decisions will coincide with the socially optimal plan and intervention will be unnecessary. However, this conclusion was derived from a model with no other distortions, static or dynamic, and so, from the general theory of the second best, it need not survive their introduction. In particular, if future wage rates, though perfectly foreseen, do not reflect the social opportunity cost of labor, then some interference with the competitive path of capital reallocation is likely to be justified. (That rational expectations need not emasculate discretionary macroeconomic policy if wages and prices are sticky has been argued by Neary and Stiglitz 1982.)

Where Mussa assumes continual full employment and concentrates on the capital reallocation decision, Lapan ignores the latter by assuming that capital is permanently sector-specific and focuses instead on the labor market. Unlike the present paper, he assumes that the labor markets in the two sectors are segmented, with migration between the two markets taking place in response to differences in sectoral unemployment rates. Lapan shows that the optimal policy requires a wage subsidy to the declining sector at a rate which may or may not decline over time. As comments by Cassing and Ochs (1978) and Ray (1979) with replies by Lapan (1978, 1979) have made clear, intervention in this model is justified by two different features: first, the assumption that due to "institutional" factors labor, though immobile, must be paid the same wage in both sectors; and second, the assumption that the responsiveness of the

58   J. Peter Neary

rate of labor migration into the expanding sector to the unemployment
rate in the declining sector decreases with the rate of unemployment,
reflecting (if unemployment is voluntary) the fact that congestion occurs
in the search for new jobs.

It is clear that all of these results are fully consistent with the theory of
distortions and welfare, whose implications for static policy intervention
in open economies have been surveyed by Bhagwati (1971) and Corden
(1974). In a first-best world, with no distortions and with rational expectations of future factor prices, the market is the best judge of the rate
of intersectoral resource transfers. But once one of these assumptions is
abandoned, a case for adjustment assistance on purely efficiency grounds
can be constructed.

3.6 Summary and Conclusion

This paper has examined the consequences of appending transitional
wage stickiness to the two-sector Heckscher-Ohlin model of international
trade theory, concentrating on the adjustment path of the economy
following an exogenous fall in the price of the labor-intensive import-
competing sector. It was shown that in the absence of substantial permanent factor-market distortions the economy moves in a stable fashion
toward the new long-run equilibrium predicted by static Heckscher-
Ohlin analysis. However, the combination of wage stickiness and sluggish
intersectoral capital movements implies an adjustment path with properties very different from those exhibited by the full-employment short-
run capital specificity adjustment path. In particular, factor prices, factor
allocations, and output levels may exhibit cyclical paths as the economy
alternates between phases of unemployment and excess demand for
labor. Moveover, these cycles in output levels may be reflected in cycles
in the value of national income, giving rise to phases of "immiserizing
reallocation" during which the presence of two separate dynamic distortions induces production and employment decisions which actually reduce the level of national income. This phenomenon does not arise from
any perversity in the assumed adjustment processes: capital always
moves toward the high-rental sector, and wages always rise or fall in
response to excess demand for or supply of labor. Both of these processes
tend of themselves to raise national income (the rise in wages under
excess demand for labor does so because it induces the sector which is not
rationed on the labor market to release labor to the other sector, where
its marginal product is higher.) Rather, immiserizing reallocation occurs
because the accompanying change in industry mix may lead to either an
increase in unemployment (when the labor-intensive sector contracts) or
an intensification of the aggregate excess demand for labor (when the
labor-intensive sector expands), and each of these tends to lower national
income.

The implications for government policy of these assumptions about the dynamic adjustment of the economy were then examined. It was noted that as far as the formal structure of the present model is concerned the government could in principle ensure instantaneous adjustment if it had access to two dynamic policy instruments and if revenue could be raised costlessly to finance the disbursement of subsidies. Of course, such a high degree of controllability of the economy is clearly farfetched. If either of these conditions are not met, then transitional adjustment costs are unavoidable, but some intervention may still be justified and will in many circumstances take the form of subsidies designed to slow down rather than speed up the rate of intersectoral capital reallocation. However, these conclusions are based on a model where the microeconomic under-pinnings of sluggish wage adjustment and intersectoral capital realloca-tion were not specified. When this is done, as it is, for example, in the recent work of Lapan (1976) and Mussa (1978), the key question be-comes whether there is a divergence between social and private costs of adjustment. Such a divergence can arise from any one of a number of sources, including imperfect foresight on the part of capital owners of the future course of factor prices, government- or trade-union-induced re-strictions on wage flexibility or labor mobility, and congestion in the process of search for new jobs.

While the likelihood that one if not all of these sources of market imperfection will be present in any particular situation suggests a pre-sumption in favor of adjustment assistance, some strategic and political considerations should be kept in mind before recommending assistance in practice.[10] Principal among these are the related questions of the auton-omy of the policy agency concerned with administration of the assistance program, and the likelihood that the nature of the dynamic distortions present may not be independent of the existence or expected duration of such a program. Moreover, since the terms on which assistance is granted are likely to vary from case to case, there is a grave danger that the establishment of an assistance program may lead to a diversion of re-sources toward lobbying activities, or, in the terminology of Hirschman (1970), to an increased used of "voice" as a means of postponing "exit." (This is especially likely when declining industries are geographically concentrated and government policies restrict interregional labor mobility.)

Finally, it should be recalled that we have concentrated in this paper on defenses of adjustment assistance which rely on its raising allocative efficiency in an environment where the revenue to finance subsidies can be raised costlessly. This neglects the well-known fact that, when nondis-torting revenue sources are unavailable, the optimal levels of any subsidy must be modified to reflect the by-product distortion costs of revenue raising. In addition it ignores what is probably the strongest economic and certainly the most potent political argument for adjustment assistance—its use as a redistributional tool in compensating factors tied to declining industries, and thus in ensuring that the gains from trade liberalization do not accrue only to consumers and to factors employed in export industries.

Appendix A   *The Time Path of National Income during the Adjustment Process*

Changes in real national income Z at the prices prevailing after the initial change in the terms of trade are a weighted average of the changes in sectoral output levels, the weights being the share of each sector in national income:

(A1) $$\hat{Z} = \theta_x \hat{X} + \theta_y \hat{Y}.$$

To evaluate this change, it is necessary to distinguish between cases where all firms are on their "notional" labor-demand schedules and those where they are not. Considering first the former cases, the change in output in each sector is a weighted average of the changes in input levels, the weights being the shares of each factor in the value of output:

(A2) $$\hat{X} = \theta_{lx}\hat{L}_x + \theta_{kx}\hat{K}_x,$$
$$\hat{Y} = \theta_{ly}\hat{L}_y + \theta_{ky}\hat{K}_y.$$

Substituting from (A2) into (A1), and using equation (12) to eliminate $\hat{K}_y$, yields

(A3) $$\hat{Z} = \theta_x\theta_{lx}\hat{L}_x + \theta_y\theta_{ly}\hat{L}_y + \left[\theta_x\theta_{kx} - \theta_y\theta_{ky}\frac{\lambda_{kx}}{\lambda_{ky}}\right]\hat{K}_x.$$

This may be simplified by invoking the identities

(A4) $$\theta_i\theta_{li} = \theta_l\lambda_{li} \quad (i = x,y),$$

where θ_l is the share of wages in national income, and

(A5) $$\theta_x\theta_{kx}\frac{r_y}{r_x} = \theta_y\theta_{ky}\frac{\lambda_{kx}}{\lambda_{ky}}.$$

Equation (A3) thus becomes

(A6) $$\hat{Z} = \theta_l(\lambda_{lx}\hat{L}_x + \lambda_{ly}\hat{L}_y) + \theta_x\theta_{kx}\left[1 - \frac{r_y}{r_x}\right]\hat{K}_x.$$

Since employment is demand-determined, the first bracketed term in (A6) is simply the change in the aggregate demand for labor, L^d:

(A7) $$\hat{Z} = \theta_l \hat{L}^d + \theta_x \theta_{kx} \left[1 - \frac{r_y}{r_x} \right] \hat{K}_x.$$

When full employment is maintained by wage flexibility, L^d is constant, and so

(A8) $$\hat{Z} = \theta_x \theta_{kx} \left[1 - \frac{r_y}{r_x} \right] \hat{K}_x.$$

Since capital is assumed to be reallocated at all times toward the high-rental sector, (A8) confirms the assertion in section 3.4 that immiserizing reallocation cannot take place under the full-employment short-run capital specificity adjustment mechanism.

When unemployment prevails, we may substitute from equation (13) into (A7) to obtain

(A9) $$\hat{Z} = \left[\frac{\theta_l}{\lambda_{ky}} |\lambda| + \theta_x \theta_{kx} \{ 1 - \frac{r_y}{r_x} \} \right] \hat{K}_x - \theta_l \Delta \hat{w}.$$

Hence, under excess supply of labor, national income is raised by a reallocation of capital toward the high-rental sector or by a rise in employment; and the latter in turn may be brought about by either a fall in wages or a reallocation of capital toward the labor-intensive sector. Immiserizing reallocation can therefore occur when the expanding high-rental sector is relatively capital-intensive (as in region 1 of figure 3.7) but not when it is labor-intensive (as in region 2 of figure 3.7).

Comparing equations (A9) and (13), it may be noted that when excess supply of labor prevails, iso-national-income and iso-employment loci are tangential in figure 3.7 when the capital market is in equilibrium. When the capital market is out of equilibrium, the iso-national-income locus at a given point in (w, K_x) space is more steeply sloped than the iso-employment locus at the same point if and only if sector X is the high-rental sector.

We turn next to cases where excess demand for labor prevails, so that at least one sector is off its notional labor-demand schedule. If this is true of sector X, then the levels of both labor and capital inputs are predetermined in the short run, and the first equation in (A2) must be replaced by

(A10) $$\hat{X} = \bar{\theta}_{lx} \hat{L}_x + \bar{\theta}_{kx} \hat{K}_x.$$

The input elasticities of supply may now be interpreted as sectoral value shares evaluated not at market factor prices but at "virtual" factor prices, $\bar{w}_x$ and $\bar{r}_x$, where the latter are the factor prices which would induce unconstrained firms to behave in the same way as employment-constrained ones. Thus

(A11) $$\bar{\theta}_{lx} = \frac{\delta X}{\delta L_x} \frac{L_x}{X} = \frac{\bar{w}_x}{p} \frac{L_x}{X} = \frac{\bar{w}_x}{w} \theta_{lx}.$$

We must now distinguish between three cases.

a) Both sectors constrained: In this case neither sector is willing to relinquish any labor, so that sectoral employment levels are constant and hence the level of national income is independent of the wage rate. Substituting from (A10) and the corresponding equation for sector Y, and using (12) to eliminate $\hat{K}_y$, (A1) becomes

$$(A12) \qquad \hat{Z} = \left[\theta_x \bar{\theta}_{kx} - \theta_y \bar{\theta}_{ky} \frac{\lambda_{kx}}{\lambda_{ky}} \right] \hat{K}_x.$$

Invoking an equation similar to (A5), but in terms of virtual rather than actual rentals, this becomes

$$(A13) \qquad \hat{Z} = \theta_x \bar{\theta}_{kx} \left[1 - \frac{\bar{r}_y}{\bar{r}_x} \right] \hat{K}_x.$$

Since there is no necessary relationship between the rankings of the two sectors by market rentals (which determine the direction of capital movement) and virtual rentals (which reflect the extent to which the sectors are forced off their notional labor-demand schedules), it is possible for immiserizing reallocation to take place in this case.

b) Only sector X constrained: In this case the amount of labor available to sector X is determined through the full-employment constraint,

$$(A14) \qquad \lambda_{lx} \hat{L}_x + \lambda_{ly} \hat{L}_y = 0,$$

by sector Y's notional labor-demand function (11). Substituting into (A10) and making use of (12) yields

$$(A15) \qquad \hat{X} = \left[\bar{\theta}_{kx} + \bar{\theta}_{lx} \frac{\lambda_{ly}}{\lambda_{lx}} \frac{\lambda_{kx}}{\lambda_{ky}} \right] \hat{K}_x + \bar{\theta}_{lx} \frac{\lambda_{ly}}{\lambda_{lx}} \frac{\sigma_y}{\theta_{ky}} \hat{w}.$$

Note that an increase in the wage rate *raises* the output of X, since it induces sector Y to release labor, so relaxing the labor-demand constraint on sector X. Substituting from (A2) and (A15) into (A1) yields an expression which may be simplified by invoking equations (A4) (for sector Y), (A5), and (A16):

$$(A16) \qquad \theta_x \bar{\theta}_{lx} w = \theta_l \lambda_{lx} \bar{w}_x.$$

Manipulation yields

$$(A17) \qquad \hat{Z} = \left[- \frac{\theta_l}{\lambda_{ky}} |\lambda| \left\{ \frac{\bar{w}_x}{w} - 1 \right\} + \theta_x \theta_{kx} \left\{ 1 - \frac{r_y}{r_x} \right\} \right] \hat{K}_x$$

$$+ \theta_l \lambda_{ly} \frac{\sigma_y}{\theta_{ky}} \left[\frac{\bar{w}_x}{w} - 1 \right] \hat{w}.$$

Since $\bar{w}_x$ exceeds w, (A17) shows that immiserizing reallocation is possible in this case when the high-rental sector is relatively labor-intensive (e.g., in region 3 of figure 3.7). This is because, by contrast with (A9), national income is increased by a *fall* in the aggregate effective demand for labor when excess demand for labor prevails, and such a fall is encouraged by either a rise in wages or a reallocation of labor toward the relatively capital-intensive sector.

c) *Only sector Y constrained.* A similar series of derivations yields in this case

(A18) $$\hat{Z} = \left[-\frac{\theta_l}{\lambda_{ky}} |\lambda| \{\frac{\bar{w}_y}{w} - 1\} + \theta_x \theta_{kx} \{1 - \frac{r_y}{r_x}\} \right] \hat{K}_x$$

$$+ \quad \theta_l \lambda_{lx} \frac{\sigma_x}{\theta_{kx}} \left[\frac{\bar{w}_y}{w} - 1 \right] \hat{w}.$$

Appendix B *The Capital-Market Equilibrium Locus under Excess Demand for Labor*

When excess demand for labor prevails, the capital-market equilibrium locus is not given by equation (6), since the assumption made in deriving that equation, namely, that the rental in each sector equals the marginal product of capital there, does not hold in a sector which is rationed in its demand for labor. Instead, the rental is simply the residual income per unit of capital accruing to the sector after wage payments are made. Thus, for sector X

(A19) $$r_x = \frac{pX - wL_x}{K_x} \ .$$

Totally differentiating, holding p constant, and substituting from (A10) and (A11) yields

(A20) $$\theta_{kx} \hat{r}_x = -\theta_{lx} \hat{w} + \theta_{lx} \{\frac{\bar{w}_x}{w} - 1\}(\hat{L}_x - \hat{K}_x).$$

When firms in sector X are on their notional labor-demand curves, this reduces to equation (4) in the text. However, when sector X is rationed in the labor market, $\bar{w}_x$ exceeds w, implying that at a given market wage a fall in the sector's capital-labor ratio (which represents a relaxation of the labor-demand constraint) raises the return to capital.

In order to derive an expression for the capital-market equilibrium locus, it is again necessary to distinguish between three cases.

a) Both sectors constrained. Combining (A20) with the corresponding equation for sector Y, recalling that L_x and L_y are constant, and using (12) to eliminate $\hat{K}_y$ yields

$$(A21) \qquad \hat{r}_x - \hat{r}_y = - \frac{|\theta|}{\theta_{kx}\theta_{ky}} \hat{w} - \left[\frac{\theta_{lx}}{\theta_{kx}}\{\frac{\bar{w}_x}{w} - 1\} \right.$$

$$\left. + \frac{\lambda_{lx}}{\lambda_{ly}} \frac{\theta_{ly}}{\theta_{ky}}\{\frac{\bar{w}_y}{w} - 1\} \right] \hat{K}_x.$$

The coefficient of $\hat{K}_x$ is zero in the neighborhood of the long-run equilibrium point, and is otherwise negative, implying that when both sectors are rationed, the capital-market equilibrium locus is downward-sloping if and only if sector X is relatively labor-intensive.

b) Only sector X constrained. In this case

$$(A22) \qquad \hat{r}_x - \hat{r}_y = - \frac{|\theta|}{\theta_{kx}\theta_{ky}} \hat{w} + \frac{\theta_{lx}}{\theta_{kx}} \left[\frac{\bar{w}_x}{w} - 1 \right] (\hat{L}_x - \hat{K}_x).$$

Using (A12), (11), and (12) to eliminate $\hat{L}_x$, this becomes

$$(A23) \qquad \hat{r}_x - \hat{r}_y = - \frac{1}{\theta_{kx}\theta_{ky}} \left[|\theta| - \theta_{lx} \frac{\lambda_{ly}}{\lambda_{lx}} \sigma_y\{\frac{\bar{w}_x}{w} - 1\} \right] \hat{w}$$

$$- \frac{\theta_{lx}}{\theta_{kx}} \frac{|\lambda|}{\lambda_{lx}\lambda_{ky}} \left[\frac{\bar{w}_x}{w} - 1 \right] \hat{K}_x.$$

A reallocation of capital toward sector X has the direct effect of tightening the labor-market constraint which the sector faces and thereby lowering the return to capital there; in addition, by inducing sector Y to release some labor, it indirectly tends to relax the constraint on sector X. A necessary and sufficient condition for the direct effect to dominate is that sector X be relatively labor-intensive. As for an increase in the wage rate, it has the usual effect of lowering the relative rental in the labor-intensive sector. In addition, by encouraging sector Y to release some labor, it raises output and the return to capital in sector X.

By inspecting (A23) it may be established that this locus is horizontal in the neighborhood of long-run equilibrium and downward-sloping when the extent of excess demand for labor is small. If the labor market is extremely tight (so that $\bar{w}_x$ greatly exceeds w), the locus is downward-sloping if and only if sector X is relatively capital-intensive.

c) Only sector Y constrained. A similar series of derivations yields

$$(\text{A24}) \qquad \hat{r}_x - \hat{r}_y = -\frac{1}{\theta_{kx}\theta_{ky}}\left[\, |\theta| + \theta_{ly}\frac{\lambda_{lx}}{\lambda_{ly}}\sigma_x\{\frac{\overline{w}_y}{w}-1\}\,\right]\hat{w}$$

$$+\frac{\theta_{ly}}{\theta_{ky}}\,\frac{|\lambda|}{\lambda_{ly}\lambda_{ky}}\left[\frac{\overline{w}_y}{w}-1\right]\hat{K}_x.$$

Notes

1. Mussa (1979) illustrates the usefulness of these isocost curves in international trade theory.
2. This criticism of adjustment costs as a rationale for noninstantaneous movement from one long-run equilibrium to another was first made by Rothschild (1971) in the context of investment theory.
3. These facts are reflected in the shape of the transformation curve in the minimum-wage model of Brecher (1974). Note, however, that if the wage is pegged at a level which implies excess demand for labor, then (as shown in appendix B) the capital-market equilibrium locus does depend on the intersectoral allocation of capital, and so a determinate unspecialized equilibrium is possible.
4. As shown by Jones and Neary (1979) this does not rule out a temporary reversal of the sign of $|\theta|$ in the course of the adjustment process.
5. See Dixit (1978), for example. I am indebted to Avinash Dixit for pointing out the need to "Clowerize" the capital-market equilibrium locus under excess demand for labor in the present model.
6. Production would remain at A'' if both capital and labor were sector-specific in the short-run but their returns in each sector were perfectly flexible, ensuring continual full employment of both factors. The consequences of these assumptions have been examined by Kemp, Kimura, and Okuguchi (1977) and Neary (1978b).
7. Since real income is evaluated at post- rather than prechange prices, the measure of adjustment costs proposed here is of the compensating rather than the equivalent variation kind. The construction of a true measure of adjustment costs is, of course, greatly facilitated by the assumption that commodity prices are exogenous. The difficulties of constructing measures of static efficiency losses in a closed economy are illustrated by Desai and Martin (1979).
8. The optimal policy under the minimum-time objective for the special case where techniques are fixed in both sectors (so that the competitive solution is as illustrated in figure 3.4) has been derived by Koichi Hamada in a paper published in Japanese.
9. Optimal policy choice in models with adjustment costs has also been examined by Bhagwati and Srinivasan (1976) and Mayer (1977). However, they were not concerned with adjustment assistance.
10. Wolf (1979) presents a valuable survey of actual experience with adjustment assistance and discusses some of the issues touched on here.

References

Bhagwati, J. 1971. The generalized theory of distortions and welfare. In J. Bhagwati et al., eds., *Trade, balance of payments, and growth:*

Essays in honor of Charles P. Kindleberger, pp. 69–90. Amsterdam: North-Holland.

Bhagwati, J., and T. N. Srinivasan. 1976. Optimal trade policy and compensation under endogenous uncertainty: The phenomenon of market disruption. *Journal of International Economics* 6: 317–36.

Brecher, R. A. 1974. Minimum wage rates and the pure theory of international trade. *Quarterly Journal of Economics* 88: 98–116.

Cassing, J., and J. Ochs. 1978. International trade, factor-market distortions, and the optimal dynamic subsidy: Comment. *American Economic Review* 68: 950–55.

Corden, W. M. 1974. *Trade policy and economic welfare*. London: Oxford University Press.

Desai, P., and R. Martin. 1979. On measuring resource-allocational efficiency in Soviet industry. Mimeographed. Russian Research Centre, Harvard University.

Dixit, A. 1978. The balance of trade in a model of temporary equilibrium with rationing. *Review of Economic Studies* 45: 393–404.

Haberler, G. 1950. Some problems in the pure theory of international trade. *Economic Journal* 60: 223–40.

Hirschman, A. 1970. *Exit, voice, and loyalty: Response to decline in firms, organizations, and states*. Cambridge, Mass.: Harvard University Press.

Jones, R. W. 1965. The structure of simple general equilibrium models. *Journal of Political Economy* 73: 557–72.

———. 1975. Income distribution and effective protection in a multicommodity trade model. *Journal of Economic Theory* 11: 1–15.

Jones, R. W., and J. P. Neary. 1979. Temporal convergence and factor intensities. *Economics Letters* 3: 311–14.

Kemp, M. C., Y. Kimura, and K. Okuguchi. 1977. Monotonicity properties of a dynamical version of the Heckscher-Ohlin model of production. *Economic Studies Quarterly* 28: 240–53.

Lapan, H. E. 1976. International trade, factor market distortions, and the optimal dynamic subsidy. *American Economic Review* 66: 335–46.

———. 1978. International trade, factor-market distortions, and the optimal dynamic subsidy: Reply. *American Economic Review* 68: 956–59.

———. 1979. Factor-market distortions and dynamic optimal intervention: Reply. *American Economic Review* 69: 718–20.

Mayer, W. 1974. Short-run and long-run equilibrium for a small open economy. *Journal of Political Economy* 82: 955–67.

———. 1977. The national defense tariff argument reconsidered. *Journal of International Economics* 7: 363–77.

Mussa, M. 1974. Tariffs and the distribution of income: The importance of factor specificity, substitutability, and intensity in the short and long run. *Journal of Political Economy* 82: 1191–1203.

————. 1978. Dynamic adjustment in the Heckscher-Ohlin-Samuelson model. *Journal of Political Economy* 86: 775–91.

————. 1979. The two-sector model in terms of its dual: A geometric exposition. *Journal of International Economics* 9: 513–26.

Neary, J. P. 1978*a*. Short-run capital specificity and the pure theory of international trade. *Economic Journal* 88: 488–510.

————. 1978*b*. Dynamic stability and the theory of factor-market distortions. *American Economic Review* 68: 671–82.

Neary, J. P., and J. E. Stiglitz. 1982. Towards a reconstruction of Keynesian economics: Expectations and constrained equilibria. *Quarterly Journal of Economics* (forthcoming).

Ray, E. J. 1979. Factor-market distortions and dynamic optimal intervention. Comment. *American Economic Review* 69: 715–17.

Rothschild, M. 1971. On the cost of adjustment. *Quarterly Journal of Economics* 85: 605–22.

Wolf, M. 1979. Adjustment policies and problems in developed countries. World Bank Staff Working Paper no. 349.

Comment   Carlos Alfredo Rodríguez

In Neary's two-sector, two-factor, small-country, open-economy model, the wage level adjusts slowly in response to the rate of unemployment while physical capital moves slowly between sectors in response to differences in its marginal value product in each sector. Neary shows that in the resulting dynamic adjustment path, national income evaluated at world prices may actually fall for some time in spite of the quite reasonable adjustment mechanism postulated for the factor markets and the absence of distortions in the goods markets. This possibility is baptized "immiserizing reallocation" (IR) by the author and is, in my view, the main contribution of the paper. However, I feel that the paper does not provide a clear, intuitive explanation for the phenomenon of IR, and doing so is the purpose of this comment.

Explaining Immiserizing Reallocation

There are two state variables in the model: the wage rate, w, and the capital used in sector X, K_x, (K_y equals the fixed total stock minus K_x). According to Neary, IR may happen when w falls (so there must be unemployment) and K_x also falls (so that the marginal product of K in Y exceeds that in the X sector). Clearly, the fall in wages can only contribute to a higher level of employment and therefore will raise national

Carlos Alfredo Rodríguez is professor of economics with C.E.M.A. in Buenos Aires, Argentina, and was professor of economics at Columbia University. He has published extensively on international trade and monetary theory.

income (remember, there are no distortions in goods markets so that here cannot be any "adverse" Rybczynski effect); therefore the fall in wages cannot be the direct cause of IR, which then must be the result of the shift of capital between sectors in the face of short-run wage rigidity.

The question is how can shifting capital from a low- to a high-marginal-value product activity reduce national income in the absence of distortions in the goods markets? The answer is that in a fixed wage economy, the marginal product of capital does not equal its social marginal product (i.e., the increase in national income due to a unit increase in the capital stock). In Neary's world, because of the fixed wage assumption, the social opportunity cost of labor is zero since any increase in employment in one sector comes exclusively from the pool of unemployment and not from reduced employment (and output) in the other sector. The social marginal product of labor being zero implies that the social marginal product of capital in each sector is equal to its average private product in the sector (this will be formally proved below). The criterion for IR therefore becomes that capital moves from a high average product activity to a low average product activity. Notice that it is perfectly possible for the sector with the higher average product of capital to have the lower marginal product of capital. Since capital moves in response to differences between private rates of return (marginal products), the possibility of IR is therefore explained as a result of the difference between the private and social rates of return to capital in each sector. To the extent that unemployment persists, the possibility of IR is eliminated when capitalists perceive the average product of capital as its opportunity cost and this can be obtained through a subsidy to the use of capital in each sector equal to the difference between its average and marginal product. This second-best subsidy will eliminate the possibility of IR but will not, of course, eliminate the social loss of unemployment due to the wage rigidity, the solution to which would require subsidizing labor by the full amount of its marginal product.

I will now derive algebraically the above results.

(1) $\bar{w} = F_L(L_x, K_x)$ demands for labor.
(2) $\bar{w} = G_L(L_y, K_y)$

(3) $X = F(L_x, K_x)$ production functions.
(4) $Y = G(L_y, K_y)$

The functions $F(\cdot)$ and $G(\cdot)$ are assumed to be homogeneous in the first degree so that

(5) $F_{LL} = -(K_x/L_x)F_{KL},$

(6) $G_{LL} = -(K_y/L_y)G_{KL}.$

The capital constraint requires that

(7) $\qquad K_x + K_y = \bar{K}$,

while there is no labor constraint since there is unemployment. National income, assuming world prices equal unity, is

(8) $\qquad I = X + Y = F(L_x, K_x) + G(L_y, K_y)$.

The phenomenon of IR can arise when capital is shifted away from the X sector into the Y sector. The net effect on national income of this capital reallocation is obtained by computing the derivative dI/dK_y in (8) subject to the conditions (1), (2), and (7). Differentiating (1), (2), and (8) and using (7), we obtain

(8') $\qquad dI/dK_y = (dL_x/dK_y)\bar{w} + (dL_y/dK_y)$
$$\bar{w} + (G_K - F_k),$$

(1') $\qquad dL_x/dK_y = F_{KL}/F_{LL} = -(L_x/K_x) \qquad \text{(using [5])},$

(2') $\qquad dL_y/dK_y = G_{KL}/G_{LL} = -(L_y/K_y) \qquad \text{(using [6])}.$

The first two terms on the RHS of (8') represent the effect on national income of the reallocation of labor induced by the movement of capital; the last term in (8') captures the direct effect of the reallocation of capital (which is positive since by assumption G_K exceeds F_K). The possibility of IR requires therefore that the sum of the first two terms on the RHS of (8') be sufficiently negative to offset the positive contribution of the last term $(G_K - F_K)$. We can go one step further to see whether a more definite expression can be obtained. Replacing (1') and (2') into (8') using (1) and (2), we obtain

(9) $\qquad dI/dK_y = -(F_L L_x/K_x) + (G_L L_y/K_y) + G_K - F_K =$
$$= \frac{G_L L_Y + G_K K_y}{K_y} - \frac{F_L L_x + F_K K_x}{K_x},$$

which, given the linear technology, becomes

(10) $\qquad dI/dK_y = (Y/K_y) - (X/K_x).$

According to (10), shifting capital away from the X sector into the Y sector will increase national income if and only if the average product of capital in the Y sector exceeds the average product of capital in the X sector. This result is totally independent of the relationship between the marginal products of capital in both sectors and, as explained before, is due to the fixed wage assumption.

Comment   Avinash Dixit

This is a typically competent Neary paper on the specific factor model. The added feature is wage stickiness, which is shown to produce interesting new problems such as cyclical adjustment paths involving "immiserizing" phases where the value of output may be falling. Like all fix-price models, this one could be criticized for its lack of explicit attention to the process of price formation. The ad hoc nature of the capital allocation process could also be discussed. Neary is aware of both problems, and would offer the standard replies. Instead of indulging in this ritual, therefore, I shall point out how some of the technical aspects of the paper could be developed more neatly. Thus the discussion is an alternative version of Neary's appendix A.

Instead of Neary's λ-θ approach following Jones (1965), I shall use the revenue or national product function following Chipman (1972) and Dixit and Norman (1980). In the flexible-wage case, the matter is very simple. The value of output is given by

$$(1) \qquad Z = R(p_x, p_y, K_x, K_y, L),$$

where the function on the RHS gives the maximum of $p_x X + p_y Y$ subject to production feasibility given factor supplies K_x, K_y, and L. The important property of this function for our purposes is that its partial derivatives with respect to K_x and K_y are the value marginal products of these factor quantities, i.e., the rental rates r_x and r_y in the respective sectors. Differentiating with respect to time, therefore, we have

$$(2) \qquad \dot{Z} = (\partial R/\partial K_x)\dot{K}_x + (\partial R/\partial K_y)\dot{K}_y = (r_x - r_y)\dot{K}_x$$

using $\dot{K}_y = -\dot{K}_x$. Since $\dot{K}_x$ has the same sign as $(r_x - r_y)$, national product increases monotonically along the adjustment path.

When the sticky wage is below its full-employment level, labor must be rationed between the two sectors. Neary considers alternative cases and finds ambiguous answers. The nature of this ambiguity is brought out most sharply by considering a case where labor is allocated efficiently, i.e., so as to maximize the value of output. Now we once again have (1), but the partial derivatives of R with respect to K_x and K_y are the shadow rentals $\bar{r}_x$ and $\bar{r}_y$. Differentiating,

$$(3) \qquad \dot{Z} = (\bar{r}_x - \bar{r}_y)\dot{K}_x.$$

The sign of $\dot{K}_x$ is that of the difference between the market rental rates $(r_x - r_y)$. There is no logical connection between this and the difference

Avinash Dixit is professor of economics and international affairs at Princeton University. He is coauthor (with Victor Norman) of *The Theory of International Trade*, and of other books and articles on international trade, industrial organization, public finance, and growth and development theory.

between the shadow rental rates; therefore the immiserizing decrease in Z along the adjustment path is a possibility.

When the sticky wage is too high, there is unemployment. In this case it is better to replace the revenue function by the closely related profit function $\pi(p_x, p_y, K_x, K_y, w)$, this being the maximum of $(p_x X + p_y Y - wL)$ subject to feasibility given (K_x, K_y) and the prices. Its partial derivatives with respect to K_x and K_y are the rentals r_x and r_y, while the labor demand function is minus the partial derivative with respect to w:

$$(4) \qquad L^d(p_x, p_y, K_x, K_y, w) = -\pi_w(p_x, p_y, K_x, K_y, w).$$

National product is then profit plus the wage bill:

$$(5) \qquad Z = \pi(p_x, p_y, K_x, K_y, w) + w L^d(p_x, p_y, K_x, K_y, w).$$

In the specific factor model, labor demand is found by equating the marginal product of labor in each sector to the product wage there:

$$(6) \qquad w/p_x = f'_x(L_x/K_x) \text{ or } L_x = K_x g_x(w/p_x),$$

where f_x is the production function in intensive form and g_x is the function inverse to f'_x. Similarly for the other sector. Therefore

$$(7) \qquad L^d(p_x, p_y, K_x, K_y, w) = K_x g_x(w/p_x) + K_y g_y(w/p_y).$$

Using all this and differentiating (5), we have

$$(8) \qquad \dot{Z} = (r_x - r_y)\dot{K}_x + w L^d_w \dot{w} + w[g_x(w/p_x) - g_y(w/p_y)]\dot{K}_x.$$

The first term is positive as before. The second term is also positive, since L^d_w is negative, and in the region of unemployment so is $\dot{w}$. The only possible ambiguity arises from the third term. The term in brackets is the difference between the labor-capital ratios in the two sectors, which is positive by Neary's assumption that sector X is more labor-intensive. Therefore the third term will be positive when $\dot{K}_x$ is positive, i.e., in Neary's region (2). In that region, therefore, national product is increasing along the adjustment path. In region (1), however, $\dot{K}_x$ is negative and so is the third term, and it is possible for it to outweigh the first two and thus produce an immiserizing decrease of national product during the adjustment process.

References

Chipman, J. S. 1972. The theory of exploitative trade and investment. In L. E. Di Marco, ed., *International economics and development*. New York: Academic Press.

Dixit, A., and Norman, V. 1980. *Theory of international trade*. Welwyn, Herts., UK: Nisbets and Cambridge University Press.

Jones, R. W. 1965. The structure of simple general equilibrium models. *Journal of Political Economy* 73, no. 4: 557–72.

4 Government Policy and the Adjustment Process

Michael Mussa

4.1 Introduction and Summary

Most standard analyses of the effects of changing conditions of international trade and of international trade policies such as tariffs and import quotas either focus on conditions of long-run equilibrium or implicitly assume that resources can be moved costlessly from one activity to another. Recent experience with the problems of adjusting to the increase in the world price of energy, to cite one dramatic instance, demonstrates that this practice of abstracting from the process of adjustment ignores many important questions of international trade policy. The purpose of this paper is to examine some of these questions in the context of a modified version of the standard two-sector model and, specifically, to analyze the interaction of various government policies with the adjustment process.[1]

The model of adjustment technology, as set forth in section 4.2, is obtained from the standard Heckscher-Ohlin-Samuelson model by assuming that the process of moving capital from one industry to another requires an input of some of the economy's available labor. This assumption gives rise to a distinction between short-run production possibilities, with a fixed distribution of capital, and long-run production possibilities, when capital is mobile. It also implies an explicit cost for capital movement in terms of reduced production of final outputs. Recognition of this cost implies that the adjustment process cannot be viewed as governed by an arbitrarily specified "speed of adjustment" that should be made as large as possible. Rather, the adjustment process must be treated as an

Michael Mussa is the William H. Abbott Professor of International Business at the University of Chicago and a research associate of the National Bureau of Economic Research. He has published extensively on the theory of international trade, international finance, and monetary economics.

economic process in which the marginal cost of more rapid adjustment is balanced against its marginal benefit.

In section 4.3, the optimal adjustment path of the economy is analyzed under the assumption that the economy is managed by a planner who maximizes the present discounted value of the economy's final output. This analysis establishes the central point that decisions about adjustment are fundamentally investment decisions in which the marginal benefit of capital movement reflects the present discounted value of the differential between the rental earned by capital in the two industries.

The main point of section 4.4 is that private maximizing behavior will lead to a socially efficient adjustment path provided that three conditions are met. First, there must be no distortions in the product or factor markets that cause privately perceived values to diverge from true social values. Second, the private discount rate used in calculating the benefit of capital movement to private capital owners must be the same as the social discount rate. Third, the expectations on which private capital owners base their estimates of the benefits of capital movement must be "rational" in the sense that they appropriately reflect the structure of the economy.

As discussed in section 4.5, when there are distortions that directly affect the adjustment process, then, in accord with the general principles of policy intervention, it is appropriate for the government to intervene to countervail these distortions. In particular, a proportional tax on factor income (which is nondistorting in a static context) distorts the adjustment process by reducing the privately perceived benefit of capital movement relative to the true social benefit. To countervail this distortion it is appropriate to grant an investment tax credit for all adjustment costs. An excess of the private discount rate over the social discount rate also reduces the privately perceived benefit of capital movement relative to the true social benefit, and requires either a subsidy to capital movement or a subsidy to the income of capital in the expanding industry. Errors of expectations by private capital owners also distort the adjustment process. However, except in the case where such errors arise from an incorrect perception of future government policy, there is no general argument that government policy can be used systematically to correct distortions resulting from errors of expectations.

When a country can affect the price that it pays for imports, the first-best policy for that country requires that the government impose an optimum tariff to make the privately perceived price of imports equal to the social marginal cost of imports. As discussed in section 4.6, the adjustment process influences optimal tariff policy. Specifically, under fairly general conditions, the optimal tariff (measured as a specific tariff) declines as the economy moves along its optimal adjustment path, starting from free trade equilibrium. Moreover, at any point along this adjustment path, the optimal tariff is greater than the tariff that would be charged with a fixed distribution of capital because the process of capital movement increases the marginal cost of domestically produced import substitutes. To achieve the optimal adjustment path, it is not necessary for the government to intervene in the adjustment process to promote the movement of resources into the import-competing industry. This reflects the general principle that no intervention in the adjustment process is required provided that the first-best policy that countervails a product or factor market distortion is implemented.

When the first-best policy is not available, the second-best combination of policies may or may not require intervention in the adjustment process. This general principle is illustrated in section 4.7 by considering second-best policies to exploit monopoly power in trade when the first-best policy of an optimally varying tariff is not available. If a constant tariff that yields the optimal steady state is imposed, the speed of convergence toward this steady state (starting from free trade) is less than socially optimal. It is appropriate therefore for the government to intervene in the adjustment process by subsidizing the movement of capital into the import-competing industry. In contrast, if the government imposes the optimal steady state import quota, the speed of convergence toward the steady state is greater than socially optimal; and it is appropriate to tax the movement of capital into the import-competing industry. If the government can employ a production subsidy but not a tariff, an import quota, or a consumption tax, the optimal second-best policy is an optimally varying production subsidy, with no intervention in the adjustment process. If the government can employ a consumption tax but not a tariff, an import quota, or a production subsidy, the optimal second-best policy includes not only the consumption tax but also intervention in the adjustment process in order to restrain the movement of capital out of the import-competing industry. This difference between the consumption tax and the production subsidy reflects the fact that under the production subsidy (but not under the consumption tax) the price facing domestic producers of the import substitute corresponds to the social marginal value of domestically produced import substitutes. Under the production subsidy, therefore, private capital owners receive the correct signal concerning the benefits and costs of capital movement, without any government intervention in the adjustment process.

The concluding section of the paper considers extensions and generalizations of the analysis in the preceding sections. First, we examine the effects of government policies directed at the adjustment process on the distribution of income among factor owners and the possible effects on the adjustment process of government policies directed at affecting the distribution of income. Next, we investigate the implications of a more general adjustment technology that allows for investment in altering the size of the capital stock, as well as in moving capital from one industry to another. Finally, we summarize the general principles concerning government policy toward the adjustment process that are implied by the present theoretical analysis and that appear likely to carry over to more elaborate and realistic models.

4.2   A Model of Adjustment Technology

To provide a formal basis for the analysis of the role of government policy in the adjustment process, it is useful to develop a simple model of adjustment technology, based on the standard two-sector model.[2] Suppose that the output of each good is produced in accord with a neoclassical, linear homogeneous production function:

(1) $$X = F(L_X, K_X),$$

(2) $$Z = G(L_Z, K_Z),$$

where L_X, L_Z, K_X, and K_Z are the quantities of labor and capital used in the respective industries. Let Z be the numeraire commodity, and let P, W, R_X, and R_Z denote, respectively, the price of X, the wage of labor, and the rental rates on capital in X and capital in Z, all measured in terms of Z. The total stock of capital, $\underline{K} = K_X + K_Z$, is fixed. Its distribution between X and Z is indicated by the variable K, with $K_X = K$ and $K_Z = \underline{K} - K$. At any moment of time, K is given, but it can be changed over by a process that uses some of the economy's supply of labor; specifically, suppose that [3]

(3) $$L_I = \beta \cdot I^2,$$

where $I = |\dot{K}|$ is the rate at which capital is being moved from X to Z or vice versa. Labor is freely mobile, but total labor use is constrained by the fixed aggregate supply:

(4) $$L_X + L_Z + L_I = \underline{L}.$$

From this specification of productive technology, we obtain the transformation function

(5) $$Z = T(X, I, K),$$

which indicates the maximum amount of Z that can be produced as a function of X, I, and K. Without going into details or derivations, we may summarize the key properties of this transformation function, using the notation T_i and T_{ij} to denote the first and second partial derivatives of T. First, the marginal cost of X in terms of Z is given by $-T_X$ and is equal to the ratio of the marginal products of labor in Z and X:

(6) $$-T_X(X, I, K) = \mathrm{MPL}_Z / \mathrm{MPL}_X.$$

The marginal cost of X is an increasing function of X ($-T_{XX}>0$), an increasing function of I ($-T_{XI}>0$), and a decreasing function of K ($-T_{XK}<0$). Second, the marginal cost of I in terms of Z is given by $-T_I$ and satisfies

$$(7) \qquad -T_I(X,I,K) = \beta \cdot I \cdot \mathrm{MPL}_Z.$$

The marginal cost of I is zero for $I = 0$ and is greater than zero for $I > 0$; it is an increasing function of I ($-T_{II} > 0$) and an increasing function of X ($-T_{IX} > 0$). If X is relatively capital-intensive, then $-T_{IK} < 0$; and conversely if X is relatively labor-intensive. Third, a shift of capital from Z to X increases potential output of Z, given X and I, if and only if the value of the marginal product of capital in X (measured by $R_X = -T_X \cdot \mathrm{MPK}_X$) is greater than the value of the marginal product of capital in Z (measured by $R_Z = \mathrm{MPK}_Z$); specifically,

$$(8) \qquad T_K(X,I,K) = -T_X \cdot \mathrm{MPK}_X - \mathrm{MPK}_Z = R_X - R_Z.$$

For each feasible combination of X and I, there is a $K^*(X,I)$ such that

$$T_K(X,I,K) \gtreqless 0 \text{ according as } K \lesseqgtr K^*(X,I),$$

where $K_X^* > 0$ and $K_I^* < 0$. Further, $T_{KX} = T_{XK} < 0$, $T_{KI} = T_{IK} \gtrless 0$ depending on relative factor intensities, and $T_{KK} < 0$ at least in the neighborhood of points where $T_K = 0$.

Some of the properties of the transformation function are illustrated in figure 4.1. In the upper panel, the transformation curves $T(X, 0, K_0)$ and $T(X, 0, K_1)$ show the effect of a redistribution of capital ($K_1 > K_0$) on production possibilities, after the process of capital movement is complete. The marginal cost curves $-T_X(X, 0, K_0)$ and $-T_X(X, 0, K_1)$ in the lower panel show the effect of this capital redistribution on the marginal cost of producing X. The transformation curve $T(X, I_0, K_0)$ and the associated marginal cost curve $-T_X(X, I_0, K_0)$ show the effect of a positive rate of capital movement ($I_0 > 0$) on production possibilities for final outputs and on the marginal cost of X.

The outer envelope of all of the transformation curves $T(X, 0, K)$ is the transformation curve $T^*(X)$ implied by the standard two-sector model in which labor and capital are both freely mobile between X and Z. Formally, this "long-run" transformation curve is defined by

$$(9) \qquad Z = \bar{T}(X) \equiv T(X, 0, K^*(X, 0)).$$

Corresponding to this long-run transformation curve, in the lower panel of figure 4.1, is the long-run marginal cost curve $-\bar{T}_X(X)$. This long-run marginal cost curve is flatter than any of the short-run marginal cost curves $-T_X(X, 0, K)$ drawn for a fixed distribution of capital. The intersection of the long-run marginal cost curve with each of these short-

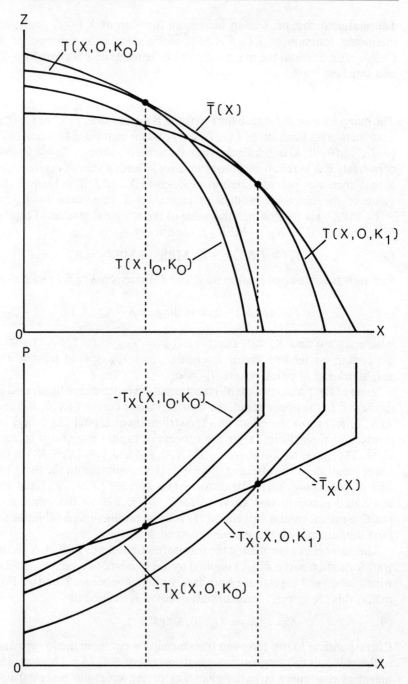

Fig. 4.1   Transformation curves and marginal cost curves for different distributions of capital and different rates of capital movement.

run marginal cost curves occurs at the level of X for which $K = K^*(X, 0)$. At the corresponding point in the upper panel of figure 4.1, the transformation curve $T(X, 0, K)$ is tangent to the outer envelope transformation curve $\bar{T}(X)$. At such points, $T_K(X, 0, K) = 0$, indicating that it is not possible to increase output of Z through any redistribution of capital without reducing output of X.

4.3 Social Optimization

Suppose that the economy whose technology was described in the preceding section is a small country that faces a fixed relative price of X in world trade, P, and a fixed world interest rate, r. The relevant objective for a social planner (leaving aside issues of income distribution) is to maximize

$$(10) \qquad \int_0^\infty (P \cdot X + Z) \exp(-r \cdot t) \, dt$$

subject to the constraint

$$(11) \qquad Z = T(X, |\dot{K}|, K)$$

starting from an initial distribution of capital, K_0.

To determine the solution of this problem, define the current value Hamiltonian

$$(12) \qquad H = P \cdot X + Z + \theta \cdot (T(X, |\dot{K}|, K) - Z) + \lambda \cdot \dot{K},$$

where θ is a Lagrangian multiplier assigned to the constraint (11) and λ is the costate variable that represents the shadow price of a unit of capital located in X rather than Z. Assuming an interior solution, the optimum path of the economy must satisfy the following conditions (see Arrow 1968):

$$(13) \qquad \partial H / \partial X = P + \theta \cdot T_X = 0,$$

$$(14) \qquad \partial H / \partial Z = 1 - \theta = 0,$$

$$(15) \qquad \partial H / \partial \dot{K} = \text{sign}(\dot{K}) \cdot \theta \cdot T_I + \lambda = 0,$$

$$(16) \qquad \dot{\lambda} = r \cdot \lambda - \theta \cdot T_K.$$

The optimum path must also be consistent with the constraint (11), the initial condition, $K(0) = K_0$, and the boundary conditions

$$(17) \qquad \lambda \leq 0 \text{ if } K = \bar{K},$$

$$(18) \qquad \lambda \geq 0 \text{ if } K = 0.$$

The conditions (13), (14), and (15) jointly determine output of X and the rate of capital movement, $I = |\dot{K}|$, by the requirement that the marginal cost of X, $-T_X(X, I, K)$, equal P, and the requirement that the marginal cost of capital movement, $-T_I(X, I, K)$, equal $|\lambda|$. These requirements implicitly determine X and I as functions of K, $|\lambda|$, and P:

(19) $\qquad X = \tilde{X}(K, |\lambda|, P), \quad \tilde{X}_K > 0, \quad \tilde{X}_{|\lambda|} < 0, \quad \tilde{X}_p > 0,$

(20) $\qquad I = \tilde{I}(K, |\lambda|, P), \quad \tilde{I}_K \gtreqless 0, \quad \tilde{I}_{|\lambda|} > 0, \quad \tilde{I}_p > 0.$

Output of Z is determined by the constraint (11) to be

(21) $\qquad Z = \tilde{Z}(K, |\lambda|, P) = T(\tilde{X}(K, |\lambda|, P), \tilde{I}(K, |\lambda|, P), K).$

The direction of capital movement is determined by the sign of λ:

(22) $\qquad \dot{K} = sign(\lambda) \cdot \tilde{I}(K, |\lambda|, P).$

Further, since $-T_I(X, I, K) = 0$ if and only if $I = 0$, it follows that

(23) $\qquad \dot{K} = 0$ iff $\lambda = 0.$

Given these results, the determination of the optimal path of the economy reduces to determining the optimal paths of K and λ. This may be accomplished with the aid of figure 4.2. From (23) it follows that the K axis (where $\lambda = 0$) corresponds to the combinations of K and λ for which $\dot{K} = 0$. Above this axis, $\dot{K} > 0$, and below it, $\dot{K} < 0$. From (16) it follows that

(24) $\qquad \dot{\lambda} = r \cdot \lambda - \varphi(K, |\lambda|, P),$

where

(25) $\qquad \varphi(K, |\lambda|, P) = T_K(\tilde{X}(K, |\lambda|, P), \tilde{I}(K, |\lambda|, P), K).$

Thus $\dot{\lambda} = 0$ along the line where $\lambda = \varphi(K, |\lambda|, P)/r$. Above this line, $\dot{\lambda} > 0$, and below it, $\dot{\lambda} < 0$. The $\dot{\lambda} = 0$ line intersects the K axis at the steady state distribution of capital, $\bar{K}(P)$, which is the efficient distribution of capital determined in the standard two-sector model where labor and capital are both freely mobile. At the steady state distribution of capital, the short-run marginal cost of producing the steady state output $\bar{X}$, $-T_X(\bar{X}, 0, \bar{K}(P))$, is equal to the long-run marginal cost of producing this level of output, $-\bar{T}_X(\bar{X})$; and both short-run and long-run marginal cost are equal to the given output price, P.[4]

From the dynamic system illustrated in figure 4.2, it is possible to determine the paths of K and λ, starting from any initial combination of K and λ. For each initial K, however, there is only one initial λ for which the subsequent path of K and λ converges to the steady state where $K = \bar{K}(P)$ and $\lambda = 0$. This is the value of λ that lies along the stable branch of the dynamic system illustrated in figure 4.2, which is denoted by $\tilde{\lambda}(K)$. For any initial K, a choice of an initial λ not equal to $\tilde{\lambda}(K)$ leads to a subsequent path of K and λ that ultimately violates one of the boundary

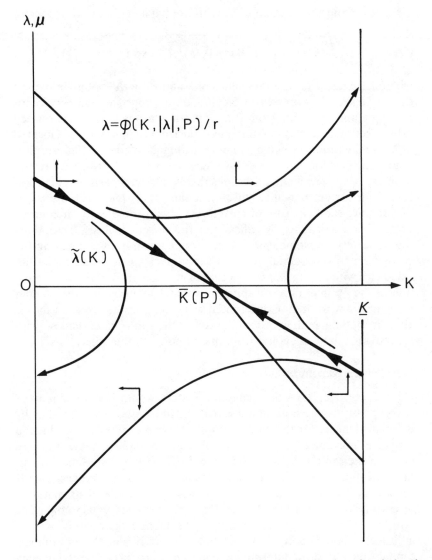

Fig. 4.2   The optimal adjustment path for the distribution of capital and the shadow price for relocating capital.

conditions (17) or (18). Such paths are clearly not optimal since it is obviously senseless to devote productive resources to moving more capital into the industry that already has all of the capital and out of the industry that has none. Thus the optimal path of K and λ is the path associated with the stable branch, and this path of K and λ determines the optimal paths for all other variables.

Finally, from the solution of the differential equation (24), it follows that

(26) $\tilde{\lambda}(t) = \int_t^\infty \varphi(\tilde{K}(s), |\tilde{\lambda}(s)|, P) \exp(-r \cdot (s-t)) ds$,

where $\tilde{\lambda}(s)$ and $\tilde{K}(s)$ are the values of λ and K on the optimum path at time s. This result expresses the fact that the appropriate shadow price for moving a unit of capital from Z to X is equal to the present discounted value of difference between the rental earned by a unit of capital located in X and the rental earned by a unit of capital located in Z. This result is important because it reveals that decisions about adjustment are not ordinary, static production decisions that involve comparisons of current costs with current benefits, but are fundamentally *investment decisions* that require the balancing of current costs with the present discounted value of future benefits. Specifically, in the present analysis, the optimal rate of capital movement is not determined simply by comparing the current rental differential between capital located in X and capital located in Z with the current cost of capital movement. Rather, determination of the optimal rate of capital movement requires that the planner recognize how this rental differential will change as the economy moves along its optimal path in order to establish the appropriate shadow price for moving a unit of capital from one industry to the other.

4.4 Private Maximization

Next, consider how the economic system would behave if it were governed by the decisions of individual maximizing agents rather than by a social planner. Since labor is mobile between the three production activities, maximization by individual workers implies that wage rates must be the same for labor used in X, in Z, and in capital movement. Maximization by private capital owners implies that labor in each industry will be employed up to the point where the value of its marginal product ($P \cdot \text{MPL}_X(\ell_X)$ for X and $\text{MPL}_Z(\ell_Z)$ for Z) is equal to the wage rate, W. These conditions determine the labor/capital ratios in each industry, $\ell_X(W/P)$ and $\ell_Z(W)$, as functions of W and P. These labor/capital ratios, in turn, determine the marginal product of capital in each industry, $\text{MPK}_X(\ell_X)$ and $\text{MPK}_Z(\ell_Z)$, and hence the rental rates earned by a unit of capital in each industry, $R_X(W, P) = P \cdot \text{MPK}_X(\ell_X(W/P))$ and $R_Z(W) = \text{MPK}_Z(\ell_Z(W))$. The service of capital movement is assumed to be provided on a competitive basis by profit maximizing firms that equate the marginal cost of providing this service, $W \cdot (dL_I/dI)$, to the price, q, that they receive for a unit of this service.[5] This assumption, together with the specification of labor requirements for capital movement given in (3), implies that the demand for labor for use in capital movement is given by $L_I(W,q) = (1/\beta) \cdot (q/2W)^2$.

In order for the economy to be in equilibrium when its behavior is governed by the decisions of individual maximizing agents, the total demand for labor must equal the available supply; that is,

(27) $\ell_X(W/P) \cdot K + \ell_Z(W) \cdot (\underline{K} - K) + L_I(W,q) = \underline{L}.$

This condition determines the equilibrium wage rate as a function of K, q, and P:

(28) $W = \tilde{W}(K,q,P) \qquad \partial W/\partial K \underset{<}{\gtreqless} 0, \partial W/\partial q > 0, \partial W/\partial P > 0.$

It is important to note that this formula for the equilibrium wage rate is also the formula that determines the wage rate for the social planner, with $q = |\lambda|$. This must be so because the social planner equates the value of the marginal product of labor in all production activities and is constrained by the total labor supply. It follows that with $q = |\lambda|$, private maximization results in the same allocation of labor as determined by the social planner. Hence outputs of X and Z and the rate of capital movement under private maximization are determined precisely by the functions $\tilde{X}(K,q,P)$, $\tilde{Z}(K, q, P)$, and $\tilde{I}(K, q, P)$ that were derived in the analysis of the behavior of the social planner.

It is apparent that the critical issue in determining the behavior of the economy under private maximization is the determination of the price that private capital owners will pay for capital movement. The benefit that a private capital owner believes he would enjoy from moving a unit of capital from X to Z, denoted by $\mu(t)$, is the present discounted value of the expected difference between the rental rate on capital in X and the rental rate on capital in Z; that is,

(29) $\mu(t) = \int_t^{\infty} (R_X^e(s;t) - R_Z^e(s;t)) \exp(-i \cdot (s - t)) ds,$

where $R_X^e(s;t)$ and $R_Z^e(s;t)$ are the expected time paths of the rental rates on capital in X and Z, based on expectations held at time t, and i is the discount rate used by private capital owners. The price that capital owners will pay for capital movement is $|\mu|$. The sign of μ determines the direction of capital movement, in accord with

(30) $\dot{K} = \text{sign}(\mu) \cdot \tilde{I}(K, |\mu|, P).$

Further, differentiation of (29) with respect to t, given the expected time paths of R_X and R_Z, implies that

(31) $\dot{\mu}^e = i \cdot \mu - \varphi(K, |\mu|, P).$

This expresses the requirement that the total expected rate of return from holding capital in X rather than Z, including expected capital gains, $(R_X - R_Z + \dot{\mu}^e)/\mu$, must equal the private discount rate, i.

Different assumptions about expectations yield different conclusions about the behavior of μ. If expectations are "static" in the sense that the current economic situation is expected to persist indefinitely, then $\dot{\mu}^e = 0$ and hence μ is determined by

(32) $\mu = \varphi(K, |\mu|, P)/i.$

If $i = r$, then the path of μ determined by (32) is shown by the $\lambda = \varphi(K, |\lambda|, P)/r$ line in figure 4.2. It follows that the steady state distribution of capital is the same $\bar{K}(P)$ determined by the social planner, but that convergence to this steady state under private maximization with static expectations is more rapid than is socially optimal. Further, for any i, the steady state distribution of capital is $\bar{K}(P)$. The greater the value of i relative to r, the slower is the speed of convergence toward this steady state. Thus, up to a point, a high private discount rate tends to offset the distortion created by static expectations.

The social planner does not make the mistake of believing that current conditions will persist indefinitely because he calculates the effect of future capital movement on the value of λ. If private agents had the same correctness of foresight, their expectations would be "rational," in the sense that they would appropriately reflect the structure of the economic system. With rational expectations, we require that $\dot{\mu}^e = \dot{\mu}$. Hence, if $i = r$ and expectations are rational, the conditions that determine the evolution of μ and K must be precisely the same as the conditions that determine the evolution of λ and K for the social planner, as represented in figure 4.2. In addition, for expectations to be rational, they must be consistent with the boundary conditions (17) and (18).

Specifically, when all capital is removed from X and $K = 0$, capital owners should not expect that resources will continue to be devoted to the futile task of moving more capital into Z; and, conversely, when $K = \underline{K}$. This implies that the only path of μ and K that is consistent with rational expectations is the path that corresponds to the stable branch in figure 4.2 namely, the socially optimal path that maximizes the present discounted value of the economy's final output.

This key result may be summarized in the form of a general proposition:

(P1)   *Private maximizing behavior will lead to a socially efficient adjustment process provided that the prices of outputs and factors and the discount rate perceived by private agents correspond to their true social values, and provided that the expectations that influence private decisions about adjustment are rational.*

This proposition has been established in the context of a specific model of adjustment technology, under the restrictive assumption that the prices of outputs and the discount rate are exogenously given and constant. It is clear, however, that the procedure used to establish this proposition in the present narrow context carries over to alternative specifications of productive technology, provided that the technology does not involve externalities or scale economies that would cause prices perceived by private agents to diverge from true social values. The assumption of constant output prices and a constant discount rate can easily be relaxed to any time paths of prices and the discount rate that are exogenously given to the production sector of the economy.[6]

4.5 Distortions of the Adjustment Process

The general theory of policy intervention suggests that government policies to improve the efficiency of the adjustment process should be directed to correcting distortions that induce the privately perceived costs or benefits of adjustment to diverge from the true social costs or benefits. It is relevant to consider the circumstances that give rise to such distortions and the policies that are appropriate to deal with them.

One important example is the distortion arising from a proportional tax on income from capital or on all factor income. Since total factor supplies have been assumed fixed, such a tax is nondistorting in the standard static production model, with either fixed or freely mobile capital. Such a tax, however, distorts the adjustment process because it causes the privately perceived benefit of capital movement to be lower than the social benefit. It τ is the proportional tax rate, then the privately perceived benefit of owning a unit of capital in X rather than Z is given by

$$(33) \qquad b = (1 - \tau) \cdot \mu,$$

where μ is defined in (29) as the present discounted value of the expected before-tax difference between the rental on capital in X and the rental on capital in Z. If private capital owners have rational expectations and the private discount rate is equal to the social discount rate, then the adjustment path toward the steady state is as illustrated in figure 4.3. The K axis is still the line along which $\dot{K} = 0$. But the line along which $\dot{b} = 0$ is now determined by the condition

$$(34) \qquad b = (1 - \tau) \cdot \varphi(K, |b|, P)/r$$

rather than by the condition $b = \mu = \varphi(K, |\mu|, P)/r$. The steady state distribution of capital, $\bar{K}(P)$, is the same as in figure 4.2, but the path of convergence to this steady state in figure 4.3 involves a less than socially optimal rate of capital movement.

Elimination of the tax on income from capital would, of course, remove this distortion of the adjustment process. Other considerations of government policy, such as the need for revenue, however, may make the elimination of this tax impractical. An alternative policy would be to

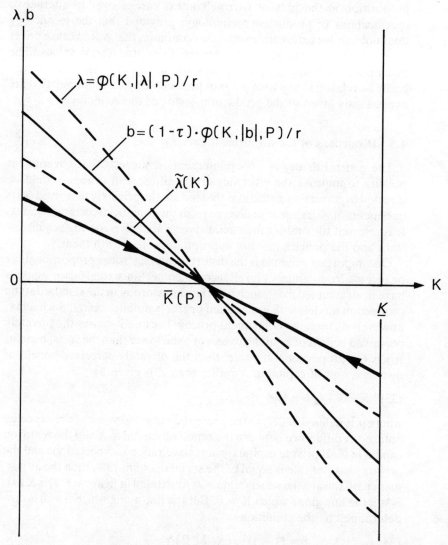

$$\lambda = \varphi(K, |\lambda|, P)/r$$

$$b = (1-\tau) \cdot \varphi(K, |b|, P)/r$$

$$\tilde{\lambda}(K)$$

Fig. 4.3   The adjustment path when a tax is imposed on the income from capital.

remove the distortionary effect of the tax on the adjustment process by allowing an investment tax credit which permits the deduction of adjustment costs from taxable income. The value of this credit is the price paid for a unit of capital movement, q, multiplied by the tax rate, τ. With this credit, the total privately perceived benefit of moving capital from Z to X becomes

(35) $b = (1 - \tau) \cdot \varphi + \tau \cdot b.$

It follows immediately that $b = \mu$. This establishes the proposition

(P2)   *To correct the distortion of the adjustment process created by a proportional tax on income from capital (or all factor income) it is appropriate to grant an investment tax credit that allows the deduction of all adjustment costs.*

The general argument for this investment tax credit is essentially the argument for a consumption-based expenditure tax, rather than an income tax. An income tax distorts intertemporal choices because of the double taxation of savings. An investment tax credit that allows income used for productive investment to avoid taxation removes this distortion.

A second possible cause of distortion of the adjustment process is an excess of the private discount rate, i, over the social discount rate, r.[7] From the analysis in sections 4.3 and 4.4, it is clear that an excess of i over r reduces the privately perceived benefit of capital movement relative to the true social benefit. Like a tax on income from capital, an excess of i over r does not affect the steady state distribution of capital, but it does reduce the rate of convergence toward this steady state to less than the socially optimal rate.

One policy that would correct this distortion would be to eliminate whatever is responsible for the excess of i over r. If this is not possible, an alternative policy would be to subsidize capital owners in the industry where capital earns a higher rental or tax capital owners in the industry where capital earns a lower rental. The required subsidy is equal to the difference $i - r$ multiplied by the privately perceived benefit of owning capital in the high-rent industry. Assuming that owners of capital in X are either subsidized or taxed (whichever is appropriate), the privately perceived benefit of owning capital in X rather than Z becomes

(36) $b(t) = \int_{t}^{\infty} (\varphi(s) + (i - r) \cdot b(s)) \exp(-i \cdot (s - t)) \, ds.$

Assuming rational expectations, differentiation of (36) with respect to t yields

(37) $\dot{b} = r \cdot b - \varphi.$

Thus, with the income subsidy for owners of capital in the high-rent industry and with rational expectations, the differential equation that determines the evolution of b is the same as the differential equation that determines the evolution of λ for the social planner. It follows that with the subsidy and with rational expectations, the adjustment path of the economy under private maximization will be socially optimal.

88   Michael Mussa

It is difficult to conceive, however, of a government that would systematically subsidize capital owners who already earn high rental rates or
systematically tax those who earn low rental rates. An alternative and
probably more attractive policy would be to subsidize the movement of
capital out of the low-rent industry. From (36) it follows that the required
subsidy to capital movement is given by

$$(38) \qquad \sigma(t) = \int_t^\infty (i - r) \cdot |\lambda(s)| \exp(-i \cdot (s-t)) \, ds,$$

where the path of $\lambda(s)$ is determined by the stable branch in figure 4.2.
The required subsidy is approximately proportional to the price of capital
movement, $q(t)$; specifically,

$$(39) \qquad \sigma(t) \cong ((i - r)/(i + \epsilon)) \cdot q(t),$$

where ϵ is the speed of convergence of q toward its steady state value of
zero. This establishes the proposition

(P3)
> *To correct the distortion of the adjustment process created by an
> excess of the private discount rate over the social discount rate, it is
> appropriate to subsidize the movement of capital at a rate that is
> approximately proportional to the cost of capital movement, using
> a subsidy rate that is itself approximately proportional to the differ-
> ence between the private and social discount rates.*

The specific result for the appropriate subsidy rate given in (39) depends on the details of the present model of the adjustment process.
More generally, it can be argued that an excess of i over r discourages all
forms of investment and hence makes a general subsidy to all forms of
investment a desirable policy.

Errors of expectations are a third potentially important cause of distortions of the adjustment process. For example, the analysis of static
expectations in the discussion of private maximizing behavior demonstrated that this particular deviation from rationality causes the benefits
of capital movement to be overvalued and hence results in too rapid
convergence of the distribution of capital to its steady state distribution.
To correct this distortion (assuming that expectations could not be
altered) would require the imposition of a tax on capital movement.
Other errors of expectations that cause the benefits of capital movement
to be undervalued by private capital owners would justify a reverse policy
of subsidizing capital movement.

In general, however, it is difficult to argue that errors of expectations
would lead systematically to either overvaluation or undervaluation of
the benefits of capital movement. The only general circumstance in which

intervention may be required to correct errors of expectations is when such errors are intrinsically related to other government policies. For instance, if a government intends to provide temporary assistance to an industry injured by import competition, it should adopt policies to ensure that such assistance does not lead to increased investment in the distressed industry. Otherwise, the assistance that is granted may strengthen political pressures to make such assistance permanent rather than temporary. Indeed, the expectation that even temporary assistance may be granted to industries adversely affected by import competition may distort the adjustment process by inducing owners of factors in such industries to delay adjustment in the hope that protective measures may make adjustment unnecessary. Thus the social cost of measures to protect particular industries from import competition is not limited to the industries in which such measures are adopted, but also extends to other industries where adjustment is influenced by the expectation that such measures may be adopted.

Finally, the adjustment process may be afflicted by the usual problems of externalities, monopoly and monopsony power, and taxes and subsidies that distort the economic system in general. In fact, the adjustment process may be more exposed to such afflictions than other economic activities. Social insurance programs that provide benefits on the basis of previous experience in a particular industry or region (whatever their social value) tend to limit the incentive for adjustment by those who would lose benefit entitlements as a result of moving to other industries or regions. Special privileges granted to existing producers in a particular industry or region, such as preferential access to lower cost energy sources or freedom from certain zoning or environmental restrictions, provide an artificial incentive for inefficient but established producers to remain in an industry or region and an artificial impediment to the establishment of new an more efficient producers. Legal restrictions on plant closings such as have been proposed in many states limit both the outward movement of resources from declining activities and the willingness to invest in new areas. In general, the political opposition to economic change and the measures to which it gives rise tend to reduce the speed of adjustment and to distort the adjustment process.

4.6   Adjustment to an Optimum Tariff

The adjustment process must be taken into account not only in designing policies to correct distortions of that process, but also in adopting policies to serve other objectives. A specific example of this general problem that illustrates many important principles is the imposition of an optimum tariff by a country that desires to exploit its monopoly power in international trade.

The relevant objective for a social planner who recognizes that the marginal cost of imports rises as the volume of imports rises is to maximize

(40) $$\int_0^\infty (U(C) + B)\, \exp\cdot(-r\cdot t)\,dt$$

subject to the constraints

(41) $$Z = T(X, |\dot{K}|, K),$$

(42) $$Z - B = J(C - X), J(0) = 0, J' > 0,\ J'' > 0,$$

where C measures home consumption of X, B measures home consumption of Z, and the foreign offer function, J, indicates the volume of home exports, $Z - B$, required to pay for home imports, $C - X$. For simplicity, it is assumed that the social discount rate is constant and that the marginal utility of consumption of Z is constant and equal to unity. The initial distribution of capital, K_0, is assumed to be the steady state distribution appropriate to free trade.

To determine the solution of the planner's optimization problem, define the current value Hamiltonian

(43) $$H = U(C) + B + \theta \cdot (T(X, |\dot{K}|, K) - Z)$$
$$+ \alpha \cdot (J(C - X) - (Z - B)) + \lambda \cdot \dot{K},$$

where θ and λ retain their previous interpretations and α is a Lagrangian multiplier assigned to the offer function constraint. In addition to the initial condition $K(0) = K_0$, the boundary conditions (17) and (18), and the constraints (41) and (42), the optimum path of the economy must satisfy the conditions

(44) $$\partial H/\partial C = U' + \alpha \cdot J' = 0,$$

(45) $$\partial H/\partial B = 1 + \alpha = 0,$$

(46) $$\partial H/\partial X = \theta \cdot T_X - \alpha \cdot J' = 0,$$

(47) $$\partial H/\partial Z = -\theta - \alpha = 0,$$

(48) $$\partial H/\partial \dot{K} = \text{sign}\,(\dot{K}) \cdot \theta \cdot T_I + \lambda = 0,$$

(49) $$\dot{\lambda} = r \cdot \lambda - \theta \cdot T_K.$$

To interpret the conditions (44) through (48), it is useful to think of the planner as establishing a relative price P for a unit of X in terms of Z. The planner sets C so that the marginal utility of consumption of X, $U'(C)$, is equal to P, thus determining C as a function of P:

(50) $$C = U'^{-1}(P).$$

The planner sets imports of X so that their marginal cost, $J'(C - X)$, is equal to P, thus determining

(51) $\qquad C - X = J'^{-1}(P).$

The planner determines X and $I = |\dot{K}|$ so that the marginal cost of X, $-T_X(X, I, K)$, is equal to P and the marginal cost of I, $-T_I(X, I, K)$, is equal to $|\lambda|$. These conditions jointly determine X and I through the functions $\tilde{X}(K, |\lambda|, P)$ and $\tilde{I}(X, |\lambda|, P)$ introduced in section 4.2, with Z given by $\tilde{Z}(K, |\lambda|, P)$. The value of P that is set by the planner must satisfy the condition

(52) $\qquad U'^{-1}(P) - J'^{-1}(P) = \tilde{X}(K, |\lambda|, P).$

This condition implicitly determines P as a function of K and $|\lambda|$:

(53) $\qquad P = \hat{P}(K, |\lambda|), \partial\hat{P}/\partial K < 0, \partial\hat{P}/\partial\lambda > 0.$

This result, in turn, determines $C, C - X, X, I, Z,$ and $B = Z - J(X - C)$ as functions of K and $|\lambda|$.

The paths of K and λ may be determined with the aid of the phase diagram shown in figure 4.4. The rate of capital movement from Z to X is determined by

(54) $\qquad \dot{K} = \text{sign}(\lambda) \cdot \tilde{I}(K, |\lambda|, \hat{P}(K, |\lambda|)).$

This rule is slightly different from the rule (22) that determines $\dot{K}$ in figure 4.2 because P is no longer fixed; but it is still true that $\dot{K} = 0$ along the K axis, is positive above the K axis, and is negative below the K axis. The evolution of λ is determined by

(55) $\qquad \dot{\lambda} = r \cdot \lambda - \psi(K, |\lambda|),$

where

(56) $\qquad \psi(K, |\lambda|) = \varphi(K, |\lambda|, \hat{P}(K, |\lambda|)).$

The line along which $\dot{\lambda} = 0$ is determined by the condition $\lambda = \psi(K, |\lambda|)/r$, which is similar to the condition that determines the $\dot{\lambda} = 0$ line in figure 4.2, except that P is no longer fixed. The steady state distribution of capital, $\bar{K}$, is the unique value of K for which $\psi(K, 0) = 0$. The relative output price that is associated with $\bar{K}$ is $\bar{P} = \hat{P}(\bar{K}, 0)$. This capital stock distribution and relative output price are precisely the same as would be obtained in the standard static analysis of the optimum tariff, under the assumption that capital is freely mobile between industries. The path of convergence to this steady state is along the stable branch of the dynamic system determined by (54) and (55), as illustrated by the function $\hat{\lambda}(K)$ shown in figure 4.4. Specifically, starting from $K_0 < \bar{K}$ (because the amount of capital allocated to X under free trade is less than under the

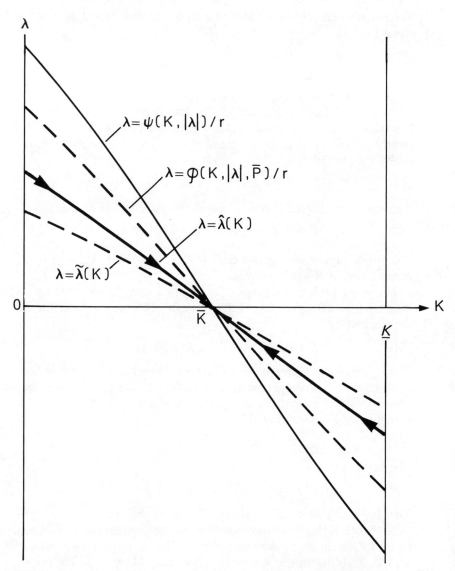

Fig. 4.4   The adjustment path under an optimally varying tariff.

optimum tariff), we move down the $\hat{\lambda}(K)$ line in figure 4.4 until we reach the steady state position where $K = \bar{K}$ and $\lambda = \hat{\lambda}(\bar{K}) = 0$.[8]

If private capital owners have rational expectations and the same discount rate as the social planner, and if there are no other distortions, the optimum path of the economy can be obtained by imposing an optimum tariff that varies with the distribution of capital. Stated as a specific tariff of τ units of Z per unit of X, the required tariff rate is given by

$$(57) \qquad \tau(K) = \hat{P}(K, |\hat{\lambda}(K)|) - \hat{P}^*(K, |\hat{\lambda}(K)|),$$

where $\hat{P}^*(K, |\hat{\lambda}(K)|)$ is the relative price of X facing foreign suppliers of home imports, as determined by

$$(58) \qquad P^* = J(C - X)/(C - X),$$

where $X = \tilde{X}(K, |\hat{\lambda}(K)|, \hat{P}(K, |\hat{\lambda}(K)|))$ and $C = U'^{-1}(\hat{P}(K, |\hat{\lambda}(K)|))$. When this tariff is imposed, the privately perceived cost of imports becomes $P^* + \tau(K)$. The requirement of equilibrium in the market for X, as expressed by the condition (52), ensures that the equilibrium relative price of X facing domestic producers and consumers is given by $\hat{P}(K, |\hat{\lambda}(K)|)$, provided that private capital owners have rational expectations and hence assign the same value to capital movement as the social planner.

The optimum tariff at the steady state position of the economy, $\tau(K)$, is the same as the optimum tariff calculated in the standard static trade model; it is the tariff that equates the privately perceived cost of imports, $P^* + \tau$, to their social marginal cost, $J'(C - X)$, and to both the marginal utility of X consumption, $U'(C)$, and the long-run marginal cost of domestic X production, $-\bar{T}_X(X)$. The optimum steady state tariff $\tau(\bar{K})$ and the associated steady state position of the economy are the same as those obtained in the standard two-sector model in which labor and capital are both freely mobile.

The importance of the adjustment process for optimum tariff policy is indicated by the variation in $\tau(K)$; specifically,[9]

(P4)   *As K rises toward $\bar{K}$, imports declines and, provided that the difference between the marginal and average cost of imports increases with increases in imports, $\tau(K)$ declines.*

This proposition may be established with the aid of figure 4.5. In the left-hand panel, the curve labeled $U'(C)$ indicates the demand for consumption of X as a function of the price, P, facing domestic consumers; the curve labeled $J(C - X)/(C - X)$ indicates the supply of imports of X as a function of the price, P^*, received by foreign suppliers; and the curve labeled $J'(C - X)$ indicates the marginal cost of imports of X. Under the optimum tariff, imports are carried to the point where their marginal cost is equal to the price facing consumers. It follows that the optimum tariff required at any given level of imports is equal to the vertical distance between the $J'(C - X)$ and the $J(C - X)/(C - X)$ curves at that level of imports. By assumption, this distance increases as the level of imports increases. In the right-hand panel, the curve labeled $D(P)$ indicates the demand facing domestic producers of X as a function

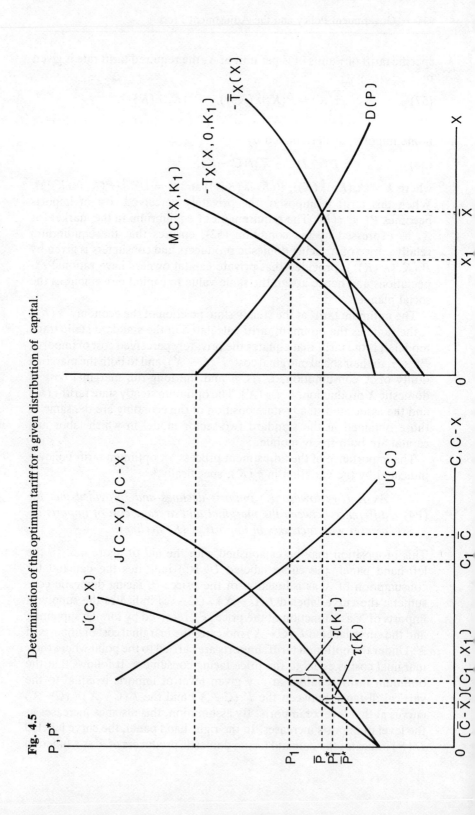

Fig. 4.5 Determination of the optimum tariff for a given distribution of capital.

of P, under the assumption that imports are carried to the point where their marginal cost equals P. This $D(P)$ curve is the horizontal difference between the $U'(C)$ and the $J'(C-X)$ curves in the left-hand panel. The curve labeled $MC(X, K_1)$ indicates the marginal cost of domestically produced X, given a distribution of capital K_1, between K_0 and $\bar{K} > K_0$, when $I = |\dot{K}|$ is set at its optimum value, $\tilde{I}(K_1, |\hat{\lambda}(K_1)|, P(K_1, |\hat{\lambda}(K_1)|))$. The intersection of the $MC(X, K_1)$ curve and the $D(P)$ curve determines the appropriate value of P (which satisfies [52]) when the distribution of capital is K_1. Feeding this price into the left-hand panel, the intersection of this price line with the $U'(C)$ curve determines domestic consumption of X, and the intersecton with the $J'(C-X)$ curve determines imports of X. The vertical distance between the $J'(C-X)$ curve and the $J(C-X)/(C-X)$ curve at this level of imports determines the optimum (specific) tariff $\tau(K_1)$ that is appropriate for the given distribution of capital. As K increases along the path of convergence to the optimum steady state, the $MC(X, \bar{K}_1)$ curve in the right-hand panel shifts downward and to the right both because the increase in K directly reduces the marginal cost of producing $X (-T_{XK} < 0)$ and because the reduction in resources devoted to capital movement ($d\tilde{I}/dK < 0$ for $K < \bar{K}$) reduces the marginal cost of producing $X (-T_{XI} > 0)$. It follows that as K rises toward $\bar{K}$, the value of P determined in the right-hand panel declines. Hence, in the left-hand panel, the level of imports declines and so does the optimum (specific) tariff $\tau(K)$.

It is not possible to prove that $\tau(K)$ is a decreasing function of K for K greater than $\bar{K}$ because as K declines toward $\bar{K}$ along the optimal adjustment path a declining I and a declining K have opposite effects on the marginal cost of producing X. However, it is possible to show that

(P5)   *For any $K \neq \bar{K}$, the optimum (specific) tariff $\tau(K)$ is greater than the optimum (specific) tariff that would be charged if the distribution of capital were held fixed.*

In particular, if the distribution of capital were fixed at $K_1 < \bar{K}$ and no resources were devoted to capital movement, the relevant marginal cost curve for domestically produced X would be the curve $-T_X(X, 0, K_1)$ in the right-hand panel of figure 4.5. The intersection of this marginal cost curve with the $D(P)$ curve determines the appropriate value of P when the distribution of capital is fixed at K_1. This price is necessarily less than the price determined by the intersection of the $MC(X, K_1)$ curve and the $D(P)$ curve because a positive rate of capital movement which draws resources out of the production of final goods increases the marginal cost of producing X. It follows that the optimum tariff when the distribution of capital is fixed at K_1 is less than $\tau(K_1)$. The same argument applies for any $K \neq \bar{K}$ since a positive $I = |\dot{K}|$ always increases the marginal cost of producing X.

These propositions concerning the influence of the adjustment process an optimum tariff policy remain valid under more general assumptions about the utility function and productive technology. If consumers can borrow and lend at a world interest rate equal to their subjective discount rate, the amount spent on consumption will be a constant proportion of the consumer's unchanging wealth. Regardless of the form of the flow of utility function, generally represented by $V(C, B)$, the demand curve for consumption of X, shown by the curve in the left-hand panel of figure 4.5, will not shift over time. Hence the proofs of propositions (P4) and (P5) go through as before.[10] If consumers are restricted to spending only their current income (equal to the value of domestic output, $P \cdot X + Z$, plus the redistributed tariff proceeds, $\tau \cdot (C - X)$), the demand curve in the left-hand panel will shift over time unless, as previously assumed, $V(C, B) = U(C) + B$. This assumption (which implies that the marginal propensity to spend on X is zero and the marginal propensity to spend on Z is one) can easily be relaxed. If both X and Z are normal, the demand curve will shift to the right as income grows along the adjustment path, implying a rightward shift of the $D(P)$ curve in the right-hand panel. This rightward shift of the $D(P)$ curve (at the previous equilibrium price), however, is smaller than the rightward shift of the $MC(X, K)$ curve. The reason is that only a fraction of the increase in the value of X output (equal to the excess of short-run marginal cost over long-run marginal cost, less the reduction in tariff revenue) corresponds to the increase in consumer income, and, since X and Z are both normal, only a fraction of this increase in income is spent on X. It follows that P declines as we move along the path of convergence to the steady state (starting from $K_0 < \bar{K}$) and propositions (P4) and (P5) remain valid. Generalizing this argument, it is clear that these propositions remain valid provided that Z is not strongly inferior. With respect to productive technology, the key features that are vital in establishing propositions (P4) and (P5) are that the shift of resources into X reduces the marginal cost of producing X ($-T_{XK} < 0$) and that the process of moving these resources increases the marginal cost of producing X ($-T_{XI} > 0$). The propositions concerning the behavior of the optimum tariff along the economy's adjustment path should remain valid under alternative specifications of productive technology that retain these two essential features.

Finally, it is important to note a general proposition concerning government intervention into the adjustment process:

(P6)   *To correct the distortion due to a divergence between the privately perceived cost of imports and the social marginal cost, the government must impose an optimum (specific) tariff τ (K) that varies appropriately along the economy's adjustment path. Given this tariff, the government should not intervene in any other manner to affect the adjustment process.*

This proposition reflects the general principle that government policy should aim directly at distortions that impair the efficiency of the economic system. The correct policy to deal with a divergence between the private and social cost of imports is an optimum tariff which makes the privately perceived cost of imports correspond to their true social marginal cost. The appropriate tariff, $\tau(K)$, reflects the nature of the adjustment process. However, once the optimum tariff has been adopted, it is not necessary or desirable for the government to intervene in the adjustment process, unless there is some distortion that directly affects this process (such as those discussed in section 4.5). Moreover, it is clear that these principles apply to other distortions of product and factor markets. In each case the correct (first-best) policy is the policy that directly countervails the distortion. The required magnitude of the policy intervention will, in general, reflect the nature of the adjustment process. However, provided that there is no direct distortion of the adjustment process, no additional intervention into that process will be required to ensure the full efficiency of the economic system.

4.7 Second-best Policies and the Adjustment Process

When the first-best policy that directly countervails a distortion of the product or factor markets cannot be implemented, it may be that the second-best combination of policies includes intervention into the adjustment process, even though such intervention would not be desirable if the first-best policy were available. To illustrate this general point, it is useful to consider second-best policies to deal with the distortion resulting from the failure to impose an optimum tariff, when such a tariff (and other equivalent policies) cannot be implemented.

4.7.1 A Constant Tariff

First, consider the case where the optimum steady state tariff $\tau(\bar{K})$ is imposed, but where it is not possible to vary the tariff as the economy moves its adjustment path. It is easily established that

(P7)

> *If the constant tariff τ $(\bar{K})$ is imposed, the steady state of the economy is the same as under the optimally varying tariff τ (K); but, under the hypothesis of (P4), the speed of convergence to the steady state, starting from $K_0 < \bar{K}$, is less than under the optimally varying tariff.*

The conclusion that the steady state of the economy is unchanged follows the fact that in the standard two-sector model (with labor and capital both freely mobile) there is a unique equilibrium for each specific tariff rate. The present specification of adjustment technology ensures that this steady state equilibrium will be achieved as the end result of the adjustment process. Further, from proposition (P4) we know that $\tau(K) > \tau(\bar{K})$ for any $K < \bar{K}$ and hence that the price established under the optimally varying tariff $\tau(K)$ is greater than the price that would be established, at that K, under the tariff $\tau(\bar{K})$. Since the relative price of X is higher under the tariff $\tau(K)$, it follows that the incentive to move capital from Z to X must be stronger. Hence speed of convergence toward the steady state is faster under the optimally varying tariff than under the constant tariff τ $(\bar{K})$.

If the tariff is fixed at $\tau(\bar{K})$, then it is appropriate for the government to intervene in the adjustment process in order to obtain a more efficient adjustment path. Without going into the details of the derivation of the government's optimal intervention policy, it may be stated that the government should subsidize the rental on capital used in X at a rate $\delta(K) \cdot T_{XK}$ and tax the movement of capital from Z to X at a rate $-\delta(K) \cdot T_{XI}$, where

(59) $\delta(K) \gtreqless 0$ according as $K \gtreqless \bar{K}$.

The subsidy on the rental of capital in X is necessary to raise the privately perceived benefit of capital movement to the level of the true social benefit. Given this subsidy on the rental of capital in X, the tax on capital movement is necessary to correct a divergence between the privately perceived cost of capital movement and the true social cost which arises because capital movement that draws resources out of domestic X production increases imports of X, and these increased imports have a social marginal cost that exceeds their privately perceived cost. As the economy converges to its steady state, the required subsidy on the rental of capital in X and the required tax on the movement of capital from Z and X both decrease to zero.

Alternately, if no subsidy is paid on the rental of capital in X, it is necessary to subsidize the movement of capital from Z to X at the rate given by

(60) $\delta(K) \cdot T_{XI} + \int_{t}^{\infty} \delta(K) \cdot T_{XK} \exp(-r \cdot (s-t)) \, ds.$

This subsidy to capital movement does not make the privately perceived benefit equal to the true social benefit or the privately perceived cost equal to the true social cost; but it does leave exactly offsetting distortions to benefits and costs. Hence it produces the second-best optimum path for the economy (if expectations are rational and $i = r$), given the constraint that the tariff cannot be varied (and that other equivalent policies cannot be used).

4.7.2   A Constant Import Quota

Second, consider the case where the government restricts imports by means of an import quota rather than a tariff. If we allow the quota, Q, to vary with the distribution of capital, then we can determine the optimally varying quota, $Q(K)$, by simply setting the import quota at any given K equal to the level of imports that would occur under the optimally varying tariff $\tau(K)$. Thus, as one would expect from the standard propositions concerning the equivalence of tariffs and import quotas, there is no difference between the optimal path that can be achieved with an optimally varying quota and the optimal path achieved with an optimally varying tariff.[11]

The path that results from setting the quota at its optimal steady state level, $Q(\bar{K})$, however, is different from the path that results from setting the tariff at $\tau(\bar{K})$. This difference reflects more than the general principle that a quota that is equivalent to a tariff under one set of economic conditions is not necessarily equivalent to the same tariff under different economic conditions. This difference also reflects the endogeneity of the process governing the change in economic conditions, and the differential impact of the import quota $Q(\bar{K})$ and the tariff $\tau(\bar{K})$ on this process. In particular, it may be established that

(P8)   *Starting from an initial $K_0 < \bar{K}$, the speed of convergence to the steady state under a constant import quota $Q(\bar{K})$ is more rapid than the socially optimal speed of convergence under an optimally varying quota or tariff, and, a fortiori, more rapid than the speed of convergence under the constant, steady-state-equivalent tariff $\tau(\bar{K})$.*

To demonstrate this result, note that in the proof of (P4) it was established that the level of imports falls as K rises toward $\bar{K}$ along the adjustment path produced by the optimally varying tariff $\tau(K)$. It follows that the optimally varying quota $Q(K)$ falls as K rises toward $\bar{K}$. Thus, for any $K < \bar{K}$, the steady state quota $Q(\bar{K})$ restricts imports more than the optimally varying quota $Q(K)$ (which is equivalent to the optimally varying tariff $\tau(K)$). It follows that the domestic relative price of X under the quota $Q(\bar{K})$, at any $K < \bar{K}$, is greater than the price under the optimally varying quota. This higher relative price of X means a stronger incentive to move capital from Z and X and hence a more rapid speed of convergence to the steady state than under the optimally varying quota. The last statement in (P8) follows immediately from (P7).[12]

Further, from proposition (P8) it is clear that if a constant import quota $Q(\bar{K})$ were imposed to move the economy from its free trade equilibrium to its optimal steady state position, the government should also intervene in the adjustment process to slow the speed of convergence toward the steady state. It should adopt policies that are the reverse of the policies described in the preceding subsection for the case of the constant tariff $\tau(\bar{K})$.

4.7.3   A Production Subsidy

Third, consider the case where the government can subsidize domestic production of the import good, but cannot tax domestic consumption, impose a tariff, or adopt any equivalent policies.[13] The problem for the social planner is to maximize (40) subject to the constraints (41) and (42) and the additional constraint

(61) $$U'(C) = P^* = J(C - X)/(C - X),$$

which expresses the requirement that domestic consumption of X will be carried to the point where its marginal utility, $U'(C)$, is equal to the foreign relative price, $P^* = J(C - X)/(C - X)$.

To determine the solution of this problem, define a modified version of the current value Hamiltonian given in (43):

(43′) $$H = U(C) + B + \theta \cdot (T(X, |\dot{K}|, K) - Z)$$
$$+ \alpha \cdot (J(C - X) - (Z - B))$$
$$+ \beta \cdot (U'(C) - (J(C - X)/(C - X))) + \lambda \cdot \dot{K},$$

where β is a Lagrangian multiplier assigned to the constraint (61), and every other variable has its previous role and interpretation. The optimum path of the economy must satisfy the same conditions given for the optimum tariff in section 4.6, with the addition of the constraint (61), and the modification of the conditions (44) and (46) to the following:

(44′) $$\partial H/\partial C = U' + \alpha \cdot J' + \beta \cdot (U'' - a) = 0,$$

(46′) $$\partial H/\partial X = \theta \cdot T_X - \alpha \cdot J' + \beta \cdot a = 0,$$

where

(62) $$a = dP^*/d(C - X) = (J'/(C - X)) - (J/(C - X)^2) > 0.$$

Two important implications of these conditions (which may be stated without going into a detailed description of the second-best optimal path of the economy) are summarized in the following proposition:

(P9)   *To induce private agents (with rational expectations and $i = r$) to follow the second-best optimal path, it is necessary for the government to give a subsidy to domestic producers of X which varies appropriately with the distribution of capital and which makes the price received by domestic producers, P, equal to the social marginal value of domestically produced X. Given this production* *subsidy, no direct intervention into the adjustment process is required to achieve the second-best optimal path of the economy.*

The required production subsidy (measured in units of Z per unit of domestically produced X) may be determined from the conditions (61), (44'), and (46') to be

(63) $\sigma = (- U''/(a - U')) \cdot (J' - P^*)$.

Given this subsidy, the price received by domestic producers of X, $P = P^* + \sigma$, is an appropriate weighted average of the value to consumers of additional X consumption, $U'(C) = P^*$, and the marginal cost of imports, $J'(C - X)$; specifically,

(64) $P = (a/(a - U'')) \cdot P^* + (- U''/(a - U'')) \cdot J'$,

where the weights are the fractions by which an additional unit of domestically produced X would increase domestic consumption and reduce imports, respectively. This production subsidy will vary with the distribution of capital; but it is not possible to establish general propositions similar to (P7) and (P8) that characterize the nature of this variation. Nor is it possible to say, in general, whether the steady state value of K under the second-best production subsidy is greater or less than $\bar{K}$ under the optimum tariff.

The conclusion that no intervention in the adjustment process is required follows from the fact that the production subsidy makes the prices confronting the production sector of the economy (which includes the adjustment process) correspond to true social marginal values. In particular, since the condition (48) remains intact, it follows that the government need not tax or subsidize the movement of capital; and since the condition (49) remains intact, it follows that the government need not tax or subsidize the rental received by capital in either industry.

4.7.4   A Consumption Tax

Fourth, consider the case where the government can tax domestic consumption of the import good, but cannot subsidize domestic production, impose a tariff, or adopt any equivalent policies. The problem for the social planner is now to maximize (40) subject to the constraints (41) and (42) and the additional constraint

(65) $- T_X(X, |\dot{K}|, K) = P^* = J(C - X)/(C - X)$,

which expresses the requirement that the price facing domestic producers of X is the price prevailing in foreign trade.

To determine the solution of this problem, define a new modified current value Hamiltonian

$$(43'') \qquad H = U(C) + B + \theta \cdot (T(X,\dot{K},K) - Z)$$
$$+ \alpha \cdot (J(C - X) - (Z - B))$$
$$+ \gamma \cdot (- T_{\dot{X}}(X,\dot{K},K) - (J(C - X)/(C - X)))$$
$$+ \lambda \cdot \dot{K},$$

where γ is a Lagrangian multiplier assigned to the constraint (65) and every other variable has its previous role and interpretation. The optimum path must satisfy the usual initial and boundary conditions, the constraints (41), (42), and (65), and the following modified forms of the conditions (44) through (49):

$$(44'') \qquad \partial H/\partial C = U' + \alpha \cdot J' - \gamma \cdot a = 0,$$

$$(45'') \qquad \partial H/\partial B = 1 + \alpha = 0,$$

$$(46'') \qquad \partial H/\partial X = \theta \cdot T_X - \alpha \cdot J' - \gamma \cdot (T_{XX} - a) = 0,$$

$$(47'') \qquad \partial H/\partial Z = - \theta - \alpha = 0,$$

$$(48'') \qquad \partial H/\partial \dot{K} = \text{sign}(\dot{K}) \cdot (\theta \cdot T_I - \gamma \cdot T_{XI}) + \lambda = 0,$$

$$(49'') \qquad \dot{\lambda} = r \cdot \lambda - \theta \cdot T_K + \gamma \cdot T_{XK},$$

where $a = dP^*/d(C - X) > 0$ is defined in (62).

From $(45'')$ and $(47'')$, it follows that $\theta = -\alpha = 1$. Given this result, it follows from (65) and $(46'')$ that

$$(66) \qquad \gamma = (J' - P^*)/(a - T_{XX}) > 0.$$

Further, define $P^c = U'(C)$ as the price facing domestic consumers. This price is enforced by a consumption tax of τ^c units of Z per unit of X consumed, which makes $P^c = P^* + \tau^c$. From $(44'')$, $(46'')$, and (66), it follows that

$$(67) \qquad \tau^c = - \gamma \cdot T_{XX} = (- T_{XX}/(a - T_{XX})) \cdot (J' - P^*).$$

This makes sense since it implies that P^c is an appropriate weighted average of the marginal cost of domestically produced X, $- T_X = P^*$, and the marginal cost of imports, $J'(C - X)$,

$$(68) \qquad P^c = P^* + \tau^c = (a/(a - T_{XX})) \cdot P^*$$
$$+ (- T_{XX}/(a - T_{XX})) \cdot J',$$

where the weights are the fractions by which domestic production and imports would be increased if consumption of X were increased by a unit.

The consumption tax, however, is not the only policy that the government must employ to place the economy on its second-best optimal path. As indicated in the following proposition, the government must also intervene in the adjustment process:

> *When the price facing domestic producers is constrained to equal the foreign price P*, the second-best combination of policies*
(P10)   *includes a tax on domestic consumption of X, a tax on the movement of capital, and a subsidy on the rental of capital used in X.*

From (48''), it follows that the required tax on the movement of capital is given by $-\gamma \cdot T_{XI} > 0$. From (49''), it follows that the required subsidy on the rental of capital used in X is given by $-\gamma \cdot T_{XX} > 0$. These interventions are required in order to make the privately perceived costs and benefits of capital movement correspond to the true social costs and benefits.

The rationale for this intervention into the adjustment process can easily be understood by considering what would happen, starting from steady state free-trade equilibrium, if the government imposed only a consumption tax. This tax would reduce consumption and hence reduce imports. This is beneficial since (at the initial equilibrium) the marginal cost of imports exceeds their marginal value of consumers. By reducing the foreign price P^*, which is the price facing domestic producers, the consumption tax would also reduce domestic production of X, thereby tending to increase imports. This is harmful, but the harm is unavoidable since (by assumption) the government cannot intervene to make the price to domestic producers differ from P^*. The reduction in price of X facing domestic producers also reduces the rental on capital in X below the rental on capital in Z. This motivates private capital owners to move capital from X to Z. In the short run, this is harmful because the process of capital movement diverts resources from domestic production of X and increases imports which have a marginal cost that is higher than P^*. In the long run, this is harmful because even after the process of movement is complete, the lower capital stock in X means less domestic production of X and hence larger imports. To counteract the short-run harm associated with the process of capital movement, it is appropriate for the government to tax capital movement. To counteract the long-run harm that would result from a redistribution of capital away from X and toward Z, it is appropriate for the government to remove the motivation for this redistribution by subsidizing the rental earned by capital employed in producing X.

The steady state position resulting from the combination of policies in (P10) is the same as the equilibrium position in the standard two-sector model when the government uses the second-best combination of a consumption tax and a subsidy to capital used in X. The subsidy to capital used in X is beneficial because it operates, in part, like a production subsidy; but this benefit must be balanced against loss of efficiency resulting from the factor market distortion associated with a subsidy to factor use.[14]

If a subsidy cannot be paid on the rental of capital used in X, then as a third-best policy the government should combine a tax on the consumption of X with a tax on the movement of capital out of X. Indeed, if the optimal steady state level of capital in X under the policies of (P10) were above the initial level K_0, it would be appropriate for the government to levy a prohibitive tax on the movement of capital in order to prevent the consumption tax from moving the distribution of capital even further from the optimal steady state distribution.

Finally, it is important to indicate why it is appropriate for the government to intervene in the adjustment process in conjunction with a consumption tax, but not in conjunction with a production subsidy. This is because the adjustment process resides in the production sector of the economy and the production subsidy removes all distortions from this sector of the economy; specifically, it makes the relative price of X facing domestic producers correspond to the social marginal value of an additional unit of domestically produced X. In contrast, under the consumption tax, the price facing domestic producers of X does not equal the social marginal value of an additional unit of domestically produced X. This divergence between price and social marginal value distorts the adjustment process and hence justifies additional government intervention to correct this distortion. If the adjustment process resided exclusively in the consumption sector of the economy rather than the production sector, then no intervention into the adjustment process would be required in conjunction with a consumption tax, but such intervention would be required in conjunction with a production subsidy. More generally, if the adjustment process is partly in the production sector and partly in the consumption sector, then some intervention into the adjustment process will be desirable in conjunction with either a second-best consumption tax or a second-best production subsidy. Moreover, this principle applies not only to second-best policies to deal with a divergence between the social and private cost of imports, but also to second-best policies to deal with other distortions.

4.8   Extensions, Generalizations, and Conclusions

So far, the analysis in this paper has focused exclusively on the issue of the economic efficiency of the adjustment process and has ignored the important quetions concerning the effects on the distribution of income of government policies directed at the adjustment process. The preceding analysis has also been limited in that it has been based on a single, specific model of adjustment technology. The purpose of this section is to partially remedy these deficiencies and to summarize the general principles concerning the role of government policy in the adjustment process that are suggested by the present theoretical analysis.

4.8.1 Income Distribution and the Adjustment Process

In discussing questions of income distribution, it is important to distinguish between the "personal distribution of income" and the "functional distribution of income." The "personal distribution of income" refers to the distribution of income among individuals in the society, by income levels, but not to the levels of income of specific individuals. Theoretical analyses of economic equity are usually concerned with this concept of the distribution of income. The "functional distribution of income" refers to the distribution of income among different types of factors of production, as determined by the prices paid for the productive services they supply. Changes in the functional distribution of income, in general, imply important changes in the incomes of specific individuals in the society, and hence are of great interest to these individuals. But, without strong assumptions about the distribution of ownership of various factors of production among individuals, it is not possible to reach conclusions concerning the consequences for the personal distribution of income of changes in the structure of factor prices.

Since the model analyzed in previous sections does not include specific assumptions about the distribution of factor ownership, it cannot be used to investigate questions concerning the personal distribution of income. It can, however, be used to examine two general and important questions relating to the functional distribution of income: What is the effect of various government policies designed to affect the efficiency of the adjustment process on the functional distribution of income? What is the effect of government policies designed to affect the functional distribution of income on the efficiency of the adjustment process? These questions are of considerable importance because individual factor owners are obviously concerned with the effects of government policies on the incomes of the particular factors that they own, and because much government policy (particularly in the area of international trade policy) is directed to protecting the incomes of particular factor owners, regardless of any general objectives of economic equity related to the personal distribution of income.

With respect to long-run equilibrium, the model of productive technology described in section 4.2 is identical to the standard two-sector model. Hence the Stolper-Samuelson theorem describes the long-run equilibrium response of factor rewards to any change in the relative output price. Specifically, assuming that X is relatively capital-intensive, it follows that an increase in P will increase the rental received by capital, measured in terms of either X or Z, and will decrease the wage received by labor, measured in terms of either X or Z.

In discussing the short-run effects of policy and parametric changes on the functional distribution of income, it is necessary to distinguish between three factors. The mobile factor, referred to as "labor," earns the same wage in both final goods industries and in the activity of capital movement. Holding the amount of labor devoted to capital movement constant, an increase in P increases the wage measured in terms of Z and reduces the wage measured in terms of X, implying that labor has no clear-cut short-run interest in policies that either increase or reduce P. Since capital movement uses only labor, however, an increase in the rate of capital movement increases the wage in terms of both goods, implying a short-run benefit to labor. Capital employed in X enjoys a short-run gain, measured in terms of both goods, from an increase in P, holding constant the amount of labor used in capital movement; and conversely for capital employed in Z. An increase in the wage rate induced by an increase in the demand for labor in capital movement is disadvantageous to capital employed in either industry.[15]

When there is a divergence between the short-run response and the long-run response of a factor price to a policy or parametric change, the interest of the factor owner is presumably determined by the effect on the present discounted value of his income stream. If X is relatively capital-intensive, owners of capital initially employed in X will be very likely to benefit, in terms of present discounted value, from an increase in the relative price of X.[16] If the movement of capital requires only small amounts of labor (i.e., if the coefficient β in [3] is small), then capital will shift rapidly from Z to X, with little impact on the wage rate from the use of labor in capital movement. In this case, owners of capital initially employed in Z will also benefit from an increase in P. Moreover, if β is small, owners of capital initially employed in either industry are likely to benefit and workers are likely to lose, in terms of present discounted value, from a subsidy to capital movement imposed subsequent to an increase in P. This is because the short-run effect of the subsidy to capital movement in increasng the wage rate will be outweighed by the decline in the wage rate and the increase in the rental rates associated with the more rapid shift of capital from the labor-intensive to the capital-intensive industry. On the other hand, if β is small, then a subsidy to capital movement will benefit workers and harm capital owners in the event of a decrease in P. If β is large, then a subsidy to capital movement may benefit workers and harm capital owners in the event of any change in P. This is because labor will have sharply declining marginal productivity in capital movement. Hence a subsidy to capital movement will increase the wage rate over a substantial period of time, by increasing the demand for labor in capital movement, but will not increase to a commensurate extent the speed of movement of capital from one industry to another.

These results illustrate the implications of the model discussed in previous sections for the incidental consequences for the functional distribution of income of government policies directed at affecting output prices and/or the process of adjustment. A related issue is the effect on the process of adjustment of policies directed toward affecting the functional distribution of income. Specifically, suppose that there has been a decline in the relative price of X in world trade and that, for political reasons, the government desires to protect owners of capital (including human capital) employed in X, the import-competing industry, from the consequences of this price change. Of course, the government might simply impose a tariff that would keep the domestic relative price of X at its previous level. But suppose this tariff cannot be imposed, either because the government recognizes the production and consumption distortion losses it would generate or because other domestic political considerations preclude the tariff or because the government fears foreign retaliation. Further, suppose that the objective of government policy is not to protect owners of capital employed in X from the long-run deterioration of the income of capital in both industries that would result from a reduction in the relative price of the capital-intensive good, but only to protect them from the additional loss that they suffer relative to owners of capital initially located in Z. The first-best policy to achieve this objective is a lump-sum wealth transfer to the owner of each unit of capital initially employed in X equal to the present discounted value of the difference between the rental of a unit of capital employed in Z and the rental of a unit of capital employed in Z. An equivalent policy is a flow transfer to owners of capital initially employed in X equal to the difference between the rental on capital employed in Z and the rental on capital employed in X. Both of these policies are nondistorting with respect to the process of adjustment.

It is important to recognize that a flow transfer paid to owners of capital *initially* employed in X is very different from a flow transfer paid to owners of capital that *remains* employed in X. The latter policy which makes receipt of the transfer contingent on capital remaining in X seriously distorts the adjustment process. In fact, if the level of the subsidy were set equal to the current rental differential between capital located in Z and capital located in X, then all incentive for capital movement would be removed and there would be no adjustment toward the new long-run equilibrium appropriate for the lower world relative price of X. More generally, if the transfer to owners of capital in X was set equal to a fraction of the rental differential or was made to decline gradually over time, some incentive for capital movement would be retained, but the rate of capital movement would be reduced to below the socially optimal rate. This is because the linking of transfer payments to the current location of capital, rather than its initial location, creates an artificial incentive to keep capital employed in X.

If practical or political considerations rule out wealth and income transfers as a means for compensating those adversely affected by changing conditions of international trade, a government might resort to "adjustment assistance" as an alternative means of providing such compensation. It is noteworthy that in the model developed in this paper, adjustment assistance in the form of a subsidy to capital movement is not likely to be beneficial to owners of capital initially employed in the capital-intensive industry when there is a decline in the relative price of that industry's output. In the short run, such a subsidy will work to the disadvantage of capital owners by increasing the demand for labor in capital movement and thus the wage rate. In the longer run, more rapid movement of capital out of the capital-intensive industry and into the labor-intensive industry implies that the return to capital in both industries will decline more rapidly, in accord with the dictates of the Stolper-Samuelson theorem. From this theorem, it also follows that a subsidy to capital movement is more likely to be beneficial to owners of capital initially employed in the labor-intensive industry when that industry suffers a decline in its relative output price.

These results concerning the effects of adjustment assistance do not necessarily apply under alternative assumptions about productive technology, particularly the technology of the adjustment process, or under other assumptions about the form of adjustment assistance. They do illustrate, however, the general proposition that assistance to factors of production in moving out of declining industries is *not* necessarily beneficial to the owners of these factors. Moreover, it should be emphasized that whatever the income distributional consequences of adjustment assistance, such assistance is likely to interfere with the efficiency of the adjustment process, unless it countervails some other distortion that affects the adjustment process.

4.8.2   Alternative Adjustment Technologies

In the model of adjustment technology presented in section 4.2, the economy's total capital stock is assumed fixed and the only adjustment activity consists of using labor to move capital from one industry to another. It is useful to consider briefly the implications of a more general model of adjustment technology, which retains the same basic assumptions about the technology for producing final outputs, but allows adjustment both in the distribution of capital between industries and in the total size of the capital stock. Specifically, suppose that capital in each industry depreciates at a constant exponential rate δ and that the amount of labor required to replace depreciating capital, create new capital, and move capital from one industry to another is given by

$$(69) \qquad L_I = H(I_X + I_Z) + Q_X(\dot{K}_X) + Q_Z(\dot{K}_Z),$$

where $I_X = \dot{K}_X + \delta \cdot K_X$ measures gross investment in capital in X and $I_Z = \dot{K}_Z + \delta \cdot K_Z$ measures gross investment in capital in Z. The function $H(\ )$ determines the amount of labor required to produce the new capital for the two industries; it is assumed that $H' > 0$ and $H'' \geq 0$. The functions $Q_X(\ )$ and $Q_Z (\ )$ are the "Penrose functions" which indicate the amount of labor required to alter the scale of production facilities in order to accommodate changes in the size of the capital stock employed in a particular industry; it is assumed that $Q_X(0) = Q_Z(0) = 0$, $Q'_X(0) = Q'_Z(0) = 0$, $Q''_X > 0$, and $Q''_Z > 0$.[17]

To illustrate the general implications of the adjustment technology embodied in (69), it is useful to consider three special cases. First, suppose that the depreciation rate is zero and that the aggregate capital stock $K_X + K_Z$ is fixed. In this case (69) reduces to

(70) $\qquad L_I = Q_X(\dot{K}_X) + Q_Z(-\dot{K}_X).$

This labor requirements function is a generalization of the labor requirements function for capital movement given in (3). Since the two labor requirements functions (3) and (70) share all of the same essential properties, they share all of the same implications.

Second, suppose that the Penrose functions, Q_X and Q_Z, are eliminated from (69), and further suppose that marginal labor requirements for capital goods production, $H' (I_X+I_Z)$, are strictly increasing as a function of total gross investment.[18] To analyze the process of adjustment under this assumption about adjustment technology, it is useful to define $\mu_X(t)$ and $\mu_Z(t)$ as the present discounted values of the stream of rentals that would be produced by a unit of capital initially located in the two respective industries at time t; that is, [19]

(71) $\qquad \mu_X(t) = \int_t^\infty R_X(s)\exp(-(r+\delta)\cdot(s-t))ds,$

(72) $\qquad \mu_z(t) = \int_t^\infty R_Z(s)\exp(-(r+\delta)\cdot(s-t))ds.$

Since newly produced capital can be located at zero cost in either industry, it will be located only in the industry for which $\mu_X(t)$ or $\mu_Z(t)$ is the largest, and the level of gross investment will be determined by the condition

(73) $\qquad W\cdot H' (I_X+I_Z) = \max(\mu_X(t),\mu_Z(t)),$

where W is the wage rate consistent with the requirement of labor market equilibrium, namely,

(74) $\qquad \ell_X(W/P)\cdot K_X + \ell_Z(W)\cdot K_Z + H(I_X+I_Z) = \underline{L}.$

Given P, the conditions (73) and (74) jointly determine W and I_X+I_Z as functions of $K_X, K_Z, \mu_X,$ and μ_Z. When $\mu_X \neq \mu_Z$, net investment in each industry is determined by the allocation of all newly produced capital to the industry with the highest μ. The rental rates on capital in the two industries, the allocation of labor between industries, and their outputs are also determined as functions of the state variables, K_X and K_X, and the costate variables, μ_X and μ_Z, given P.

For the economy to have a steady state, associated with a given value of P, in which the capital stock in both industries is positive, it must be the case that at this steady state $\mu_X = R_X/(r+\delta)$ is equal to $\mu_Z = R_Z/(r+\delta)$. For this to happen, the rental rates on capital in the two industries, as well as the wage rates paid to labor, must be the same. Thus, at the steady state equilibrium, the conditions of the two-sector model with respect to product and factor prices must apply, implying that the steady state wage rate and the steady state rental rates on capital in both industries are determined by the output price ratio and the properties of the production functions for final outputs; say, $W = W^*(P)$ and $R_X = R_Z = R^*(P)$. It follows that the steady state values of μ_X and μ_Z, denoted by an underscore, are given by

(75) $$\underline{\mu}_X = R^*(P)/(r+\delta) = \underline{\mu}_z.$$

Further, since gross investment in the steady state must equal total depreciation, it follows that the steady state capital stocks in the two industries, denoted by $\underline{K}_X$ and $\underline{K}_Z$, must satisfy

(76) $$W^*(P) \cdot H'(\delta \cdot (\underline{K}_X + \underline{K}_Z)) = R^*(P)/(r+\delta).$$

The combinations of K_X and K_Z that satisfy this condition are illustrated by the line labeled $\underline{KK}$ in figure 4.6, which has a slope of -1. In addition, the steady state capital stocks must be consistent with full employment of the economy's supply of labor; that is,

(77) $$\ell_X(W^*(P)/P) \cdot \underline{K}_X + \ell_Z(W^*(P)) \cdot \underline{K}_Z$$
$$+ H(\delta \cdot (\underline{K}_X + \underline{K}_Z)) = \underline{L}.$$

The combinations of K_X and K_Z that satisfy this condition are illustrated by the line labeled $\underline{LL}$ in figure 4.6. This line is flatter than the $\underline{KK}$ line because, by assumption, X is relatively capital-intensive, implying that $\ell_X(W^*(P)/P) < \ell_Z(W^*(P))$. The intersection of the $\underline{KK}$ line and the $\underline{LL}$ line in figure 4.6 determines the steady state capital stocks for the two industries and the aggregate steady state capital stock, $\underline{K} = \underline{K}_X + \underline{K}_Z$, appropriate for the given output price ratio.

A change in the output price ratio alters the steady state position of the economy. The steady state responses of the wage rate and the rental rates of capital in the two industries are the same as in the standard two-sector model. This reflects the assumption that newly produced capital can be installed at zero cost in either industry and hence must earn the same steady state rental in either industry. It is not the case, however, that the aggregate capital stock and the supply of labor used to produce final

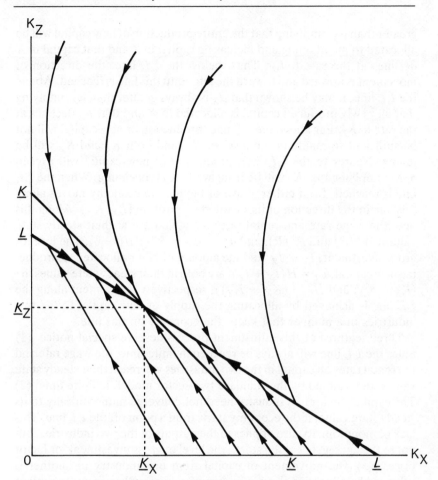

Fig. 4.6   Steady state capital stocks and adjustment paths when there are not installation costs.

outputs remain unchanged in the face of a change in P, as they are assumed to do in the standard two-sector model. Specifically, an increase in P, the relative price of the capital-intensive good X, increases the aggregate steady state capital stock, $\underline{K} = \underline{K}_X + \underline{K}_Z$, and increases the amount of labor required to support this capital stock, $L_I = H(\delta \cdot \underline{K})$, thereby reducing the amoung of labor, $\underline{L} - L_I$, used to produce final outputs. From the Rybczynski theorem, it follows that output of X rises and output of Z declines by significantly more than would be the case if the aggregate capital stock and the amount of labor used to produce final outputs both remained constant in the face of the increase in P.[20]

The nature of the process of convergence to the steady state appropriate for a given value of P is also illustrated in figure 4.6. It may be shown that for combinations of K_X and K_Z lying below the $\underline{L}\underline{L}$ line, μ_Z is always greater than μ_X, implying that the entire production of new capital will be allocated to maintaining and increasing capital in Z and that capital in X declines at the rate $\delta \cdot K_X$. Thus, below the $\underline{LL}$ line, the direction of movement is upward and toward the left, until this line is reached. Above the $\underline{LL}$ line, it may be shown that μ_X is always greater than μ_Z, implying that all newly produced capital is allocated to X and that K_Z declines at the rate $\delta \cdot K_Z$. Far above the $\underline{LL}$ line, production of new capital will not be sufficient to maintain the level of K_X, and both K_X and K_Z will be falling. Nearer to the $\underline{LL}$ line, production of new capital will exceed $\delta \cdot K_X$, implying that K_X will be rising while K_Z is declining. When the $\underline{LL}$ line is reached, from either above or below, the economy moves along this line in the direction of its steady state position $(\underline{K}_X, \underline{K}_Z)$. Along this line, the wage rate and rental rates on capital are at their steady state values, $W^*(P)$ and $R^*(P)$, and $\mu_X = \mu_Z = R^*(P)/(r+\delta)$. The level of gross investment, $I_X + I_Z$, and the amount of labor allocated to producing new capital, $L_I = H(I_X + I_Z)$, are both at their steady state values, $\delta \cdot (\underline{K}_X + \underline{K}_Z)$ and $H(\delta \cdot (\underline{K}_X + \underline{K}_Z))$, respectively. Movement along the $\underline{LL}$ line is achieved by allocating the supply of new capital to the two industries in a manner that keeps the economy on this line.

Three features of this adjustment process deserve special notice. (1) Since the $\underline{LL}$ line will always be reached in finite time, the wage rate and the rental rates on capital in the two industries will reach their steady state values, determined by the standard two-sector model, in finite time. (2) The capital stock in an industry need not converge monotonically to its steady state value, if the economy starts from a point off the $\underline{LL}$ line. This lack of monotonicity also applies to the outputs of the two industries, but not to the aggregate capital stock, the level of gross investment, or factor prices. (3) The movement of capital from one industry to another is achieved by allocating the production of new capital so as not to replace capital that depreciates in the industry that should have a declining capital stock. Thus, in this special case of the general adjustment technology (69), the movement of capital is not "costly" in the sense that it does not require an explicit use of scarce factors of production.

The third special case of (69) is the general case where the Penrose functions, $Q_X(\dot{K}_X)$ and $Q_Z(\dot{K}_Z)$, are added on to the function $H(I_X+I_Z)$. For a given relative output price and given values of the state variables, K_X and K_Z, and the costate variables, μ_X and μ_Z, as defined in (71) and (72), the momentary equilibrium wage rate and the levels of gross and net investment in the two industries are determined by the requirements

(78) $W \cdot [H'(I_X+I_Z) + Q_X'(\dot{K}_X)] = \mu_X,$

(79) $W \cdot [H'(I_X+I_Z) + Q_Z'(\dot{K}_Z)] = \mu_Z,$

(80) $\ell_X(W/P) \cdot K_X + \ell_Z(W) \cdot K_Z + H(I_X + I_Z)$

$\qquad + Q_X(\dot{K}_X) + Q_Z(\dot{K}_Z) = \underline{L}.$

Given the solutions for the wage rate and the levels of gross and net investment in the two industries, the amounts of labor employed in producing the two final outputs, the levels of these outputs, and the rental rates for capital in the two industries are also determined as functions of K_X, K_Z, μ_X, and μ_Z, given P.

By assumption, $Q_X(0) = Q_Z(0) = 0$ and $Q'_X(0) = Q'_Z(0) = 0$. It follows that in steady state equilibrium, where $\dot{K}_X = \dot{K}_Z = 0$, the Penrose functions and their derivatives disappear from (78), (79), and (80). Thus, with respect to steady state equilibrium, (80) reduces to (74), and (78) and (79) reduce to (73), plus the requirement that $\mu_X = \mu_Z$. It follows that the conditions that must apply in steady state equilibrium under the general form of (69) are the same as those that apply in the special case where the Penrose functions are omitted from (69). Hence the analysis of steady state equilibrium under the general form of (69) is exactly the same as under this previously considered special case.

Where the Penrose functions do matter is in analyzing the process of convergence toward the steady state. When these functions are eliminated from (69), any difference between μ_X and μ_Z (that is, anywhere off the $\underline{LL}$ line in figure 4.6) implies that all of gross investment is allocated to the industry with the higher shadow price for a unit of capital. This applies even in the neighborhood of the steady state (off of the $\underline{LL}$ line), where the difference between μ_X and μ_Z is small, but the level of gross investment is relatively large (equal approximately to its steady state level, $\delta \cdot (\underline{K}_X + \underline{K}_Z)$). When the Penrose functions are present in the adjustment technology, we no longer have this peculiarity. In the neighborhood of the steady state, where the difference between μ_X and μ_Z is small, gross investment will be divided between the two industries so that the level of net investment in each industry is close to its steady state value of zero, for otherwise the conditions (78) and (79) would not be satisfied. In fact, there must be a region in the neighborhood of the steady state where net investment in both industries is positive, and another region where net investment in both industries is negative. These regions exist because, when the Penrose functions are present in the adjustment technology, the movement of capital is a costly activity, and this cost cannot be avoided simply by reallocating newly produced capital between the two industries.

The exact pattern of adjustment of the capital stocks in the two industries to their respective steady state values, $\underline{K}_X$ and $\underline{K}_Z$, depends on the exact properties of the Penrose functions. One possible pattern of adjustment is illustrated in figure 4.7. In this figure, the $\dot{K}_X = 0$ line and the $\dot{K}_Z$

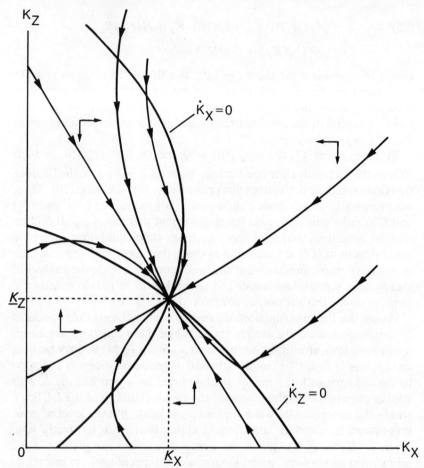

Fig. 4.7   Steady state capital stocks and adjustment paths with increasing marginal installation costs.

$= 0$ line show the combinations of K_X and K_Z for which net investment in the two industries, respectively, is equal to zero. These lines intersect at the steady state point ($\underline{K}_X$ and $\underline{K}_Z$) and divide the plane into four regions: a region where $\dot{K}_X > 0$ and $\dot{K}_Z > 0$; a region where $\dot{K}_X < 0$ and $\dot{K}_Z < 0$; a region where $\dot{K}_X > 0$ and $\dot{K}_Z < 0$; and a region where $\dot{K}_X < 0$ and $\dot{K}_Z > 0$. The arrows in the diagram indicate the direction of movement of the capital stock in each industry in each of the four regions. Convergence to the steady state is necessarily noncyclic, though it need not be the case that the capital stock in each industry converges monotonically to its steady state value.

4.8.3   General Conclusions

It is worthwhile to investigate the generality of the conclusions reached earlier in this paper under the alternative adjustment technology specified in (69). First, the key proposition that private maximizing behavior will lead to a socially optimal adjustment path, provided that there are no distortions in the economy, that the private discount rate is equal to the social discount rate, and that private agents have rational expectations, remains valid under the adjustment technology specified in (69). Under private maximization, the shadow prices μ_X and μ_Z that are used by the social planner to guide level and disposition of investment are replaced by the values that private asset owners assign to units of capital located in the two industries. Provided that there are no distortions in the economic system that cause the rental received by private capital owners to differ from the values of the marginal products of capital in the two industries, provided that the discount rate used by private asset owners is equal to the social discount rate, and provided that expectations concerning future rentals earned by capital in the two industries are rational, the values of units of capital located in the two industries assigned by private asset owners will equal the shadow prices established by the social planner. The process of adjustment that occurs under the guidance of these capital values will be the same as that determined by the social planner. Moreover, it is clear that this principle of the social optimality of the adjustment process under private maximizing behavior (which is a special case of Adam Smith's principle of the invisible hand) carries over to more general assumptions about adjustment technology and to more general models of production of final outputs.

Second, when there are distortions that directly affect the adjustment process, there is rationale for government intervention to directly countervail these distortions. In particular, it remains true under the adjustment technology specified in (69) that a proportional tax on income from capital (or on all factor income) distorts the adjustment process, even if such a tax allows an appropriate deduction for depreciation. The reason is that such a tax reduces privately received (after tax) rentals from capital ownership to below the true social rentals and hence induces private asset owners to assign lower values to units of capital located in either industry than would be assigned by the social planner. This results in a steady state capital stock that is smaller than the socially optimal capital stock and, in general, also distorts the process of convergence toward the steady state. An investment tax credit that allows capital owners to deduct from their current tax liability both the cost of newly produced capital and the costs of variations in the scale of production associated with the Penrose functions, but eliminates subsequent depreciation allowances, will correct this distortion. In the long run, however, such a credit will have a serious effect on the government's tax revenue since it amounts to an elimination of the tax on income from capital for all capital that is installed after the credit is instituted. If the lost revenue cannot be replaced by lump-sum nondistorting taxes, then the benefits of reducing the disincentives to capital accumulation by the investment tax credit will have to be weighed against the distortions created by the alternative taxes used to replace the lost tax revenue.

Third, when there are distortions in the product or factor markets that do not specifically affect the adjustment process, such as the failure to impose an optimum tariff, then the first-best policy is to countervail these distortions directly. In general, the countervailing tax or subsidy will not be constant, but will vary with the size and distribution of the economy's capital stock. However, provided that the first-best policy to correct the product market distortion is implemented, no further intervention into the adjustment process will be required in order to ensure a socially optimal adjustment path.

Fourth, preliminary analysis suggests that the specific propositions concerning the behavior of the optimum tariff along the path of convergence to the steady state that were stated in section 4.6 probably do generalize to the adjustment technology specified in (69). In particular, it may be shown that the relative positions of the steady state equilibria under free trade and under the optimum tariff are such that convergence of the capital stock in each industry and of the aggregate capital stock to their steady values under the optimum tariff, starting from the free trade steady state, are monotonic when the Penrose functions are eliminated from (69). This point is critical in establishing the analogs of the propositions (P4), (P5), (P7), and (P8) for the adjustment technology specified in (69). It cannot be presumed, however, that specific propositions concerning properties of the adjustment path are generally invariant to the specification of adjustment technology.

Fifth, when the first-best policies to correct product or factor market distortions are not available, the second-best combination of policies *may* involve intervention into the adjustment process. This is the case whenever the adjustment process becomes distorted as a result of a second-best policy directed at some other distortion. In particular, the imposition of a consumption tax as a second-best policy to correct for a divergence between the social marginal cost of imports and their privately perceived cost should generally be combined with a policy to discourage the movement of resources out of the import-competing sector that would otherwise be induced by the depressing effect of the consumption tax on the price facing domestic producers of the import good. A second-best production subsidy, however, will not require additional intervention into the adjustment process because this subsidy removes all distortions from the production sector of the economy, which is assumed to include the adjustment process.

Finally, it is worthwhile to summarize the general philosphy concerning government policy toward the adjustment process that is suggested by the preceding analysis. Adjustment to changing conditions of international trade and to other causes of economic change generally involves investment decisions in which the costs of adjustment must be weighed against the expected future benefits. In many economies, such decisions are to a large extent made by private agents who pursue their individual self-interest. A principal objective of government policy should be to create an environment in which the decisions of these agents lead to a socially appropriate outcome by removing the general distortions, including the distortions associated with government taxes and transfers, that cause the privately perceived benefits or costs of adjustment to diverge substantially from the true social benefits or costs. In addition, there may be instances of clearly identifiable distortions of the adjustment process for particular industries, perhaps resulting from government policies pursued for other purposes, that justify specific interventions to either enhance or impede the adjustment process. Lastly, care must be taken in designing policies to compensate factor owners who suffer losses as a result of changing economic conditions in order to ensure that such compensation does not interfere unduly or unnecessarily with the private incentive to achieve socially efficient adjustment.

Notes

1. The process of adjustment to changing conditions of international trade and the influence of the adjustment process on government policy have not been totally neglected in the literature; see, in particular, Baldwin, Mutti, and Richardson (1978), Kemp and Wan (1974), Lapan (1976), Mayer (1974), Mussa (1978), and Neary (1978).

2. This model of adjustment technology is the same as that presented in Mussa (1978).

3. It is inconvenient to assume that labor requirements for capital movement are proportional to the rate of capital movement because this implies that the marginal cost of capital movement is always strictly positive. With a strictly positive marginal cost of capital movement, the economy will not, in general, converge to a steady state position that is the same as the equilibrium position in the standard two-sector model. Instead, as Kemp and Wan (1974) point out, there are "hysteresis effects" which make the steady state position of the economy dependent on its initial position. To avoid the difficulties associated with such "hysteresis effects" and preserve as much as possible the properties of the standard two-sector model, it is convenient to assume that labor requirements for capital movement are determined by (3).

4. The $\dot{\lambda} = 0$ line in figure 4.1 is shown as everywhere negatively sloped. It cannot be proved that the $\dot{\lambda} = 0$ line will necessarily have this property. However, it can be shown that there is a unique intersection of the $\dot{\lambda} = 0$ line with the $\dot{K} = 0$ line (identical with the K axis), occurring at the optimal steady state value of K that corresponds to the distribution of capital determined in the standard two-sector model. At this steady state, the $\dot{\lambda} = 0$ line is negatively sloped. Everywhere except in the neighborhood of the steady state K, the $\dot{\lambda} = 0$ line is bounded away from the K axis. These facts are sufficient to establish that there is a unique optimum path converging to the steady state which lies above the K axis for $K < \bar{K}(P)$ and below the K axis for $K > \bar{K}(P)$. It follows that the distribution of capital always converges monotonically to its optimal steady state distribution.

5. The assumption of competitive behavior is questionable since the production function for capital movement is not linear homogeneous. The assumption of competitive behavior

could be justified, however, if firms producing the service of capital movement were assumed to use a Cobb-Douglas production function, $I = (L_I \cdot S_I)^{1/2}$, where L_I is the amount of labor employed by such a firm and S_I is the amount of capital so employed. Capital used in producing the service of capital movement is specific to that activity, and the total amount of such capital is equal to $\bar{S}_I$. The demand for labor by firms supplying the service of capital movement would, under these assumptions, be given by $L_I(W, q) = \bar{S}_I \cdot (q/2W)^2$.

6. In the analysis of the optimum tariff in section 4.6 and of various second-best policies in section 4.7, the path of the output price is endogenously determined by the general equilibrium of the economic system. This endogenous determination of prices creates no difficulties for proposition (P1). All that is necessary is that individual agents take these prices as given and act in their own best interest.

7. This difference might be due to the finite life of individuals or to an excess of the private cost of risk over the social cost or to other factors. Somewhat less plausibly, it might be assumed that the private discount rate is less than the social discount rate. Obviously, this would require the exact reverse of the policies appropriate to correct for an excess of the private discount rate over the social discount rate.

8. The $\lambda = \psi(K, |\lambda|)/r$ line is steeper than the $\lambda = \varphi(K, |\lambda|, \bar{P})/r$ line because $\hat{P}(K, |\lambda|) > \bar{P}$ for $K < \bar{K}$ and $\lambda > 0$. It follows that the speed of convergence to the steady state under the optimally varying tariff along the $\lambda = \hat{\lambda}(K)$ line is greater than the speed of convergence to the steady state along the $\lambda = \tilde{\lambda}(K)$ line constructed for a constant $P = \bar{P}$.

9. If we make the stronger assumption that the proportional difference between the marginal cost of imports, J', and the average cost of imports, $J/(C-X)$, increase as imports increase, we may conclude that the optimal ad valorem tariff, $\tau(K)/\hat{P}^*(K, |\hat{\lambda}(K)|)$, declines as K rises toward $\bar{K}$. However, neither of these assumptions is guaranteed by the standard properties of the foreign offer function. If the marginal cost of imports tends toward a constant value as imports rise, both the optimum specific tariff and the optimum ad valorem tariff may rise as K rises toward $\bar{K}$. The level of imports, however, should always decline as K rises toward $\bar{K}$, and so should the domestic relative price of the import good.

10. Since the relative output price is changing along the adjustment path, there is some difficulty in defining the appropriate measure of the discount rate. The basic point remains, however, that the amount spent on consumption will depend on wealth, not current income. Hence, if wealth is not changing significantly as the economy moves along the adjustment path, the position of the demand curve in the left-hand panel of figure 4.5 will remain approximately constant.

11. For a general discussion of the circumstances under which tariffs and quotas are and are not equivalent, see Bhagwati (1965), Falvey (1975, 1976), and Fishelson and Flatters (1975).

12. Even if the hypothesis of (P7) is not valid and the tariff $\tau(K)$ rises as K rises to $\bar{K}$, it is still true that, for any $K < \bar{K}$, the import quota $Q(\bar{K})$ results in lower imports and a higher domestic price of X than the tariff $\tau(\bar{K})$. Hence the quota $Q(\bar{K})$ induces more rapid convergence to the steady state than the tariff $\tau(\bar{K})$, starting from any $K_0 < \bar{K}$.

13. For a general analysis of production subsidies, consumption taxes, factor market interventions, and other second-best policies, see Johnson (1960), (1965), Bhagwati and Ramaswami (1963), Bhagwati, Ramaswami, and Srinivasan (1969), and Dornbusch (1971).

14. The desirability of factor market interventions when an optimum tariff is ruled out is well established; see Bhagwati and Ramaswami (1963) and Bhagwati, Ramaswami, and Srinivasan (1969).

15. A detailed analysis of the short-run and long-run effects of relative price changes on factor incomes, under the assumption that the amount of labor used for capital movement is constant, is implied by the results given in Mussa (1974).

16. If no capital movement took place, owners of capital employed in X would gain permanently in terms of both goods. When the process of capital movement is complete, the long-run gains to all capital owners are larger than the gains that owners of capital in X

would enjoy if no capital movement took place. The only possible cause of loss to owners of capital initially employed in X is from the increase in the wage rate induced by the use of labor in capital movement. It is unlikely that this increase in the wage would be sufficiently large and endure sufficiently long for owners of capital initially employed in X to suffer a loss in terms of present discounted value of rental income from an increase in P.

17. The implications of alternative assumptions about adjustment technology are also investigated in Mussa (1978). The concept of the "Penrose function" is discussed in Uzawa (1968, 1969).

18. If marginal labor requirements are constant, then, as discussed in Mussa (1978), there will be only one output price ratio at which both final outputs will be produced in the steady state.

19. There is an error in Mussa (1978) in that the discount factor used in defining μ_X and μ_Z does not take account of the depreciation of capital.

20. Formally, the effects of an increase in P on $\underline{K}_X$ and $\underline{K}_Z$ may be determined by applying the standard technique of comparative statics analysis to (76) and (77). Specifically, from the properties of the two-sector model, it follows that since X is capital-intensive, an increase in P reduces $W^*(P)$, increases $R^*(P)$, and increases both $\ell_X(W^*(P)/P)$ and $\ell_Z(W^*(P))$. From (76) and the fact that $H'' > 0$, it follows that the steady state capital stock, $\underline{K} = \underline{K}_X + \underline{K}_Z$, must rise as a result of an increase in P; geometrically, in figure 4.6, the $\underline{KK}$ line shifts outward from the origin. The increase in ℓ_X and ℓ_Z implies that the $\underline{LL}$ line, defined by equation (77), shifts toward the origin. The shifts of the $\underline{KK}$ and $\underline{LL}$ lines imply that $\underline{K}_X$ rises by more than the increase in $\underline{K}$ and that $\underline{K}_Z$ declines. Moreover, the changes in both $\underline{K}_X$ and $\underline{K}_Z$ are larger than would occur if the aggregate capital stock remained constant, as determined by shifting only the $\underline{LL}$ line in figure 4.6.

References

Arrow, K. J. 1968. Applications of control theory to the decision sciences. In *Mathematics of the decision sciences*, part 2. Providence, R.I.: American Mathematical Society.

Baldwin, R. E., J. Mutti, and J. D. Richardson. 1978. Welfare effects in the United States of significant multilateral tariff reduction. Department of Economics, University of Wisconsin, Madison, processed in April.

Bhagwati, J. N. 1965. On the equivalence of tariffs and quotas. In R. Baldwin et al., eds., *Trade growth and the balance of payments*, pp. 53–67. Chicago: Rand McNally.

Bhagwati, J. N., and V. K. Ramaswami. 1963. Domestic distortions and the theory of optimum subsidy. *Journal of Political Economy* 71, no. 1: 33–50.

Bhagwati, J. N., V. K. Ramaswami, and T. N. Srinivasan. 1969. Domestic distortiors, tariffs, and the theory of optimum subsidy: Further results. *Journal of Political Economy* 77, no. 6: 1005–10.

Dornbusch, R. 1971. Optimal commodity and trade taxes. *Journal of Political Economy* 79, no. 6: 1360–68.

Falvey, R. E. 1975. A note on the distinction between tariffs and quotas. *Economica* 42, no. 167 (August): 319–26.

120   Michael Mussa

————. 1976. A note on quantitative restrictions and capital mobility. *American Economic Review* 66, no. 1: 217–20.

Fishelson, G., and F. Flatters. 1975. The (non) equivalence of optimal tariffs and quotas under uncertainty. *Journal of International Economics* 5, no. 4: 385–93.

Johnson, H. G. 1960. The cost of protection and the scientific tariff. *Journal of Political Economy* 68, no. 5: 327–45.

————. 1965. Optimal trade intervention in the presence of domestic distortions. In R. Baldwin et al., eds., *Trade growth and the balance of payments*, pp. 3-34. Chicago: Rand McNally.

Kemp, M. C., and H. Wan. 1974. Hysterisis of long-run equilibrium from realistic adjustment costs. In G. Horwich and P. Samuelson, eds., *Trade, stability, and macroeconomics*. New York: Academic Press.

Lapan, H. E. 1976. International trade, factor market distortions, and the optimal dynamic subsidy. *American Economic Review* 66, no. 3: 335–46.

Mayer, W. 1974. Short-run and long-run equilibrium for a small open economy. *Journal of Political Economy* 82, no. 5: 955–67.

Mussa, M. L. 1974. Tariffs and the distribution of income: The importance of factor specificity, substitutability, and intensity in the short and long run. *Journal of Political Economy* 82, no. 6: 1191-1203.

————. 1978. Dynamic adjustment in the Heckscher-Ohlin-Samuelson model. *Journal of Political Economy* 86, no. 5: 775–91.

Neary, J. P. 1978. Short-run capital specificity and the pure theory of international trade. *Economic Journal* 88, no. 334: 488–510.

Uzawa, H. 1968. The Penrose curve and optimum economic growth. *Economic Studies Quarterly* 31: 1.

————. 1969. Time preference and the Penrose effect in a two-class model of economic growth. *Journal of Political Economy* 77, no. 4: 628–52.

Comment   Alasdair Smith

Michael Mussa's paper strongly questions on efficiency grounds the desirability of government intervention in the process by which resources are reallocated intersectorally in response to changing world market conditions. The argument is a natural (though far from trivial) extension to an intertemporal context of the well-known Bhagwati-Johnson-Ra-

Alasdair Smith is professor of economics at Sussex and was a lecturer in economics at the London School of Economics. He is a former editor of *Economica*, and the author of several papers on international trade theory. In 1979–80 he was a visiting associate professor of economics at the University of Rochester.

maswami-Srinivasan optimal policy rules. A crucial feature of the model is the assumption of rational expectations. Although there are doubts that one could reasonably raise about this hypothesis, there are also very good reasons for this to be a benchmark hypothesis in any intertemporal policy model, and I do not question its validity here.

Rather, my concern is whether a model in which income distributional issues are absent can do justice to the real-world motivations for trade-related adjustment assistance and to the consequent second-best issues.

In at least some of the literature on the second best there is a reasonable justification for policy choices being restricted. Tariffs, for example, may be chosen rather than subsidies to deal with domestic distortions because the direct cost to the government budget or the political cost may be less. It is not clear, however, why a government should be subject to the constraints which Mussa discusses: if, for example, it has the capability to calculate optimal tariffs and quotas, it surely has the capability to vary these restrictions over time.

There are two important sets of second-best issues touched on at the end of section 4.5, but because of the neglect of income distribution, they are dismissed as pure distortions.

One possible motivation for giving trade adjustment assistance is simply to provide compensation from the gainers to the losers from trade, in an attempt to reduce or eliminate political opposition to the efficient allocation of resources. It is clear that in general such bribes cannot be paid in a nondistorting way, so we have the second-best problem of balancing the need for such payments against the desire for full efficiency. (Incidentally, it may be this aspect of trade adjustment assistance which justifies benefits in excess of ordinary unemployment benefits. When there are intranational shocks, there are strong producer lobbies within the country in favor of the change, so it is harder to assemble a coalition of losers who, unbribed, can stop change.)

The second aspect of trade adjustment assistance not adequately treated by Mussa is the social insurance motivation. This may partly be for the entirely fortuitous reason that the three-factor model which is the natural framework of analysis for this issue is normally presented with labor as the mobile factor and capital as sector-specific. Yet the real problems with adjustment to shocks surely arise for workers with sector-specific skills, high moving costs, and so on. The capital market provides insurance for stockholders, who can choose the extent to which they face risks. Workers, by contrast, for reasons having to do with moral hazard and adverse selection, may not be able to obtain their desired amount of insurance against unemployment or dislocation. Even if riskier industries pay higher wages there remains the problem of *ex post* equity: a wage which compensates for a 10 percent chance of becoming unemployed may not, after the event, be regarded as adequate compensation to the 10 percent who actually become unemployed. Again, we have interesting second-best questions: whether the points sketched above justify the existence of a social insurance program, whether and how equity and efficiency come into conflict, and how such a conflict is optimally resolved.

So although the message of this paper, that there are no obvious *efficiency* grounds for instituting trade adjustment assistance programs, may be thoroughly convincing, that message should not be misunderstood.

As a postscript, I offer an alternative explanation of the issue discussed at the start of section 4.5. In the pure Heckscher-Ohlin-Samuelson model, taxes on factor income are taxes on rents and so are nondistorting. In the present model, a tax on capital income is distortionary. Mussa says this is essentially because it has an effect like the effect of an income tax on saving. But there is no capital accumulation here. It may be more insightful to interpret the rent on the fixed capital stock as the lower of the two sectoral rates of return. The rate of return differential is a return to the elastically supplied activity of moving capital, so a tax on this is not a tax on rents. The "investment tax credit" proposed by Mussa is nondistorting simply because it removes the tax on the rate of return differential.

It is also worth pointing out that the "capital-moving" sector has decreasing returns but operates competitively, so rents are being accrued here too. I conjecture that with Mussa's "investment tax credit," although only rents are taxed, not all rents are taxed, and that other nondistorting taxation schemes exist where the rents of the (fixed number of) capital-moving entrepreneurs as well as the rents of capital and labor are taxed.

5 Protection, Trade Adjustment Assistance, and Income Distribution

Peter A. Diamond

5.1 Introduction

The income redistribution ability of government is severely limited. In the public finance literature, there has been considerable recent research exploring questions of taxation and public production where the potential gains from income redistribution are sizable. In some, but not all, cases the need for income redistribution changes the desirable rules for tax and production policy. In this paper a similar approach is taken to questions of protection and trade adjustment assistance. The focus is on the distribution of income among workers and the use of output and labor movement subsidization to maximize social welfare.

Protection policy can come in many forms including subsidies, tariffs, and quotas. In this paper I shall only consider subsidies. It is politically understandable that firms seek tariffs or quotas rather than subsidies. For the model analyzed here, subsidies are the efficient method of protection when protection is desired. Thus the analysis is simplified by considering them rather than tariffs which would introduce further distortion. The differences among subsidies, tariffs, and quotas are sufficiently well known that the reader will have no difficulty extending the analysis, should that be wanted. Similarly, I analyze a competitive industry, leaving to the reader the adaptation to other market settings.

Trade adjustment assistance is available separately to firms and to workers.[1] This paper considers only financial aid going to workers. There

Peter A. Diamond is professor of economics at Massachusetts Institute of Technology. He has published on public finance (including social security), on law and economics, and on uncertainty theory. He has also written on trade theory in the *Journal of International Economics*.

The author thanks Jagdish Bhagwati for helpful comments and the NSF for financial support.

are many issues involved in the question of when it is socially advantageous to use public resources to improve and maintain firms that might otherwise go out of business. These issues are, in part, very different from those relevant for analysis of workers, whose continued existence is taken as given. Analysis of aid to firms that comes to grips with the efficiency and behavior of firms would be very interesting.

Adjustment assistance to workers comes in the form of services and advice as well as cash—McCarthy (1975) suggests that the former may well be very important in helping workers respond to their changed environment. Nevertheless, this analysis will only consider financial assistance for workers who are well able to look after their own interests. To go further would again raise a number of very different (and very interesting) issues.

When an industry is in long-term decline, the workers in the industry are likely to be poorer than taxpayers generally. Thus there is an equity basis for subsidizing the output of the industry to raise wages in the industry. Taken alone, this subsidy has the side effect of inefficiently decreasing exit from the industry. Even workers exiting from a declining industry are likely to be poorer than taxpayers generally. Thus there is an equity basis for subsidizing moving costs. Taken alone, this subsidy has the side effect of inefficiently encouraging too much exit from the industry. Combining these two policies, we have a gain in equity with offsetting incentives on exit. This paper explores the workings of and limitations on this combination of policies.

In section 5.2 is developed a simple model of a two-industry economy with labor as the sole factor of production. The model is used to derive optimal policies of protection and adjustment assistance. The special assumptions of the model are discussed in section 5.3. Sections 5.4 and 5.5 examine the case for adjustment assistance once one recognizes the prior existence of income taxation and unemployment compensation. This analysis was developed after reading McCarthy's analysis of the Massachusetts shoe industry, an industry in long-term decline. I have not asked how typical this industry is of recipients of adjustment assistance. At several places in the analysis, the results would be different if adjustment assistance were going to industries with only temporary difficulties.

5.2 One-Period Model

The basic elements of the analysis are brought out in this section in a one-period linear model. We consider an economy with two industries. The *A* industry is the one suffering from foreign competition. The *B* industry represents the rest of the economy. This is small-country analysis, and the relative output price of these two goods is set by the world market. For ease of interpretation of the equations we will distinguish the two absolute prices p_A and p_B. The economy has workers, but no other factors of production.

At the start of the single period, each worker is located in one industry or the other. There are two consequences to being a worker in a particular industry. One is that workers are assumed to be skilled in their trades and to become unskilled should they switch industries. A skilled worker has s times the marginal product of an unskilled worker. We shall measure output so that the marginal product of an unskilled worker is equal to one (which is assumed to be independent of the number of other workers). The second consequence of different initial placements is that there is a moving cost associated with switching industries. The costs are different for different workers. We will refer to a c worker as one with moving costs equal to c and denote by $N(c)$ the number of workers in the A industry with moving costs less than or equal to c. For convenience we will assume that there are some workers with moving costs c for every positive value of c, $N'(c) > 0$ for $c > 0$. N_A and N_B are the numbers of workers in each industry at the start of the period. Apart from location and moving costs, all workers are the same.[2] We denote by $v(I; p_A, p_B)$ the indirect utility function of a worker having income I and facing prices p_A and p_B. This will often be shortened to $v(I)$ when there is no confusion. We assume that the relevant normalization for social welfare has v concave in I.

We begin by considering full welfare optimization assuming the use of ideal lump-sum taxation. Since this model does not violate any assumptions of the Arrow-Debreu model, any Pareto optimum is achievable as a competitive equilibrium with appropriate lump-sum redistribution. Thus we need not consider any other policy tools until we start second-best analysis. Ideal lump-sum taxation has two characteristics—taxes can be different for different individuals and taxes do not vary with individual behavior. Since taxes do not vary, individuals decide whether or not to move by comparing income without moving to income net of moving costs.

We assume that the A industry is in decline in the sense that $p_A < p_B$. With workers receiving their marginal products, this implies that the workers who stay in the A industry have lower earned income than workers who stay in the B industry. Lump-sum taxation to maximize the sum of utilities will then transfer income from B workers to A workers to equate incomes.

If p_A is sufficiently close to p_B for the loss of skill from moving to be more important than the lower price, $sp_A \geq p_B$, then no workers will choose to move. In this case the lump-sum transfers will be the same for all A workers and will equate incomes across industries while balancing the government budget:

$$sp_A + I_A = sp_B + I_B,$$
(1)
$$N_A I_A + N_B I_B = 0,$$

where I_A and I_B are lump-sum transfers to workers in the two industries (with $I_B < 0$ corresponding to lump-sum taxation). Since these are lump-sum taxes, they depend on the individual and not his choice of industry—someone choosing to switch industries does not change his lump-sum transfer.

If p_A declines below p_B/s, individuals will choose to move. Since lump-sum transfers do not change with the moving decision, workers with moving costs below c_0^* will move, where the c_0^* worker has the same income in either industry:

(2) $$sp_A = p_B - c_0^*.$$

Recalling that A workers are skilled in the A industry but unskilled in the B industry, the higher price of B output just offsets a c_0^* worker's moving costs and loss in skill.

In the absence of lump-sum transfers B workers would be better off than movers who would be better off than those staying as A workers. Ideal lump-sum taxation will equate the incomes of all workers. Denote by I_c the lump-sum transfer to a c worker. For $c > c_0^*$, the worker stays in the A industry. All such workers are in the same position and have the same lump-sum income I_A. For $c < c_0^*$, lump-sum income I_c will vary with c. These transfers equate all incomes and satisfy the government budget constraint:

(3) $$sp_A + I_A = sp_B + I_B = p_B - c + I_c,$$

(4) $$(N_A - N(c_0^*))I_A + N_B I_B + \int_0^{c_0^*} I_c \, dN(c) = 0.$$

For familiar reasons of limited information and administrative costs, this type of redistribution is assumed to be infeasible. Thus we shall consider a restricted set of policy tools.

5.2.1   Second Best

For constrained welfare maximization, we consider the use of two policy tools. The protection tool is the subsidization of output of the A industry. Let α be one plus the *ad valorem* subsidy rate. The adjustment assistance tool is the subsidization of moving costs. Let β be one minus the *ad valorem* subsidy rate.[3] These programs are financed by a poll tax—an equal per capita tax on all workers in the economy. Such a tax is feasible even when it is not feasible to ideally set lump-sum taxes which differ across individuals. As before we need to distinguish cases depending on the level of p_A. For $p_A \geq p_B/s$, it is inefficient to have any workers move. There is then no reason not to protect the A industry at a sufficient level to equate worker incomes in the two industries, $\alpha p_A = p_B$. In this case the poll tax T_1 must satisfy

(5) $$(N_A + N_B)T_1 = (\alpha - 1)sp_A N_A.$$

With all incomes equated, social welfare satisfies

(6) $$W_1 = (N_A + N_B)v\left(s\frac{(p_B N_B + p_A N_A)}{N_A + N_B}\right).$$

Note that this equilibrium is feasible for any p_A, not only high ones. The question is when this policy is optimal also for values of p_A below p_B/s.

The alternative policy is to restrict α so that some mobility occurs. This is only possible when $sp_A < p_B$. In this case, the worker who is just indifferent to moving has costs satisfying.

(7) $$\alpha sp_A = p_B - \beta c^*.$$

The level of poll tax T_2 needed to finance these programs satisfies

(8) $$(N_A + N_B)T_2 = (\alpha - 1)sp_A(N_A - N(c^*))$$
$$+ (1 - \beta)\int_0^{c^*} c\,dN(c).$$

At fixed subsidy rates, an increase in c^*, increasing the number of moving workers, lowers the cost of protection and raises the cost of adjustment assistance.

Protection encourages workers to stay in the A industry. Adjustment assistance encourages them to leave. For each level of movement between industries $N(c^*)$, there is a locus of pairs of subsidy levels which will give the same amount of movement. These loci are shown in figure 5.1. All are straight lines passing through the point $(p_B/sp_A, 0)$. The locus that also passes through the point $(1,1)$ has the same amount of movement as would occur in the absence of intervention. We shall consider the optimal pair of policies (α, β) as well as the optimal α for arbitrary β and vice versa.

Moving to the right along a constant movement locus, both protection and adjustment assistance increase, as do the lump-sum taxes to finance the subsidies. On the locus where the c^* worker is the marginal worker, taxes satisfy

(9) $$(N_A + N_B)T_2 = (\alpha - 1)sp_A(N_A - N(c^*))$$
$$+ \left(1 - \frac{p_B - \alpha sp_A}{c^*}\right)\int_0^{c^*} c\,dN(c).$$

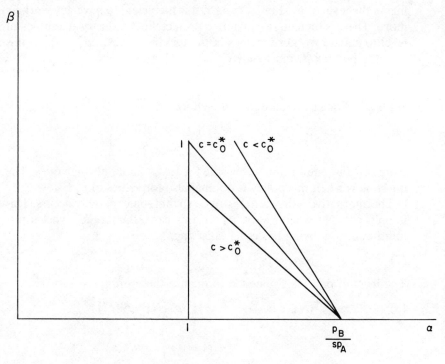

Fig. 5.1   Constant mobility loci

Thus the increase in taxes as subsidization increases satisfies

$$(10) \qquad \left.\frac{\partial T_2}{\partial \alpha}\right|_{c^*} = \frac{sp_A}{c^*(N_A + N_B)}\left[c^*(N_A - N(c^*)) + \int_0^{c^*} c\, dN(c)\right].$$

The B workers have incomes that fall at the rate of

$$\left.\frac{\partial T_2}{\partial \alpha}\right|_{c^*}$$

as we move to the right along such a locus. The A workers have incomes that rise at the rate

$$(11) \qquad \left.\frac{\partial(\alpha sp_A - T_2)}{\partial \alpha}\right|_{c^*} = \frac{sp_A}{c^*(N_A + N_B)}$$

$$\left[c^*N_B + \int_0^{c^*} (c^* - c)\, dN(c)\right].$$

The c' workers who move have incomes that change at the rate

(12)
$$\left. \frac{\partial(p_B - \beta c' - T_2)}{\partial \alpha} \right|_{c^*} = \frac{s p_A}{c^*(N_A + N_B)}$$

$$\left[c' N_B + \int_0^{c^*} (c^* - c) \, dN(c) - (c^* - c') N_A \right].$$

This expression is positive for high values of c' and negative for low ones. Thus movement to the right along this locus implies redistribution from the better to the worse off and welfare improves as we move toward the point where $\beta = 0$ and $\alpha = p_B/sp_A$, i.e., the point where everyone is indifferent to moving.[4] At this point the movers and the A workers have utility $v(p_B - T_2)$, while the B workers have utility $v(sp_B - T_2)$, where T_2 satisfies (9). To determine the optimum, we need to select c^*.

In deciding how many workers should move, the government wants to minimize the tax burden since minimizing T_2 maximizes both $v(p_B - T_2)$ and $v(sp_B - T_2)$. This occurs at the same level of movement as in the laissez-faire equilibrium $N(c_0^*)$, since this maximizes the value of net output at world prices.[5]

To complete the analysis of welfare maximization we must determine the values of p_A for which this equilibrium is better than the equilibrium with no movement and equalized incomes. With equalized incomes and no interindustry movement, welfare satisfies (6). In the constrained optimum with movement, welfare satisfies

(13) $W_2 = N_A v(p_B - T_2) + N_B v(sp_B - T_2),$

where

$$(N_A + N_B)T_2 = (p_B - sp_A)(N_A - N(c^*))$$

$$+ \int_0^{c^*} c \, dN(c),$$

(14) $c^* = c_0^* = p_B - sp_A/p_B.$

To compare alternative policies, let us assume that workers do not consume the output of the A industry, so the only effect of a higher p_A is higher incomes of all workers. With equalized incomes and no movement we have full equality but inefficiency. With movement we have efficiency but inequality. We would expect the former policy to be better when sp_A is close to p_B and so movement is unimportant. This is the case since $W_1 > W_2$ at $p_B = sp_A$. Protection alone can be the preferred policy even at $p_A = 0$ for suitable utility function and sufficiently large s. Table 5.1 compares the alternative policies.

For the stronger result that W_1 is preferred if and only if p_A exceeds a critical value, we have a sufficient condition of increasing absolute risk

Table 5.1   **Alternative Policies**

	Only Protection	Protection and Assistance
α	p_B/p_A	p_B/sp_A
β	1	0
c^*	0	c_0^*
T	T_1	T_2

aversion. To see that this is the case, we differentiate social welfare with respect to p_A in both cases:

$$(15) \qquad \frac{\partial W_1}{\partial p_A} = sN_A v'(sp_B - T_1),$$

$$\frac{\partial W_2}{\partial p_A} = s(N_A - N(c_0^*))(\frac{N_A v'(p_B - T_2) + N_B v'(sp_B - T_2)}{N_A + N_B}).$$

When W_1 equals W_2, W_1 is increasing more rapidly with decreasing absolute risk aversion since

$$(N_A + N_B)v(x) = N_A v(y) + N_B v(z)$$
$$(16) \qquad => (N_A + N_B)v'(x) > N_A v'(y) + N_B v'(z).$$

As p_A gets larger, the efficiency loss from no movement gets smaller ($sN_A > s(N_A - N(c_0^*))$). For the redistribution gain to get larger, we need redistribution to be more important the greater the income level. This latter condition is not generally plausible, so the areas of dominance of each policy are not necessarily connected.

5.2.2   Single-Policy Tool

We have considered the simultaneous optimization of protection and trade adjustment. We now consider the use of each of these tools separately, the other tool held constant and assuming a sufficiently low p_A to justify some movement out of the A industry. The result of these calculations is that the optimum occurs with greater concern for income distribution than is the case if the free policy variable is set to produce the no-intervention level of movement.[6] This is shown in figure 5.2, where it is assumed that the social indifference curves are well behaved. Even when this is not the case, the optimum has the properties mentioned above.

With the policy tools set at arbitrary levels, social welfare satisfies

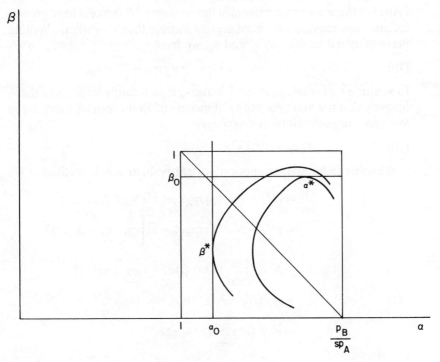

Fig. 5.2   Social indifference curves

$$W = \left[N_A - N(c^*) \right] v\,(\alpha s p_A - T)$$

$$\text{(17)} \qquad + \int_0^{c^*} v\,(p_B - \beta c - T)\,dN(c)$$

$$+ N_B v\,(s p_B - T),$$

where c^* satisfies (7) and T satisfies (8). The derivative of W with respect to the poll tax T equals minus the average marginal utility of income of taxpayers in the economy, which is defined as

$$\overline{v}' \equiv \left[N_A - N(c^*) \right] v'\,(\alpha s p_A - T)$$

$$\text{(18)} \qquad + \int_0^{c^*} v'\,(p_B - \beta c - T)\,dN(c)$$

$$+ N_B v'\,(s p_B - T).$$

Provided there are some movers in the economy,[7] B workers have greater income than movers who have greater income than A workers. Writing these marginal utilities as v_A' and v_B', we have

(19) $$v_A' \equiv v'(\alpha sp_A - T) > \overline{v'} > v'(sp_B - T) \equiv v_B'.$$

In addition we assume that the B industry is sufficiently larger than the A industry that the marginal utility of income of all the movers exceeds the average marginal utility of a taxpayer:

(20) $$v'(p_B - T) > \overline{v'}.$$

With this additional assumption, we can evaluate the derivatives of W:

$$\frac{\partial W}{\partial \alpha} = (N_A - N(c^*))sp_A v_A' - \overline{v'}(N_A + N_B)\frac{\partial T}{\partial \alpha}$$

$$= (N_A - N(c^*))sp_A v_A' - \overline{v'}\left[sp_A(N_A - N(c^*))\right.$$

$$\left. + N'(c^*)\frac{\partial c^*}{\partial \alpha}((1-\beta)c^* - (\alpha - 1)sp_A)\right]$$

(21) $$= sp_A(N_A - N(c^*))(v_A' - \overline{v'})$$

$$- \overline{v'}N'(c^*)\frac{\partial c^*}{\partial \alpha}(c^* - c_0^*),$$

$$\frac{\partial W}{\partial \beta} = \int_0^{c^*} -v'(p_B - \beta c - T)c\,dN(c)$$

$$- \overline{v'}(N_A + N_B)\frac{\partial T}{\partial \beta}$$

$$= \int_0^{c^*} -v'(p_B - \beta c - T)c\,dN(c) - \overline{v'}\left[-\int_0^{c^*} c\,dN(c)\right.$$

$$\left. + N'(c^*)\frac{\partial c^*}{\partial \beta}((1-\beta)c^* - (\alpha - 1)sp_A)\right]$$

(22) $$= -\int_0^{c^*}(v'(p_B - \beta c - T) - \overline{v'})c\,dN(c)$$

$$- \overline{v'}N'(c^*)\frac{\partial c^*}{\partial \beta}(c^* - c_0).$$

Considering the derivative with respect to α, we note that the first term is positive and the second is also positive when $c^* > c_0^*$ since c^* decreases with α. Thus, to find a value of α for which $\partial W/\partial \alpha$ is zero, we must have c^*

$< c_0$. Thus protection is carried beyond the point where the decline of the industry equals that in the absence of intervention. With protection as the only available tool, incomes of A workers are raised above the level which gives the no-intervention level of movement.

Considering the derivative with respect to β, we note that the first term is negative (by assumption [20]) and the second is also negative for $c^* < c_0$ since c^* is decreasing with β. Thus, to raise the incomes of movers, trade assistance is carried beyond the point which would yield the same movement as in the absence of intervention. Assuming they are well behaved (as need not be true), social indifference curves would appear as in figure 5.2, where β^* and α^* mark optimal policies for arbitrary policies α_0 and β_0, respectively.

5.3   Discussion of the Model

The analysis above uses a particularly simple model of an economy and has no policy variables other than the ones being analyzed. In this section we consider informally more general models of the economy. In the next two sections we reconsider these policy tools in the presence of income taxation and unemployment compensation. In Appendix C is a further discussion in responce to questions raised at the conference.

First, let us recap the basics of the analysis. We start with an industry where workers have low wages because of a fall in the world price of their output. The alternative to staying at low wages is to move out of the industry, bearing moving costs and a loss in skill. To improve income distribution, it is desirable to help these workers. If the fall in output price is not too large, the most efficient way to help them is to protect the industry, stifling movement out of the industry if there would be any. If the fall in output price is large, this policy is too expensive in terms of the efficiency loss from immobility. A better policy is then to have a lower rate of protection and to encourage mobility by subsidizing movement costs—that is, having trade assistance. By coordinating these two policies with the single margin of movement, it is possible to preserve the efficient level of movement. If only one of these two tools is available, it should be used with greater concern for income distribution than would preserve the efficient level of movement.

We turn now to considering various special aspects of the model. We shall consider the absence of capital, the use of a linear technology, the assumption of an inelastic labor supply, the use of a one-period model, the absence of firms and new workers, and the simple form of moving costs. The absence of domestic distortions (like excise taxation) avoids the familiar second-best complications of coordinating different policies or adapting to their noncoordination.

5.3.1   Absence of Capital

We have used a model with a single factor of production. To add more factors (capital for example) we would need to consider the extent to which other factors were mobile. If capital were immobile, we would only have to take account of the fact that protection raises the return to capital in the A industry. To evaluate this effect we would need to know the extent to which ownership of the A industry was narrow or wide through the stock market or indebtedness of the firms and then the income levels of the capital income recipients relative to that of taxpayers. To the extent that capital is mobile, protection would also retard movement out of the industry and so efficiency. Presumably these effects weaken the case for protection (relative to that stated above) and thus also weaken the case for trade adjustment assistance. Whether the case for protection disappears altogether would depend on the particulars of the case. Even if no protection is warranted, we have seen that there remains a case for trade adjustment assistance.

5.3.2   Linear Technology

The model assumed that the marginal products of labor in the two industries were independent of the numbers of workers in the two industries. With strictly concave production functions, labor mobility raises the wages of those remaining behind and lowers the wages in the industry receiving the additional labor. This change in the model does not alter the basic argument. In addition, with concave production functions there is a residual profit in both industries. Any change in the level of movement will change the two levels of profits and, in general, the aggregate too. The determinants of the sign of the effect are derived in appendix A. This indirect effect is in addition to the indirect effect of protection in raising profits. Being ambiguous in sign, this indirect effect could work either way in determining the desirable size of policies.

5.3.3   Inelastic Labor Supply

With labor supply variable, redistribution by raising wages involves a distortion not present with lump-sum redistribution. Institutional limitations on hours may make this point of little significance. Otherwise, optimal protection is presumably reduced somewhat, although the desirability of some protection is unaffected.

Labor supply can also be variable because new workers are coming into the A industry. If protection raises the number of such workers, we have a further distortion. This is unlikely to be a real issue in a seriously declining industry.

5.3.4   One Period Model

By considering a one-period model, we have ignored historical reasons for workers in the two industries to be systematically different as well as the effects of the anticipation of these policies on earlier entry into this industry. Both of these points are illustrated by considering a perfect foresight two-period model where workers know that the time trend of p_A is down relative to p_B. Let us assume that without government intervention individuals are just indifferent to the choice of industry at the start of period one, $(p_A(1) + p_A(2)/(1 + r)) = (p_B(1) + p_B(2)/(1 + r))$. Having the same lifetime incomes, workers who plan to stay in either industry in both periods have the same consumption plan. Having different time streams of earnings, they have different savings, with the A workers having greater wealth at the start of period two. Even though A workers have lower wages than B workers, they both have the same consumption level, giving no reason for redistribution. Even more striking is the position of those low-moving-cost workers who shift from A to B. They are the best off in the economy as revealed by their willingness to move. This *ex post* behavior has the *ex ante* implication that low-moving-cost workers are particularly attracted to the A industry, which is appropriate. Full subsidization of moving costs would undercut this incentive to attract those who are most efficient in moving.

While this model illustrates what can go wrong with naive application of the one-period model, it is unrealistic for the plight of the Massachusetts shoe workers. (It may be accurate for the Alaska pipeline workers.) It is not simple to evaluate the effects of protection and adjustment assistance on prior entry into particular industries in the face of uncertainty about future prices. Both expectation formation and savings behavior are underdeveloped areas of empirical economics, making it hard to quantify these effects. The fact of many missing markets in the presence of price uncertainty makes it hard to evaluate whatever effects occur. In this setting laisser-faire has no privileged claim to efficiency; the indirect effects of income redistribution policies may be favorable rather than unfavorable.[8]

5.3.5 Absence of Firms

The model recognizes two industries but distinguishes neither firms within the industry nor separate plants of indivdual firms. Declining industries are marked by the closing of plants and the bankruptcies of firms. While many workers are reemployed in other plants of the same firm or other firms, it is unlikely that this mechanism works with the efficiency assumed of mobility in the model. While this issue would be of relevance for analysis of the desirability of assistance to prevent the closing of plants or firms, it plays little role in consideration of aid to workers who move after shutdown. While protection tends to decrease plant shutdown, adjustment assistance makes workers less willing to accept low wages to keep plants open. Thus there remains a trade-off in policies to approximately preserve the mobility level.

Another facet of the existence of firms is the existence of uniform wage schedules. Layoff by firms will tend to be based on marginal products (which vary) relative to wages (which may not). Moving costs and skill losses are thus not the sole selection criterion for workers to move. Since concern about the costs of moving affect both productivity and wage bargaining, it is not obvious how far reality differs from the simple model.

5.3.6 Moving Costs

We have modeled individual moving costs as unaffected by their subsidization. There are three types of costs—foregone wages, financial moving costs, and psychological costs. We would expect increases in the level or extent of unemployment benefits to affect job acceptance criteria. This will be discussed below. Whether the subsidization of relocation expenses involves any distortions depends on the rules under which they are paid. Some forms of payment could lead to inefficiency because of the substitution of subsidized costs for unsubsidized costs. Depending on details, this might decrease the desirable level of subsidization, but does not remove the case for its existence. Psychological costs cannot be subsidized in the same way as financial costs. If formally introduced, they would enter the model in a parallel way to the loss in skill.

Another complication arises once we recognize that different individuals have different relative skills in the two industries. Since moving decisions reflect both skill losses and moving costs, differential treatment of these two elements will induce inefficiency. Appendix B extends the model to this case.

5.4 Income Taxation

In the absence of any other policies it is straightforward to make the income redistribution case for many market intervention policies. It is difficult to ignore the fact that the United States has a personal income tax, as do most other countries. There are then two bases for a primarily redistributive policy. One is that the political process has resulted in an income tax which has less redistribution than might be desired.[9] The other is that even the optimal use of an income tax can be improved upon by the coordinated use of supplementary policies in a complicated economy.[10] Both of these arguments strike me as valid. Since it would be off the main topic to discuss my views of the appropriate level of redistribution in the United States, I will confine my remarks to the second issue.

Apart from political limitations, income redistribution is limited by the induced inefficiencies of high marginal tax rates. Thus one can ask whether incentives create less of a problem for helping the beneficiaries of these policies than for individuals at the same income level in the general economy. There is a major argument which appears plausible, although I have not done any formal modeling to check its validity. When a poor group is separated out, its taxes can be reduced without necessarily affecting the taxes of those higher up the income distribution (except through the government budget constraint). This eases the strain between the taxes of low- and high-income individuals which comes from a nonlinear income tax structure. The critical element for this argument is that identification as a sufferer from import competition be negatively correlated with income, a plausible hypothesis.[11]

Most discussions of income taxation take place in one-period models. Yet for many government policies there appears to be greater concern for declining income than for low income per se (for example, social security), requiring use of a multiperiod model. While this outcome might just represent the relative political powers of those with low incomes and those subject to income declines, consideration of intertemporal models does raise insurance bases for concern about declining income. This is particularly the case once one recognizes the intertemporal dependence of individual utility functions and so the particular dislike of declining living standards. The relatively undeveloped state of this area limits this issue to a suggestion for future research.

5.5 Unemployment Compensation

In the United States, the annual income tax is already supplemented by unemployment compensation. Adjustment assistance increases the level and duration of benefits. Thus it is appropriate, again, to ask whether there is a case for a larger program for workers in industries hurt by foreign competition. In answering, it seems useful to distinguish declining industries from those temporarily hurt—that is, to distinguish between industries from which there is steady exit and those needing temporary layoffs.

In the previous section it was argued that the presence of a progressive income tax did not eliminate the case for using additional tools to provide income to poor groups. By identifying a separate group, it becomes possible to transfer income to that group without lessening the taxes of those higher up the income distribution. Here we consider a different issue. Assuming the recipients of unemployment compensation to have approximately the same lifetime income levels as the recipients of trade adjustment assistance, is there a case for supplementing unemployment compensation for those laid off from declining industries? Since the theory of unemployment compensation is relatively underdeveloped, I will identify questions that need answering rather than reasons for the existing program. Thus I shall review the issues about unemployment compensation to see the extent to which they might apply differently to trade-impacted workers. First, we will consider conditions of their layoff, then the characteristics of the workers.

Unemployment compensation provides automatic stabilization for business cycles. Presumably the layoffs of trade-impacted workers are less correlated with general business declines than general layoffs. This offers no basis for supplementary benefits.

Baily (1977) and Flemming (1978) have argued that unemployment compensation is a form of worker insurance. The risk aversion of workers, compounded by capital market imperfections, gives considerable scope for insurance to ease the burden of this risk. From this perspective, the insurance provided is limited by its effects on worker behavior, to which we turn next. Conceivably remaining a long time in a declining industry might make trade-impacted workers more risk averse than others. The question could be approached by comparing the wealth levels of different groups of the unemployed.

Unemployment compensation affects incentives for layoffs, search intensity, and job acceptance.[12] Precisely because these workers come from a declining industry there is not the same concern for the excessive use of temporary layoffs. The argument would not be the same if adjustment assistance were available for industries which were temporarily impacted by foreign trade.

Much of the discussion of the incentives created by unemployment compensation assumes that there are no externalities caused by the behavior of the unemployed. Then, benefits play the same role as a distorting tax and we have the familiar trade-off of efficiency with equity and insurance. However, once one recognizes the lags and imperfections in the flows of information in the labor market it is not plausible to assume an absence of externalities caused by the behavior of the unemployed. Greater search intensity by the unemployed generates external economies to jobs which are filled as a consequence of this additional search.[13] Greater selectivity in job acceptance increases vacancies, and so the rate and quality of job offers received by other unemployed workers. Since greater selectivity involves passing up poor job matches, the average quality of matching is improved.[14] Greater unemployment benefits worsen the external diseconomy from too little search but, up to a point, improve the external economy from rejecting bad jobs. Without substantial evidence, I take the second effect to be more important than the first. This then creates a case for unemployment compensation even if workers are risk neutral. The question at hand, however, is whether trade-impacted workers differ from other workers. They may well since they may be making larger changes in both locations and industries than the typical worker. Whether empirically this is the case and whether theoretically this would imply a larger optimal benefit are questions I cannot answer. They must await further research.

Unemployment compensation distinguishes a number of worker characteristics in determining benefits—recent work for eligibility, wage level for benefit level and replacement rate, presence of dependents for additional benefits in some states. There are many other characteristics which are not distinguished. In particular, age affects employability. Another question for future research is whether trade-impacted workers differ from typical insured workers in ways which would justify larger or longer benefits but which are not distinguished in the determination of benefits.

Of course, there remains the argument that additional adjustment assistance is needed to offset desired protection.

5.6   Open and Closed Economies

Industries decline for many reasons. Is there any good reason to distinguish industries by whether the decline comes from rising imports or increased production elsewhere in the domestic economy? (This is separate from the issue that domestic politics are different in the two cases and the question whether one should distinguish declining industries from other sources of low wages and unemployment.) My casual impression is that the answer is no (ignoring macroissues as is encouraged by international agreements). That is, if one introduced the A' industry to the model in section 5.2 in place of international trade, the analysis would be similar if the fall in p_A came from increased productivity in the A' industry. The lack of difference between open and closed economies may be enhanced by the fact that the optimal policies in the face of serious decline retain the flow of workers out of industry A by combining adjustment assistance with protection. Of course, with a domestic A' industry it may be administratively difficult to distinguish the A and A' industries in the design of protective policies.

While the similarity of conclusions in open and closed economies seems strong, let me end on a cautionary note. Protection and adjustment assistance are predicated on government policies that contribute to industry decline (e.g., reduced tariffs) and not just industry decline. This distinction has been ignored in this paper. There is an analogy in the much studied provision of the United States Constitution that the government not take property without just compensation. It might be worthwhile to explore that analogy.[15]

5.7   Concluding Remarks

I have focused on the purely economic basis for both protection and adjustment assistance policies. In the absence of perfect income redistribution and perfect certainty about future economic development, there is a case for the use of these policies. This analysis needs supplementation to consider the political role of these two policies in affecting trade policy.

Appendix A   *Nonlinear Model*

Assume that capital is immobile and output is determined by the production functions $F_A(s(N_A - N(c)))$ and $F_B(sN_B + N(c))$. Then movement is determined by the equation

(A1) $\alpha s p_A F_A' = p_B F_B' - \beta c^*.$

In addition to the direct effect on incomes when protection is decreased or trade adjustment assistance increased, there is the indirect effect that the induced increase in movement raises wages in the A industry and lowers them in the B industry.

Next, we examine the effect of mobility or total capital income

(A2)
$$I^k = I_A^k + I_B^k = \left[\alpha p_A F_A - \alpha s(N_A - N(c))p_A F_A'\right]$$
$$+ \left[p_B F_B - (sN_B + N(c))p_B F_B'\right]$$

In addition to the direct effect of changes in α and β on capital income, there is an indirect effect

$$\frac{1}{N'(c)}\frac{\partial I^k}{\partial c} = -\alpha s^2(N_A - N(c))p_A F_A''$$
$$+ (sN_B + N(c))p_B F_B''$$
$$= -\alpha s p_A F_A' \varepsilon_A + p_B F_B' \varepsilon_B,$$

where ε_i is the elasticity of the marginal product with respect to effective labor. This indirect effect reflects three elements. Workers lose their skills upon switching industries. Thus, they contribute less to effective labor in the new industry than in the old. Any difference in elasticities between industries implies different magnitudes of wage bill increases and decreases in the two industries from a transfer of the same amount of effective labor between industries. The presence of moving costs implies that the values of marginal products are not equal in the two industries. Thus the effect in the high-marginal-product industry is of greater importance.

This analysis rests critically on the particular assumption made concerning the way that skilled and unskilled labor enter the production function.

Appendix B

The model in section 5.2 assumed that all workers were the same, apart from moving costs. Here we introduce a second difference—skill in the B industry should the worker move. Thus we have a double index for workers (s_B, c), with $m(s_B, c)$ as the density of the index among A workers (m is not normalized to integrate to one). Workers with high s_B and low c will choose to move.

For a given α and β we define the critical value for movement s_B^* (c; α,β) by the equality of incomes in the two industries:

(A4) $\alpha s p_A = s_B^* p_B - \beta c.$

We write the level of movement in the absence of intervention as s_B^0 (c). We shall only consider cases where some movement is desirable. As before, we assume poll taxes are used to finance the subsidies.

Social welfare can be written as a function of α and β:

$$W(\alpha,\beta) = v(\alpha s p_A - T)(N_A - \int_0^\infty \int_\xi^\infty m(s_B,c)\, ds_B\, dc)$$

(A5) $$+ \int_0^\infty \int_\xi^\infty v(s_B p_B - \beta c - T) m(s_B,c)\, ds_B\, dc$$

$$+ v(s p_B - T)N_B,$$

where $\xi = s_B^*(c,\alpha,\beta)$ and where taxes satisfy

(A6) $$(N_A + N_B)T = (\alpha - 1)s p_A (N_A - \int_0^\infty \int_\xi^\infty m(s_B,c)\, ds_B\, dc)$$

$$+ (1 - \beta)\int_0^\infty \int_\xi^\infty cm(s_B,c)\, ds_B\, dc.$$

As before, we define $\overline{v'}$ as the average marginal utility of income of taxpayers. For convenience we write the equilibrium number of movers as M. Differentiating W, we have

$$\frac{\partial W}{\partial \alpha} = s p_A v'(\alpha s p_A - T)(N_A - M) - \overline{v'}(N_A + N_B)\frac{\partial T}{\partial \alpha}$$

$$= s p_A v'(\alpha s p_A - T)(N_A - M) - \overline{v'}\Big[s p_A(N_A - M)$$

(A7) $$+ \int_0^\infty ((\alpha - 1)s p_A - (1 - \beta)c)m(s_B^*,c)\frac{\partial s_B^*}{\partial \alpha}\, dc\Big]$$

$$= s p_A(N_A - M)(v_A' - \overline{v'}) - \overline{v'}s p_A p_B^{-1} \int_0^\infty ((\alpha - 1)s p_A$$

$$- (1 - \beta)c)m(s_B^*,c)\, dc$$

$$= s p_A\{(N_A - M)(v_A' - \overline{v'}) - \overline{v'}$$

$$\int_0^\infty (s_B^* - s_B^0) m(s_B^*, c) \, dc\},$$

$$\frac{\partial W}{\partial \beta} = - \int_0^\infty \int_{s_B}^\infty cv' (s_B p_B - \beta c - T) m(s_B, c)$$

$$ds_B \, dc - \overline{v'}(N_A + N_B) \frac{\partial T}{\partial \beta}$$

$$= - \int_0^\infty \int_{s_B}^\infty c(v' - \overline{v'}) m \, ds_B \, dc - \overline{v'}$$

$$\int_0^\infty ((\alpha - 1)s p_A - (1 - \beta)c) m \frac{\partial s_B^*}{\partial \beta} \, dc$$

(A8)

$$= - \int_0^\infty \int_{s_B}^\infty c(v' - \overline{v'}) m \, ds_B \, dc - \frac{\overline{v'}}{p_B}$$

$$\int_0^\infty c((\alpha - 1)s p_A - (1 - \beta)c) m \, dc$$

$$= - \int_0^\infty \int_{s_B}^\infty c(v' - \overline{v'}) m \, ds_B \, dc - \overline{v'}$$

$$\int_0^\infty c(s_B^* - s_B^0) m(s_B^*, c) \, dc.$$

These equations are similar in form to those in section 5.2 when only one policy variable was employed. (The similarity would be more striking if the cutoff were written as $c^*(s_B)$ rather than $s_B^*(c)$.) In the absence of intervention ($\alpha = 1$, $\beta = 1$, $s_B^* = s_B^0$) we see that $\partial W/\partial \alpha > 0$ and $\partial W/\partial \beta < 0$, assuming that movers have lower incomes than the average taxpayer.

Given the level of protection, adjustment assistance encourages movement by those with higher costs and lower skills in the B industry than would be efficient. This inefficiency is the source of the second-best nature of the results. The net effect of both policies on the size of the A industry can be written as

(A9) $$M^* - M^0 = \int_0^\infty \int_{s_B^*}^{s_B^0} m(s_B, c) \, ds_B dc.$$

Without restrictions on m, this need not be signed at the optimal policy. If the distribution is uniform over some region (with c ranging from $\underline{c}$ to $\overline{c}$), we can use (A7) to sign the difference in movement:

(A10) $$(M^* - M^0) = m \int_{\underline{c}}^{\overline{c}} (s_B^0 - s_B^*) \, dc < 0.$$

Thus the inefficiency in induced movement and the desire to aid those with low incomes result in a larger A industry than would occur without intervention. Presumably different assumptions on the differences among workers would lead to the opposite conclusion in some cases.

Appendix C   *Relation to More General Models*

The model in the text has been made startlingly simple to bring out the essentials of the analysis. In the conference discussion, questions were raised as to the implications of taking the simple version literally. In this appendix I discuss general ways of extending the model to deal with the questions raised. These extensions are consistent with the basic idea of a small *A* industry and a large *B* industry representing the rest of the economy.

1. *Moving costs.* The technology of moving workers between industries was unspecified. With no change in the analysis we could have moving be done by *B* workers who have equal productivity in the *B* industry or the moving industry. Alternatively, moving can simply use the output of the *B* industry.

2. *Intertemporal setting.* The model has a single period. If we append a future to the economy, moving workers will presumably acquire skills in the *B* industry. The difference between the marginal products of skilled and unskilled workers then represents the difference in present discounted values given the different trajectories of marginal products of already skilled and presently unskilled workers.

3. *Initial position.* The model has a single period. If we append a past to the economy, we must be sure we can find one which yields the posited initial position. In conventional trade theory, the assumed linear technology would have led to specialization. This implausible and unrealistic knife-edge character of equilibrium is easily removed by the introduction of nonlinear technology or differences among workers. As an example of the latter, there might be moving costs from geographically disbursed initial positions at completion of schooling to job locations in the two industries. Then both industries will exist for a range of initial positions. Similarly, there could be differing comparative advantages in learning different initial skills. Alternatively, once we recognize the reality of transport costs we can again have both industries. Since the *B* industry represents the rest of the economy, it could be disaggregated to several industries, some of which are coming into existence at the same time that the *A* industry is declining.

4. *Nonconsumption of A goods.* The analysis of each of the two policies used no restrictions on worker utility functions (other than regularity). In attempting to distinguish the cases when each of them is superior, the simplifying assumption was added that workers did not consume the output of the *A* industry. This was the limiting case of the perspective that the *A* industry is small in this economy—we can ignore the utility effect of a fall in the price of shoes. Even with this assumption no satisfactory condition was found for the two regions of superiority of the two alternative policies to be connected sets. Introduction of another

set of consumers (e.g., capitalists) would permit the same assumption on workers and the continued production and import of A goods.

Notes

1. Assistance is also available to towns. This raises the interesting question of the relative merits of encouraging movement of workers and of jobs.
2. This is a substantial assumption. There are many other ways in which workers differ. For an extension of this model to one further dimension of difference, see appendix B.
3. We assume the restrictions $\alpha \geq 1$, $0 \leq \beta \leq 1$. That is, subsidization of moving costs beyond 100 percent is assumed to result in unacceptable levels of moving costs because of the moral hazard problem.
4. We assume that the government is free to select the movers when everyone is indifferent to moving. Otherwise there is, strictly, no optimum and we want to be as close as possible to this point.
5. Taxes per capita are given in (14). This expression is minimized when $c^* = c_0^*$.
6. This assumes that the A industry is small relative to the B industry.
7. That is, we assume $\alpha s p_A < p_B$ when α is arbitrary or optimal.
8. See Hart (1975) and Diamond (1980).
9 It is not an acceptable argument against further redistributive policies that the existing income tax is the outcome of a democratic political process. If further redistributive policies are accepted, then they too become the outcome of a democratic political process.
10. For an analysis of income taxation in a many-commodity economy see Mirrlees (1976).
11. In addition to the Mirrlees reference above see Akerlof (undated).
12. See Feldstein (1976), Mortensen (1979), and Diamond (1981).
13. From an efficiency perspective this is more important than the external diseconomies to workers who otherwise would have found these jobs. (See Mortensen 1979.)
14. See Diamond (1981). Both this paper and that of Mortensen assume workers are, *ex ante*, identical. It would be good to have analysis of these issues where workers and jobs differ systematically *ex ante*.
15. It has been suggested that there is a fruitful analogy between the problem studied here and the question of the assignment of liability. The latter question involves a technological externality. However, the question studied here is, at base, a pecuniary externality.

References

Akerlof, G. Undated. The economics of "tagging," as applied to the optimal income tax and other things. Unpublished.
Baily, M. 1977. Unemployment insurance as insurance for workers. *Industrial and Labor Relations Review* 30, no. 4 (July): 495–504.
Diamond, P. 1980. Efficiency with uncertain supply. *Review of Economic Studies* 47, no. 4 (July): 645–52.
———. 1981. Mobility costs, frictional unemployment, and efficiency. *Journal of Political Economy* 89, no. 4 (August): 798–812.
Feldstein, M. 1976. Temporary layoffs in the theory of unemployment. *Journal of Political Economy* 84, no. 5 (October): 937–57.

Flemming, J. S. 1978. Aspects of optimal unemployment insurance: Search, leisure, savings, and capital market imperfections. *Journal of Public Economics* 10, no. 3 (December): 403–26.

Hart, O. 1975. On the optimality of equilibrium when the market structure is incomplete. *Journal of Economic Theory* 11, no. 3 (December): 418–43.

McCarthy, J. 1975. Trade adjustment assistance: A case study of the shoe industry in Massachusetts. Federal Reserve Bank of Boston, Research Report 58.

Mirrlees, J. 1976. Optimal tax theory: A synthesis. *Journal of Public Economics* 6, no. 4 (November): 327–58.

Mortensen, D. 1979. The matching process as a noncooperative bargaining game. Unpublished.

Comment   *John S. Chipman*

Diamond postulates a two-commodity open economy with a Ricardian technology, in which there are two special features: (*a*) workers' skills are specific to the industries in which they are initially employed, and their marginal productivity in these industries is s times what it would be in the alternative industries ($s > 1$); (*b*) there are moving costs to switching from one industry to the other.

Most of the complicated analytics of the paper flow from feature (*b*). The moving costs are stipulated to be "financial," and yet we are told that "this model does not violate any assumptions of the Arrow-Debreu model." If the latter statement is true, moving must use up real resources—either domestic or foreign. If domestic, one would like to see some explicit assumptions about the form of the production function for moving. The one-period formulation also appears to exaggerate the importance of moving: moving is a once-for-all decision, whereas income is earned period after period. For younger people, the cost of moving may be considered to be quite low compared with the present value of the interindustry differential in wages. Since I have doubts concerning the importance of moving costs—which in any event are not given a precise formulation in terms of resource use in this paper—and since, moreover, many of the difficulties I have with the paper subsist even if moving costs are ignored, I shall confine the remainder of my remarks to a discussion of these difficulties.

John S. Chipman is Regents' Professor of Economics, University of Minnesota. He is the author of "A Survey of the Theory of International Trade" (*Econometrica*, 1965–66) and of numerous other papers in international trade theory, welfare economics, and econometrics.

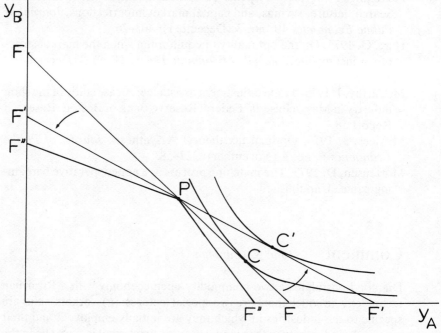

Fig. C5.1

One unanswered question is, How is it that in the initial situation, all workers are skilled in their trades? The only plausible answer is that they learned them on the job. One then wonders why they are assumed not to be able to acquire skills in new trades.

If some learning process led the economy to the initial equilibrium—so that the initial equilibrium may be regarded as one of the classical Mill-Graham variety—then if the country is truly a "small country," it would have been specializing in a single export good (commodity *B*). But on the contrary it is assumed to produce both goods; so it must have been a "large country," whose cost ratio dominated the world price ratio in Graham fashion. But then what reason would there be for the world price ratio to change?

Setting aside the above perplexities, let us accept the hypotheses and see what they imply. In figure C5.1 I show a straight-line Ricardian production-possibility frontier *FF* indicating the long-run transformation rate (in the absence of learning) between the outputs y_A and y_B of commodities *A* and *B* (the import and export good, respectively), which I also take to indicate the initial price ratio. Behind it is the broken linear-programming type of production-possibility frontier *F″PF″* re-

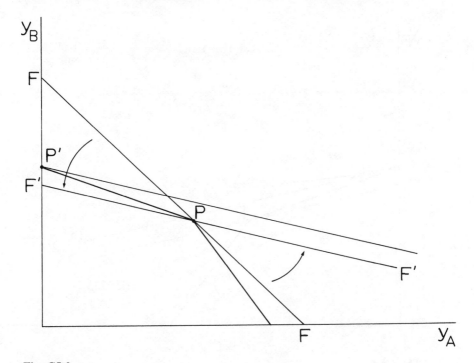

Fig. C5.2

sulting from feature (*a*). If the import price falls, the price line will swing counterclockwise around the initial production equilibrium point *P*, to the position *F'F'*, say. Given any Bergson-Samuelson social-welfare function, with optimal lump-sum transfers the economy would move to a higher social indifference curve, from *C* to *C'*, as shown. On the other hand, it is an immediate consequence of the Stolper-Samuelson theorem that real wages of the workers specific to the import-competing industry would decline and those of the workers specific to the export industry would rise. Diamond is concerned with devising a compensation scheme that would equalize workers' incomes and at the same time encourage workers to move out of the import-competing industry should the fall in import prices be so great as to require it (see figure C5.2). In the absence of moving costs, as figure C5.2 makes clear, the country would have to specialize in its export good henceforth, at the point *P'*; Diamond's moving costs are what prevent the efficient outcome from being a corner solution.

Or are they? Diamond states, "To compare alternative policies, let us assume that workers do not consume the output of the *A* industry, so that the only effect of a higher p_A is higher income of all workers." Under this

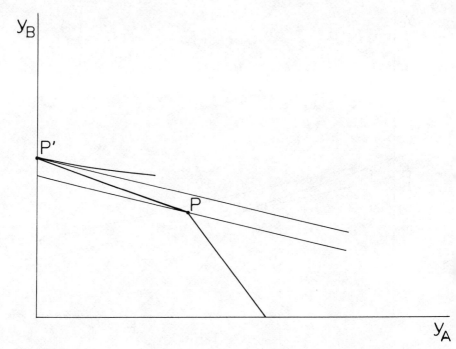

Fig. C5.3

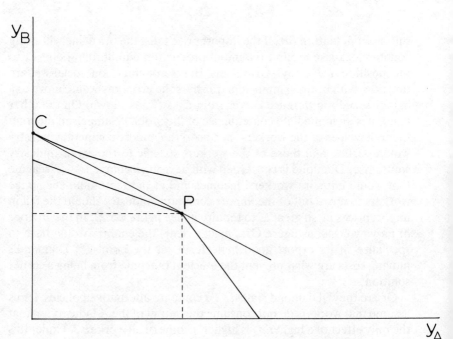

Fig. C5.4

assumption, either no amount of the A good will be produced (i.e., production and consumption will be at P' in figure C5.3) and hence there will be no trade—either before or after the price change; or some of the A good will be produced (say at P in figure C5.4) but it will all be exported (consumption being at C in figure C5.4). In neither case will there be any imports of commodity A. How can workers be damaged by the influx of cheap Japanese cars unless someone is buying cheap Japanese cars?

My final perplexity has to do with the absence of any consideration of incentives. Unless there is a wage differential between the two industries, or some other inducement, what is to provide the incentive for workers to improve their skills in their new jobs?

II. Responses to Import Competition: Lobbying et al.

6   Shifting Comparative Advantage, Protectionist Demands, and Policy Response

Jagdish N. Bhagwati

6.1   Introduction

Although the threat of "new protectionism" has arisen with reference to a whole range of industrial activities in the Western countries and although there is a tendency to consider all such threats as part of a general political-economic phenomenon to be attributed to factors such as generalized unemployment, increased demands for job security from the state, etc., it is useful to distinguish between two extreme, idealized situations.

On the one hand, the pressure of import competition, no matter how significant, can be seen as being addressed to industries undergoing a basic shift in comparative advantage, not because of technological advances arising in different parts of the world which are not being shared by competing nations, but rather because of shifts in labor costs or because "learning by doing" by latecomers is altering the traditional competitive edge of industries in the West. These are the "senescent," "declining" industries such as textiles, and shoes and footwear which are labor-intensive and mostly unintensive in skills and R & D, where the newly industrializing countries of the South are increasingly demonstrating comparative advantage. Since these industries are characterized by low technical progress—which is perfectly compatible with increasing

Jagdish N. Bhagwati is the Arthur Lehman Professor of Economics at Columbia University. He has written on trade theory, developmental theory and policy, internal and international migration, and education models. He is editor of the *Journal of International Economics* and author (with T. N. Srinivasan) of *Lectures on the Theory of International Trade*, to be published by MIT Press.

Thanks are due to NSF Grant no. SOC 79-07541 for financial support, to Robert Feenstra for helpful conversations, and to Robert Baldwin, T. Bayard, Charles Kindleberger, Gene Grossman, Jean Waelbroeck, and John Williamson for valuable comments.

capital intensity, of course—Schumpeterian responses in the nature of induced technical progress à la Weiszacre-Kennedy-Samuelson are not in evidence. Hence the responses of the enterpreneurs, labor, and communities or townships in which these industries are located, as well as the nature of the governmental policy options and responses, are likely to be quite different from those occurring when the industries are of the type considered immediately below.

This second class of industries is at the other end of the technological scale, being largely characterized by changing comparative advantage because R & D leads to technical change that gives the competitive edge to new countries. These industries are at the front end of the dynamic, Schumpeterian capitalist process. The resulting shifts in comparative advantage yield a very different set of responses by the industries losing comparative advantage, and the policy options available to the countries where they are located are also correspondingly different.

In considering these two idealized models, it will be critical to note that the response to shifting comparative advantage will involve differential interaction with international "factor" mobility. In the former case, a possible and indeed empirically important response (hitherto neglected altogether in the literature) is lobbying for a greater inflow of foreign *labor*. In the latter case, however, among the important responses are a variety of patterns of direct foreign *investment*: for example, the use of threats of protection to induce a reverse flow of foreign investment into the country or mutually penetrating investments in differential but similar products where the different countries have differential advantages.

Moreover, it will be useful to distinguish the following "actors" among the lobbies seeking governmental response to the shift in comparative advantage: (i) the entrepreneurs, who may be interested in sales à la Burnham and Galbraith but are generally identified in the formal arguments below with the owners of equity capital in the industry; (ii) labor, distinguished in practice by nationality, skills, and age but again treated in the formal analysis below as a homogeneous entity; and (iii) the community-cum-township where the affected industry may play a dominant role. The analysis will try to identify which policy responses will be sought by one or more of these actors and therefore what political forces the government is likely to confront by choosing one policy response option in preference to another.

6.2 Technically Unprogressive, "Traditional" Industries

Since technical change is not important in these industries, the *shift* in their comparative advantage largely reflects changing factor endowments and/or learning in the newly industrializing countries. They are thus also primarily labor-intensive, low-skills industries—in competition with the less developed countries (LDCs). How are these industries in the developed countries likely to react to the adversely shifting comparative advantage?

6.2.1 The Relaxation of Immigration Quotas as a Policy Response Option

As comparative advantage shifts against these unprogressive industries, pressuring them toward a (relative or absolute) contraction of their output, it might appear that all the potential lobbies that were distinguished above—entrepreneurs, labor, and the community—would be seeking relief via only one type of governmental response, namely, some sort of protection. However, this is plainly not the case. For these unprogressive industries are often at a comparative disadvantage precisely because cost conditions have moved against them, and in labor-intensive industries this is often because labor abroad has become relatively cheaper. Now, introduce into this picture the fact that international mobility of labor is severely regulated by immigration quotas and that the real wages of labor are substantially higher in the West than in many developing countries. It follows immediately that one additional policy response in which entrepreneurs could be interested is for the government to increase the availability of imported labor.

Note that the entrepreneurs' response will typically not include in this case their leaving for the foreign countries where the comparative advantage has shifted. This is due to the fact that these are unprogressive industries where, with no Hymer-like firm-specific know-how to take advantage of, the migration of domestic entrepreneurship is likely to mean merely that the migrant entrepreneurs will have to operate in unfamiliar, relatively riskier foreign situations, without any offsetting technological advantage, and hence at a competitive disadvantage with local producers.[1]

On the other hand, domestic labor should find its own interests better served by a policy of protection rather than by the alternative policy of relaxed immigration quotas. Therefore, while a governmental response in the form of allowing the increased importation of foreign labor will satisfy entrepreneurs, it will not generally satisfy domestic labor. To consider these issues rigorously, turn now to the formal analysis below.

6.2.2 Some Formal Models

Heckscher-Ohlin-Samuelson Model

Take first the $2 \times 2 \times 2$ model of trade theory to develop the main implications of our policy-choice problem rigorously. Assume two goods X and Y, and two factors K and L, and let Y be L-intensive and the importable good, in conformity with the empirical reality of the problem at hand. I would like to distinguish between the two types of shift in comparative advantage that may affect the L-intensive importable industry Y: (1) that which arises *externally*—either from a shift in the foreign offer curve facing our country or from a tariff cut by our country as in the across-the-board tariff cuts of the Kennedy Round; and (2) that which results *internally*, e.g., from capital accumulation or productivity change. In each case, it will also be relevant whether the comparisons between the two policies involve a tariff-free or a tariff-ridden economy when the policy chosen is to import more labor. Throughout, I assume a small country and negligible lobbying costs.

Case I: External shift in comparative advantage, zero initial tariff. Figure 6.1 shows the economy moving from external price ratio P_1 to P_2, adversely affecting production of good Y.

The tariff policy will then restore production of Y to the initial level Y^0 at Q_1 but, as seen in figure 6.2, will yield welfare U_t. The alternative policy of restoring Y production to Y^0 by importing labor, on the other hand, will lead to welfare level U_{Lm} as follows. As labor is imported, holding the goods price ratio unaltered at its new free-trade position P_2, we can trace the Rybczynski line Q_2R which, at Q_3, yields Y production equal to Y^0. Importation of the corresponding amount of labor (Lm) would then restore domestic importable output to the initial, preshift level. But the *national* welfare level, defined *exclusive* of imported labor's welfare, would be U_{Lm}, with the national budget line Q_2C_{Lm}, since imported labor earns the value of its marginal product, which, in turn, equals the increment in output along the Rybczynski line.

A comparison of the two policies, both achieving identical production in the importable industry and thus satisfying entrepreneurs equally in that respect,[2] then shows that the policy of reduced restrictions on the importation of labor dominates that of increasing trade protection insofar as economic welfare conventionally defined is concerned ($U_{Lm} > U_t$), and hence should be the preferred option of an economic-welfare-oriented government.[3] At the same time, from the viewpoint of international relations, it should again be a preferred option, since relaxing immigration restrictions gives the government good marks whereas increasing trade protection gives it bad marks. On the other hand, at Q_3 and Q_2 under the policy of reduced immigration restrictions, the real wages of labor are less than at Q_1 under the tariff policy, à la the Stolper-Samuelson argument.[4]

The choice between the policy option of reducing immigration restrictions and increasing trade protection in response to an adverse shift in comparative advantage therefore primarily involves the conflicting interests of the *government* (or, more precisely, that part of the government [e.g., in the United States, the executive rather than the legislative] which

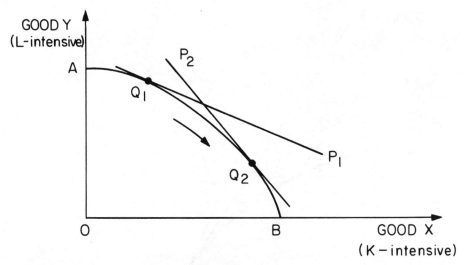

Fig. 6.1

is presumably interested in welfare as defined by conventional economics) and *consumers*, who face lower prices for importables, on the
one hand, and *domestic labor*, on the other hand, while leaving the
entrepreneurs somewhat indifferent between the two policy options insofar as industry output is concerned but in favor of the policy of importing more foreign labor since this implies greater reward to capital. I shall
later amplify other aspects of the conflicting interests involved in the
choice between these policies, especially those involved at the community-cum-township level, which cannot be accommodated in the present
model. For the present, however, let me go on to show that this basic
pattern of conflicts between the different sectors resurrects itself when
the external shift is in the presence of a trade restriction, though there are
important differences to note, as argued immediately below.

Case II: External shift in comparative advantage, positive initial tariff.
The presence of an initial tariff makes a significant difference to the
analysis of the effects of different policy responses to an external shift in
comparative advantage. This is because the policy of increasing the
importation of labor is itself to be judged in the context of a tariff-ridden
economy. For the choice now, when the external price ratio shifts from P_1
to P_2, is between increasing the tariff to restore production of Y to Y^0 at
Q_1 and, instead, increasing the importation of labor to achieve Y^0 while
maintaining the tariff at the initial level.

While in case I, with zero initial tariff, the importation of labor left the
national welfare unchanged at the free-trade level (since imported labor
earned the value of its marginal product at domestic prices as well as at

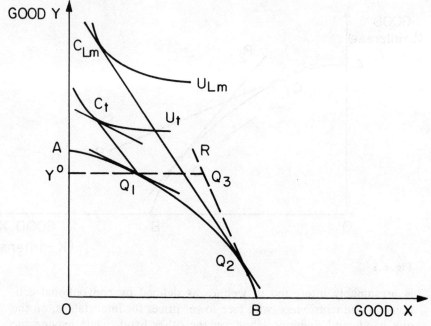

Fig. 6.2

international prices thanks to free trade), the importation of labor when the labor-intensive importable industry is protected by a tariff is necessarily immiserizing! This result, derived by Uzawa (1969) and Brecher and Alejandro (1977) independently of one another, is seen in figure 6.3. There, after the shift of the external price ratio to P_2, the continuing initial tariff makes P_2^D the new tariff-inclusive domestic price ratio. With labor imported, the corresponding Rybczynski line is then Q_2R. Now, if no labor were imported, the equilibrium consumption would be at C_2, which lies on P_2 and on the income-consumption line IC (P_2^D) which is drawn with reference to price ratio P_2^D. If, however, labor is imported and is paid the value of its marginal product at domestic tariff-inclusive prices, the *national* income at domestic prices will be identical to P_2^D through Q_2. Thus, if labor importation takes production on the Rybczynski line to Q_3, and (for simplicity) we assume that foreign labor consumes entirely in the country of residence, the *national* (net-of-foreign-labor-consumption) bundle of production will be along the stretch EF on the national income line P_2^D through Q_2. And, by putting the new international price line P_2 through E and F, and cutting IC (P_2^D), we see that the resulting national consumption will lie in the range of $C'_{Lm}C''_{Lm}$. Evidently therefore importing labor will necessarily be immiserizing.

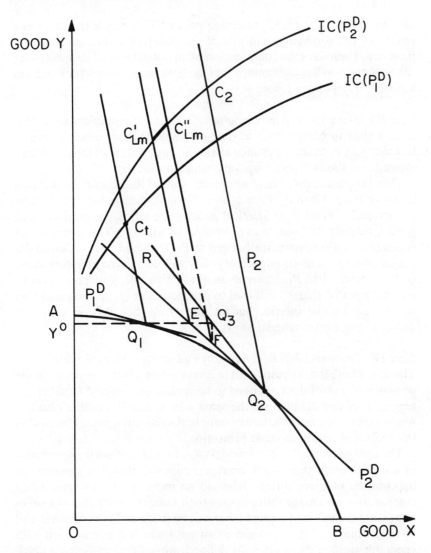

Fig. 6.3

However, it is equally evident that the alternative policy of resorting to trade protection to restore Y production to Y^0 by shifting back to Q_1, with the new international price ratio P_2, yields consumption at C_t on the income-consumption curve IC (P_1^D) which is drawn with reference to P_1^D (tangent to AB at Q_1). Evidently this is *inferior* to any equilibrium consumption, on $C'_{Lm} C''_{Lm}$, reached under the labor importation policy.

Note therefore that the welfare loss from importing labor is constrained so as to make the labor-importing policy nonetheless a better alternative than the trade protection policy.[5] This means that the basic nature of the conflicting interests of the different actors, as emerging from case I, survives the complication of an initial tariff while weakening the economic-welfare advantage that the government would derive from a policy of importing labor.

Case III: Domestic shift in comparative advantage, zero initial tariff. Nor does a shift in comparative advantage resulting from either domestic factor supply or technical change affect the basic nature of the conflicting interests on the two policy options being considered.

Thus take figure 6.4, where a domestic shift of the production possibility curve from AB to $A'B'$ leads to a strong decline in the "production advantage" of good Y: at identical goods price ratios, the production of good Y actually declines, as at Q_2 compared with Q_1.[6] The international goods price ratio remains unchanged at P_1. It should be manifest to the reader now that a labor-importing policy will lead to consumption along $Q_2 P_1$ at price ratio P_1, whereas an alternative policy of protection to retain output of Y at Y^0 will lead to production at Q_4 and consumption not merely on the inferior budget line $Q_4 P_1$, but also on a further distorted price-ratio tangent at Q_4 to $A'B'$.

Case IV: Domestic shift in comparative advantage, positive initial tariff. The case where the domestic shift in comparative advantage occurs in the presence of a tariff does not need to be spelled out, since it modifies the argument of case III in much the same way as case II modifies case I: it weakens the economic-welfare case for importing labor while leaving it as the preferred option to trade protection.

The analysis in the $2 \times 2 \times 2$ model therefore underlines the robustness of the conclusion that, while entrepreneurs will marginally prefer the importation of more foreign labor to an increase in protection when comparative advantage shifts against their industry, the policy option of increasing the influx of foreign labor will be preferred by consumers and by that branch of the government (if any) which concerns itself with economic welfare conventionally defined, while being considered detrimental to its interests by domestic labor.

However, I might add that cases III and IV, where the shift is domestically induced, suggests an important difference from cases I and II, where the shift is externally induced. In the former case, if the shift results from capital accumulation leading to a decline in the output of the labor-intensive importable activity (à la Rybczynski), the real wages of labor will be *maintained*; it is just that the "drawing power" of the importable activity for domestic labor has been reduced as a result of the change in the accumulation. In this case, it is not likely that domestic labor will oppose the import of foreign labor; the labor import will be seen rather as

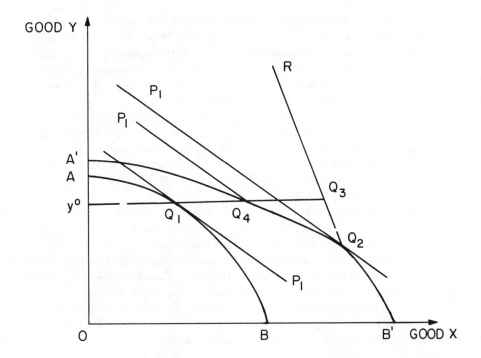

Fig. 6.4

supportive of the output of the labor-intensive industry without coming at the expense of domestic wages. (Of course, the protection option will *increase* the real wages of labor; but this is unlikely to make the same impression on labor as actually *losing* ground through reduced real wages). In cases where the shift in comparative advantage is external, however, the loss of real wages in the present model is necessarily actual, not just in an opportunity-cost sense, when the shift occurs; and therefore the importation of labor as a policy option is likely to be opposed passionately.

Jones-Neary Model

Consider instead the model of Jones (1971) and Neary (1978) in which capital is specific but labor is mobile between the two sectors. This may be considered to be the "short-run" version of the standard 2×2 model, if labor is assumed to be mobile in the short-run but capital is not, an interpretation given by Neary (1978), Mussa (1974), and Mayer (1974).[7] What happens to the choice between labor importation and protection in this model when the terms of trade shift adversely against the labor-intensive importable activity?[8]

The effect of the shift in the terms of trade is now an unambiguous fall in the rental on capital in the labor-intensive importable industry while the return to labor (after reallocation) will rise in terms of the importable but fall in terms of the exportable good. (If the importable sector is "small," then evidently the real wages of labor are likely to fall, as the weight of the exportable good in consumption will be greater). In this model, therefore, both capitalists and labor are likely to have the incentive to lobby for protection. But capitalists may also settle for increased importation of labor. For as Mayer (1974) has shown, such an increment in labor, at a constant goods price ratio, will increase the rental unambiguously to capital in both sectors while the real wages fall unambiguously.[9]

Insofar as economic welfare is concerned, the choice is again clear-cut in the Jones-Neary model, as long as an otherwise free-trade situation without distortions is considered. Thus the protection option implies the standard cost of distorted production and consumption. However, with the real wages declining as labor is imported, the importation of a finite quantity of foreign labor yields a "surplus" to the host country: labor importation is therefore welfare-improving. Thus that branch of government that responds to an economic-welfare motivation will favor labor importation over instituting a protective tariff.

Industry-specific Foreign Labor Paid a Differential Wage

The preceding two models considered foreign labor to be industry-nonspecific and equally assumed that the return to foreign and domestic labor was equal. However, approximating the West European *gastarbeiter* system more closely, we may assume that foreign labor is imported on an industry-specific contractual basis and can be effectively paid lower wages than domestic labor.

Take this model then and assume a Haberler-Brecher model with Haberler (1950)–type sector-specific factors and Brecher (1974a, b)–type sticky real wages for labor. Let Q_1 be the initial production vector, AQ_1B being the production possibility curve, given the immobility of factors. When the terms of trade shift from P_1 to P_2, turning against the importable, labor-intensive good Y, labor in Y production insists on maintaining its real wages in terms of good X. This leads to workers being laid off in industry Y until the marginal physical product of labor in Y rises sufficiently at Q_2 to restore Y labor's real wages in terms of good X.

In this situation, if the Y capitalists are allowed to import foreign labor to restore their output to Q_1, and foreign labor allows itself to be hired at lower real wages than what local labor insists on, then part of the incremental output of good Y (this increment being Q_2Q_1) will accrue to

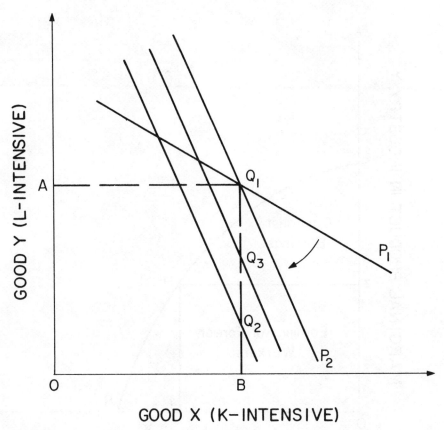

Fig. 6.5

the capitalists, as demonstrated in figure 6.6. There, OS represents the
real wages of domestic labor in terms of Y at Q_2 in figure 6.5; OZ is the
lower, fixed real wages at which foreign labor can be imported in numbers
permitted by the immigration quota; OJ is the immigration quota; SHR is
the marginal product curve for imported labor in industry Y, given the
employment of domestic capital and labor at Q_2 in figure 6.5. The total
increment in Y output that results is then $SHJO$, which is assumed to
correspond to Q_2Q_1 in figure 6.5. But of this increment, only $OZHJ$
accrues as earnings of foreign workers, and the rest, SHZ, accrues to the
domestic capitalists; this division corresponds to Q_3Q_1 for foreign workers and Q_2Q_3 for domestic capital in figure 6.5. Thus, reverting to figure
6.5, national welfare is now defined, in the labor-importation option, by
the availability line P_2 passing through Q_3.

By contrast, the protection option will maintain domestic labor's real
wages while restoring labor employment as well; it will also increase

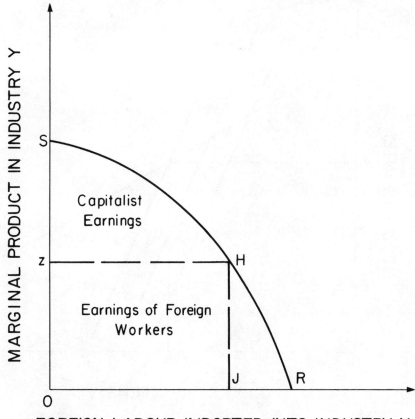

FOREIGN LABOUR IMPORTED INTO INDUSTRY Y

Fig. 6.6

capitalist earnings, but this increase cannot be rank-ordered with the increase under the labor-importation option; and economic welfare may be above or below that at Q_3 (the labor-importation option) since protection will mean that production will be restored to Q_1 but there will be a consumption-distortion cost which may be large enough to outweigh the production gain vis-à-vis the labor-importation option.[10]

6.2.3   Likely Lobbying Outcomes

What type of lobbying may then be expected in the labor-intensive industries, once we recognize the possibility of using immigration quotas as a policy instrument? Evidently the answer depends critically on the production-cum-trade model that applies to a specific situation; it is also clearly dependent on the precise immigration control system that the country operates. Thus, if we contrast the results of the three models, it is interesting that, in the Heckscher-Ohlin-Samuelson (HOS) model, capitalists would find protection harmful and labor importation of no effect on their earnings whereas in the other two models *both* options are helpful. Again, labor is actually hurt by labor importation in the Jones-Neary model but is neither hurt nor helped in the other models, whereas protection helps it in all three models. The precise conflicts of interests, reflecting the implications of the two policy options of protection and labor importation, will therefore depend on the specifics of the situation concerning factor-market and immigration-system behavior. No general conclusions are possible, as indicated by table 6.1, which categorizes the outcomes.

On the other hand, the models uniformly suggest that entrepreneurs have an interest in getting governments to agree to relax immigration quotas, that governments themselves have a potential interest in the relaxation of immigration quotas since economic welfare is such an important objective, and that labor, in contrast, has a relatively greater interest in the adoption of protection measures instead. I would therefore expect governments to expedite the inflow of foreign labor whenever (*a*) domestic labor's opposition to this policy option is weak and its lobbying for protection is correspondingly weak (as when labor is not effectively organized due to geographical dispersion of the industry, for example), (*b*) the government's ability to grant protection is weak (because, for example, of fear of retaliation or respect for GATT Article XIX), and (*c*) the government's ability to augment immigration is not constrained greatly by the social consequences of increased immigration. More specifically, the following types of hypotheses may well be worth exploring.

1. When the shift in comparative advantage is domestically induced (as in cases III and IV of the HOS model above), the opposition of domestic labor to the importation of labor will be the less, for reasons spelled out earlier. By contrast, when the shift comes from external changes (as in cases I and II), the opposition of domestic labor to the importation of labor will be the greater. Therefore I would expect that the policy response to a shift in comparative advantage would be, *ceteris paribus*, greater for imported labor when the shift is domestic rather than external.

2. Moreover, where the external shift in comparative advantage is combined with the presence of a native labor force which has low-mobility characteristics (e.g., higher age, residency traditionally in towns or communities in which the roots and ties are strong, which raises the nonpecuniary costs of mobility), the likelihood of protection emerging as the outcome of the lobbying response will be all the greater. For in this case, the option of importing foreign labor will appear particularly unattractive to the low-mobility labor, whose real wages will otherwise face a significant decline. The role of the community or township as a lobbying

Table 6.1   Effects of Output-restoring Labor-Importation and Protectionist Responses to Import Competition in Labor-intensive Industries

Model	Policy Response	Capitalists*	Labor	"Economic Welfare"
Heckscher-Ohlin-Samuelson	Labor Importation	Earnings unchanged	Earnings unchanged	Welfare Unchanged (cases I & III)
	Protection	Earnings reduced	Earnings increased (back to preshift level)	Reduces welfare
Jones-Neary	Labor Importation	Earnings increased	Earnings lowered	Increases welfare
	Protection	Earnings increased	Earnings increased	Reduces welfare
Haberler-Brecher	Labor Importation	Earnings increased	Earnings unchanged	Increases welfare
	Protection	Earnings increased	Earnings increased (via increased employment)	May increase or lower welfare (while increasing domestic employment)

Note: The comparison is with the situation where import competition (i.e., shift in comparative advantage) occurs and there is no policy response. The comparison is *not* therefore with the situation *before* import competition

*The entries here relate, in the Jones-Neary and Haberler-Brecher models, to capitalist earnings in the importable industry.

force in cases where labor has strong historical ties to an area, as in traditional "textile towns," may also be very important quite independently of the labor force itself. For where such geographical specificity is involved, other jobs are likely to be seen as being dependent not merely on the size of the industry's output but also on traditional spending patterns, and imported labor, with its usual high savings and remittance rates, is unlikely to be quite an adequate replacement in that regard! Moreover, the social cohesion of the community itself may militate against introducing a sizable foreign labor component into such communities.[11]

What type of evidence would indicate that such hypotheses make empirical sense? The foregoing arguments suggest that one may be able to examine episodes such as the response to across-the-board tariff cuts in the Kennedy Round and hypothesize a set of testable propositions.

I would expect, for example, that when across-the-board tariff cuts are made, as after the Kennedy Round, the tariff-cut exemptions (adjusted insofar as they were offset by domestic subsidies—as they were often, and in varying degree, in West Germany according to Riedel 1977) would be generally greater in those traditional industries where the labor force is largely domestic, is geographically concentrated in close-knit communities, or is relatively immobile. In contrast, when quota restrictions are relaxed, I would expect there to be a relatively greater growth of the foreign labor component in those industries in which the labor force already has a significant foreign element, is geographically dispersed, or has a domestic component that is relatively skilled and mobile.

Furthermore, if cross-sectional regressions were run, I would not be surprised if (the subsidy-adjusted) tariff-cut exemptions were inversely related to the initial proportion of foreign labor in the total labor force and to the skill level of the labor force, and positively related to the average age of the labor force, as seems to be indicated to some degree in Cheh's (1974) analysis of the United States and Riedel's (1977) analysis of West Germany. And this is the important *new* possibility: that the growth rate of foreign labor (absolute or relative to domestic labor) in these industries, reflecting the relaxation of immigration quota restrictions, may be positively related to the initial proportion of foreign labor in the total labor force and to the skill level of the labor force, and inversely related to the average age of the labor force. And thus, also, there may then exist an inverse correlation between the tariff-cut exemptions an industry receives and the growth rate of its foreign labor force, in cross-sectional analysis.

6.2.4   Labor Lobbying and the Efficient Tariff: An Aside

Where the labor interest in protection is deep-seated, the foregoing arguments suggest that the governmental response will be to yield to protectionist pressures from the labor lobby; the relaxation of immigration quota restrictions will not be the preferred option.

In these cases, the "bargaining" between the government and labor may be visualized as being over the degree of protection to be granted to the industry when the comparative advantage has shifted, with labor's primary interest consisting in fully restoring its preshift economic position and the government's in minimizing the cost of such restoration of labor's economic position.

Viewing the conflict this way, we can develop the notion of an "efficient tariff" (as is done rigorously by Feenstra and Bhagwati in chapter 9), once we recognize that the levy of a tariff will generally raise revenue. Thus, consider for simplicity the $2 \times 2 \times 2$ model where labor's real wage declines with the relative price of the importable good. A shift in comparative advantage improving the terms of trade will hurt labor, triggering the lobbying for a tariff. If then the tariff is used for restoring the real wages of labor, there will be an associated loss of welfare to society. However, since the tariff raises revenue, we may consider the following alternative. Suppose that this tariff revenue itself is used to compensate labor through a direct subsidy such that labor's real income (defined as the *sum* of its real wages in employment and this subsidy, as in Bhagwati 1959) is equivalent to its preshift real wages. Then the resulting welfare cost to society would generally be lower. Thus a tariff which restores the real *wages* of labor to their original level would generally be inferior to the efficient tariff which is chosen so as to minimize the welfare cost of a tariff which restores labor's real *income* to the original (real wage) level by additionally utilizing the tariff revenue proceeds to subsidize labor's income.[12] This notion of the efficient tariff makes a good deal of sense insofar as the revenue used for redistribution is being generated as a side effect of the protection itself and is *not* being raised *ab initio* for the redistribution![13]

What this notion of the efficient tariff does therefore is to provide a rationale for a direct subsidy to lobbying labor, as long as it is kept within the bounds of the tariff revenue raised from the partial protection granted, when the labor lobby seeking protection is strong and the government feels that there is no political alternative to maintaining the labor lobby's economic position in face of a shift in comparative advantage.

6.2.5 Protectionist Response to Import Competition and the Welfare of the Exporting Country: Some Paradoxes

While the foregoing analysis was addressed to lobbies, policy options, and likely outcomes, focusing exclusively on the country facing import competition, the novel element of foreign labor additionally introduces an interesting, and surely important, element of paradox into the situation regarding protectionist responses to import competition as far as the welfare of the *other* trading countries is concerned.

For it is no longer possible to identify the levying of protective tariffs on one's exports by another country as necessarily welfare-worsening—short of standard paradoxes in trade theory—for the simple reason that the protection also redounds to the welfare of foreign labor, and this labor may very well be one's own emigrant labor. Thus, if the United States levies protective tariffs on Mexican textile exports, this will worsen the welfare of the Mexican nonemigrant population but, since some Mexican labor is employed in textiles production in the United States, it will also improve the welfare of the Mexican emigrant population. So, depending on what distributional welfare weights are assigned, one could easily argue that United States protection *improves* the welfare of the Mexicans (emigrants *plus* nonemigrants)![14] Interestingly, this paradox is the mirror image of the paradox (analyzed in Bhagwati and Tironi 1980, Bhagwati and Brecher 1980 and Brecher and Bhagwati 1981) in which the reduction of a tariff in the presence of foreign-owned factors of production may be accompanied by a decline in national welfare even though the country is small and no other domestic distortions are present.[15]

Another interesting paradox that arises in the presence of foreign labor from LDCs and the DCs (developed countries) is that the country from which foreign labor is coming and the country producing the imports may not coincide. Thus textiles in the United States may be using Mexican labor while they face competition from South Korea. Hence there may be inter–LDC conflicts inherent in the decision of the DCs to use or not to use protection in the face of a shift in comparative advantage. For instance, West Germany uses a great deal of Turkish, Yugoslav, and Greek labor in industries that face competition from the less developed newly industrializing countries such as Brazil, Taiwan, South Korea, Hong Kong, and Singapore.

6.3 Technically Progressive, Schumpeterian Industries

The scenarios concerning lobbying and policy response options discussed in the preceding section change dramatically as attention is shifted to technologically progressive industries. These industries might be described as Schumpeterian since they represent the essence of the dynamic capitalist system that Schumpeter described so beautifully. Technological change, resulting from R & D (whether private or public), is critical to the shifts in comparative advantage in these industries, and this essential fact fundamentally transforms the nature of the lobbying responses and policy options that open up in the face of the ongoing shifts in comparative advantage.

6.3.1   Two Alternative Models of Direct Foreign
        Investment in Progressive Industries

It will be appropriate to distinguish in the analysis that follows between
two models in the direct investment literature, both an offshoot of
Hymer's (1960) ground-breaking work on direct foreign investment: the
"product cycle" (PC) model of Vernon (1966) and the "mutual penetration of investment" (MPI) model set forth in my review of Vernon's
Sovereignty at Bay (Bhagwati 1972) and then amplified in Bhagwati
(1978, 1979).

The "Product Cycle" Model

In the PC model, firms develop R & D–based new products in one
country, with a corresponding conferral of comparative advantage of
manufacture in that country. As long as the product and its associated
processes need to be "debugged" and simplified, the location of production at home, close to the R & D facilities, is important. With the passing
of this stage, the production of the products is freed from this locational
requirement and production facilities will shift to wherever wages are
cheapest. Thus this model is premised on a shift in comparative advantage in the location of production that reflects a process where R &
D–created comparative advantage self-destructs and the process is essentially a result of domestic R & D rather than a result of external changes
induced by R & D.

The "Mutual Penetration of Investment" Model

In contrast, the MPI model is based on the observation that competition occurs among differentiated but similar products and that increased
competition can typically occur in the progressive industries through R &
D–induced intensification of the advantages enjoyed by the competitors
for their differentiated products. For example, European and Japanese
small cars compete with American large cars; and this competition intensifies with time as the Japanese get better at the game (e.g., Toyota
started production only after World War II) of R & D in production,
marketing, and sales and the Americans get steadily better at producing
the "gas guzzlers." The MPI thesis then is that the response to such
intensified competition could be a mutual investment by the competing
firms in one another's R & D–induced advantages. Contrasting the
resulting MPI pattern of direct investment and Vernon's PC model, I
wrote the following in 1972:

> There is also at least one more dramatic form of international invest-
> ment which neither Vernon nor other researchers in the MNC field has
> noted but which may well be the pattern to emerge as a dominant form.
> In contrast to the case where the MNC's, having developed new

products via R&D, export them and then transit to producing them abroad, there is an alternative "model" where MNC's in different countries have R&D–induced advantages in producing different types of sub-products (e.g. one MNC in Japan is excellent with small cars and one MNC in U.S. has an edge on large cars; or tire firms in different types of tires). In competing in each other's home countries or in third markets in both types of sub-products, it is natural that each MNC would find it difficult to compete effectively with the other in sub-products where it does not have the edge. I would expect that, in this situation, there is likelihood of these MNC's deciding that mutual equity inter-penetration, with productionwise accommodation in sub-product specialization according to the advantage possessed, is profit-able. Thus, the MNC in U.S. (say, GM) that finds it difficult to compete in the small-car field with the MNC in Japan (say, Toyota) that finds it difficult to compete with the MNC in U.S. in the large-car field, would each decide that the best strategy if you cannot compete with comfort is to follow the policy: "if you cannot beat them, buy them." Thus GM would want to buy equity in Toyota for the small car production and Toyota in GM for the large-car production: and GM in U.S. would go off spending resources in producing and improving its own small cars while Toyota in Japan would similarly hold back on its own large-car efforts. One thus gets mutually interpenetrating MNC's within industries, with accompanying division of labour and a novel form of "cartelisation" which goes by sub-products. Linder has made us familiar with trade in commodities between similar countries as consisting of sub-product exchanges: and Hymer and Rowthorn have noted that MNC's from different countries penetrate into each other's countries. My "model" essentially combines these two and predicts that MNC's with R&D–induced specialization in different types of sub-products within an industry in different countries will interpene-trate.

I then noted that the MPI model was perfectly illustrated by an account in *Forbe's* magazine of 15 November 1970 (p. 22) of the following "international marriage":

Long the friendliest of competitors. Dunlop and Pirelli neatly comple-ment each other. Dunlop is primarily a manufacturer of conventional cross-ply tires. Pirelli concentrates on radials. In Europe, Dunlop has perhaps 18% of the market, Pirelli 12%, as against 12% for Michelin, the next largest competitor. In Europe, Pirelli crosses Dunlop's path only in West Germany: Elsewhere, where Dunlop is active, Pirelli stays out; where Pirelli is active, Dunlop stays out. Outside of Europe, Pirelli is active mostly in Latin America. Dunlop in the Commonwealth and North America.

The two companies have even diversified into different areas—Dunlop into sporting goods and precision engineering products, Pirelli into paper, electronics and cables.

Eventually, of course, both marketing organizations will work as one, with Dunlop pushing Pirelli products where Dunlop is strong, and Pirelli pushing Dunlop products elsewhere. "The greatest benefits should come from a pooling of R&D, however," explains J. Campbell Fraser, a Dunlop director: "In the 'seventies and 'eighties, competition will be more and more in terms of innovations. In the U.K. we have a home base of about 55 million people—that isn't big enough for the kind of R&D we'll need. Pirelli has an even smaller home base, about 45 million. By merging, we'll have a home base of 100 million, enough for the kind of R&D we'll need around the world. . . . There will not even be any exchange of public shares. Instead each will acquire an interest in the other's operating subsidiaries. The British and Italian companies will operate on their own.

The report went on to note (p. 23) that there will be four companies: Dunlop Home (the United Kingdom and Europe) with Dunlop owning 51 percent and Pirelli 49 percent; Dunlop International (the rest of the world) with Dunlop holding 60 percent and Pirelli Milan and Pirelli Switzerland 20 percent each; Pirelli Milan (the Common Market) with Pirelli Milan holding 51 percent and 49 percent; and Pirelli Switzerland (all other Pirelli operations) with Dunlop holding 40 percent, Pirelli Milan 20 percent, and Pirelli Switzerland 40 percent.

6.3.2 Shifting Comparative Advantage, Lobbying, and Policy Response Options: Three Patterns

The preceding review of major models of direct foreign investment evidently bears directly on the questions being addressed in the present paper: namely, what kind of lobbying responses can one expect, and what options are open for governmental response, when a shift in comparative advantage occurs in technically progressive industries? For one can now think of three idealized patterns: (i) the *"product cycle" scenario*, where the shift in comparative advantage occurs from the emergence of cheaper factor costs abroad overtaking the relative cheapness of domestic production due to the proximity to R & D facilities once the new product processes are simplified and debugged; (ii) the *"mutual penetration of investment" scenario*, where international competition is among similar products and technical change intensifies competition among them without conferring a dominant advantage to one class of products (and hence firms and nations) as against another; and (iii) the *"growing dominance of external products" scenario*, where, as in the MPI case, there is international competition among similar products but the technical change (or even a shift in demand, as in the case of the shift in demand away from "gas guzzlers" toward small cars and hence in favor of non-American car makers, who have traditionally specialized in small cars) favors the external producers and represents a growing, adverse shift in comparative advantage.

The first two patterns evidently include, as possible responses to the shift in comparative advantage, the corresponding patterns of direct foreign investment, i.e., the outward migration of entrepreneurs and firms. The last pattern, on the other hand, opens up a more complex set of responses.

The "Product Cycle" Scenario

In this case, the shift in comparative advantage toward producing abroad and the subsequent transfer of production abroad essentially reflect entrepreneurial decision making. Besides, the direct foreign investment response is consistent with governmental interest insofar as it represents an economic-welfare-improving move (unless there are domestic or foreign distortions present).

The lobbying response is therefore to be expected from domestic labor insofar as labor feels that it is "losing jobs" as a result of this response by the entrepreneurs.[16] Again, therefore, the actors likely to be involved in the lobbying process, in response to the shift of production abroad as comparative advantage shifts abroad, are likely to be labor lobbies.

However, the policy instruments that the labor lobby can turn to are not identical to those in the case of the "traditional" industries. Thus, if the market for the product shifts mainly overseas before the production shift overseas takes place, as in some of the PC folklore, then protecting domestic production evidently does not help! Rather, labor would have to ask for a subsidy on production or trade, neither of which is likely to appeal very much to the government because of its budgetary implications and because it opens up the possibility of countervailing action under GATT rules. An obvious alternative instrument which labor is likely to seek therefore is the imposition of restrictions on foreign investment—which is indeed what labor unions in the United States have occasionally done. Together with this route, one can also expect the unions and labor lobbies to attempt to make such direct foreign investment less attractive by complaining that the practices resulting in cheaper costs abroad are in violation of GATT and other standards, and thus require the imposition of countervailing duties, a procedure which again can help only insofar as the domestic (as against the overseas) market is still of some importance for the product. Again, this option is also occasionally exercised, as in the frequent complaints about the exploitation of child labor abroad in violation of International Labour Organization (ILO) standards, about regional subsidies that aid competing firms abroad, about special concessionary treatment of profits made by foreign firms, etc.

Given, therefore, the nature of the shift in comparative advantage to produce abroad, the lobbying game reduces in the present instance essentially to one between the government and the entrepreneurs, on one hand, and labor lobbies, on the other. But instead of the lobbying essentially focusing on trade protection, it is likely to focus primarily on the need for controls on investment abroad except in cases where the domestic market still accounts for a major fraction of total sales. Such a situation therefore contrasts with the case of "traditional" industries, where the tariff is a more effective instrument for protecting labor's economic interests. Here, the question of controlling foreign investment by the domestic entrepreneurs is a meaningless option; entrepreneurs in these industries do not seek to respond by out-migration since they do not have Hymer-type know-how that would make it economical to do so, as already noted in section 6.2.

But it *is* pertinent to ask whether the importation of foreign labor is not an option that entrepreneurs would seek as an alternative to investing abroad when the product is standardized and debugged and cheap foreign labor becomes correspondingly decisive. It must be admitted that the failure to consider this option altogether is a major weakness of the PC doctrine, which has focused wholly on the choice between producing at home with local factors and producing abroad with foreign factors. This omission does make sense when immigration quotas are taken as exogenously specified, but it does not when firms can seek to have the quotas liberalized in response to a shift in comparative advantage. Eschewing formal analysis of a firm's choice between going abroad and seeking more importation of foreign labor, I think it would be fair to assert that, since the wage costs of imported labor are likely to be substantially higher than the wage costs of similar labor abroad, the labor importation option will be outweighed by the out-migration of production option unless the industry and the countries involved are such as to make the potential risks and costs of direct foreign investment unduly high. It would appear from casual observation that United States entrepreneurs have followed the direct investment route à la Vernon's PC model fairly automatically whereas West European entrepreneurs in technically progressive industries have followed a mixed strategy, investing in cheap-labor countries abroad but also relying on increasing numbers of *gastarbeiters* much as in the "traditional," labor-intensive industries of section 6.2. It may well be that the greater willingness of West European governments to increase importation of *gastarbeiters* in the 1960s and much of the 1970s and the relative stringency of United States immigration policy in regard to unskilled labor account for this differential. Whether domestic labor unions would have permitted a shift in United States policy in this regard, leading to a shift from the Vernon-style direct investment abroad to importation of cheap labor to the United States in the technically progressive industries for their standardized, debugged, labor-intensive operations, is a question that I cannot answer but one that would be interesting to explore. In fact, it is not at all clear that domestic labor would be worse off under a policy where entrepreneurs out-migrate à la the PC scenario than it would be under a policy where entrepreneurs are allowed to import cheaper foreign labor!

The "Mutual Penetration of Investment" Scenario

In contrast to the case of PC–type shifts in comparative advantage, I have earlier distinguished shifts in comparative advantage that occur from increased competition from similar products, a state of affairs often brought about by R & D–induced changes in know-how. I have also distinguished between two polar cases: the case in which the intensification of competition does not confer an advantage to one product (and nation) as against another, and that in which the competitive advantage of one product (and nation) increases at the definite expense of the other. Before I proceed to analyze these two cases, however, it is necessary to discuss how trade in similar products comes about.

Alternative theories of trade in similar products. Recent analytical work in trade theory by Lancaster (1980), Dixit and Norman (1980), and Krugman (1979) has undertaken formalization of the original notion, inherent in Linder's (1961) pioneering work and in subsequent writings by Balassa (1967) and Grubel and Lloyd (1975), that much of the trade in manufactures among developed countries occurs in what might be called "similar" products. This formalization has proceeded on the basis of models that assume *identical* know-how among different countries and that specialization in different "similar" products ensues primarily as a result of scale economies, with basic indeterminacy as to which country produces which of the similar products and with Linder-like conclusions concerning the *volume* of trade in place of the Heckscher-Ohlin emphasis on predicting the *pattern* of trade. Therefore these theories share the Heckscher-Ohlin assumption of identical know-how but emerge with a contrasting set of outcomes concerning whether the volume or the pattern of trade can be explained.

On the other hand, I find it difficult to accept this type of formalization of trade in similar products among nation-states, neat as it is, and prefer an alternative "theory," which I will sketch below with a broad brush. Essentially, it seems to me that if we want to introduce the notion of "similar" products, with different nations trading such products to one another, we really have to give up the Heckscher-Ohlin assumption that all firms, and nations, share identical know-how *ex ante*. I would thus start with the notion that, just as in biological theorizing the "environment" interacts with "genetic factors" to produce a phenotype, we can think of an economic process whereby a specific choice of a product type emerges within a nation-society.[17] Thus, think of the income level and the level of R & D in manufacturing as defining the capacity of the society to come up technologically with a given set of characteristic product combinations, e.g., small, medium, and large cars.

The United States and Japan share this "genetic" set of traits; Zaire and Gabon do not. But which phenotype is selected in the market depends on the interaction of this common set of genetic traits with the specific "environment" of Japan and the United States. Thus the land-man ratios, the size and structure of the family, etc., may lead to the evolution of "gas guzzlers" in the United States and of smaller, fuel-economy cars in Japan, as, in fact, has been the case. At the next stage of the argument, then, the successful development of small cars in Japan and of gas guzzlers in the United States gets reinforced by localized technical change in precisely these types of cars with the result that one is now dealing with a situation of *ex ante* differentials in the know-how of producing and selling different types of cars. Next, since "cars" represent a generic product, representing a certain manner of transportation, the taste for small cars diffuses to the United States and for gas guzzlers to Japan as part of the Schumpeterian process of dynamic capitalism, aided by advertising in search of new markets. Thus trade in similar products arises. Scale economies with identical *ex ante* production functions do not play any role in this "theory," of course, and I believe that this scenario may have a greater claim to truth than the recent formal theorizations regarding trade in similar products. A formal characterization of this theory building on his recent theoretical work is presented in the appendix by Feenstra.

The MPI scenario. Whether the trade in similar products arises owing to scale economies in the presence of *ex ante* identical production functions or because of an "ecobiological process" theory like the one I have delineated above, what happens when the competition among similar products intensifies? When it results in a standoff, with the products of neither country's firms gaining dominance through R & D breakthroughs or taste shifts (whether exogenous or advertising-induced), the response of the entrepreneurs is likely to be of the MPI variety if the competition gets tough.[18]

Because no jobs are threatened, this then is an outcome to which unions ought to be indifferent. The entrepreneurs reduce the threat to their profits from import competition by *de facto* product-wise cartelization, and the government may not be unduly disturbed about the outcome (unless the result is the total elimination of competition in the industry *and* the government has an antitrust policy which it seeks to implement to this instance.)[19] The results are therefore far more sanguine in the MPI scenario than in the PC scenario!

The "Growing Dominance of External Products" Scenario

However, as soon as the comparative advantage has shifted dramatically in favor of the foreign products so that the domestic and foreign products do not both have a comfortable niche in the market, the picture changes drastically.

In this case, the entrepreneurs will want protection but may settle for greater access to cheaper foreign labor to offset the loss of comparative advantage if they can get the government to oblige them. While entrepreneurs may be indifferent between protection and greater access to foreign labor, the labor lobby will generally prefer protection to labor importation for reasons which need not be spelled out again. However, labor may be indifferent between a policy of actual protection and one in which they can merely use the *threat* of protection to get the foreign firms to invest where labor is, for the policies will equally secure their jobs. On the other hand, the entrepreneurs will prefer actual protection to the policy that merely uses protectionist threats to draw in foreign firms. For, while the United Auto Workers, for example, does not care whether its members are employed by Datsun or Ford, Ford does!

Thus we have the intriguing response possibility of domestic labor trying to import foreign entrepreneurs (with superior know-how), whereas in the "traditional" industries (of section 6.2) we had the spectacle of domestic entrepreneurs trying to import foreign labor (which will imply lower wages)!

As it happens, the protectionist threat resulting from the deteriorating competitive position of the United States car industry is a splendid example of the scenarios spelled out above. The American car industry, thanks largely to the steady erosion of the market for gas guzzlers in recent years, has been turning increasingly to producing small cars for survival, and this has shifted the problem of competition from one where the makers of American and foreign cars each had their own special niche in the market, with MPI (and variants thereof in the form of mutually supportive and profitable arrangements for marketing, joint production, etc.) as the relevant model, to one where the competition is more fierce and over a product type (the small car) where the makers of foreign cars have always had the edge. The result has been indeed for labor unions to go abroad and threaten the makers of foreign cars to produce in the United States or face protection. The following *New York Times* reports are revealing:

Douglas A. Fraser, head of the United Automobile Workers union, warned Japanese car makers today that they must invest in auto assembly plants in the United States or face the threat of immediate legislation to restrict rising imports of their small fuel-efficient cars.

He told Prime Minister Masayoshi Ohira and Foreign Minister Saburo Okita at separate meetings today that 220,000 auto workers were unemployed in the United States and that there was a 10.3 percent unemployment rate in Michigan, his home state and the center of American auto industry. Japanese auto makers should open operations in the United States to reduce unemployment there, even if only by small amounts, Mr. Fraser said. "You ought to have a sense of urgency," Mr. Fraser said he had told the Japanese leaders. He is making a short trip to Japan at the suggestion of Mike Mansfield, the United States Ambassador.

American vehicle imports totaled 2.2 million units in 1979, including about 1.7 million cars, and shipments in 1980 may increase as Americans turn to light, front-wheel-drive Japanese cars. By contrast, Japan imported fewer than 20,000 American cars last year.

The tall, heavily built U.A.W. chief said that Nissan Motor, a leading auto maker here that markets Datsun cars, offered yesterday to build a truck assembly plant in the United States, to avoid a pending 25 percent import tariff.

"That won't be sufficient," Mr. Fraser said. (*New York Times.* 1980*a*)

A stiff Congressional warning went out to Japan today to cut back voluntarily on automobile exports to the United States or face protectionist quota legislation that would damage the trading interests of both countries.

The chairman of a House trade sub-committee, Charles A. Vanik, Democrat of Ohio, called on the Japanese to roll back their American exports to 1977 levels over a two-year period to avoid what he called the "last resort" of legislated quotas.

In addition, he said, underscoring recent demands by Douglas A. Fraser, president of the United Automobile Workers, the Japanese must be convinced of the necessity to build important quantities of cars in the United States to avoid protectionist reaction here.

Declining international values for the yen, which make it more profitable to export from Japan, and the current emphasis on producing competing small cars by the American industry are behind the resistance of the two biggest Japanese producers—Toyota and Nissan—to construct assembly plants in the country. But Honda, a smaller company, has announced plans to manufacture relatively modest numbers of cars in an assembly plant in Ohio.

Mr. Vanik's call for voluntary restraint, made at committee hearings crowded today with Japanese reporters, came shortly after two bills were introduced by Michigan legislators to impose quota restraints.

But Congressional analysts believe that sentiment is not yet ready to jell, though it well might if automotive unemployment continues to rise. More than 200,000 auto workers have already been laid off.

At 1977 levels, Japanese sales here would be some 25 percent below the current rate of 2 million cars a year, which represents well over 20 percent of all cars sold in the United States.

No other country permits such penetration, Fred G. Secrest, executive vice president of the Ford Motor Company, told the panel.

He reported that, by agreement between British and Japanese producer associations, Japanese imports into Britain were held to about 11 percent of the market. France, he said, applies an informal but very effective share limit of 3 percent to Japanese cars. By bilateral agreement, Italy limits Japanese imports to 2,000 cars and trucks, while Spain limits imports of automobiles to a value of $500,000 from any exporting country.

Thomas J. Downey, Democrat of Suffolk County, said that American consumers were welcoming Japanese products "with open arms" and that even during the committee proceedings news photographs were being made by Nikon cameras and voice recordings by Panasonic.

He warned that failure to cut back the flow of Japanese cars would mean "a wave of protectionism that will sweep across the country and do irreparable harm to the Japanese economy and ultimately to us." (*New York Times*, 1980c)

The reaction to this protectionist lobbying by Japanese car makers is likely to be a response which combines some voluntary export restraints (VERs) and some accommodation to the demands for direct investment in the United States either à la Honda in Ohio or in some joint ventures in the United States with United States car makers like the proposed deal in Italy between Alfa Romeo, the state-owned car maker, and Nissan, which produces the Datsun, to produce a new medium-sized car at Alfa's plant in Alfasud in Pamigliano, Naples, with Alfa engines and Nissan bodies.[20]

6.4 Concluding Remarks

The primary emphasis of this paper has been to examine the strong relationship that exists between the response to intensifying import competition in goods and the nature of international labor and entrepreneurial mobility. In doing this, the paper has sought to provide a framework to systematize alternative patterns of responses to shifts in comparative advantage, without undertaking a rigorous, theoretical formulation of many of the ideas set forth.

Perhaps the major analytical limitation of the paper is the lack of consideration of what political scientists would call the issue of how a nation is governed. Whether, for example, the importation of foreign labor is legal, as in Western Europe, or illegal, as in the United States, and whether the unions are successful in their bid for protection instead of permitting a market-oriented adjustment to shifting comparative advantage are issues that require an analysis of how the corporate state works, i.e., how representative democracy interacts with industry and labor. Such a "political" and public-choice-theoretic analysis would nicely complement the analysis I have set forth here, essentially by explaining cross-country contrasts in the choices of policy response that have actually occurred as comparative advantage has shifted in recent years.

Notes

1. The only important exception to this hypothesis (i.e., that in the declining, senescent, unprogressive, labor-intensive industries the typical response would not be for entrepreneurs to move) would appear to come from Japanese experience. However, the shift of some Japanese textiles, for example, to South Korea and other countries in the Far East appears to have been partly a question of "investment shunting" prompted by GSP. It may also be useful to examine whether the shift has occurred from the technologically more progressive firms among these industries. Again, the few United States apparel producers who have gone abroad to take advantage of United States tariff provisions under GSP or 806.30-807 (the offshore assembly provision) seem to be the smaller firms with special designing or marketing skills. For a discussion of how Japanese direct investment differs in this respect (i.e., insofar as it occurs also in the "traditional" labor-intensive industries) from Western direct investment, see Kojima (1978).
2. In fact, the reward to capital is higher at Q_2 and Q_3 under the labor-importation policy and thus should please entrepreneurs more.
3. Note that, even if a production subsidy were used for protection, the corresponding welfare (U_{ps}) would, while avoiding the consumption cost of the tariff, still be inferior to that under the policy of relaxing the immigration restrictions on labor.
4. Note that the real rewards at Q_2 and Q_3 are identical, since the goods price ratio does not change along a Rybczynski line.
5. This strong ranking would not have followed if the policy comparison had not required identical Y^0 production. Thus it is easy to see in figure 6.3 that further shifts up along the Rybczynski line and hence IC (P_2^D) could lead eventually to welfare levels below that at C_f. Note also that the strong ranking might not hold if we were to use a sticky-wage model of either the Brecher (1974a, b) or the Harris and Todaro (1970) variety since that would introduce a domestic distortion in the sense of Bhagwati and Ramaswami (1963), Johnson (1965), and Bhagwati (1971).
6. Types of factor accumulation or technological progress which can lead to an increase in the production of the exportable good X and a fall in the production of Y are as follows: an increase in the stock of capital (used intensively in the export industry), and neutral or labor-using technological progress in the export industry (see Findlay and Grubert 1959).
7. It is a moot point whether labor is, in fact, always more mobile than capital is malleable!
8. The analysis of this model and the next could be extended to cases where the shift in comparative advantage is domestically induced, as in cases III and IV above. This can be done readily by the interested reader.

9. Note that the output of the importable industry expands under a policy of protection or labor importation.

10. The production is, of course, identical under both options; i.e., both policies are assumed to take the economy back to Q_1. However, under the labor-importation option, the net-of-remuneration-for-foreign-workers "production" point is Q_3 ($<Q_1$).

11. The project at Sussex University's Center for European Studies under the direction of Professor Ronald Dore ought to shed more light on these questions.

12. In chapter 9 of this volume, the analysis considers the lobbying costs of the labor lobby as well.

13. If we could raise any amount of revenue in a lump-sum fashion, it would of course be trivially true that we could bribe the labor lobby out of any protectionist pressure! The notion of the efficient tariff, on the other hand, is a second-best one, and the beauty of it is that the revenue being used for the bribe to labor is generated by the tariff itself. For further discussion, see chapter 9.

14. In the standard $2 \times 2 \times 2$ model, it is possible to work out the conditions under which the paradox of welfare-worsening tariff imposition will arise. See Bhagwati and Rivera-Batiz (1980). This paradox was first noted in Bhagwati (1979).

15. Needless to say, varying the tax on foreign capital to its optimal level would eliminate the paradox. This is, however, as removed from reality as differential taxation of foreign labor in the argument in the text and in Bhagwati and Rivera-Batiz (1980).

16. Of course, it is easy enough to construct analytical cases where the shift outward of technology-cum-capital, by profit-maximizing entrepreneurs, neither increases domestic unemployment in a Brecher-type model nor lowers the real wages of labor with full employment in the $2 \times 2 \times 2$ model.

17. Thus a typical popularized statement of the modern genetic theory is the following: "The phenotype is the result of a particular heredity acting on a particular environmental background. Any variation we observe among the members of a related group of organisms living under natural conditions must be phenotypic variation, because it will be the result of different environmental pressures and different genetic histories. Phenotypic variation in a population is the sum of genotypic variation inherent in the combined heredity of the group plus that part of the environmental variation which affects the phenotype" (Alland, Jr., 1972, p. 9).

18. Impure forms of the MPI phenomenon may involve a one-way equity purchase in exchange for marketing facilities.

19. Governments, of course, manage to get worried about direct foreign investments for all sorts of reasons; so perhaps I ought not to be overly optimistic about their benign neglect in this case!

20. However, the foreign investment response, as already indicated, may not meet with the approval of the entrepreneurs in the Honda type of investment or with that of the entrepreneurs other than the one going into joint venture in the Alfa-Nissan type of investment. In fact, as the *New York Times* (1980b) reported on the Alfa-Nissan proposal: "Fiat, not surprisingly, reacted strongly against the proposal, charging that the Nissan deal could become the opening wedge for a Japanese invasion of the Italian automobile market. Fiat, auto industry experts say, is particularly vulnerable to fresh competition because it has been losing some of its market share to other European car makers. . . .

"Fiat is also beset by sabotage and work stoppages by its workers. The company says that the violence and wildcat strikes caused a 12 percent decline in production last year and pushed its operating costs up sharply.

"To head off the Nissan-Alfa venture, Fiat made a proposal of its own to Alfa early this month, offering to buy 40,000 to 50,000 Alfa engines—the same number that would be involved in the Nissan deal—and mount them on new flat models over the next several years. There has also been talk about possible construction of a new Fiat body factory near the Alfasud plant."

Trade unions, if organized by firms, may also then have conflicting interests; and differential location of different firms may also pose questions of conflicting interests, e.g., workers in Alfa Romeo versus workers in Fiat.

References

Alland, Jr., A. 1972. *The human imperative.* New York: Columbia University Press.

Balassa, B. 1967. *Trade liberalization among industrial countries.* New York: McGraw-Hill.

Bhagwati, J. 1959. Protection, real wages, and real incomes. *Economic Journal* 69: 733–44.

———. 1971. The generalized theory of distortions and welfare. In J. Bhagwati et al., ed., *Trade, balance of payments, and growth.* Amsterdam: North-Holland.

———. 1972. Review of Vernon, *Sovereignty at bay. Journal of International Economics* 2 no. 4: 455–62.

———. 1977. Review of Hymer. *Journal of Development Economics* 4: 391–95.

———. 1978. *Anatomy and consequences of exchange control regimes.* Cambridge, Mass.: Ballinger.

———. 1979. The economic analysis of international migration. Plenary lecture to Nordisk Migrasjonsforskerseminar, Nordic Council of Ministers, Oslo, Norway, October.

Bhagwati, J., and R. Brecher. 1980. National welfare in an open economy in the presence of foreign-owned factors of production. *Journal of International Economics* 10 (May): 103–16.

Bhagwati, J., and V. K. Ramaswami. 1963. Domestic distortions, tariffs, and the theory of optimum subsidy. *Journal of Political Economy* 71, no. 1 (February): 44–50.

Bhagwati, J., and F. Rivera-Batiz. 1980. Protection in the presence of immigrant workers and sending country's welfare: Some paradoxes. Mimeographed, May.

Bhagwati, J., and E. Tironi. 1980. Tariff change, foreign capital, and immiserization: A theoretical analysis. *Journal of Development Economics*, February, pp. 103–15.

Brecher, R. 1974a. Minimum wage rates and the pure theory of international trade. *Quarterly Journal of Economics* 88, no. 1: 98–116.

———. 1974b. Optimal commercial policy for a minimum-wage economy. *Journal of International Economics* 4: 139–49.

Brecher, R., and C. D. Alejandro. 1977. Tariff, foreign capital, and immiserizing growth. *Journal of International Economics* 7 (November): 317–22.

Brecher, R., and J. Bhagwati. 1981. Foreign ownership and the theory of trade and welfare. *Journal of Political Economy* 89, no. 3 (June): 497–511.

Cheh, J. 1974. United States concessions in the Kennedy Round and short-run labor adjustment costs. *Journal of International Economics* 4 (November): 323–40.

Dixit, A., and V. Norman, 1980. *The theory of international trade: A text.* Cambridge: Cambridge University Press.

Findlay, R., and H. Grubert. 1959. Factor intensities, technological progress, and the terms of trade. *Oxford Economic Papers*, nos. 111–21. Also in J. N. Bhagwati, ed. 1970. *International trade: Selected readings*, pp. 327–40. Harmondsworth, UK: Penguin

Grubel, H., and P. Lloyd. 1975. *Intra-industry trade.* London: Macmillan.

Haberler, G. 1950. Some problems in the pure theory of international trade. *Economic Journal* 60 (June): 223–40.

Harris, J., and M. Todaro. 1970. Migration, unemployment, and development: A two-sector analysis. *American Economic Review* 60 (March): 126–42.

Hymer, S. 1960. The international operations of national firms: A study of direct foreign investment. Dissertation, MIT. Published with the same title in 1976 by MIT Press, Cambridge, Mass. (See pp. xxii and 253 of the latter.)

Johnson, H. G. 1965. Optimal trade intervention in the presence of domestic distortions: In R. E. Caves, P. B. Kenen, and H. G. Johnson, eds., *Trade, growth, and the balance of payments*, pp. 3–34. Amsterdam: North-Holland.

Jones, R. 1971. A three factor model in theory, trade, and history. In J. Bhagwati et al., eds., *Trade, balance of payments, and growth*, pp. 3–21. Amsterdam: North-Holland.

Kojima, K. 1978. *Direct foreign investment.* London: Croom Helm.

Krugman, P. 1979. Increasing returns, monopolistic competition, and international trade. *Journal of International Economics* 9 (November): 469–80.

Lancaster, K. 1980. Intra-industry trade under perfect monopolistic competition. *Journal of International Economics* 10: 151–76.

Linder, S. 1961. *An essay on trade and transformation.* New York: Wiley.

Mayer, W. 1974. Short-run and long-run equilibrium for a small open economy. *Journal of Political Economy* 82: 955–68.

Mussa, M. 1974. Tariffs and the distribution of income: The importance of factor specificity, substitutability, and intensity in the short and long run. *Journal of Political Economy* 82: 1191–1204.

Neary, J. P. 1978. Short-run capital specificity and the pure theory of international trade. *Economic Journal* 88 (September): 488–510.

184   Jagdish N. Bhagwati

New York Times. 1980*a*. Fraser bids Japan build cars in U.S. 14 February, Section D.
———. 1980*b*. Italy debating auto future. 29 February, Section D.
———. 1980*c*. Rep. Vanik warns Japan to curb auto exports. Clyde Farnsworth. 14 February, Section D.
Riedel, J. 1977. Tariff concessions in the Kennedy Round and the structure of protection in West Germany: An econometric assessment. *Journal of International Economics* 7, no. 2 (May): 133–44.
Uzawa, H. 1969. Shihon jiyuka to kokumin keizai. *Ekonomisuto*, 23 December, pp. 106–22.
Vernon, R. 1966. International investment and international trade in the product cycle. *Quarterly Journal of Economics* 80 (May): 190–207.

Appendix *Product Creation and Trade Patterns: A Theoretical Note on the "Biological" Model of Trade in Similar Products*
Robert C. Feenstra

Introduction

In this appendix I shall draw on the recent research of Feenstra (1980) to formalize the "biological" model of trade in similar products outlined by Bhagwati in this chapter.[1] The main features of the model to be presented are as follows: (1) As in models of "learning by doing" (see Arrow 1962) or induced technological innovation (see Kennedy 1964; Samuelson 1965), the technologies available within a country are endogenously determined by tastes, research and development (R & D) costs, and other parameters. (2) The returns to R & D activity are the monopoly profits associated with developing and marketing a new product, and an equilibrium of the R & D process is determined as a Chamberlinian "tangency solution" where profits on the last R & D project are zero. (3) If we allow countries to reach an R & D equilibrium in autarky, then it follows from (1) and (2) that countries with differing tastes, R & D costs, etc., will have different sets of available products and technologies. We shall assume that technological knowledge cannot be transferred abroad. Then opening the countries to international trade, we may observe trade in "similar" products arising from the fact that some countries may

Robert C. Feenstra is assistant professor of economics at Columbia University and was a Post-Doctoral Fellow in International Economics at the University of Chicago. He has published in the *Journal of International Economics* and has written on international trade theory and econometrics.

The author acknowledges helpful discussions with Richard Eckaus, Paul Krugman, and Martin Weitzman and the financial support of National Science Foundation Grant SOC 79-07541.

produce unique varieties of a differentiated product, and therefore export these varieties and import others. This bilateral trade in similar products, or intraindustry trade, is not related to scale economies in the post–R & D technologies (which are assumed to exhibit constant returns to scale), but, rather, depends on differences in the post–R & D technologies across countries and therefore, from (1), on cross-country differences in tastes, R & D costs, and other parameters.

It can be seen from this brief outline that our model is closely related to the ideas sketched by Bhagwati, and offers an alternative explanation for trade in similar products from the models of monopolistic competition and trade given in, among others, Krugman (1979) and Lancaster (1980), and in these authors' contributions to this volume. In the next section we shall present our model in detail and show how the autarky equilibrium is established. The pattern of trade between two countries is analyzed in the third section. In the last section we contrast our results to those from models of monopolistic competition and trade, and give brief conclusions.

Autarky Equilibrium

We shall consider the group of markets for a differentiated product, where the aggregate demand for product (i.e., variety) i is given by

(A1) $$q_i = a_i d^i(p, I; S(t)),$$

where p is the vector of prices, I is total consumer income, a_i is a parameter reflecting tastes for different varieties, and $S(t)$ denotes the set of products which are currently available for purchase and which change over time due to R & D. It is assumed that the demand functions d^i correspond to a *symmetric* utility function.[2] It is also assumed that demand is homogeneous of degree one in income and negative one in prices, and that goods are substitutes in the sense that an expansion in the set $S(t)$ of goods available implies a fall (or no change) in the demand for any good previously available.[3]

Note that the aggregate demand functions given in (A1) can be aggregated from individual demand functions under either of the following conditions: (1) all consumers have identical homothetic utility functions, in which case the parameters a_i, reflecting tastes for different varieties, are identical across consumers; (2) the distribution of income across consumers is fixed, and the individual utility functions are homothetic and differ only in the parameters a_i, in which case the *aggregate* parameters a_i reflect *differences* across individuals in their tastes for different varieties.[4]

We shall model an R & D project as spending fixed costs of f to discover the technology to produce good i. It is assumed that the post–R & D unit costs c_i of producing good i are nonstochastic and known even before the R & D takes place: this assumption is made for simplicity, but may not be unrealistic in situations where, prior to R & D, one has an accurate estimate of the inputs needed to produce a good even though the manner in which the inputs will be combined (i.e., the design of the product) is unknown. The post–R & D technologies are assumed to be linearly homogeneous, and the factor prices which determine c_i are held constant throughout the analysis. If the fixed costs $\tilde{f}$ of R & D are stochastic, then f denotes the certainty equivalent of $\tilde{f}$.[5] We shall assume that after the technology for producing any particular good is known, no further R & D on this good takes place; our model is thus one of *product creation* rather than process innovation on the technologies of existing goods.

In general terms, the R & D process we wish to model is one in which R & D proceeds sequentially over different products, where private firms decide which products to develop and when to stop creating new goods. It will be convenient to assume that, at any point in time when R & D is occurring, only *one* product (and corresponding technology) is being developed, and only *one* firm is engaged in this R & D. We shall suppose that the knowledge embodied in any new technology is protected by a one-period patent and that after the patent expires this knowledge is fully appropriable by all firms in the domestic (but not foreign) market. It follows that the returns to creating a new product through R & D are simply the one-period monopoly profits associated with the product:

(A2a) $\Pi_i(S(t)) = (p_i^* - c_i)a_i d^i(p^*, I; S(t) \cup \{i\}) - f,$

where p_i^* denotes the profit-maximizing price (where marginal revenue equals marginal cost), p^* is the corresponding vector of prices, and the notation $S(t) \cup \{i\}$ denotes the set obtained by adding product i to the set of products $S(t)$ previously available for purchase.

After a patent expires and other firms begin production of that good, it is assumed that the market structure is perfectly competitive, so that the good is sold at its marginal (and average) cost of c_i. Thus the prices p_j in the vector p^* are determined as follows:

(A2b) $p_j = \begin{cases} c_j & \text{for } j \in S(t) \\ p_i^* = c_i \left[\dfrac{e_i}{e_i - 1} \right] & \text{for } j = i \\ +\infty & \text{for } j \notin S(t) \text{ and } j \neq i, \end{cases}$

where e_i denotes the elasticity of demand for product i, $e_i > 1$, and we adopt the convention of setting prices equal to $+\infty$ for products which are not available for purchase. The monopolistic equilibrium given in (A2a, b) is assumed to exist.

To complete our model, we must specify how R & D proceeds over time, that is, how the set of products $S(t)$ available for purchase at the competitive price changes. Loosely speaking, we shall assume that starting from any set of initial products S_0, R & D occurs on the product of highest profitability and then proceeds sequentially (i.e., one good at a time) to the products next highest in the rank order of profitability, stopping when the remaining profits are nonpositive. This description is not precise, since it is possible for the rank order of products by profitability to depend on the set of goods $S(t)$, and therefore the rank ordering can change over time.

More formally, given any set of products $S(t)$ available for purchase at the competitive price, we shall assume that the next product selected for development is i^*, which satisfies

(A3) $\Pi_{i^*}(S(t)) = \max_{i \notin S(t)} \Pi_i(S(t))$.

If more than one product i^* satisfies (A3), any one can be selected. Let $\Delta(t)$ denote the length of time between the introduction (availability) of the last, and next, product sold at its competitive price. We shall assume that $\Delta(t)$ is inversely related to the current profitability of R & D:

(A4a) $\Delta(t) = 1/\psi(\Pi_{i^*}(S(t)))$,

where

(A4b) $\psi(x) = 0$ for $x \leq 0$,

$\psi'(x) > 0$ for $x > 0$.

Finally, note that the set of products $S(t)$ available for purchase at the competitive price changes in the following manner:

(A5) $S(t + \Delta(t)) = S(t) \cup \{i^*\}$, $t \geq 0$

$S(t) = S_0$, $0 \leq t < \Delta(0)$,

where the set S_0 of initial products is given and nonempty. Equations (A2)–(A5) are a complete description of our R & D process.[6]

From (A4) we see that as the profitability of the most attractive remaining R & D project falls, the length of time $\Delta(t)$ between the introduction of new products increases, and when $\Pi_{i^*} \leq 0$, then $\Delta(t) = +\infty$ in which case no further R & D takes place and we shall say that the set $S(t)$ of available products has converged.[7] We shall refer to the set $\bar{S}$ of available products and the associated competitive prices as an *autarky equilibrium* of the R & D process.

What products do we expect to be produced in the autarky equilibrium (i.e., included in the set $\bar{S}$)? Clearly, those products which are most profitable—which have a high a_i or low c_i—will be produced. Thus, suppose that $c_i = c$ for all i so that products differ only in the demand parameter a_i. We can rank-order products from the highest to lowest a_i, and this clearly corresponds to the rank ordering by profitability and is invariant to the set $S(t)$ of goods produced. Then R & D will begin at the product with highest a_i and proceed down the rank ordering, stopping when the profits from R & D become nonpositive. Similarly, if $a_i = a$ for all i and products differ only in their unit costs c_i, then the rank ordering of products from lowest to highest c_i corresponds to the rank ordering by profitability and is invariant to the set of goods produced, and R & D will begin at the product with lowest c_i and proceed along the rank ordering until the profits from R & D are nonpositive.

For given demand parameters a_i and unit costs c_i, the number of goods produced in the autarky equilibrium is determined by total consumer income I and the fixed R & D costs f. From our assumption that goods are substitutes, an increase in the number of products (i.e., an expansion of $S(t)$) lowers the returns to R & D on any remaining product. A rise in consumer income or fall in fixed costs of R & D increases the profits from R & D, and therefore expands the number of goods produced in the autarky equilibrium.[8]

To make explicit the relationship between our formalization and the "biological" model of trade in similar products outlined by Bhagwati, note that we can identify the total consumer income I spent on all varieties of the differentiated product, and the fixed costs of R & D, as "genetic" traits defining the capacity of an economy to create products through R & D. Given countries with similar "genetic" traits, the actual set of product varieties developed (i.e., phenotype selected) depends on the interaction between this common set of genetic traits and the specific "environment" of a country, where we identify the demand parameters a_i and post–R & D unit costs c_i as determined by the environment (e.g., factor endowments; transportation and communication infrastructure, including advertising; social habits) of a country. We have seen that slight differences in the environmental parameters may lead to marked differences in the set of product varieties developed in autarky, and thus a situation of technological differentials across countries in the production of different varieties.[9] These cross-country differences in the sets of products developed in autarky will lead to trade in similar products, as we shall analyze in the following section.

Trade Equilibrium

We shall consider trade between two countries A and B, where it is assumed that the functions d^i in (A1) are identical in the two countries so that tastes differ only in the demand parameters a_i. The countries may also differ in consumer income I, unit costs c_i, or fixed R & D costs f, which are measured in terms of a common numeraire in the two countries and are denoted with a superscript A or B. Note that given any set $S(t)$ of products available in both countries, the *world* demand for product i is

(A6) $a_i^A d^i(p, I^A; S(t)) + a_i^B d^i(p, I^B; S(t))$

$= (a_i^A I^A + a_i^B I^B) d^i(p, 1; S(t)),$

since the demand functions d^i are homogeneous of degree one in income. The sets $S^A(t)$ and $S^B(t)$ denote those products which have been *developed* in countries A and B, respectively, and the set $S(t)$ of goods *available* in both countries with trade is given by $S(t) = S^A(t) \cup S^B(t)$.

Because of the dynamic nature of our R & D process, in order to determine the set of products available in a trade equilibrium we must specify the *timing* of trade liberalization. Accordingly, we shall assume that each of the two countries A and B reaches an autarky equilibrium $\bar{S}^A$ and $\bar{S}^B$, respectively, and that trade is opened only *after* the autarky equilibria have been established. This assumption corresponds to the empirical observation that firms usually develop new products for the home market before considering export possibilities, and can be justified on the basis of various forms of uncertainty when marketing products abroad. We shall also assume that technologies cannot be transferred internationally, so that if firms in any country wish to produce a good which is not yet produced at home (but may be available through trade), they must first develop the technology through R & D.[10]

Within our model, the trade equilibrium is determined in the following manner. After the opening of trade, the profits from R & D activity are evaluated using world rather than domestic demand so that, from (A2a) and (A6), the returns to R & D on product i are given by

(A2a′) $\Pi_i^k(S(t)) = (p_i^* - c_i^k)(a_i^A I^A + a_i^B I^B) d^i(p^*, 1; S(t) \cup \{i\})$

$- f^k, k = A, B,$

where at the time T when trade is opened the set $S(t)$ of products available in both countries is $S(t) = \bar{S}^A \cup \bar{S}^B$.

Note that in general R & D in one country may occur in goods which are already produced abroad, where this *product imitation* may be profitable if one country has a sufficient cost advantage in production over the other country. However, if countries have similar post–R & D unit costs (measured in terms of a common numeraire), then product imitation is unlikely to occur, and we shall assume that this is the case. It follows that in (A2a′) product i is not included in the set of products already available for purchase ($i \notin S(t) = S^A(t) \cup S^B(t)$) and that the vector of prices p^* is given by

$$(A2b') \qquad p_j^* = \begin{cases} \min\{c_j^A, c_j^B\} & \text{for } j \in S^A(t) \cap S^B(t) \\ c_j^A & \text{for } j \in S^A(t), j \notin S^B(t) \\ c_j^B & \text{for } j \in S^B(t), j \notin S^A(t) \\ c_i^k \left[\dfrac{e_i}{e_i - 1} \right] & \text{for } j = i \text{ and when evaluating} \\ & \Pi_i^k, k = A, B \\ +\infty & \text{for } j \notin S(t) \text{ and } j \neq i. \end{cases}$$

In this specification of p^* it is recognized that for products which have been developed in both countries ($j \in S^A(t) \cap S^B(t)$), production and export will take place in the country of minimum unit cost and competitive price.

Turning to the dynamics of R & D, we shall assume in general that, after the opening of trade, R & D will occur in a country if and only if the monopoly profits from R & D as given in (A2') are positive for some product. When the maximum profits over all remaining products are nonpositive in both countries, then the sets $S^A(t)$, $S^B(t)$, and $S(t)$, of the R & D process will have converged to some sets $\bar{\bar{S}}^A$, $\bar{\bar{S}}^B$, and $\bar{\bar{S}} = \bar{\bar{S}}^A \cup \bar{\bar{S}}^B$, respectively, and we shall refer to these sets of products developed and available, and the associated competitive prices, as a *trade equilibrium* of the R & D process.[11]

While it is difficult to specify a general set of equations governing the R & D process with trade, one can easily describe certain special cases. For example, suppose that the countries "take turns" in R & D in the sense that the first country—say, country A—engages in R & D in a manner analogous to the autarky process until the profits (as given in [A2']) from remaining R & D activity are nonpositive, after which country B develops products sequentially until profitable R & D opportunities have been exhausted. From our assumption that goods are substitutes, this process will converge after the two "turns" we have indicated, since the introduction of new products by country B will lower the profits from R & D activity in country A.

As another example, suppose that the time intervals $\Delta^A(t)$ and $\Delta^B(t)$ between the introduction of the last, and next, product sold at its competitive price are equal and constant in both countries whenever profits from R & D are positive; that is,

$$(A4') \qquad \Delta^k(t) = \begin{cases} \bar{\Delta} & \text{if } \Pi_{i_k^*}^k > 0, \\ +\infty & \text{if } \Pi_{i_k^*}^k \leq 0, \end{cases} \qquad k = A, B,$$

where i_k^* satisfies

$$(A3') \qquad \Pi_{i_k^*}^k(S(t)) = \max_{i \notin S(t)} \Pi_i^k(S(t)), \qquad k = A, B.$$

Then the change in the set of products $S(t)$ available for purchase at the competitive price is determined by

(A5′) $S(t) = S^A(t) \cup S^B(t),$

$$S^k(t + \bar{\Delta}) = \begin{cases} S^k(t) \cup \{i_k^*\} & \text{if } \Pi_{i_k^*}^k > 0 \\ S^k(t) & \text{if } \Pi_{i_k^*}^k \leq 0, \end{cases} \quad t \geq T,$$

$S^k(t) = \bar{S}^k \quad \text{for} \quad T \leq t < T + \bar{\Delta}, k = A,B.$

In this case the R & D process with trade is completely described by (A2′)–(A5′), and is assumed to converge to a trade equilibrium.

What trade patterns do we expect to observe in a trade equilibrium? First, let us consider the pattern of trade which emerges in the *temporary* competitive equilibrium immediately following the opening of trade, but before any additional R & D has occurred. Suppose that the sets $\bar{S}^A$ and $\bar{S}^B$ of products developed in countries A and B, respectively, have no products in common, where the difference between these sets may be attributed to differing demand parameters a_i^k and post–R & D unit costs c_i^k in the two countries, $k = A,B$, which leads to different products being developed in autarky (e.g., small and big cars, different varieties of furniture, etc.). In this equilibrium, all products in the set $\bar{S}^A$ will clearly be exported from country A to country B, and conversely for products in the set $\bar{S}^B$. The volume of exports from one country to the other is determined by the number of goods the exporting country produces (i.e., in $\bar{S}^k$), where for given tastes and post–R & D unit costs, the number of goods produced in the autarky equilibrium is directly related to total consumer income I^k and inversely related to the fixed costs of R & D f^k, $k = A,B$.

More generally, suppose that the sets $\bar{S}^A$ and $\bar{S}^B$ of products developed have some goods in common. For these goods, production and export in the temporary equilibrium will take place in the country of minimum unit cost and competitive price, while for goods developed in only one country, the trade pattern is determined as before. In this case the volume of trade depends on the relative unit costs of production between the countries, since the country with a cost advantage in the larger number of products will tend in aggregate to be a net exporter of those products both countries have developed.

Do we expect to observe additional R & D after trade is opened to move the economies away from the temporary equilibrium we have just described? Such R & D will occur if and only if the evaluation of profits from R & D is changed from nonpositive to positive as a result of using world rather than domestic demand (i.e., shifting from [A2] to [A2′]). This shift in demand has two effects on profits: (1) profits are increased due to the expansion of market income, that is, evaluating profits using $I^A + I^B$ rather than I^A or I^B; (2) profits are decreased due to the greater variety of products available, that is, evaluating profits using

$S(T) = \bar{S}^A \cup \bar{S}^B$ rather than $\bar{S}^A$ or $\bar{S}^B$. It is quite possible for effect (2) to dominate effect (1) so that there is *no* additional R & D after trade is opened, and the *temporary* equilibrium which we have just analyzed is identical to the *trade* equilibrium.

In fact, the following result can be established.[12] Suppose that demand and unit costs of production are identical across products and countries, $a_i^A = a_i^B = a$ and $c_i^A = c_i^B = c$ for all i, that as more products are introduced goods become stronger substitutes, that the sets of goods $\bar{S}^A$ and $\bar{S}^B$ produced in each country in the autarky equilibrium have no products in common, and that the number of goods produced in each country in the autarky equilibrium is large. Then after trade is opened there is *no* additional R & D activity. By continuity, we can allow slight differences in the demand parameters a_i^k and c_i^k across commodities and countries, $k = A, B$, and under the remaining hypotheses still find that the amount of R & D activity after trade (if any) is small. The difference between the sets $\bar{S}^A$ and $\bar{S}^B$ of products developed in autarky is now determined by cross-country differences in tastes and post–R & D unit costs (as well as differences in total consumer income and fixed costs of R & D), and the implications for trade patterns are as previously described: products in $\bar{S}^A$ will be exported to country B, and conversely. We have thus arrived at the model of trade in "similar" products outlined in the introduction to this appendix and a formalization of the ideas sketched by Bhagwati.

Last, we must consider the case where additional R & D activity *does* occur after the opening of trade. The products which firms in each country select to develop need not be identical across countries, though identical rank orderings by profitability will obtain if the post–R & D unit costs of production are equal in the two countries. In general we expect the rate of product creation in each country to depend on the profits from R & D, which may differ across countries due to different unit costs of production or fixed costs of R & D, and some exogenously specified "rate of product creation" function (or parameter) such as ψ in (A4) (or $\bar{\Delta}$ in [A4']). Countries with a quicker rate of product creation will tend in aggregate to be a net exporter of those products which are developed after trade is opened.

Conclusions

A general conclusion from models of monopolistic competition and trade, such as Krugman (1979) and Lancaster (1980), is that the *volume* of trade between countries is determined in the trade equilibrium, but the geographical origin of any particular product is indeterminate; the latter result follows since countries are assumed to have identical technologies. The above model of product creation differs in several respects. First, the geographical origin of production is determinate for any good which is developed in one country but not the other, where this situation is likely to occur whenever one country has a demand bias or cost advantage in certain product varieties while the other country has a demand bias or cost advantage in other varieties. In particular, countries will tend to export those products which are developed in autarky.[13] The resulting intraindustry trade is not related to scale economies in the post–R & D technologies, but, rather, is determined by scale economies (due to the spreading of fixed costs) of R & D and cross-country differences in tastes, post–R & D unit costs, etc. Note that for goods which are developed in *both* countries, the location of production is indeterminate if the post–R & D unit costs are identical.

The volume of trade in any particular product is determined by the number of goods produced, and, as in models of monopolistic competition, this number is established in a Chamberlinian "tangency solution" and is directly related to total consumer income and inversely related to the fixed costs of production or R & D.[14] For the case where additional R & D activity occurs after the opening of trade, the aggregate volume of trade in equilibrium is determined by the rates of product creation in the two countries, whereas this effect does not enter the models of monopolistic competition and trade (which are primarily of a static nature).

In conclusion, we should indicate that the model of product creation we have presented can be fruitfully extended in a wide variety of directions (see Feenstra 1980), e.g., modeling "product imitation" by one country to lead to a model of the "product cycle", or an examination of the Linder (1961) hypotheses concerning the importance of domestic demand in determining potential and actual trade.

Notes

1. This formalization demonstrates how the "biological model" of trade in similar products can be cast in theoretical terms, but is incomplete in that certain aspects of the proposed model are not fully investigated.

2. In order to correspond to a symmetric utility function, the demand functions d^i must satisfy the following condition: if the vector $\bar{p}$ is equal to p except that the components p_i and p_j have been interchanged, then

$$d^i(p,I;S(t)) = d^j(\bar{p},I;S(t)).$$

An example of a utility function leading to demand equations as in (A1) is

$$U = \sum_{i=1}^{N} a_i v(q_i/a_i), \qquad v'>0, v''<0.$$

The corresponding demand functions are

$$q_i = a_i \phi(\lambda p_i),$$

where ϕ is the inverse function of v' and λ is the marginal utility of income.

3. That is, for $i \in S$ and $S \subseteq S'$, we have

$$d^i(p,I;S') \leq d^i(p,I;S).$$

4. Lancaster (1980) assumes that each consumer has a most preferred product variety, that demand for neighboring varieties decreases in a uniform manner, and that the distribution of consumers' preferred varieties is also uniform across products, in which case *aggregate* demand is identical across product varieties.

5. If firms evaluate profits using the utility function U, an approximate certainty equivalent to $\tilde{f}$ is given by

$$f = \bar{f} + \frac{1}{2} \sigma_f^2 R_A,$$

where $\bar{f} = E(\tilde{f})$, $\sigma_f^2 = E(\tilde{f} - \bar{f})^2$, and $R_A = -U''/U'$ is the index of absolute risk aversion.

6. I have permitted myself one sleight of hand in specifying the equations for the R & D process. Specifically, given equation (A4), it would be natural to let $\Delta(t)$ denote the length of time between the introduction of the last, and next, product sold at its *monopolistic* (rather than competitive) price. However, this definition would complicate the specification of p^* in (A2b) since, depending on the length of time needed to complete the R & D for one product, at any point in time a variable number of products are sold at their monopolistic price. Because of this complication, we have adopted the simpler, but less natural, definition of $\Delta(t)$.

7. We shall assume that convergence is obtained; that is, the R & D eventually stops. This seems to be a reasonable assumption of a market where total demand is stationary (i.e., consumer income I is fixed) and the introduction of new goods does not affect the demand or cost parameters a_i, c_i, and f_i.

8. But note that, starting from an autarky equilibrium, a *fall* in I or *rise* in f has *no* effect on the set $\bar{S}$ of available products: these parameter changes decrease the profits from remaining R & D projects and also decrease the *hypothetical* profits from duplicating the R & D activity on any existing product (and hypothetically selling the product at its monopoly price for one period), but neither of these outcomes has any effect on the set of products available. This illustrates a basic difference between our model and models of monopolistic competition: in the model being presented the set of products available can expand but never contract, since the fixed costs of R & D are borne in only one period, whereas in models of monopolistic competition where fixed costs are paid every period, the number of products available can expand or contract as a result of parameter changes. However, if we compare two *different* economies which are identical except that the first has lower consumer income or higher fixed costs of R & D than the second and these parameters have not changed over time, then in their autarky equilibria the first economy will have a smaller number of products available than the second.

9. Note that even if the demand parameters a_i and unit costs c_i are *identical* across commodities, in which case *any* undeveloped product satisfies (A3) and may be selected for development, we may still obtain cross-country differences in the sets of products developed in autarky due to random differences in the products selected for R & D. If the number of potential product varieties is large relative to the number actually developed, this random selection procedure will probably lead to little overlap across countries in the sets of products developed in autarky, and therefore to a considerable amount of trade in these similar products (as analyzed in the next section).

10. That is, in the model being presented we shall assume that the fixed costs of R & D in any country do not depend on whether the product has previously been developed abroad. In some cases it may be more realistic to assume that the additional fixed costs of adapting a foreign technology for production at home are considerably less than if the technology had not been developed abroad, and our model can be extended in this direction (see Feenstra 1980).

11. Note that our analysis is partial equilibrium, and we do not require that trade is balanced in the trade equilibrium.

12. A similar result, using a CES utility function, is established in Feenstra (1980).

13. Note that in the models of Krugman and Lancaster it is assumed that aggregate demand and production costs are identical across goods. If we adopted this assumption within our model, then we would not be able to predict which goods would be developed in autarky (as discussed in note 9), though it would still be the case that countries would tend to export the autarky set of products. On the other hand, if we weakened the "symmetry" assumption of identical aggregate demand and production costs within Lancaster's model, but retained the assumption that countries have identical technologies and factor prices, then we would still find that the geographical origin of production is indeterminate (in contrast to the model of product creation). The "symmetry" assumption cannot be weakened within Krugman's model, since this would lead to the nonexistence of a long-run equilibrium with zero profits for every firm in the industry; this existence problem may be recognized as a weakness of the Chamberlinian approach to monopolistic competition theory, as also discussed by Chipman in his comment to chapter 7.

14. A difference in the determination of the number of goods produced between our model and that of monopolistic competition is discussed in note 8.

References

Arrow, K. J. 1962. The economic implications of learning by doing. *Review of Economic Studies* 29, (June): 155–73.

Feenstra, R. C. 1980. Product creation and trade patterns. Mimeographed, November.

Kennedy, C. 1964. Induced bias in innovation and the theory of distribution. *Economic Journal* 74 (September): 541–47.

Krugman, P. 1979. Increasing returns, monopolistic competition, and international trade. *Journal of International Economics* 9: 469–79.

Lancaster, K. J. 1980. Intra-industry trade under perfect monopolistic competition. *Journal of International Economics* 10, no. 2 (May): 151–75.

Linder, S. B. 1961. *An essay on trade and transformation.* New York: Wiley.

Samuelson, P. A. 1965. A theory of induced innovation along Kennedy-Weizsacker lines. *Review of Economics and Statistics* 47 (November): 343–56.

7   Trade in Differentiated Products and the Political Economy of Trade Liberalization

Paul Krugman

Why is trade in some industries freer than in others? The great postwar liberalization of trade chiefly benefited trade in manufactured goods between developed countries, leaving trade in primary products and North-South trade in manufactures still highly restricted. Within the manufacturing sector some industries seem to view trade as a zero-sum game, while in others producers seem to believe that reciprocal tariff cuts will benefit firms in both countries. In a period of rising protectionist pressures, it might be very useful to have a theory which explains these differences in the treatment of different kinds of trade.

This paper is an attempt to take a step in the direction of such a theory. I develop a multi-industry model of trade in which each industry consists of a number of differentiated products. The pattern of *interindustrial* specialization is determined by factor proportions, so that there is an element of comparative advantage to the model. But scale economies in production ensure that each country produces only a limited number of the products within each industry, so there is also *intraindustry* specialization and trade which does not depend on comparative advantage. The model thus draws on recent work on the theory of intraindustry trade by Dixit and Norman (1980), Lancaster (1980), and the author.

In the model, liberalizing trade within an industry leads each country to expand both its imports and its exports in that industry. A country which is a net exporter in an industry will still have some demand for the products produced abroad, so net exporters will still be gross importers and vice versa. This creates the possibility that reciprocal removal of trade barriers can lead to increased sales by producers in *both* countries.

Paul Krugman is the Ford International Associate Professor of Management at Massachusetts Institute of Technology. He has published several articles establishing him as a leading trade theorist.

If this is the case, presumably trade liberalization will be relatively easy to achieve. The paper shows that whether this happens depends in economically sensible ways on industry characteristics. Specifically, producers in both countries will gain from mutual trade liberalization in an industry if neither country has too great a comparative advantage and the products within the industry are strongly differentiated. This fits in well with casual observation: trade is more liberal in differentiated manufactures than in homogeneous primary products, more restricted between countries with very unequal wage-rental ratios than between countries with similar factor prices. Thus, although the model is admittedly dependent on a number of very special assumptions, it does produce results which seem to shed light on the variation in protection across industries.

The paper is organized in four sections. Section 7.1 sets out the basic model for a single economy. In section 7.2, the pattern of specialization and trade between two such economies is considered. Section 7.3 considers the effects of mutual trade liberalization on a single industry. Finally, section 7.4 suggests some conclusions.

7.1 Structure of the Model

The model developed in this paper is based on the recently developed theory of intraindustry trade. In this theory, an "industry" is a group of products which are all produced with the same factor proportions. Whether a country is a net importer or exporter in an industry thus depends on the conventional forces of comparative advantage. Because of scale economies in production, however, each country specializes in a limited subset of the products within each industry. The result is "intraindustry" trade—countries which are *net* exporters in a particular industry will still be *gross* importers, because foreigners will be producing differentiated products.

This theory of trade helps explain why there is so much trade between similar countries and why the trade between these countries consists largely of two-way trade in similar products. The price one pays for these insights is that one must deal with illuminating special cases rather than general models. Economies of scale mean that markets cannot be perfectly competitive, and we are only able to model monopolistic competition by making special assumptions about utility and production functions. In dealing with models of intraindustry trade, then, one must always be satisfied with illustrating propositions rather than proving them.

As one might expect from these remarks, the model about to be developed is one characterized by a number of very special assumptions.

These assumptions may at first seem too special; but I believe that their simplicity and the intuitive appeal of the results they yield justify them.

Let us consider, then, an economy consisting of a number of "industries," each of which consists of many products. The appropriate definition of an industry has been a major problem in discussions of intraindustry trade: should a "supply-side" or a "demand-side" concept be used? In the particular model considered here, there is a natural grouping of products which meets both concepts; we have "industries" whose products are relatively close substitutes on both the supply and demand sides. One might justify this as an empirically reasonable assumption by arguing that products with similar characteristics are likely to have relatively similar inputs. In the theoretical model presented here, however, the characteristics which differentiate products are not explicitly set out. Thus the convenient existence of a natural definition of industries should be regarded as one of the model's special assumptions.

On the demand side, then, everyone in the economy will be assumed to have the same tastes, which can be represented by a two-level CES utility function:

(1) $$U = \left[\sum_{j=1}^{K} \delta_i C_i^\gamma \right]^{1/\gamma} \qquad \gamma < 1,$$

where we define

(2) $$C_i = \left[\sum_{j=1}^{N_i} c_{ij}^{\theta_i} \right]^{1/\theta_i} \qquad 0 < \theta_i < 1, \qquad i = 1, \ldots, K,$$

Here c_{ij} is an individual's consumption of the jth product of industry i, and N_i is the (large) number of potential products in the ith industry. We note that the *interindustry* elasticity of substitution is $1/1 - \gamma$, while the *intraindustry* elasticity of substitution (which varies across industries) is $1/1 - \theta_i$ for the ith industry.

On the supply side, I will assume that the products of each industry are produced by a single factor, "labor," which is wholly specific to that industry. That is, we have a labor supply L_i corresponding to each industry i. This is a relatively crude way of introducing a supply side into the model; it has the virtue, as we will see, of allowing an easy parameterization of the amount of comparative advantage in an industry. If we assume full employment of resources, we can write the resource constraint as

(3) $$L_i = \sum_j \ell_{ij} \qquad i = 1, \ldots, K,$$

where ℓ_{ij} is labor used in producing product j of industry i.

Labor used in the production of a particular product will be assumed to involve a fixed set-up cost and constant marginal costs thereafter:

$$\ell_{ij} = 0 \text{ if } q_{ij} = 0 \qquad i = 1, \ldots, K$$

(4) $$= \alpha_i + \beta_i q_{ij} \text{ if } q_{ij} > 0 \qquad j = 1, \ldots, N_i,$$

where q_{ij} is the output of the jth product of industry i and the parameters α_i and β_i are assumed constant across the products within an industry.

Equilibrium in this model will take the form of monopolistic competition. Each product will be produced by only one firm, while free entry will drive profits to zero. The simplified structure of the model makes it easy to determine pricing behavior and the size and number of firms in each industry.

First, consider pricing behavior. If the number of firms in each industry is large, each firm can disregard interindustry substitution and focus solely on intraindustry competition. Thus each firm in the ith industry will face a demand curve with an elasticity equal to the industry elasticity of substitution:

(5) $$\varepsilon_i = 1/1 - \theta_i \qquad i = 1, \ldots, K.$$

Profit-maximizing pricing behavior will involve setting the price at $\varepsilon_i/\varepsilon_i - 1$ times marginal cost, so that we have

(6) $$p_i = \frac{\varepsilon_i}{\varepsilon_i - 1} \beta_i w_i$$

$$= \theta_i^{-1} \beta_i w_i \qquad i = 1, \ldots, K,$$

where p_i is the profit-maximizing price of firms in industry i—the same for all firms—and w_i is the wage rate of industry i's sector-specific labor.

Consider next the profitability of firms. Economic profits earned by a firm in industry i, charging price p_i and with sales q_i, are

(7) $$\pi_i = p_i q_i - (\alpha_i + \beta_i q_i) w_i \qquad i = 1, \ldots, K.$$

Using the pricing rule (6), we can rewrite this as

(8) $$\pi_i = \left[\theta_i^{-1} \beta_i q_i - \alpha_i - \beta_i q_i \right] w_i \qquad i = 1, \ldots, K.$$

If there is free entry and exit, the number of firms in an industry will fall if profits are negative and rise if they are positive, so that in equilibrium $\pi_i = 0$. But this lets us determine the equilibrium level of output:

(9) $$q_i = \alpha_i \theta_i / \beta_i (1 - \theta_i) \qquad i = 1, \ldots, K.$$

Given the size of firms, the number of firms and thus of products actually produced within an industry can be determined from the full employment condition:

$$n_i = L_i / (\alpha_i + \beta_i q_i)$$

(10) $$= L_i (1 - \theta_i) / \alpha_i \qquad i = 1, \ldots, K.$$

Finally, we need to determine relative wages w_i. We need not go into detail here; it is enough to note that relative demands for industry outputs are determined by the utility function (1) and that relative supplies are determined by the sector-specific labor forces L_i. We will return to this question in section 7.4.

This model, then, gives rise to an equilibrium in which all industries are monopolistically competitive, containing a number of firms producing differentiated products and charging prices above marginal cost. In the next section we will consider what happens when two such economies are allowed to trade. First, however, we should note that, while all industries are monopolistic, the degree of monopoly varies. This variation will turn out to be crucially important in determining the consequences of trade liberalization.

Consider the pricing equation (6). Price exceeds marginal cost by the ratio θ_i^{-1}. We can view θ, which is inversely related to the intraindustry elasticity of substitution, as an inverse index of product differentiation; if θ_i is low, products are highly differentiated and firms have considerable monopoly power. Further, since price equals average cost in equilibrium, θ is the ratio of marginal to average cost, and is thus an inverse index of unexploited economies of scale.

7.2 Comparative Advantage and the Trade Pattern

Suppose that there exists another economy very similar to the one described in section 7.1. It shares the same technology, and its consumers have the same utility function. The only difference is that the second economy has a different endowment of industry-specific labor supplies, which we will represent as L_i^*, $i = 1, \ldots, K$.

Suppose that these economies are able to trade at zero transportation cost. What can we say about the resulting pattern of trade?

Determining pricing and production in the second country is somewhat simpler than might appear. First, given the identity of utility and cost functions in the two countries, pricing behavior and the equilibrium size of firm in each industry are the same in our second country as in our first. Price is a markup on marginal cost:

(11) $$p_i^* = \theta_i^{-1} \beta_i w_i^* \qquad i = 1, \ldots, K.$$

Output is determined by the condition of zero profits:

(12) $$q_i^* = \alpha_i \theta_i / \beta_i (1 - \theta_i) \qquad i = 1, \ldots, K.$$

The number of products produced in the second country in each industry is proportional to its labor force in that industry:

(13) $$n_i^* = L_i^* (1 - \theta_i) / \alpha_i \qquad i = 1, \ldots, K.$$

Notice that we cannot determine *which* products in the industry will be produced in which country. What we can be sure of is that there will be no overlap. Since firms can costlessly differentiate their products, no two firms will ever produce the same product; and thus firms in different countries will specialize in different products.

Finally, given the symmetry of the problem, wages in each industry will be equalized across countries:

(14) $w_i = w_i^*$ $i = 1, \ldots, K.$

Before proceeding to the pattern of trade, it is useful to begin by regarding the two countries together as a single economy. The industries in the world economy have labor forces $L_1 + L_1^*, \ldots, L_K + L_K^*$; and these labor forces receive equilibrium wages $w_1 = w_1^*, \ldots, w_K = w_K^*$. If we let Y be the first country's income, Y^* the second country's, then we have

(15) $Y = \sum_{i=1}^{K} w_i L_i,$

(16) $Y^* = \sum_{i=1}^{K} w_i L_i^*.$

The wage rates w_i are determined by demand. Since the countries have identical, homothetic tastes, they will spend the same share of income on each industry's products:

(17) $n_i p_i q_i + n_i^* p_i^* q_i^* = \pi_i (Y + Y^*),$

where π_i, the share of expenditure falling on industry i's products, is of course dependent on relative prices. Since profits are zero, sales of an industry equal its factor payments:

(18) $w_i L_i + w_i^* L_i^* = \pi_i (Y + Y^*).$

We are now prepared to examine the pattern of trade. Let X_i be the value of the first country's exports in industry i. We know that the second country will spend a share π_i of its income on industry i's products. At the same time, it will spend an equal share of this expenditure on each of the products within the industry. So the share of i expenditure falling on the first country's products is $n_i/(n_i + n_i^*)$. Thus the value of i exports is

$$X_i = \frac{\pi_i n_i}{n_i + n_i^*} Y^*$$

(19) $$= \frac{\pi_i L_i}{L_i + L_i^*} Y^*   i = 1, \ldots, K.$$

A similar argument shows that the first country's imports are

(20) $$M_i = \frac{\pi_i L_i^*}{L_i + L_i^*} Y \qquad i = 1, \ldots, K.$$

We can use (19) and (20) to establish two interesting propositions about trade. First, notice that a country's net export position in an industry depends on its relative endowment of the industry-specific factor. Consider, for example, a widely used measure of "revealed comparative advantage":

(21) $$R_i = \ln(X_i/M_i).$$

From (19) and (20), we have

(22) $$R_i = \ln(L_i/L_i^*) - \ln(Y/Y^*).$$

Since Y/Y^* is a term common to all industries, the ranking of industries by revealed comparative advantage is determined by relative factor endowments.

The second proposition concerns the importance of "intraindustry" trade. Obviously, (19) and (20) imply that a country will import even where it has a comparative advantage, export where it has a comparative disadvantage. A widely used measure of this intraindustry trade is the index of trade overlap,

(23) $$I_i = 1 - \frac{|X_i - M_i|}{X_i + M_i}.$$

Algebraic manipulation allows us to rewrite this as

(24) $$I_i = \frac{2}{1 + \exp|R_i|}.$$

Thus intraindustry trade will predominate in those industries in which the absolute value of R is close to zero, i.e., in which comparative advantage is weak.

We have shown in the last two sections that it is possible to develop a relatively simple trade model in which there are many industries, and in which the degree of monopoly and the extent of comparative advantage vary in economically meaningful ways across industries. It remains to show why these industry characteristics matter. The next section considers how the parameters which describe an industry can make trade liberalization easy or difficult.

7.3 Effects of Trade Liberalization

Suppose that some particular industry, say industry i, is subject to trade restrictions. Ordinarily, producers in each country will oppose any unilateral elimination of their country's restrictions; by exposing them to foreign competition this will lower the wages of industry-specific labor and will not usually offer a compensating consumption gain. But a simultaneous removal of restrictions by both countries may be another matter. Not only will it increase the welfare of producers in the country with a comparative advantage; it may benefit producers in the country with a comparative disadvantage as well!

How is this possible? The products of different countries are imperfect substitutes for one another; removing trade restrictions offers consumers a wider range of choice and may lead them to spend a larger share of their income on industry i's products. If the products are sufficiently differentiated and comparative advantage is weak, this effect may be enough to raise the industry-specific wage rate in the country with a comparative disadvantage.

To establish this point, it is helpful to make several simplifying assumptions:

i) Industry i is taken to be "small," so that we disregard the effect of trade liberalization on national income and on other industries' prices.

ii) Trade liberalization is assumed to take an extreme form. Before liberalization, trade in industry i (though not in other industries) is wholly prohibited. After liberalization, trade is completely free. Thus we exclude limited or differential liberalization.

iii) To exclude effects which arise from differences in the size of countries, as opposed to specific industry characteristics, the countries are assumed to have equal national incomes: $Y = Y^*$.

We can now begin the formal analysis. The crucial aspect of the model is the existence of many products within each industry and the value consumers place on this diversity. This aspect can be viewed as creating a divergence between *physical* output in an industry and "true" output taking into account the value of diversity. Consider the utility formulation (1) and (2). One way of reading this (a way suggested by Ethier 1980) is to think of consumers assembling final consumption goods C_i from components C_{ij}. It is then apparent that the output of these final consumption goods depends on the diversity of products available as well as on physical output. Specifically, an index of "true" output for industry i can be written

$$(25) \qquad Q_i^t = \tilde{n}_i^{1/\theta_i} q_i,$$

where $\tilde{n}_i$ is the number of products available and q_i is the output of a representative product.

Similarly, there is a divergence between the actual prices of products and the "true" price index reflecting the value of diversity. For a given price of representative products in an industry, the price of the final consumption good "assembled" from these products will fall as the diversity of products increases. Again, by inspecting (1), we can see that a "true" price index will have the form

$$(26) \qquad P_i^t = \tilde{n}_i^{(\theta_i - 1)/\theta_i} p_i,$$

where p_i is the price of a representative product.

What is the definition of $\tilde{n}_i$? Since we are deriving our indices from the utility function, the relevant number of products is the number *available to the consumer*. Before trade liberalization, $\tilde{n}_i = n_i$, the number of domestic products; after trade, $\tilde{n}_i = n_i + n_i^*$, the number of products produced worldwide. As Ethier (1979) has pointed out, in this kind of situation increasing returns apply on a world scale.

Now consider the situation of the industry before trade liberalization. We already know how n_i, q_i, and p_i are determined; using (6), (9), and (10) and writing the results in logarithmic form, we have

$$(27) \qquad \ln Q_i^t = \ln \alpha_i \theta_i / \beta_i (1 - \theta_i) + \theta_i^{-1} \ln L_i (1 - \theta_i)/\alpha_i$$

for the true index of output, and

$$(28) \qquad \ln P_i^t = \ln \theta_i^{-1} \beta_i w_i - \frac{1 - \theta_i}{\theta_i} \ln L_i (1 - \theta_i)/\alpha_i.$$

The demand for true output will depend on income and prices. The form of the utility function ensures that all industries will face an income elasticity of demand of one and a price elasticity of $1/1 - \gamma$. Thus we can write a demand function in terms of true output and prices:

$$(29) \qquad \ln Q_i^t = A_i + \ln Y - \frac{1}{1 - \gamma} \ln P_i^t,$$

where A_i is a constant term.

Note that we have not specified the units in which income and prices are measured. Since the industry is assumed small, however, and we are considering a liberalization of trade *in one industry at a time*, the relative prices of all other industries' products can be taken as fixed, and thus all other output (and all other factors) can be regarded as a composite commodity. We can then use this composite commodity as *numeraire*.

We can solve (29) for the wage rate of industry i labor. Using (27) and (28), we can derive the expression

$$(30) \qquad \ln w_i = K_i + (1 - \gamma) \ln Y - \frac{\theta_i - \gamma}{\theta_i} \ln L_i,$$

where K_i includes all of the terms which will not change when trade is liberalized.

Trade liberalization amounts to moving to a larger economy, with an income of $Y + Y^* = 2Y$ and with an industry i labor force of $L_i + L_i^*$.

Let us define σ_i as the share of the first country in the ith industry's labor force:

$$(31) \qquad \sigma_i = L_i/(L_i + L_i^*).$$

Since Y and Y^* are assumed equal, σ_i can be regarded as an index of comparative advantage. We will be concerned with the case $\sigma_i \le \frac{1}{2}$; i.e., what happens to wages in the industry at a comparative disadvantage?

Using the definition of σ_i, the change in the wage rate in industry i can be written

$$(32) \qquad \Delta \ln w_i = (1 - \gamma)\ln 2 + \frac{\theta_i - \gamma}{\theta_i} \ln \sigma_i.$$

The first term is positive, the second of ambiguous sign. There are three relevant parameters: γ, which is common to all industries, and θ_i and σ_i, which are specific to industry i.

Both of the industry-specific parameters have economic interpretations. As just noted, σ_i is an index of comparative advantage; the lower is σ_i, the greater the disadvantage of domestic producers. And we have already noted that θ_i is an index of product differentiation: the lower is θ_i, the more value consumers place on diversity and the greater the monopoly power of firms.

The effect of these factors can be determined by noticing the following:

i) For $\theta_i \le \gamma$, i.e., a situation of highly differentiated products, $\Delta \ln w_i$ is always positive.

ii) For $\theta_i > \gamma$, $\Delta \ln w_i$ is increasing in σ_i and decreasing in θ_i.

iii) $\Delta \ln w_i = 0$ when $\theta_i = 1$, $\sigma_i = \frac{1}{2}$.

The implications of these points are shown in figure 7.1. On the axes are shown the industry characteristics of product differentiation and comparative advantage. In the relevant region, what we have shown is that we can draw a line dividing industries into two groups. In the lower right are industries with strong comparative advantage and weak product differentiation. In these industries the producers in the comparatively disadvantaged country stand to lose from liberalization. In the other group of industries—those with weak comparative advantage and strong product differentiation—producers in both countries gain from liberalization.

7.4 Conclusions

This paper has developed a simple multi-industry model of trade which is designed to give some insight into the reasons why trade is freer in some goods than others. While the model is dependent on many special assumptions, the two factors it points to seem intuitively plausible. The

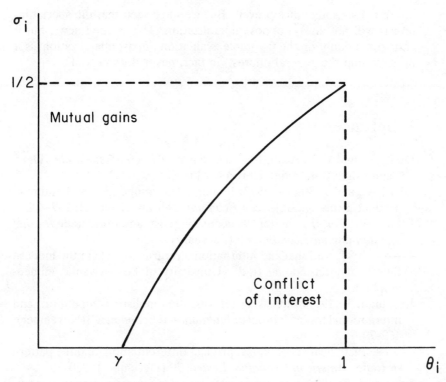

Fig. 7.1

analysis suggests that bilateral trade liberalization will be favored by producers in both countries if (i) neither country has a strong comparative advantage in the industry and (ii) the products of different firms within the industry are highly differentiated.

This analysis is very suggestive. In actual experience trade liberalization has typically taken place between countries with fairly similar economic structure; it has been biased toward industries in which comparative advantage has been weak, so that growth in trade is largely intraindustry in character; and it has been easier to liberalize trade in industries producing differentiated products than where firms' output is more homogeneous. This is casual, impressionistic evidence; but the theory does seem to accord in at least a rough way with experience.

The analysis has mixed implications for the political economy of trade, in that it suggests more optimism on the "economy" side than the "political" side. In the traditional view of trade, moves toward freer trade always involve a struggle between special interests which favor protection and the general interest, which is served by liberalization. According to this view, actual experiences of liberalization show that the general interest does sometimes prevail. But we have seen that the special interests will not always oppose liberalization. This is good news: but it casts some doubt on the favorable evaluation of past liberalization. Is it possible that the general interest, in fact, never does prevail?

References

Dixit, A., and V. Norman. 1980. *The theory of international trade: A text.* Cambridge: Cambridge University Press.
Dixit, A., and J. Stiglitz. 1977. Monopolistic competition and optimum product diversity. *American Economic Review* 67 (June): 297–308.
Ethier, W. 1979. Internationally decreasing costs and world trade *Journal of International Economics* 9 (February): 1–24.
———. 1980. National and international returns to scale in the modern theory of international trade. University of Pennsylvania, mimeographed.
Krugman, P. 1979. Increasing returns, monopolistic competition, and international trade. *Journal of International Economics* 9 (November): 469–79.
———. 1980. Scale economies, product differentiation, and the pattern of trade. *American Economic Review* 70 (December): 950–59.
Lancaster, K. 1980. Intraindustry trade under perfect monopolistic competition. *Journal of International Economics* 10 (May): 151–76.

Comment   Kelvin Lancaster

The model of product-differentiated trade presented by Paul Krugman, which is based on the Dixit-Stiglitz model of monopolistic competition,[1] represents a different approach from that developed in my own work,[2] and masks, I believe, the real problems associated with import competition when products are differentiated.

Differentiated models, like differentiated products, have characteristics in different proportions, and so do the Dixit-Stiglitz and Lancaster models. The important differences for the present purposes have been listed in table 7.1, and I believe the table saves a great deal of verbal explanation. Some of my criticisms of the Dixit-Stiglitz model are on

Kelvin Lancaster is the John Bates Clark Professor of Economics at Columbia University. He has made seminal contributions to economic theory, especially in second-best and product differentiation. His writings on international trade theory have also had a substantial impact.

record elsewhere,[3] and I am concerned here only with those features of the original model or with Krugman's extension which give what I consider to be an erroneous picture of import competition under product differentiation.

The feature of the Dixit-Stiglitz-Krugman model which differentiates it most from my own is the absence of any reference to the properties or characteristics (specification) of the products. All products, however similar to or different from other products of the same industry, are equal substitutes for all industry products. A consumer does not benefit because a new product is closer to what he or she would order on a custom basis (his preferred specification), but simply because there is a greater number of goods, all of which are purchased by every consumer. Firms do not need to agonize over the design of a new product: whatever the design, it is guaranteed a market with properties identical to those of the markets for all other goods in the industry. The simplicity of the Krugman model, which can derive some results much more expeditiously than mine, must be weighed against special predictions that do not generalize and some notable eccentricities.

Import Competition with Identical Countries

In both the Krugman and Lancaster models, identical countries can gain from trade of an intraindustry kind even though there are no comparative advantage or factor endowment differences between them, and the special features of trade in differentiated products can be seen most clearly in this case. Since the countries are identical, their economies will have the same structure in a no-trade situation, and, in particular, the number of goods in each product-differentiated industry will be the same in the two countries. In the Lancaster model, the same goods will be produced in both countries since the decisions as to specification will be made under identical circumstances. In the Krugman model, the goods need not be the same since there is no decision mechanism for determining specification, and the choice of goods to be produced can be considered as a random draw from a very large, even infinite, number of possibilities, except that no two firms in the same country will produce the same good.

If costless trade is now opened up between the two countries, both models agree that (1) there will be intraindustry trade in each product-differentiated industry, and (2) each good will be produced in one country only, half for domestic use and half for export.

The models differ considerably, however, in the predicted post-trade structure of the product-differentiated industries and in the nature of the gains from trade. In the Krugman model, the number of products depends only on the amount of the industry-specific factor so that the world industry will produce twice as many products as each country in isola-

Table C7.1   Comparison of Krugman and Lancaster Models of Product Differentiation

	Krugman	Lancaster
Nature of goods	Direct objects of utility	Possess properties or characteristics in certain, proportions (specification). Goods desired for their characteristics.
Individual consumers	Treat all goods symmetrically (within industry); purchase all goods	Each has "most preferred specification" for good in group, chooses single good on basis of both price and specification (will pay more for good closer to most preferred specification)
Consumer diversity	All consumers identical	No product variety within industry without diversity (e.g., automobiles). Extent of diversity determines degree of variety, given other conditions.
Welfare gain from product variety	Individual utility greater from $1/n$ units each of n goods than from $1/(n-1)$ units of $n-1$ goods (utility becomes infinite as $n \to \infty$)	Greater variety enables more consumers to have a good closer to most preferred specification. Variety raises average welfare level, but not necessarily that of every individual.

Elasticity of demand for single good	Fixed parameter of utility function. Independent of number of goods. Does not depend on events outside industry.	Depends on specification difference from close goods. (Approaches infinity as goods become more similar.) Increases with number of goods. Depends on interindustry relationships.
Production and cost properties	Fixed plus variable cost. System explodes (infinite utility) without fixed cost. Factors immobile between industries.*	Any form permissible. Custom production (infinite differentiation) if no economies of scale. Factors freely mobile.
Decisions faced by firms	Price/quantity and entry only	Specification of product as well as price/quantity and entry
Product variety at market equilibrium	Given system parameters, determined solely by supply of industry-specific factor. Independent of market size, output levels, or events outside industry.	Determined by size of market, diversity of preferences, cost structures, equilibria of other industries
Equilibrium output	Determined by utility and cost function parameters only. Independent of size of market, number of products, events outside industry.	Determined jointly with number of products; depends on same factors
Chief virtues	Simplicity	Realism and flexibility

*This is a special feature of the Krugman model, not part of the Dixit-Stiglitz analysis.

tion—that is, each country will produce the same number of products after trade as before. Furthermore, since equilibrium outputs are determined entirely by system parameters, the output of every good will be the same after trade as before. *There are no gains from economies of scale* as a result of trade. The gains are due to the fact that consumers now purchase twice as many different goods as before, although each in only half the pre-trade quantity, which increases welfare because of the assumed structure of the utility function.

In the Lancaster model, the equilibrium number of goods in the post-trade world market cannot be so easily determined, since the degree of product differentiation depends in a complex way on the size of the market and the structure of the cost functions. However, it can easily be shown that the number in this case must be less than twice the pre-trade number in each country, and the equilibrium output levels are always greater than in a single isolated country. Thus the Krugman outcome is impossible in the Lancaster model, in which gains from trade due to economies of scale will always occur. The extreme case in the Lancaster model occurs with production functions which are homogeneous of degree greater than unity (conventional increasing returns to scale without fixed costs), when the number of goods is independent of the size of the market and thus there will be the same number of goods after trade as before, so the number produced in each country is halved and the output of each good approximately doubled.[4]

The differences between the two models as to the predicted structural changes in the differentiated-goods industries lead to crucial differences concerning the assessment of the effects of import competition and the associated political economy.

The Krugman model depicts a very smooth transition from pre- to post-trade conditions. The world industry will consist of the same number of firms, each producing the same level of output, as in the two countries together before trade. The worst that can happen to a firm as a result of trade is that, by chance, the independent random choice of products in the two countries should have resulted in a firm in the other country producing the same product, in which case either or both firms can costlessly switch to a different product with no loss. The incomes of the industry-specific factors are unchanged by trade in the identical country case, so both the entrepreneurs and the factor owners are neutral as between trade and no trade. The gains from trade are all consumption gains (variety), so the consumers' vote in favor of trade would be unopposed.

The Lancaster model predicts a very different situation, in which some firms in each country must leave the industry. In the homogeneous production function case, the opening of trade will lead to a direct one-on-one clash between every producer in one country and his counterpart in the other, since there will be only one producer of each good at the final equilibrium. Half the firms in each country should close down, but which ones? If the economies are truly identical, there is no obvious mechanism (or even a convenient hidden hand) for choosing the particular firms,[5] a situation that could result in *all* firms in *both* countries feeling simultaneously threatened, so that there might be industry-wide lobbying against imports in both countries. On the other hand, the firms that survive will be better off than before (they will have greatly increased outputs), so if firms differ in their perceptions of their own powers to compete, there may be firms that perceive the opening of trade as an export opportunity rather than as import competition, and thus favor it.

The homogeneous production function case presents the head-on clash in its most extreme form. In the more general case, the world equilibrium will call for fewer firms than in the two countries before trade so that firms must close down in both countries, but not as many as half. On the other hand, the new equilibrium will require a different set of products, so that even the firms that remain will have to change the specifications of their products to a greater or lesser degree. The search for the appropriate new products provides a potential selection mechanism for determining which firms survive—those that choose the right specifications. This process means that all firms must adapt and none can hope to survive merely by continuing as before and hoping its opposite number will go under. The one-on-one element is removed, with less potential for universal opposition to trade.

Consumer gains from trade in the Lancaster model are more tangible than in the Krugman model, since in the former they include the effect of economies of scale as evidenced in lower prices for the traded goods, and this presumably makes the case for trade rather easier to argue. On the other hand, a particular individual may actually lose from trade under the Lancaster conditions, since the post-trade world equilibrium may not produce some product very close to his preferred specification, even though this had been produced in the pre-trade situation. Such a loss may not be counterbalanced by the lowered price of whatever product is now closest to his personal preference. There will, however, be more consumers for whom the reverse is true, since the greater variety will enable more consumers to have goods very close to their preferred specification than in the pre-trade situation.

Comparative Advantage

Comparative advantage is not required to explain the existence of a large volume of trade in a world economy in which product-differentiated industries are of major importance, but comparative advantage effects may exist along with those effects (scale economies in Lancaster, variety in Krugman) which generate intraindustry trade in its absence.

I have discussed several aspects of comparative advantage within the Lancaster framework elsewhere,[6] primarily in the context of a product-differentiated sector (manufacturing) and a nondifferentiated sector (agriculture). The broad features are simple enough: for a sufficiently large comparative advantage difference, specialization will occur with exchange of one industry's products for those of another, as in traditional trade theory. For a lesser difference in comparative advantage there will be intraindustry trade, but the country with the comparative advantage in the industry will produce a larger number of the products than the country with the comparative disadvantage. Each good will be produced in only one country but sold in both, the country having the comparative advantage in a particular industry running a surplus on the intraindustry trade which is offset against industries in which it has the comparative disadvantage.

Commencing from a no-trade situation, the opening of trade will necessarily result in a shrinking of the industry with the comparative disadvantage, a shrinking that will be more severe than in the identical country case. If the comparative disadvantage is great enough, the whole industry will close, but in general it will remain with a small number of firms. The output of the firms that remain will, however, expand, and these firms will thrive even though the industry has declined. Since factors are mobile in the Lancaster model, labor and capital will move out to the country's expanding industries (although capital might migrate to the same industry in the other country) and interindustry effects will be much the same as in the traditional analysis. The important difference in the political economy of the situation between the product-differentiated and homogeneous cases is that the surviving firms will be better off after trade in the former case, and thus firms that believe they will survive may favor trade liberalization even though they are in the disadvantaged industry.

A special form of comparative advantage may exist in the Lancaster framework due to differences in the distribution of consumer preferences between the two countries. Suppose the home country's preferences are distributed in such a way that a majority prefer large cars to small, while the preferences in the foreign country are distributed in the opposite direction. If the countries are otherwise similar, the home country will produce more models of large cars, and those in larger quantities, than the foreign country. In terms of design experience, output capacity, and unit cost, the home country will have a comparative advantage in large cars, the foreign country in small. This is an intraindustry comparative advantage that makes it relatively clear which firms in each country's automobile industry are likely to gain from trade, and which to lose.[7]

Comparative advantage in the Krugman model has very special features. Since factors are immobile between industries, specialization can never occur—indeed, the number of firms in each industry and the outputs of each firm remain the same before and after trade, with or without comparative advantage effects. The only effect of trade on the industry itself is its effect on the wages (really rent) of the industry-specific factors. Krugman defines comparative advantage as having a higher-than-average proportion of the industry-specific factor. In the normal case, trade makes the specific factor relatively less scarce in the world economy than it was beforehand in the country with the comparative disadvantage, so the rent falls relatively, while it rises in an industry with a comparative advantage. Owners of the specific factor gain in the advantaged industry and lose in the disadvantaged one. However, the fall in rent in the disadvantaged industry may be more than offset by the gain in utility per dollar due to the increased product variety with trade, so the factors in the disadvantaged industry may still gain in welfare. This gain requires the offset of two effects, and will only occur if the comparative advantage difference is relatively small. Krugman also introduces a perverse case (having the strange property that goods outside the industry are better substitutes for goods in the industry than are other goods asserted to be in the same industry) in which rent rises in the "disadvantaged" industry (which can actually be shown to have the advantage in terms of pre-trade prices). In this case, however, rent falls in the other industry. In either case, the results are similar to those of the Stolper-Samuelson analysis in that one factor makes an unambiguous welfare gain while the other makes a welfare gain only if the factor proportions are relatively similar between the countries. Krugman is incorrect in arguing that all industries may favor trade liberalization over a wide range of configurations—on the basis of his own model this can only occur when the economies are relatively similar, and even then one industry's gains will be intangible, due entirely to greater variety.

The Political Economy of Import Competition

In a product-differentiated industry, import competition is also export opportunity, unless comparative advantage effects are so great as to lead to industry specialization.[8] Thus there is a potential conflict of interest within the industry between those firms which fear to be put out of business by trade liberalization and those that expect to survive and expand their output, a quite different situation from that of the homogeneous product industry in which all firms will gain or all will lose.

Since the opening of trade for a differentiated product industry will lead to major changes within the industry—some firms vanishing, others expanding, all searching for the product designs appropriate to the world market—the political pressures in the industry for and against trade liberalization will depend on the distribution of expectations and approaches to risk over the firms. If all firms are cautious risk averters, it is possible that all firms in both countries may oppose trade—even the firms in the country with the comparative advantage in the industry. At the other extreme, all firms (even those in the disadvantaged country) may favor trade if they are all optimistic risk takers. It seems reasonable to expect, however, that the net pressures will be in favor of trade in the advantaged country and against in the disadvantaged, on average. In the identical country case, the balance is unclear.

A special feature of the political economy of differentiated products is the likely pressure for highly specific trade barriers—special tariffs on industry products with specifications lying between narrow limits, those of the products already produced by the home industry.

If the industry is composed of multiproduct firms instead of the single-product firms assumed in the analysis, the views of individual firms will depend on their mix of products as well as their expectations, but the potential for divergent views about trade liberalization is still there.

Notes

1. Dixit and Stiglitz (1977).
2. Lancaster (1979, 1980b).
3. Lancaster (1980c).
4. The world market equilibrium outputs may be more or less than twice the pre-trade level in each country, depending on the elasticity of substitution with respect to goods outside the industry, the shape of the cost function, and other factors.
5. But the balance of payments mechanism, if stable, will ensure that neither country produces more than half the total number of products. See Lancaster (1980a).
6. Lancaster (1980a).
7. An application of this reasoning to the United States automobile market at the present time should also take account of a general shift in preferences toward small cars due to increased gasoline prices, an effect easily analyzed in terms of characteristics. In addition, it should be noted that the analysis is based on monopolistic competition (single-product firms), rather than the multiproduct oligopolies which characterize the international automobile industry. It should be noted that the United States automobile industry needs to (and is attempting to) change its product mix. Tariffs on small car imports would not help, but would probably hinder, this required structural change.
8. The comments in this section are based on the use of the Lancaster model only.

References

Dixit, A., and J. Stiglitz. 1977. Monopolistic competition and optimum product diversity. *American Economic Review* 67: 297–308.

Lancaster, K. 1979. *Variety, equity, and efficiency*. New York: Columbia University Press; Oxford: Basil Blackwell.

———. 1980a. Intra-industry trade under perfect monopolistic competition. *Journal of International Economics* 10 (1980): 151–75.

———. 1980b. Competition and product variety. *Journal of Business* 53 (1980): S79–S104.

———. 1980c. Pettengill versus Dixit-Stiglitz: A third party intervention. The Economics Workshops, Columbia University, Paper no. 54, April.

Comment   Michael Mussa

Paul Krugman has provided us with a stimulating paper that argues pursuasively for the virtues of a nontraditional model of international trade that assumes increasing rather than constant returns to scale, that postulates monopolistic rather than perfect competition, and that focuses on the opportunities for consuming a greater diversity of commodities as a key benefit of international trade. I believe that the benefits of diversity are particularly important in economic theory, and that Paul Krugman's paper is especially valuable because it provides us with an alternative analytical framework that adds a new perspective to our understanding of many important issues in international economics. My task as a critic, however, is not to praise Caesar, but rather to suggest some possible limitations and deficiencies of his new imperial designs. Accordingly, I would like to emphasize three main reasons why we need to take very seriously Paul's own caution that his model is "dependent on a number of very special assumptions."

First, while the specification of productive technology implies that there are increasing returns to scale in producing each individual commodity, the profit-maximizing decisions of firms, under the assumption of monopolist competition, always lead to a constant level of production of each commodity. The opening of trade between countries therefore does not yield any benefits from a reduction in costs associated with an increase in the scale of production of individual commodities. Thus in Krugman's model we do not observe the important principle enunciated by Adam Smith that society benefits from the efficiencies generated by a more refined division of labor, made possible by broadening the extent of the market.

Second, Krugman's model has peculiar properties with respect to the degree of competition among firms in the same industry. As the number of firms in an industry grows, the cross-price elasticity of demand between the differentiated products of these firms tends to zero; that is, a change in the price of one firm's product has virtually no effect on the demands for the products of other firms in the same industry. Moreover, the own-price elasticity of demand for a firm's product converges to a constant, $\varepsilon_i = 1/(1 - \theta_i)$, that depends only on the parameters of the utility function. These properties of Krugman's model run counter to our normal intuition that, as the number of firms in an industry producing differentiated products grows, their products will tend to become closer and closer substitutes, the cross-price elasticities of demand will become large, and the monopoly power of any individual firm (measured by the

Michael Mussa is the William H. Abbott Professor of International Business at the University of Chicago and a research associate of the National Bureau of Economic Research. He has published extensively on the theory of international trade, international finance, and monetary economics.

inverse of the own-price elasticity of demand for its product) will become small. Because Krugman's model lacks these intuitively appealing properties, I question its relevance to the key question of the benefits of international trade in enforcing more competitive behavior in industries where increasing returns to scale limit the number of firms that may efficiently operate within any national economy. This question is of vital importance in discussions of antitrust policy for a number of industries in the United States and presumably in other countries.

Third, in my judgment Krugman's explanation of intraindustry and interindustry trade relies too strongly on unrealistic implications of his theoretical model. Under free trade, consumers in each country divide their expenditure equally among the products of all individual firms in a given industry. The ratio of foreign sales to domestic sales for any individual firm is equal to the ratio of foreign income to domestic income. Hence all firms in a given country, regardless of industry, are equally engaged in international trade, in the sense that all individual firms have the same ratio of foreign sales to domestic sales. This is a very strong and (I believe) unrealistic implication of Krugman's model. It leads directly to Krugman's conclusions concerning intraindustry trade. Specifically, for two countries of equal size (income), each individual firm in both countries always exports exactly half of its output. If the two countries have the same endowments of factors specific to the various industries and hence the same number of firms in each industry, then all trade will be "intraindustry" in the sense that trade will balance industry by industry. To the extent that endowments of specific factors are not the same between the two countries, there will be "interindustry" trade in the sense that trade will not be balanced on an industry by industry basis. My concern is that to reach these conclusions it should not be necessary to use a model with the unrealistic implication that all firms within a given country are equally engaged in trade.

Comment   John S. Chipman

I would like to draw attention to a seemingly innocent assumption contained in Krugman's specification (4) of the production relations in his model. The condition that "the parameters α_i and β_i are assumed constant across the products within an industry" is not invariant with respect to changes in the units of measurement; this has consequences that

John S. Chipman is Regents' Professor of Economics, University of Minnesota. He is the author of "A Survey of the Theory of International Trade" (*Econometrica*, 1965–66) and of numerous other papers in international trade theory, welfare economics, and econometrics.

somewhat impair the credibility of the model, as I shall show by means of a simple illustration.

Suppose that a technological change occurs in the production of commodity j' in industry i', so that for $ij = i'j'$ we have, henceforth,

(4') $\ell_{i'j'} = \alpha_{i'} + \beta_{i'j'} q_{i'j'}$ where $\beta_{i'j'} < \beta_{i'}$ (say),

the relations (4) remaining valid for $ij \neq i'j'$. In order to handle such a situation one would have to change the units of measurement of this commodity and replace the term $q_{i'j'}$ (the output of the j'^{th} product of industry i') by

(4'') $q'_{i'j'} = \dfrac{\beta_{i'j'}}{\beta_{i'}} q_{i'j'}$,

so that in terms of the new units of measurement

(4''') $\ell_{i'j'} = \alpha_{i'} + \beta_{i'} q'_{i'j'}$.

Krugman's relations (4) thus remain formally valid with (4) replaced by (4''') for $ij = i'j'$.

However, for the model to remain consistent, one obviously would have to make the same change in units of measurement on the consumption side. Specifically, in Krugman's equation (2) one would have to replace the term $c_{i'j'}$ (an individual's consumption of the j'^{th} product of industry i') by

(2'') $c'_{i'j'} = \dfrac{\beta_{i'j'}}{\beta_{i'}} c_{i'j'}$,

resulting in

(2''') $C_{i'} = \left[\displaystyle\sum_{\substack{j=1 \\ j \neq j'}}^{N_{i'}} c_{i'j'}^{\theta_{i'}} + \dfrac{\beta_{i'}}{\beta_{i'j'}} c'^{\theta_{i'}}_{i'j'} \right]^{1/\theta_{i'}}$.

This term must replace the previous expression for $C_{i'}$ in the utility function (1).

In short, for the model to remain consistent it must be assumed that preferences are tied to the technology; a technological change must be accompanied by an exactly offsetting change in consumer preferences.

This is no accident. It has been well known since Marschak's classic discussion of the overdeterminacy of equilibrium under imperfect competition (Marschak 1950, pp. 92–93) that if all agents perceive the technology and the market demand functions as they actually are, the system of equations describing market equilibrium is overdetermined. One solution is then to introduce some manifestly artificial conditions that will guarantee functional dependence as between preferences and the technology. This is the solution adopted by Krugman.

Fifteen years ago (Chipman 1965, pp. 736–49) I sketched an argument outlining an alternative approach, and five years later (Chipman 1970) I carried it out precisely in the context of a model not unlike Krugman's in which labor was the sole factor of production. The key to overcoming the overdeterminacy is to assume that individual producers *perceive* their production processes to operate under constant returns to scale, even if they do not. This is strictly analogous to the assumption adopted in the perfectly competitive model that each individual *perceives* that he has no influence on the market price (whereas such a perception is obviously false, since the aggregate of all individuals would then also have no influence on the market price). Similarly, one can in the case of monopolistic competition assume that each firm *perceives* the demand curve for its product to be linear, say, and such as to pass through the equilibrium point with a slope equal to the slope of the true demand curve at that point. Such an approach was introduced by Negishi (1941) and has been carried out successfully by Silvestre (1977). The idea has recently been applied to international trade theory by Inoue (1981). It is an obvious generalization of the idealization used in the perfectly competitive model.

The above is certainly not the only viable alternative approach. Another is to follow the lead of Aumann (1964) in postulating the existence of a continuum of agents, each being identified, say, with a point on the unit interval [0,1]. In the Walrasian general-equilibrium framework, Zeno's paradox that the whole cannot exceed the sum of its parts is resolved by virtue of the fact that no one of the infinitesimal agents has any influence on the price, whereas any open interval of agents does; any single agent has measure zero. The same idea can be carried over to the theory of product differentiation and increasing returns to scale, as has indeed been done recently by Helpman (1981).

With either one of these approaches one can avoid the artificial functional dependence between technology and tastes that Krugman's formulation necessarily entails.

References

Aumann, R. J. 1964. Markets with a continuum of traders. *Econometrica* 32 (January–April): 39–50.
Chipman, J. S. 1965. A survey of the theory of international trade: Part 2, the neo-classical theory. *Econometrica* 33 (October): 685–760.
———. 1970. External economies of scale and competitive equilibrium. *Quarterly Journal of Economics* 84 (August): 347–85.
Helpman, E. 1981. International trade in the presence of product differentiation, economies of scale, and monopolistic competition. *Journal of International Economics* 11 (August): 305–40.

Inoue, T. 1981. A generalization of the Samuelson reciprocity relation, the Stolper-Samuelson theorem, and the Rybczynski theorem under variable returns to scale. *Journal of International Economics* 11 (February): 79–98.

Marschak, J. 1950. The rationale of the demand for money and of "money illusion." *Metroeconomica* 2 (August): 71–100.

Negishi, T. 1941. Monopolistic competition and general equilibrium. *Review of Economic Studies* 28 (June): 194–201.

Silvestre, J. 1977. General monopolistic equilibrium under non-convexities. *International Economic Review* 18 (June): 425–34.

8　Endogenous Tariffs, the Political Economy of Trade Restrictions, and Welfare

Ronald Findlay and Stanislaw Wellisz

Evaluation of the welfare cost of trade restrictions has long been a major concern of economics and public policy. The founding fathers, both of our discipline and of our republic, were much concerned with this issue. Adam Smith complained that the deliberations of the legislature on these matters were directed by the "clamorous importunity of partial interests" rather than by "an extensive view of the general good," while James Madison in his famous tenth *Federalist* paper on the dangers of "faction" observed that "shall domestic manufacturers be encouraged, and in what degree, by restrictions on foreign manufacture, are questions which would be differently decided by the landed and manufacturing classes, and probably by neither with a sole regard to justice and the public good."

In the technical literature of applied welfare economics as represented by Harberger (1959) and Johnson (1960), for example, the welfare costs of exogenously given tariffs and quotas (or any taxes, subsidies, and quantitative restrictions) are assessed, in the tradition of Dupuit and Marshall, by calculating the areas of the "little triangles" of consumers' and producers' surplus lying beneath the demand and supply curves for the commodities on which these restrictions are placed. In this conventional theory of the cost of protection the increased rents to factors

Ronald Findlay, the Ragnar Nurkse Professor of Economics at Columbia University, is a leading international trade theorist. His work also embraces developmental and general theory. Stanislaw Wellisz is professor of economics at Columbia University. He has made contributions to developmental theory, the theory of organization of the firm, and international economics (jointly with Findlay). His publications include *The Economics of the Soviet Bloc* (New York: McGraw-Hill).

The authors acknowledge helpful comments and suggestions made by Jagdish N. Bhagwati, Richard A. Brecher, J. Peter Neary, and Alasdair Smith.

engaged in the protected industry are regarded as transfers to them from consumers or factors employed elsewhere in the economy, and are therefore not considered as constituting a cost to society as a whole.

Tullock (1967), however, rightly argues that various interest groups in the society would actively seek to promote the generation of these rents arising from the imposition of tariffs while others whose interests are adversely affected would seek to prevent them. Both sides would absorb scarce resources in the conflict over the extent and structure of trade restrictions, and the social value of these resources should be considered in addition to the conventional deadweight loss in arriving at estimates of the total welfare cost. Tullock illustrates his point by means of an extended analogy with theft, for which expenditures on safes and locks by the potential victim, and on nitroglycerine and oxyacetylene torches by the thieves constitute the social costs of the process of transferring incomes from the pockets of the law-abiding citizens to those of the criminals.[1]

Our purpose in this paper is to incorporate Tullock's valuable insight into the formal analysis of the welfare costs of a tariff. The tariff level will be determined endogenously in a general equilibrium model extended in the simplest possible way to incorporate the process of tariff formation emerging from the clash of opposing interest groups. The level of the tariff, the lobbying expenditures on "tariff seeking" and opposition thereto by the interest groups, and the associated deadweight losses will all be determined simultaneously within the same model. The analysis of this paper could be readily adapted to the topic of this conference, namely, the response to import competition, by having import competition initially trigger off tariff-seeking lobbying by the specific factor in the importable activity; this, in turn, would be opposed by the lobbying of the other specific factor in the model.

The general equilibrium structure employed will be that of the "specific factors" model used by Haberler, Ohlin, and Viner in their classic studies and recently revived by Jones (1971) and others. Two goods, "food" and "manufactures," are produced, with "land" specific to food and "capital" specific to manufactures. There is a constant returns to scale production function for each good, with the specific factor and labor as the arguments. Labor is homogeneous and freely transferable from one sector to the other. The international terms of trade are taken as given, and there is perfect competition in all factor and commodity markets. The supply of labor and of both specific factors is fixed.

In the absence of trade the relative price of food and manufactures will be determined by domestic demand conditions. With given factor supplies and technology, the rentals per unit of land and capital, equal to the marginal products of these specific factors in their respective sectors, can be determined as functions of the relative price of the two goods. If the given international terms of trade are such that the country has a comparative advantage in manufactures then the rental per unit of capital, and hence the total rents accruing to this specific factor, will fall as a result of trade while the rental per unit of land and the total rents of the landowning class will rise in terms of food and fall in terms of manufactures as labor is transferred from the former to the latter sector in response to the opportunity to engage in trade.

Suppose that both the landed and manufacturing interests are organized into Madisonian "factions" or pressure groups capable of influencing the political process with labor being purely passive. The landed interest would try to introduce a tariff on food at a prohibitive level if they could get away with it, whereas the manufacturing interest would try to preserve free trade. Depending upon the relative strengths and commitments of the two sides it is plausible to think that some tariff between zero and the prohibitive level will emerge. The social value of the resources used up by both sides in this struggle would constitute a welfare cost over and above the familiar deadweight loss associated with whatever tariff level emerges from the political process.

The following notation will be used in constructing the formal model:

F,M = outputs of food and manufactures,

T,K,L = fixed supplies of land, capital, and labor,

L_F, L_M = labor allocated to food and manufactures,

L_T, L_K = labor used in the political process by the landowning and capitalist interest groups,

π = fixed international price of food in terms of manufactures,

t = rate of tariff on imports of food,

p = domestic price of food in terms of manufactures,

w = real wages of labor in terms of manufactures,

q = rental per unit of capital in terms of manufactures,

r = rental per unit of land in terms of food.

The structure of the model is easily specified. Production functions for the two goods are

(1) $$F = F(L_F, T),$$

(2) $$M = M(L_M, K),$$

with constant returns to scale, positive first derivatives with respect to all arguments, and diminishing returns to labor in each case. The marginal product of each specific factor is an increasing function of the associated labor input.

Profit maximization and perfect competition result in

(3) $$p \frac{\partial F}{\partial L_F} = w,$$

(4) $$\frac{\partial M}{\partial L_M} = w,$$

(5) $$\frac{\partial F}{\partial T} = r,$$

(6) $$\frac{\partial M}{\partial K} = q,$$

The domestic price ratio p is connected to the given international terms of trade π by the relation

(7) $$p = (1 + t)\pi$$

where the tariff rate t is an *endogenous* variable to be determined by the operation of the political process as influenced by the pressure groups representing the landed and manufacturing interests.

Brock and Magee (1978) summarizes their own pioneering research on the political economy of tariffs, reported in a series of working papers. They apply sophisticated game-theoretic mathematical approaches to modeling the behavior of voters, parties, and lobbies in electoral processes that determine tariff levels. For our present purposes a much simpler formulation of the political process that can perhaps be considered as a "reduced form" of the Brock-Magee framework is possible.

Taking political institutions and attitudes in the country as given, we assume that a tariff level is determined as a stable function of the resources committed to the political process by each of the two interest groups. For convenience let labor be the sole input used by both sides in their political activities. This leads to the hypothesis that

(8) $$t = t(L_T, L_K),$$

which states that a determinate tariff results once the input of each interest group is specified. It is clearly reasonable to suppose that

$$\frac{\partial t}{\partial L_T} > 0, \quad \frac{\partial t}{\partial L_K} < 0,$$

$$\frac{\partial^2 t}{\partial L_T^2} < 0, \quad \frac{\partial^2 t}{\partial L_K^2} > 0,$$

implying that there are "diminishing returns" to both groups from participation in political activity. The positive increments in the tariff level resulting from successive unit increments in the input of the protariff group get smaller and smaller while the reductions attainable by the antitariff group also get smaller and smaller in absolute value. No compelling argument can be found, at the present level of generality, for attaching any restrictions on the sign of the cross-derivative. It is assumed that both L_T and L_K receive the going wage w.

Equilibrium in the labor market requires

$$(9) \qquad L_F + L_M + L_T + L_K = L.$$

To the extent that they are successful the activities of the pressure groups constitute voluntary public goods for the individual landowners and capitalists. The "free rider" problem pointed out by Olson (1965) in this context is assumed to be solved somehow, so that we leave aside the internal organization of the groups, each of which is treated as a single "rational" agent that seeks to maximize its "class" interest in the political process. It should be apparent, however, that this collective action by landowners and capitalists only takes place in the "political" sphere, atomistic competition being the rule in the "economic" sphere of the production of food and manufactures and the distribution of the income arising therefrom. The two spheres are, however, obviously linked into a single interdependent system by virtue of the endogenous nature of the tariff.

Before considering the explicit determination of L_T and L_K, it will be helpful to note some properties of the model that follow if L_T and L_K are taken as given. From (8) the value of t is determined and hence of p from (7). Defining the labor available for production as

$$(10) \qquad L_A = L - (L_T + L_K),$$

it follows readily from the structure of the model that $F, M, \underline{r}, \underline{q}$, and $\underline{w}$ are each determined as functions of p and L_A alone with the properties

$$(11) \qquad \frac{\partial F}{\partial p} > 0, \quad \frac{\partial F}{\partial L_A} > 0,$$

$$(12) \qquad \frac{\partial M}{\partial p} < 0, \quad \frac{\partial M}{\partial L_A} > 0,$$

$$(13) \qquad \frac{\partial r}{\partial p} > 0, \quad \frac{\partial r}{\partial L_A} > 0,$$

$$(14) \qquad \frac{\partial q}{\partial p} < 0, \quad \frac{\partial q}{\partial L_A} > 0,$$

$$(15) \qquad \frac{\partial w}{\partial p} > 0, \quad \frac{\partial w}{\partial L_A} < 0.$$

Assuming that there would be free trade in the absence of any political pressure by the landed interest and that the political activities of the manufacturers are purely defensive in nature, the income of the landowners in terms of manufactures when L_T equals zero would be $\pi r(\pi, L) T$. The net benefit from engaging in the political process to the landowning class is therefore

$$N_T = p(L_T, L_K) \mathrm{r}[p(L_T, L_K), (L - L_T - L_K)] T$$

(16) $$- \pi r(\pi, L) T - w[p(L_T, L_K), (L - L_T - L_K)] L_T$$

in which L_K is taken as a parameter. Note that the second term is independent of both L_T and L_K and is therefore a constant determined by the given values of π, L, and T. The dependence of $\underline{p}$ on L_T and L_K follows from (7) and (8). The first-order condition for maximizing N_T with respect to L_T is

(17)
$$\left[(1 + \frac{p}{r} \frac{\partial r}{\partial p}) \frac{LT}{p} \frac{\partial p}{\partial L_T} + \frac{LT}{r} \frac{\partial r}{\partial L_T} \right] \frac{prT}{L_T}$$

$$= \left[1 + \frac{L_T}{w} \frac{\partial w}{\partial L_T} + \frac{p}{w} \frac{\partial w}{\partial p} \frac{L_T}{p} \frac{\partial p}{\partial L_T} \right] w,$$

which states, in elasticity form, that the marginal contribution of L_T in raising land rents prT should be equal to the marginal cost of L_T. Notice that an increase in L_T has three separate effects on the income from land. It increases $\underline{p}$, which induces an increase in $\underline{r}$, both of which raise the income of landowners, but an increase in L_T does reduce $\underline{r}$ at constant $\underline{p}$, which works in the opposite direction. It is assumed that the negative effect is small relative to the positive effects so that the sign of the entire term in parentheses on the LHS of (17) is positive. This condition is quite plausible and is indeed necessary for any expenditure on lobbying to be effective at all. The marginal cost of L_T is greater than $\underline{w}$ since

$$\frac{L_T}{w} \frac{\partial w}{\partial L_T} \text{ and } \frac{p}{w} \frac{\partial w}{\partial p} \cdot \frac{L_T}{p} \frac{\partial p}{\partial L_T}$$

in the coefficient of $\underline{w}$ on the RHS of (17) are both positive.

If t denotes the optimal tariff (possibly prohibitive) obtainable by the landed interest in the absence of any defensive measures by the manufacturing interest, $\hat{L}_T$ the amount of labor used by the landed interest to achieve this, and $\hat{q}$ the resulting rental per unit of capital, then the net benefit to the manufacturers of entering the political process to protect their incomes would be

$$N_K = q[p(L_T, L_K), (L - L_T - L_K)] K$$

$$- \hat{q}[\pi(1 + \hat{t}), (1 - \hat{L}_T)] K$$

(18) $$- w[p(L_T, L_K), (L - L_T - L_K)] L_K,$$

in which the second term is a constant independent of L_K. Maximizing N_K with respect to L_K, treating L_T as a parameter, requires

(19)
$$\left[\frac{p}{q}\frac{\partial q}{\partial p} \cdot \frac{L_K}{p}\frac{\partial p}{\partial L_K} + \frac{L_K}{q}\frac{\partial q}{\partial L_K} \right]\frac{qK}{L_K}$$

$$= \left[1 + \frac{L_K}{w}\frac{\partial w}{\partial L_K} + \frac{p}{w}\frac{\partial w}{\partial p}\frac{L_K}{p}\frac{\partial p}{\partial L_K} \right] w,$$

which states that the marginal return from employing L_K amount of labor to raise the income from capital should be equal to its marginal cost. The first term in the coefficient of the LHS is the product of two negative terms and therefore positive, while the second term is negative. It is again natural to suppose that the coefficient is on balance positive, making it worthwhile for the manufacturing interest to adopt defensive lobbying activities.

Given L_K the optimum L_T for the landed interest is determined by (17), while given L_T the optimum L_K for the manufacturing interest is determined by (19). The "reaction functions" showing the optimal response by each group given the action of the other can be obtained by total differentiation of the first-order conditions (17) and (19). These can be expressed as

(20)
$$\frac{dL_T}{dL_K} = - \frac{\dfrac{\partial^2 N_T}{\partial L_K \partial L_T}}{\dfrac{\partial^2 N_T}{\partial L_T^2}},$$

(21)
$$\frac{dL_K}{dL_T} = - \frac{\dfrac{\partial^2 N_K}{\partial L_T \partial L_K}}{\dfrac{\partial^2 N_K}{\partial L_K^2}}.$$

The denominators of (20) and (21) have to be negative to fulfill the second-order conditions for maximization of N_T and N_K so that the slope of each reaction function depends upon the sign of the corresponding cross-partial in the numerator. Unfortunately, however, each of these cross-partials is the sum of a long succession of individual terms of conflicting or indeterminate signs. We therefore simply assume that, whatever their slope, the reaction functions have a unique and "stable" intersection defining a Cournot-Nash equilibrium in the "political" sphere with L_T^* and L_K^* as the optimal inputs for each group consistently with the actions of the other. The equilibrium net benefits from engaging in the political process, N_T^* and N_K^*, can be determined from (16) and (18). It is assumed that both are nonnegative; i.e., it is worthwhile for each group to engage in the political process. The value of t^* and all the other eight variables of the system can be determined by equations (1) to (9) after L_T^* and L_K^* are known. We have thus depicted the general equilibrium of an economy with an endogenous tariff level.

The welfare cost of the endogenous tariff t^* is depicted in figure 8.1. The transformation curve TT corresponds to the situation in which the entire labor force L is used for productive activity. The free trade levels of production and consumption are determined by the points $\underline{a}$ and $\underline{c}$ where the slopes of TT and the maximum attainable indifference curve are equal to the given world price ratio π. If a tariff of level t^* were to be imposed *exogenously*, the standard analysis indicates that the production point would move to $\underline{b}$ on TT, where the slope is equal to $p^* = (1 + t^*)\pi$, and the consumption point to $\underline{e}$, where the slope of the indifference curve is also equal to p^*. The terms of trade remain unchanged at π. We make here the usual assumption that the entire proceeds of the tariff revenue are returned directly to the private sector. The welfare cost of the tariff is therefore measured in principle by the difference in utility levels between $\underline{c}$ and $\underline{e}$.

When the tariff level t^* is endogenously determined by a resource-using political process, however, the transformation curve TT is shifted inward to $T'T'$, since the labor force available for production is now reduced by $(L_T^* + L_K^*)$. The production point is at $\underline{b}'$ on $T'T'$, where the slope is equal to p^*. The reduction in the available labor force reduces the outputs of *both* goods at constant prices, by virtue of (11) and (12), in the context of the "specific factors" model that we are using. If we continue to assume that the tariff revenue is returned directly to the private sector, the consumption point will shift to $\underline{e}'$, with $\underline{e}$ and $\underline{e}'$ both lying on the Engel curve corresponding to relative price p^*. It is therefore apparent that the welfare cost of an endogenous tariff is higher than that of an independently given tariff of the same rate.

At this point it would be of some interest to compare the result just obtained with those of Bhagwati and Srinivasan (1979). In their model the tariff rate is set exogenously, as in the standard analysis. However, instead of assuming that the tariff revenue is distributed to the population according to some independently specified rule, they postulate a "revenue-seeking" activity that uses scarce resources to influence the allocation of the tariff revenue. The activity is also assumed to operate under competitive conditions so that in the final equilibrium position a dollar's worth of resources is used up for every dollar of revenue that the given tariff rate generates. The analysis is conducted in terms of the two-by-two Heckscher-Ohlin-Samuelson model with the "revenue-seeking" activity incorporated into it. The world price ratio is assumed to be given, just as in the present model.

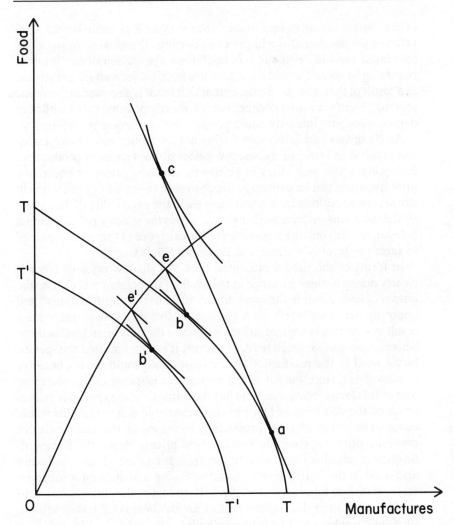

Fig. 8.1

An apparently paradoxical result that the authors obtain is that welfare can be *higher* in the presence of "revenue seeking" than it would be in the case of the conventional calculation of the welfare loss from an exogenously given tariff. As they note, the key to the paradox is the Johnson (1967) demonstration that capital accumulation in the presence of a tariff on the capital-intensive good can reduce welfare, since it is possible for the value of production at world prices to decline even though it of course goes up at the tariff-inclusive domestic price ratio. The key to Johnson's result in turn is the Rybczynski theorem, since the extra capital reduces the output of the labor-intensive exportable while increasing the output of the capital-intensive importable, thus making it possible for the total value of production at world prices to decline. If capital were to be the sole input used in "revenue seeking," then application of the Johnson reasoning in reverse would show how it is possible for welfare to increase as a result of that activity. To the extent that labor is also used in "revenue seeking," welfare would decline, but it is clearly possible that a sufficient degree of capital intensity could produce a net increase in welfare.

As Bhagwati and Srinivasan (1979) note, another way of expressing this result is in terms of the shadow prices of the factors of production. Following Little and Mirrlees (1969) the shadow prices of nontraded primary inputs can be defined as the change in the value of production at world prices resulting from a unit increase in the availability of the input.[2] When the Johnson "immiserizing" case arises the shadow price of capital is negative, thus making it possible for the existence of "revenue seeking" to raise the level of welfare á la Bhagwati-Srinivasan.

In terms of the model presented here the shadow price of labor is clearly positive, since a change in the availability of labor will change the output of *both* goods in the same direction. Thus the "tariff-seeking" and opposing activities involved in generating the endogenous tariff must result in a decline in welfare so long as labor is the only input used in those activities, as was assumed here. However, it is apparent that the specific factor used in the production of the importable could have a negative shadow price, since output of the importable is increased by one more unit of this factor being available but the output of the exportable falls as result of the diversion of labor to the importable sector that this would cause. The value of total production increases at the tariff-inclusive domestic price but could decline at world prices. Hence the Bhagwati-Srinivasan paradox could arise in the present context, if this input were also used in the "tariff-seeking" and opposing activities on a sufficient scale relative to labor: and then the welfare cost of the endogenous tariff could be less than the welfare cost of an identical tariff levied without such tariff-seeking and opposing activities.

An unconventional implication of the model presented here is that the welfare loss is not a monotonically increasing function of the tariff level. A low tariff resulting from an intense struggle that absorbs a large volume of resources in political activity could be worse, from the standpoint of overall welfare, than a higher tariff that is not vigorously opposed by the free trade forces. Some wars may simply not be worth winning, or even fighting. Constitutional amendments to outlaw tariffs would clearly be desirable, but the sort of continuing political struggle over an annual trade bill that we have described would simply be "capitalized" if such an amendment were to be a genuine possibility. A pluralist democracy of checks and balances between conflicting interest groups, as described by Dahl (1956) and other political scientists, is unlikely to produce a stable and enduring free trade regime except under exceptional circumstances such as those existing in Victorian England, where a world empire provided expanding opportunities to all social classes and serious rivals for industrial supremacy had not yet appeared.[3]

It remains true, of course, that free trade is the first-best social optimum in the absence of national monopoly power over the terms of trade. The question is whether and how that optimum can be attained. The traditional approach assumes away the question by postulating the existence of a benign, omniscient government that can use nondistortionary taxes and subsidies to place society at any point of the utility-possibility frontier. Coase (1960) argued that, in the absence of transaction and negotiation costs, private individuals themselves could work out a system of mutually beneficial deals with side payments to compensate losers that would attain a Pareto-optimal solution. However, the absence of free trade for most of the world's recorded history points to the reality of suboptimal conflict situations of the sort that we have tried to analyze in this paper with very elementary economic tools.

Notes

1. Also see the valuable paper of Krueger (1974) for a theoretical analysis of "rent seeking" where the rents on import quotas, exogenously imposed, are sought competitively. The Bhagwati and Srinivasan (1979) paper discussed below provides a critique of the Krueger contention that such rent seeking must be welfare-worsening, noting the inherently second-best nature of the problem. It also introduces the terminology of "tariff seeking" and "revenue seeking" used below.

2. See Findlay and Wellisz (1976) and Srinivasan and Bhagwati (1978) for the derivation of shadow prices for nontraded primary inputs.

3. See Kindleberger (1978) and Pincus (1977) for interesting historical examples of the political economy of tariffs.

References

Bhagwati, J., and T. N. Srinivasan. 1980. Revenue-seeking: A generalization of the theory of tariffs. *Journal of Political Economy* (December).

Brock, W. A., and S. P. Magee. 1978. The economics of special interest politics: The case of the tariff. *American Economic Review* (May).

Coase, R. 1960. The problem of social cost. *Journal of Law and Economics* (October).

Dahl, R. 1956. *A preface to democratic theory.* Chicago: University of Chicago Press.

234   Ronald Findlay/Stanislaw Wellisz

Findlay, R., and S. Wellisz. 1976. Project evaluation, shadow prices, and trade policy. *Journal of Political Economy* (June).

Harberger, A. C. 1959. Using the resources at hand more effectively. *American Economic Review* (May).

Johnson, H. G. 1960. The cost of protection and the scientific tariff. *Journal of Political Economy* (August).

————. 1967. The possibility of income losses from increased efficiency or factor accumulation in the presence of tariffs. *Economic Journal* (March).

Jones, R. W. 1971. A three factor model in theory, trade, and history. In J. Bhagwati et al., eds., *Trade, balance of payments, and growth.* Amsterdam: North-Holland.

Kindleberger, C. P. 1978. *Economic response.* Cambridge, Mass.: Harvard University Press.

Krueger, A. O. 1974. The political economy of the rent-seeking society. *American Economic Review* (June).

Little, I. M. D., and J. A. Mirrlees. 1969. *A manual of industrial project analysis in developing countries*, vol. 2. Paris: OECD.

Olson, M. 1965. *The logic of collective action.* Cambridge, Mass.: Harvard University Press.

Pincus, J. 1977. *Pressure groups and politics in antebellum tariffs.* New York: Columbia University Press.

Srinivasan, T. N., and J. Bhagwati. 1978. Shadow prices for project selection in the presence of distortions. *Journal of Political Economy* (February).

Tullock, G. 1967. The welfare costs of tariffs, monopolies, and theft. *Western Economic Journal* (June).

Comment   Richard A. Brecher

Introduction

The paper by Findlay and Wellisz is well written, interesting, stimulating, and worthwhile. It extends the theory of rent seeking in an open economy by allowing such activity to determine economic policy endogenously, thereby departing from Bhagwati and Srinivasan (1980), who instead permit revenue seeking to redistribute the proceeds of an exogenously given tax. In the Findlay-Wellisz model, an import tariff results from intergroup conflict expressed through lobbying, which gives rise to

Richard A. Brecher is professor of economics, Carleton University, Ottawa, Canada. He is the author of articles on international trade theory appearing in journals such as *Canadian Journal of Economics, Journal of International Economics, Journal of Political Economy, Oxford Economic Papers*, and *Quarterly Journal of Economics*.

an equilibrium of the Cournot-Nash variety. The following comments will focus on certain technical aspects of the paper, some possible extensions of the model, and various policy implications of the analysis. Limitations on space will keep these comments very brief, permitting only a slight sketch of the main arguments, whose details must be kept to a bare minimum here.

Technical Aspects

Equations (16) and (18) could be simplified by elimination of their constant components, $\pi r(\pi, L)T$ and $\hat{q}[\pi(1 + \hat{t}), (1 - \hat{L}_T)]K$, respectively. The central analysis would be essentially unaffected by this simplification, which leads to straightforward maximization of pressure-group income net of lobby costs, without unnecessary reference to some constant benchmark.

In discussing equation (19), the authors assume that $\partial(qK)/\partial L_K > 0$. It may be noted, however, that necessary and sufficient for this result is the plausible condition that $\partial M/\partial L_K > 0$. In other words, if and only if additional lobbying by capitalowners increases output of manufactures (as might reasonably be expected), the corresponding increase in manufacturing employment must (ceteris paribus) raise capital's gross income (before deducting the lobby costs), for well-known reasons connected with diminishing returns to labor. By similar reasoning in equation (17), however, $\partial(prT)/\partial L_T > 0$ if but not only if $\partial F/\partial L_T > 0$, since $\partial p/\partial L_T > 0$.

In the present paper, the equilibrium tariff must be nonnegative, because the authors assume that lobbying by capital (the sector-specific factor in exportables) is purely in defense of free trade. It might be more realistic and equally tractable to remove the constraint that $t \geq 0$, thereby generalizing the discussion to admit the plausible possibility of subsidized trade in the lobby-determined equilibrium. In this case, the reaction curve for capitalowners would simply be modified to have $L_K > 0$ (rather than $L_K = 0$) when $L_T = 0$, without any serious complication of the analysis.

Even in the absence of explicit rent seeking, the government might impose a tariff to anticipate the latent preferences of voters within the different interest groups. If the subsequent introduction of lobbying alters the government's perception of these preferences, the tariff might then be reduced below the initial (lobby-free) level. This possible movement toward the free-trade situation would be an efficiency gain to be weighed against the resource cost of lobbying, to arrive properly at an overall economic assessment of rent-seeking activity.

The net costs of lobbying might be overemphasized also by the paper's focus on the full-employment economy. In the presence of unemployed resources, the introduction of lobbying need not alter national income at any given tariff, but the associated increase in employment might well be considered socially desirable nevertheless.

As a final point on technical detail, it might be more appropriate for each pressure group to maximize its utility rather than its income (N_T or N_K). This modification could have some noticeable implications for the analysis. For example, as could readily be shown, stronger conditions would be needed to ensure a positive L_T intercept for the reaction curve of landowners. This line of discussion need not be pursued here, since the utility-maximizing approach to lobbying is adopted by Feenstra and Bhagwati in chapter 9.

Possible Extensions

If the cost of negotiation between landowners and capitalowners were assumed to be less than prohibitive, it might pay these two groups to collude as a type of cartel, which maximizes (and internally redistributes) joint rents (or utility). The cartel solution could even emerge automatically without need for intergroup negotiation, if landowners and capitalowners owned land and capital in the same proportion. Since defensive lobbying at cross purposes would be obviously unprofitable for the cartel, the resulting equilibrium must have $L_T \geq L_K = 0$ (or $L_K \geq L_T = 0$ if trade subsidies were allowed). Note that optimal policy for the cartel could be free trade—if a "small" tariff would create exactly offsetting gains and losses for landowners and capitalowners, respectively—even when the Cournot-Nash equilibrium involves a positive tariff. Free trade would also arise if the cartel were extended to include the remaining factor (labor) or if everyone owned all three factors in the same proportion.

Although the paper draws the battle lines between owners of land and of capital, other sorts of conflict are worth considering. For example, chapter 9 by Feenstra and Bhagwati focuses instead upon the familiar division between capital and labor, within the traditional trade-theoretic model with no sector-specific factors. It might also be rewarding to consider the interesting possibility of pressure groups that cut across national boundaries.

In the traditional (lobby-free) theory of tariffs for the small-country case, the welfare cost due to the well-known tariff-induced distortions in production and consumption increases monotonically with the tariff. If instead the magnitude of this cost were the same for all tariff levels ($t \gtrless 0$), it could be effectively ignored in this context. Once the present paper highlights lobbying as an additional tariff-induced cost, it would be worthwhile to explore the relationship between size of tariff and total rent-seeking resources. Since these variables (t and $L_T + L_K$) are endogenously determined within the model, their relationship could be explored only by allowing changes in some exogenously given parameters.

Although the most visible of these parameters are π, K, L, and T, consider also the interesting possibility of rewriting equation (8) as follows: $t = t(L_T, L_K; G)$, where G is an index of government resistance to lobbying, so that $\partial t/\partial G < 0$ (given that negative tariffs are excluded). In other words, if the government becomes more willing to bear the political consequences of resisting pressure for tariffs, the level of protection will fall *(ceteris paribus)*. For the sake of concreteness, let the reaction curves be positively sloped (implying that $\partial^2 N_T/\partial L_T \partial L_K > 0$ and $\partial^2 N_K/\partial L_K \partial L_T > 0$). From the perspective of landowners, a rise in G looks like a rise in L_K, and hence their reaction curve shifts to a higher L_T for each L_K (provided that $\partial^2 N_T/\partial L_T \partial G > 0$). The reaction curve of capitalowners, however, shifts (except at the origin) to a lower L_K for each L_T (provided that $\partial^2 N_K/\partial L_K \partial G < 0$), since they interpret the rise in G as a fall in L_T. Given this asymmetric pattern of reaction-curve shifts, the direction of change in t and $L_T + L_K$ appears to be ambiguous, at the present level of generality. It therefore seems, for example, that a "small" increase in government resistance could lead to a larger tariff and more total lobbying, even though complete resistance could cause $t = L_T = L_K = 0$. To obtain a definite relationship between t and $L_T + L_K$, however, further restrictions on the model probably would be needed.

Policy Implications

In the case analyzed by Bhagwati and Srinivasan (1980), since an exogenously given tariff generates revenue-seeking activity, the costs of this activity can be attributed to the tariff. In the Findlay-Wellisz paper, however, the tariff cannot really be blamed for the associated costs of lobbying, since both of these variables are endogenously determined within the model. These costs in this case therefore must be attributed to something more basic. For example, perhaps lobbying is simply a natural consequence of a democratic system, which permits interest groups to operate freely and legally. From a somewhat different perspective, rent seeking might be viewed as due ultimately to the particular division of power in a national constitution, which enables the government to levy taxes attractive to various lobbies. Alternatively, the ultimate source of rent seeking might be unequal factor-ownership ratios, which make it possible for tariffs to redistribute income among individuals. Depending upon which of these (or other) viewpoints is adopted, the role and focus of policy may be quite different. Needless to say, moreover, policymakers must also consider the costs of any structural change contemplated, including the lobbying costs to oppose or reverse such change, as well as the rent seeking associated with the new environment.

According to a central proposition of the paper, a higher tariff might be associated with a higher level of welfare, for reasons relating to the endogeneity of economic policy. It may be noted, however, that this unconventional result can also occur in models where the tariff is exogenously given. An example of such an occurrence could be constructed readily in figure 2 of Bhagwati and Srinivasan (1980), by shifting their income-consumption curve $C_rC_tC_r'$ rightward until consumption point C_r lies instead where line P_tJ intersects the world-price line drawn through point P_t, without reversing the direction of international trade. (Although this constructed equilibrium is potentially unstable—because the cost of further revenue seeking would be less than the tariff revenues resulting—instability could be avoided by appropriately limiting the amount of earnable revenues in the manner suggested by Bhagwati and Srinivasan 1980.) A tariff-induced improvement in welfare for nationals of a small country might also arise when foreign-owned factors of production are present within the country, as shown by Bhagwati and Brecher (1980) and Brecher and Bhagwati (1981). It would be interesting, moreover, to consider the policy implications of combining the foreign-ownership and revenue-seeking analyses for the case in which domestic lobbies are operated locally by foreign interests based within the host country.

Conclusion

In short, the paper by Findlay and Wellisz is a most welcome contribution. Although the above discussion has been necessarily brief, it is hoped that the foregoing comments help to suggest the wide scope and broad significance of the analysis pursued by the authors.

References

Bhagwati, J. N., and R. A. Brecher. 1980. National welfare in an open economy in the presence of foreign-owned factors of production. *Journal of International Economics* 10, no. 1 (February): 103–15.

Bhagwati, J. N., and T. N. Srinivasan. 1980. Revenue-seeking: A generalization of the theory of tariffs. *Journal of Political Economy* 88, no. 6 (December): 1069–87.

Brecher, R. A., and J. N. Bhagwati. 1981. Foreign ownership and the theory of trade and welfare. *Journal of Political Economy* 89, no. 3 (June): 497-511.

Comment   Leslie Young

Introduction

Findlay and Wellisz have captured an important issue of political economy within a simple and lucid model which should be useful in

Leslie Young is senior lecturer in economics, University of Canterbury. He has published articles on tariff theory and quotas in several professional journals, including the *American Economic Review* and the *Journal of International Economics*.

attacking a wide range of questions.[1] Their contribution is thus most valuable and provocative. We shall show how their model can be simplified even further using duality theory. Using this simplification, we show that the lobbying equilibrium need not be unique. This has interesting implications for the political economy of tariffs. Finally, we point out that the equilibrium of the model depends on the choice of numeraire. This undesirable feature can be removed by assuming that the political factions maximize utility rather than profits.

A Dual Approach

Findlay and Wellisz consider how lobbying affects the rents on land and capital. This approach leads to rather complicated first-order conditions for a Cournot-Nash equilibrium of lobbying. Simpler conditions can be obtained if we assume that each faction maximizes revenue net of wages. This objective function is identical to that of Findlay and Wellisz when there are constant returns to scale in production (so that pure profits are zero).

Let $R^T(p,w)$ and $R^K(w)$ be the net revenue from production of farmers and manufacturers when the domestic price of food in terms of manufactures is p and the wage in terms of manufactures is w, i.e.,

$$R^T(p,w) = pF(p,w) - wL_F(p,w),$$

$$R^K(w) = M(w) - wL_M(w),$$

where $F(p,w)$ and $M(w)$ are the supply functions of food and manufactures and $L_F(p,w)$ and $L_M(w)$ are the derived demand functions for farm and manufacturing labor. By Hotelling's lemma (Varian 1978, p. 31):

(1) $$\frac{\partial R^T}{\partial p} = F(p,w) \qquad \frac{\partial R^T}{\partial w} = -L_F(p,w)$$

$$\frac{\partial R^K}{\partial w} = -L_M(p,w).$$

Farmers take as given the lobbying L_K of manufacturers and choose lobbying L_T to maximize production profits net of lobbyists' wages:

$$\max_{L_T} R^T(p,w) - wL_T.$$

The first-order condition is

$$\frac{\partial R^T}{\partial p} \cdot \frac{\partial p}{\partial L_T} + (\frac{\partial R^T}{\partial w} - L_T)$$

$$(\frac{\partial w}{\partial L_T} + \frac{\partial w}{\partial p} \cdot \frac{\partial p}{\partial L_T}) - w = 0.$$

Using the dual relations (1), this reduces to

(2) $$F\frac{\partial p}{\partial L_T} = w + (L_F + L_T)(\frac{\partial w}{\partial L_T} + \frac{\partial w}{\partial p} \cdot \frac{\partial p}{\partial L_T}).$$

The left-hand side gives the effect on the revenue from food sales of the marginal change in domestic price from additional lobbying. The right-hand side gives the marginal rise in wage costs from additional lobbying. This equals the wage of the marginal lobbyist plus the effect on the total wage bill of the wage rise resulting from lobbying. This wage rise is the result of (1) the increased demand for lobbyists and (2) the increased demand for farm labor as a result of the induced rise in food prices.

Manufacturers take as given the lobbying L_T of farmers and choose lobbying L_K to maximize production profits net of lobbyists' wages:

$$\max_{L_K} R^K(w) - wL_K.$$

An analysis similar to that above yields the first-order condition

(3) $$0 = w + (L_K + L_M)(\frac{\partial w}{\partial L_K} + \frac{\partial w}{\partial p} \cdot \frac{\partial p}{\partial L_K}).$$

The interpretation of (3) is similar to that of (2).

Thus a Cournot-Nash equilibrium of lobbying has been characterized by first-order conditions (2) and (3), which have straightforward interpretations.

Uniqueness of the Nash Equilibrium

In discussing the welfare implications of their model, Findlay and Wellisz state: "An unconventional implication of the model presented here is that the welfare loss is not a monotonically increasing function of the tariff level. A low tariff resulting from an intense struggle that absorbs a large volume of resources could be worse, from the standpoint of overall welfare, than a higher tariff that is not vigorously opposed. . . ." If the lobbying equilibrium were unique, as Findlay and Wellisz assume, then varying tariff levels could arise only from variations in some parameter of the model such as endowments, production possibilities, or lobbying effectiveness. Given such changes in the underlying structure, there is no reason to suppose that welfare losses decrease with reduced tariff levels—*whether or not* these are the outcome of a more intense political struggle. However, if the lobbying equilibrium were not unique, then a more interesting interpretation of the Findlay-Wellisz statement would be possible: in a model with *fixed* parameters there could be two equilibria, one of which involves lower tariffs *and* lower welfare because resources have been diverted into nonproductive lobbying.

We can give an example of this using standard assumptions. Suppose that the resources and techniques available to farmers and manufacturers imply production functions:

$$F = L_F^a, \, M = L_M^a \qquad a > 0.$$

Suppose also that the domestic price p is determined by lobbying as follows:

$$p(L_T, L_K) = L_T^d L_K^{-e} \qquad d > 0, e > 0.$$

If L_0 is the total supply of labor, then define

$$L \equiv L_0 - L_T - L_K, r \equiv 1/(1 + p^{1/(1-a)}).$$

Elementary (but tedious) calculations[2] show that the first-order conditions (2) and (3) become

$$1 + r(d + 1 - a) + (1 - a)L_T/L$$

$$+ \, Lrd(r - 1/a)/L_T = 0,$$

$$2 - a + r(e + a - 1) + (1 - a)L_K/L$$

$$- \, Lre(1 - r)/L_K = 0.$$

We have computed numerical solutions for the case $L_0 = 10$, $a = .75$. If (A) $d = .5$, $e = .5$, then there are *two* solutions (all numbers are rounded to two decimal places):

$$L_T^1 = .88, L_K^1 = .19 \text{ so } p(L_T^1, L_K^1) = 2.15,$$

$$L_T^2 = 1.12, L_K^2 = 1.09 \text{ so } p(L_T^2, L_K^2) = 1.01.$$

If (B) $d = .25$, $e = .5$, then there are again two solutions:

$$L_T^1 = .53, L_K^1 = .12 \text{ so } p(L_T^1, L_K^1) = 2.47,$$

$$L_T^2 = .67, L_K^2 = 1.13 \text{ so } p(L_T^2, L_K^2) = .90.$$

Cases (A) and (B) illustrate the point made by Findlay and Wellisz within a model with fixed parameters. In each case, the solution (L_T^1, L_K^1) involves a high domestic price but few resources in lobbying whereas the solution (L_T^2, L_K^2) involves a lower domestic price arising from a more intensive political struggle. Clearly the diversion of resources to lobbying in the second solution could result in lower welfare despite the reduction in tariff level.

More generally, nonuniqueness of the Nash equilibrium implies that the data of the political and economic system need not determine the outcome of that system. If this possibility were empirically important, then attempts to "explain" tariff levels by the effectiveness and the putative gains from lobbying (see section 10.5 of this volume) could be chimerical.

Choice of Numeraire and Utility-maximizing Factions

In most economic models a change of numeraire does not alter the optimal choice of firms since it merely scales up their maximands by a factor they treat as parametric: the relative price. In the Findlay-Wellisz model, however, firms seek to manipulate this relative price, so a change of numeraire *does* alter their optimal choice. For example, if farmers seek to maximize net profits expressed in terms of manufactures, then the first-order condition is

$$\frac{d}{dL_T}\{R^T - wL_T\} = 0.$$

If they seek to maximize net profits expressed in terms of food, i.e., $\{R^T - wL_T\}/p$, then the first-order condition is

$$p\frac{d}{dL_T}\{R^T - wL_T\} - \{R^T - wL_T\}\frac{\partial p}{\partial L_T} = 0.$$

Since $\partial p/\partial L_T \neq 0$, this condition clearly leads to a different choice. Similar remarks apply for the manufacturer.

These observations bring out the inappropriateness of the assumption that each faction maximizes its profits. If prices are regarded as parametric, then, whatever the numeraire, firms should maximize profits in order to maximize the utility of their owners. However, this will not be true if the firm is actively manipulating the prices its owners face *as consumers*. In such a situation, it is more reasonable to assume that each faction is concerned with maximizing a utility function in which profits appear as an argument. The assumption that the preferences of each faction can be represented by a *single* utility function is in the spirit of the Findlay-Wellisz analysis of the struggle between monolithic factions.

Dual concepts again facilitate the analysis. Let $V^T(q_M, q_F, Y)$ be the maximum utility of farmers given a price q_F for food, a price q_M for manufactures, and an income Y. We assume that the farmers' sole income is farm profits. If manufactures were the numeraire, then their maximand would be $V^T(1, p, R^T - wL_T)$. If food were the numeraire, then their maximand would be $V^T(1/p, 1, \{R^T - wL_T\}/p)$. Since the indirect utility function is homogeneous of degree zero in prices and income, these two maximands are identical; i.e., the choice of numeraire is immaterial.

The first-order condition for a maximum of $V^T(1, p, R^T - wL_T)$ is

(4) $$0 = \frac{\partial V}{\partial p} \cdot \frac{\partial p}{\partial L_T} + \frac{\partial V}{\partial Y} \cdot \frac{d}{dL_T}\{R^T - wL_T\}.$$

If $D^T(p,Y)$ is the farmers' demand function for food, then by Roy's formula (Varian 1978, p. 93)

$$(5) \qquad D^T = - \frac{\partial V}{\partial p} / \frac{\partial V}{\partial Y}.$$

Dividing (4) by $\partial V/\partial Y$ and using the dual relations (1) and (5), we can reduce (4) to

$$(6) \qquad (F - D^T) \frac{\partial p}{\partial L_T} = w + (L_T + L_K)$$

$$(\frac{\partial W}{\partial L_T} + \frac{\partial w}{\partial p} \cdot \frac{\partial p}{\partial L_T}).$$

This differs from the profit-maximizing condition (2) in that the price effect of lobbying, $\partial p/\partial L_T$, applies not to all F units of food produced but only to those $F - D^T$ units sold outside the farming faction.

A similar analysis shows that if D^K is the demand for food by manufacturers, then their utility is maximized when

$$(7) \qquad - D^K \frac{\partial p}{\partial L_K} = w + (L_K + L_M)$$

$$(\frac{\partial w}{\partial L_K} + \frac{\partial w}{\partial p} \cdot \frac{\partial p}{\partial L_K}).$$

This differs from the profit-maximizing condition (3) in that account is taken of the price effect of lobbying on the food expenditure of manufacturers. Equations (6) and (7) would reduce to (2) and (3) only if neither faction consumed any food.

Notes

1. Errors in the oral version of these comments were pointed out by T. N. Srinivasan, John Chipman, and Paul Krugman. Avinash Dixit and Robert Feenstra also provided useful comments. D. C. McNickle and F. T. Baird carried out the numerical calculations.
2. Fuller details of the derivation are given in Young (1980).

References

Varian, H. R. 1978. *Microeconomic analysis.* New York: W. W. Norton.
Young, L. 1980. The uniqueness of political-economic equilibrium: The case of the tariff. University of Canterbury, mimeographed.

9   Tariff Seeking and the Efficient Tariff

Robert C. Feenstra and
Jagdish N. Bhagwati

9.1   Introduction

A common reaction to increased import competition is tariff lobbying by interest groups adversely affected by the competition, a phenomenon christened "tariff seeking" in Bhagwati and Srinivasan (1980). Empirical analyses by Cheh (1974), Pincus (1975), Caves (1976), and several others have pointed to the importance of interest group pressures in determining the level of tariffs and, in particular, the importance of tariff lobbying within labor-intensive industries.

In this paper we shall model the lobbying activities of labor, used intensively in the import-competing industry, as a game between labor and the government, where the actions of the government are determined jointly by its willingness to grant (or perhaps its inability to resist the granting of) tariffs in the face of political pressure and by its desire to maximize social welfare.

We shall suppose that a decrease in the relative price of imports due to increased foreign competition triggers lobbying activity by labor and that this political pressure leads the government to grant tariff protection. The tariff improves the real wages of labor, but under the assumption that we are dealing with a small country, is welfare-inferior to a position of no

Jagdish N. Bhagwati is the Arthur Lehman Professor of Economics at Columbia University. He has written on trade theory, developmental theory and policy, internal and international migration, and education models. He is editor of the *Journal of International Economics* and author (with T. N. Srinivasan) of *Lectures on the Theory of International Trade*, to be published by MIT Press. Robert C. Feenstra is assistant professor of economics at Columbia University and was a Post-Doctoral Fellow in International Economics at the University of Chicago. He has published in the *Journal of International Economics* and has written on international trade theory and econometrics.

Financial support for the research underlying this paper was provided by NSF Grant SOC 79-07541.

tariff and no lobbying. It should be expected, then, that the government will search for policies to reduce the lobbying activity and resulting tariff. If lump-sum taxation were feasible, then the government could simply bribe labor to stop its lobbying activity by offering sufficiently high compensation, thereby restoring the economy to its first-best position with no tariff.

However, in the more realistic case where the government faces a budget constraint, its ability to bribe labor is limited, and in this case it may turn to the revenue created by the tariff itself as a source of funds. By using this revenue to increase labor's real income (defined as the sum of its real wages and this subsidy, as in Bhagwati 1959), the government can change the amount of lobbying activity and tariff, and improve welfare. It cannot, however, eliminate the lobbying activity completely since in that case the tariff is zero and there is no revenue with which to compensate labor. So in general the equilibrium after *optimal* government intervention will have a nonzero tariff, and we shall refer to this as the *efficient* tariff.[1]

Note that the efficient tariff is a second-best concept in that lump-sum taxation to raise funds to compensate labor is assumed infeasible. The idea makes a good deal of sense insofar as the revenue raised for redistribution is being generated as a side effect of the protection itself and is *not* being raised *ab initio* for the redistribution.[2] Our underlying assumption that one part of the government responds to the protectionist pressures while another tries to maximize welfare subject to this response suggests, as some conference participants wittily remarked, a "left-brain, right-brain" or an "ego versus id" type of approach to the political economy at hand. It does reflect, however, the classic division and confrontation between the (protrade) executive and the (lobbying-dominated) legislature in countries such as the United States.

In section 9.2 we determine the equilibrium tariff level based on optimal lobbying activity by labor. In section 9.3 we introduce the possibility of government intervention in the form of conditional subsidies to labor and derive the efficient tariff. While one might expect that it is optimal for the government to *reduce* the amount of lobbying and the resulting tariff, it is also possible for the optimal policy to involve an *increase* in the level of lobbying and tariff. This paradox can arise if, given the existing distortion caused by the tariff, the shadow price of the lobbying activity is *negative*, so that an increase in the lobbying activity may be socially desirable (for analyses of negative project shadow prices see Srinivasan and Bhagwati 1978; Bhagwati, Srinivasan, and Wan 1978; Bhagwati and Srinivasan 1980). In section 9.4 we derive a necessary and sufficient condition for this possibility to arise. Further discussion and conclusions are given in sections 9.5 and 9.6.

9.2 Optimal Lobbying

We shall adopt the usual 2×2 HOS (Heckscher-Ohlin-Samuelson) model, with industry 1 labor-intensive and import-competing. Choosing commodity 2 as the numeraire, let p^* and $p = p^*(1 + t)$ denote the foreign and domestic relative price of commodity 1, respectively, where t is the *ad valorem* tariff rate and, under the assumption of a small country, p^* is given as a parameter by world trade. The consumption and production of good i are denoted by X_i and Y_i, $i = 1,2$, and the factor prices and given endowments of labor and capital are denoted by w, r, L, and $\bar{K}$, respectively.

Suppose that the foreign relative price of good 1 falls from p_0^* to p^* due to increased import competition and that this triggers tariff lobbying by labor, whose real wages have fallen. Following Findlay and Wellisz (chapter 8 of this volume), we shall assume that this lobbying activity takes the form of hiring labor L_t and capital K_t to determine a tariff level $t = f(L_t, K_t)$, where f is increasing and concave. This lobbying function should be interpreted as derived from given political behavior and institutions, such as the desire of politicians to maximize their probability of reelection.[3] We shall denote minimum costs at which the tariff rate t can be obtained as $C(t,w,r)$. A reasonable form for the lobbying cost function is

(1)
$$C(t,w,r) = \left\{ \frac{t\phi(w,r)}{\max\{0,(p_0^* - p^*(1 + t))\}} \right\},$$

where $\phi(w,r)$ is increasing and quasi-concave. For this cost function, as the tariff increases and $p^*(1 + t)$ approaches p_0^* so that labor's real wages approach the level obtained *before* the increased import competition, costs become arbitrarily large. Also, if import competition were to *decline* ($p^* > p_0^*$) and labor's real wages improve, then the costs of lobbying for any positive tariff would be arbitrarily large. This cost function is meant to embody the notion that *before* the change in the terms of trade the historically determined distribution of income between labor and capital was "acceptable" in the sense that lobbying would have been ineffective (lobbying costs would have been arbitrarily large), and it is only *after* the shift in the terms of trade that lobbying becomes feasible for the factor whose real wages have deteriorated. Adopting an analogous lobbying cost function for capital, and for the case we are considering where $p_0^* > p^*$, capitalists will *not* lobby after the change in the terms of trade because their real rental has improved.[4]

We shall assume that all laborers have an identical linearly homogeneous utility function, and denote the maximum utility obtainable with the relative price p and income I by $V(p,I)$. After the fall in the foreign relative price of commodity 1 from p_0^* to p^*, labor's lobbying problem is

(2) $$\max_{t\geq0} V\{p^*(1+t), w\bar{L} - C(t,w,r)\},$$

where $(w\bar{L} - C(t,w,r))$ is labor's income net of lobbying costs. Using Roy's identity,[5] the first-order conditions for this problem can be written as

(3a) $$p^*(\bar{L}\frac{dw}{dp} - X_1^L) = \frac{dC}{dt},$$

where

(3b) $$\frac{dC}{dt} = \left(w\frac{\partial L_t}{\partial t} + r\frac{\partial K_t}{\partial t}\right) + p^*\left(L_t\frac{dw}{dp} + K_t\frac{dr}{dp}\right).$$

The left-hand side of (3a) is the change in labor's real income due to a change in the tariff, $dw/dp > 0$ and $(\bar{L}(dw/dp) - X_1^L) > 0$, where X_1^L is labor's consumption of good 1;[6] the right-hand side is the marginal cost of the tariff, including both the direct effect on costs of hiring more inputs and the indirect effect of changing factor prices.

The solution t^* to labor's lobbying problem is illustrated in figure 9.1, where $C(t)$ are costs as a function of t including general equilibrium changes in factor prices, and the "benefits" curve $B(t)$ has slope $p^*(\bar{L}(dw/dp) - X_1^L)$. For the lobbying cost function given in (1), costs approach infinity as t approaches $\bar{t} = (p_0^*/p^*) - 1$, and this implies that $t^* < \bar{t}$; so the domestic price ratio $p = p^*(1 + t^*)$ after tariff lobbying lies between the foreign price ratios p_0^* and p^* obtaining before and after the increase in import competition, respectively. Note that multiple solutions to (3) are possible.[7] Assuming that lobbying costs are shared equally by all laborers, the net wage after lobbying is $(w - C(t^*,w,r)/\bar{L})$.

9.3 Government Intervention

The equilibrium with optimal lobbying by labor is welfare-inferior to a position of no lobbying and no tariff. Thus, as argued in section 9.1, the government may turn to the revenues created by the tariff itself as a source of funds to compensate labor and improve welfare. In order to be effective, this compensation will take the form of subsidy payments which are *conditional* on the tariff rate: for the case in which the government wishes to reduce the level of lobbying and tariff to $\hat{t} < t^*$ it would offer the subsidy $\hat{S}(t)$ defined by

(4) $$\hat{S}(t) = \begin{cases} S(\hat{t}) & \text{for } t \leq \hat{t} \\ 0 & \text{for } t > \hat{t}, \end{cases}$$

where $S(\hat{t})$ is chosen such that labor will *accept* the conditional subsidy. This bribe is illustrated in figure 9.1, from which it is clear that the minimum level of $S(\hat{t})$ that labor will accept is

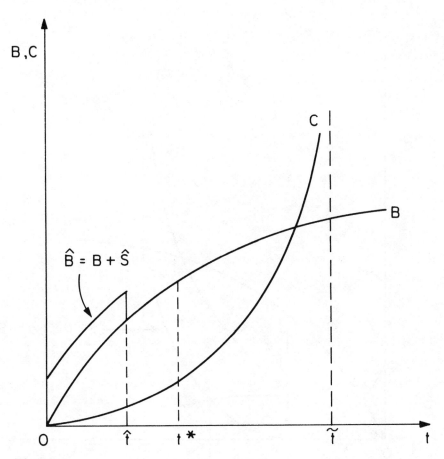

Fig. 9.1

(5) $$S(\hat{t}) = \Big[B(t^*) - C(t^*)\Big] - \Big[B(\hat{t}) - C(\hat{t})\Big],$$

in which case labor is indifferent between $\hat{t}$ and t^*. The schedule of minimum subsidy payments $S(t)$ is implicitly defined by (5) or, equivalently,

(5') $$V(p^*(1+t), w\overline{L} - C(t,w,r) + S(t)) = V_L^*,$$

where V_L^* is the utility of labor in the optimal lobbying equilibrium. The subsidy payments are illustrated in figure 9.2. Note that for the case in which the government wishes to increase the level of lobbying and tariff to $\hat{t} > t^*$, it would offer the conditional subsidy $\hat{S}(t)$ defined by

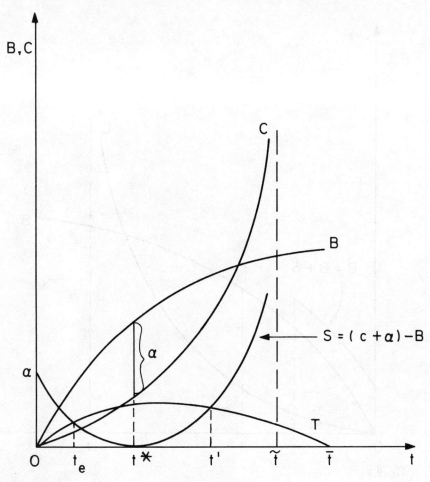

Fig. 9.2

$$\hat{S}(t) = \begin{cases} 0 \text{ for } t < \hat{t}, \\ S(\hat{t}) \text{ for } t \geq \hat{t} \end{cases}$$

where with $S(t)$ chosen according to (5) or (5') labor would be willing to accept this compensation.

Using the subsidy payments $S(t)$, the government can shift the equilibrium of the economy to any desired position with $0 \leq t < \tilde{t}$, and we assume that it wishes to choose the position which maximizes social welfare.[8] Assuming that the government places equal weight on all individuals when evaluating social welfare and that capitalists have the same linearly homogeneous utility function as laborers, social welfare is given by

$$U = V(p^*(1+t), w\bar{L} + r\bar{K} + T - C(t,w,r))$$
$$= V(p^*(1+t), w\bar{L} - C(t,w,r,) + S(t))$$
$$+ V(p^*(1+t), r\bar{K} + T - S(t))$$
$$= V_L^* + V(p^*(1+t), r\bar{K} + T - S(t)),$$

where T denotes redistributed tariff revenues. Since V_L^* is a constant, maximizing social welfare is equivalent to maximizing $V_k \equiv V(p^*(1+t), r\bar{K} + T - S(t))$, which is the utility of capitalists when they receive their rental income and redistributed tariff revenues less subsidy payments. We explicitly rule out the possibility of lump-sum taxation of capital, and so the net income distributed to capital must be *nonnegative*. Thus, the government's problem can be stated as

(6) $\max\limits_{t \geq 0} V_K$ subject to $T - S(t) \geq 0$.

The tariff rate t_e given by the solution to (6) is the *efficient* tariff. The game-theoretic equilibrium at which the efficient tariff obtains is a *Stackelberg* equilibrium with the government as the Stackelberg leader: in choosing its optimal policy, labor takes any conditional subsidy offer $\hat{S}(t)$ as given, whereas the government includes the reaction of labor to different subsidy offers in its decision framework.

The efficient tariff may be below or exceed the optimal labor-lobbying tariff t^*, where the latter possibility can arise if the shadow price of the lobbying activity is negative. Consider first the "normal" case, where it is optimal for the government to bribe labor to *reduce* the lobbying activity and resulting tariff. Then the *minimum* feasible tariff rate and maximum social welfare is clearly attained where $T = S(t)$, so that all of the tariff revenue is used to compensate labor and none is distributed to capital. This corner solution is shown as $t_e < t^*$ in figure 9.2, where $\bar{t}$ is the prohibitive tariff, and $\bar{t} > \tilde{t}$ since it is assumed that industry 1 was import-competing before the initial shift in the terms of trade.[9] For the latter case where it is optimal for the government to *increase* the level of lobbying and tariff from t^*, social welfare is maximized at a tariff rate *between* t^* and t'. The point t' is defined by $t' > t^*$ and $T = S(t')$, and the efficient tariff is necessarily less than t'. This result can be demonstrated as follows. Using the subsidy payments $S(t)$, labor obtains the same utility at t^* and t', but since at t' *all* tariff revenues are used to compensate labor and the rental on capital is less than at t^* (by the Stolper-Samuelson theorem), capital is necessarily worse off at t' as compared with t^*. Therefore, social welfare is lower at t' than at t^*, and so for the case we are considering where a marginal rise in the tariff rate from t^* increases social welfare, the maximum is clearly obtained between t^* and t'.[10]

When can the latter paradoxical case arise? As we shall demonstrate in the following section, starting at any tariff rate t, $0 \leq t < \tilde{t}$, an *increase* in the amount of lobbying activity and resulting tariff due to government intervention is welfare-improving if and only if

(7) $$-\frac{d}{dt}\left(p^*Y_1 + Y_2\right) < t(p^*)^2\left(\left.\frac{\partial X_1}{\partial p}\right|_u - \frac{\partial Y_1}{\partial p}\right),$$

whereas the optimal intervention is to decrease the amount of lobbying and tariff if the inequality in (7) is reversed.[11] The left-hand side of (7) is the change in national income evaluated at *international* prices due to a change in the level of lobbying activity and tariff, which is the *shadow price* of the lobbying activity. The right-hand side of (7) reflects the change in tariff revenue due to substitution effects in consumption and production, and is negative since

$$\left.\frac{\partial X_1}{\partial p}\right|_u < 0 \text{ and} \frac{\partial Y_1}{\partial p} > 0.$$

Thus, an increase in the lobbying activity and tariff is optimal if and only if the shadow price of the lobbying activity is negative and sufficiently large in absolute value.

9.4 Derivation of Optimal Government Intervention

The change in the subsidy given to labor needed to keep labor's utility at its optimal lobbying level can be calculated from (5′) as

(8) $$\frac{dS}{dt} = -\{p^*(\bar{L}\frac{dw}{dp} - X_1^L) - \frac{dC}{dt}\}.$$

When the tariff revenues less subsidy payments are redistributed to capitalists, their utility is $V_K = V(p^*(1+t), r\bar{K} + T - S(t))$, and

$$\frac{dV_k}{dt} = \frac{\partial V}{\partial I}\{p^*(\bar{K}\frac{dr}{dp} - X_1^K) + \frac{dT}{dt} - \frac{dS}{dt}\},$$

where X_1^K is the consumption of good 1 by capitalists and $dr/dp < 0$. Then $dV_K/dt > 0$, in which case it is optimal for the government to bribe labor to *increase* the amount of lobbying and resulting tariff, if and only if

(9) $$\left(\frac{dT}{dt} - \frac{dS}{dt}\right) > -p^*\left(\bar{K}\frac{dr}{dp} - X_1^K\right).$$

The right-hand side of (9) is the real income loss of capitalists due to a higher tariff, and so the higher tariff is preferred if and only if the net gain in tariff revenue exceeds this loss.

Equation (9) clarifies the nature of the optimal intervention for the case where it is optimal for the government to increase the level of lobbying and tariff from t^* (i.e., [9] holds at t^*). The right-hand side of (9) is positive (by the Stolper-Samuelson theorem), and in a neighborhood of t' it can be seen that $dT/dt < dS/dt$, so that (9) cannot hold. The efficient tariff in this case is obtained when (9) holds with equality, which will occur at a point between t^* and t'. We can also see that the efficient tariff satisfies $dT/dt > 0$, which implies that the efficient tariff is necessarily less than the *maximum revenue* tariff for which $dT/dt = 0$.

Tariff revenues are given by

$$T = tp^*(X_1(p^*(1 + t), w\bar{L} + r\bar{K} + T - C) - Y_1),$$

where $X_1 = X_1^L + X_1^K$, from which we can calculate that

$$\frac{dT}{dt} = \beta\{p^*(X_1 - Y_1) + t(p^*)^2(\frac{\partial X_1}{\partial p}\Big|_u - \frac{\partial Y_1}{\partial p})\}$$

$$+ \beta tp^*(\frac{\partial Y_1}{\partial \bar{L}}\frac{dL_t}{dt} + \frac{\partial Y_1}{\partial \bar{K}}\frac{dK_t}{dt})$$

(10) $$+ (\beta - 1)(p^*\bar{L}\frac{dw}{dp} + p^*\bar{K}\frac{dr}{dp} - p^*X_1 - \frac{dC}{dt}),$$

where $\beta = (1 - tp^*(\partial X_1/\partial I)^{-1} > 0$ so long as good 2 is not inferior.[12] We also have

$$\frac{dS}{dt} - p^*(\bar{K}\frac{dr}{dp} - X_1^K)$$

$$= -(p^*\bar{L}\frac{dw}{dp} + p^*\bar{K}\frac{dr}{dp} - p^*X_1 - \frac{dC}{dt})$$

using (8);

$$= -(p^*(\bar{L} - L_t)\frac{\partial Y_1}{\partial \bar{L}}$$

$$+ p^*(\bar{K} - K_t)\frac{\partial Y_1}{\partial \bar{K}} - p^*X_1 - C_t)$$

using (3b), using the reciprocity relations $dw/dp = \partial Y_1/\partial \bar{L}$ and $dr/dp = \partial Y_1/\partial \bar{K}$, and since $C_t = w(\partial L_t/\partial t) + r(\partial K_t/\partial t)$;

(11) $$= p^*(X_1 - Y_1) + C_t$$

since $$Y_1 = (\bar{L} - L_t)\frac{\partial Y_1}{\partial \bar{L}} + (\bar{K} - K_t)\frac{\partial Y_1}{\partial \bar{K}}.$$

Using (10) and (11), condition (9) becomes

$$(9') \qquad t(p^*)^2 \left(\frac{\partial X_1}{\partial p} \bigg|_u - \frac{\partial Y_1}{\partial p} \right) + tp^* \left(\frac{\partial Y_1}{\partial \bar{L}} \frac{dL_t}{dt} \right.$$

$$\left. + \frac{\partial Y_1}{\partial \bar{K}} \frac{dK_t}{dt} \right) - C_t > 0.$$

To further simplify $(9')$ we must introduce the concept of *shadow prices* of primary factors at the tariff-distorted equilibrium. Letting a_{ij} denote the cost-minimizing unit-output requirement of factor i in industry j, evaluated at the tariff-distorted domestic price ratio $p = p^*(1 + t)$, the factor prices w and r satisfy

$$p^*(1 + t) = a_{L1}w + a_{K1}r,$$

$$(12a) \qquad\qquad 1 = a_{L2}w + a_{K2}r,$$

whereas the *shadow* factor prices w^* and r^* are defined by

$$p^* = a_{L1}w^* + a_{K1}r^*,$$

$$(12b) \qquad\qquad 1 = a_{L2}w^* + a_{K2}r^*.$$

Using (12a) and (12b), it can be shown that

$$tp^* \frac{dw}{dp} = w - w^*,$$

$$(13) \qquad\qquad tp^* \frac{dr}{dp} = r - r^*.$$

Using (13) and the reciprocity relations, we then have

$$tp^* \left(\frac{\partial Y_1}{\partial \bar{L}} \frac{dL_t}{dt} + \frac{\partial Y_1}{\partial \bar{K}} \frac{dK_t}{dt} \right)$$

$$(14) \qquad\qquad = C_t - \left(w^* \frac{\partial L_t}{\partial t} + r^* \frac{\partial K_t}{\partial t} \right) + \theta,$$

where

$$\theta = t(p^*)^2 \left\{ \frac{\partial L_t}{\partial w} \left(\frac{dw}{dp} \right)^2 \right.$$

$$\left. + 2 \frac{\partial L_t}{\partial r} \left(\frac{dw}{dp} \right) \left(\frac{dr}{dp} \right) + \frac{\partial K_t}{\partial r} \left(\frac{dr}{dp} \right)^2 \right\}$$

$$= t^{-1}(w^*, r^*) \begin{bmatrix} C_{ww} & C_{wr} \\ \\ C_{rw} & C_{rr} \end{bmatrix} \begin{pmatrix} w^* \\ \\ r^* \end{pmatrix} \leq 0,$$

since $C(t,w,r)$ is concave in (w,r).

Substituting (14) into (9′), the necessary and sufficient condition for an increase in the level of lobbying and tariff to be welfare-improving is

(9″) $$(w^* \frac{\partial L_t}{\partial t} + r^* \frac{\partial K_t}{\partial t}) - \theta < t(p^*)^2 (\frac{\partial X_1}{\partial p}\Big|_u - \frac{\partial Y_1}{\partial p}).$$

Finally, note that national income evaluated at international prices is given by

$$p^* Y_1 + Y_2 = w^*(\bar{L} - L_t) + r^*(\bar{K} - K_t),$$

from which it can be shown that

(15) $$-\frac{d}{dt}(p^* Y_1 + Y_2) = (w^* \frac{\partial L_t}{\partial t} + r^* \frac{\partial K_t}{\partial t}) - \theta.$$

Substituting (15) into (9″), we obtain condition (7), as desired.

9.5   A Sufficient Condition for Welfare Improvement in the Lobbying Equilibrium

In the absence of any tariff lobbying the fall in the relative price of imports due to foreign competition, while harmful to the real wages of labor, is welfare-improving. The lobbying activity reduces welfare from that point by establishing a tariff and using resources, and so it is possible for social welfare to be *lower* after the improvement in the terms of trade and resulting lobbying and tariff than before. However, as shown in figure 9.3, a *sufficient* condition for welfare to be *higher* after the improvement in the terms of trade and lobbying is easily derived. (Note that the efficient tariff equilibrium is no worse than the lobbying equilibrium, so that our sufficiency condition extends to it as well.)

In figure 9.3 the equilibrium production points before and after the fall in the relative price of imports (and with no lobbying) are P_0 and P_1, respectively, and $0I$ is the income-consumption path corresponding to the domestic price ratio in the tariff-distorted equilibrium. For the lobbying cost function given in (1), the domestic price ratio with optimal labor lobbying lies between the international price ratios obtaining before and after the change in the terms of trade (so that $\tilde{P}$ is spanned by P_0 and P_1). Production is shifted from $\tilde{P}$ to P_t by the lobbying activity, and consumption is at C_t. For the given tariff, an increase in lobbying costs would shift consumption down along $0I$, but so long as the consumption point does not fall below $\tilde{C}$, welfare U_t must be higher than U_0. (Note that this condition is sufficient but *not* necessary and that $\tilde{C}$ is a hypothetical

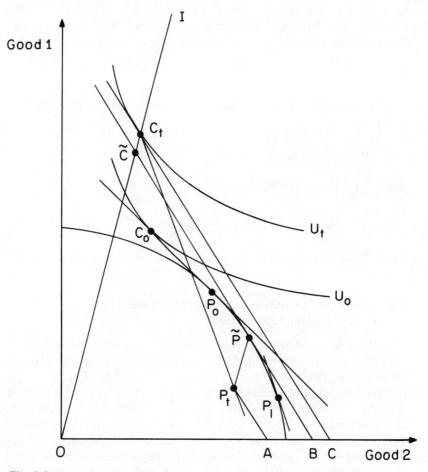

Fig. 9.3

consumption point which does *not* correspond to any trade equilibrium.)
The condition for C_t to exceed $\tilde{C}$ is that tariff revenues AC exceed
lobbying costs AB, and so this is a sufficient condition for welfare to
improve due to the initial fall in the relative price of imports.

9.6 Conclusions

We have derived the efficient tariff obtaining in the Stackelberg
equilibrium of a game between the government and labor, where labor
lobbies for a tariff and the government responds by granting some tariff
protection but also by using tariff revenues to compensate labor directly,
thereby changing the amount of lobbying. For the lobbying cost function
given in (1), the real rental on capital improves as a result of the improve-

ment in the terms of trade despite the lobbying (i.e., in moving from P_0 to P_t in figure 9.3), labor's real income is damaged by the increased foreign competition but is higher than in the absence of lobbying, and so long as tariff revenues exceed lobbying costs in the final equilibrium the improved terms of trade improve social welfare.

Notes

1. Johnson's (1960) concept of the "scientific tariff" related to that tariff structure which would minimize the cost of certain "noneconomic" objectives such as "diversification, industrialization, or agriculturization" and "national self-sufficiency and independence." As such, it was a constrained, second-best concept, the second-best nature of the tariff structure relating to the fact that the first-best solution is additionally being constrained by the noneconomic objectives. As noted in the text, however, our concept of the "efficient tariff" is also a second-best one insofar as the lobbying activity cannot be eliminated by bribing labor with lump-sum transfers in a first-best solution. The efficient tariff, however, minimizes the welfare loss from the successful lobbying for a tariff by utilizing an added policy instrument which is perfectly appropriate to the problem (and which was earlier disregarded by trade theorists following the Meade assumption that all tariff revenues are given away as lump-sum transfers), namely, the tariff revenues which can be used to bribe labor into accepting a lower tariff.

2. Gene Grossman has pointed out to us that something very similar in spirit to the efficient tariff notion is implied by the Carter administration's proposal to use the revenue raised from the oil tariff and the windfall profits tax to compensate the losers from higher-priced oil. In chapter 12 Richardson also notes that a provision of the Trade Act of 1974 earmarked funds out of tariff revenues for the retraining of trade-displaced workers.

3. Brock and Magee (1978) model politicians as maximizing their probability of reelection in a very general game-theoretic framework.

4. Aside from the direct costs of hiring factors to lobby, the lobbying cost function can also be interpreted as including costs of labor *union* activity which induces tariff lobbying by *entrepreneurs*. For example, if workers strike in response to lowered real wages, this could lead to greater tariff lobbying by entrepreneurs in an attempt to meet union wage demands without reducing the return on capital. Labor would have to bear the costs of not receiving wage income during the strike (though these costs may be mitigated by government compensation), as well as some portion of the opportunity costs of capital unemployed during the strike. Within the context of our model we are assuming that the costs to labor $C(t,w,r)$ include the *full* opportunity cost of unemployed capital as well as the lobbying costs of entrepreneurs in industry 1; we also do not consider the role of government unemployment compensation.

5. Roy's identity states that $X_1 = (-\partial V/\partial p)/(\partial V/\partial I)$.

6. We have $(\bar{L}(dw/dp) - X_1^L) > 0$ since, by the Stolper-Samuelson theorem, labor's real wages improve in terms of *either* good and so the rise in real income exceeds the increased cost of consumption.

7. Of course, if $C(t)$ is convex and $B(t)$ concave, then the solution is unique. The convexity of $w(p)$, which is a component of $B(t)$, is investigated in Kemp and Khang (1975).

8. Note that the government's desire to maximize social welfare is consistent with its willingness to grant tariff protection, in that the latter can represent its reaction to distributive equity whereas the former corresponds to allocative efficiency.

9. Note that the tariff revenue T need *not* be "single-peaked" as shown in figure 9.2. If $T = S(t)$ at numerous values of t, then the optimal value of t when the government wishes to reduce the lobbying activity and resulting tariff is the *minimum* t for which $T = S(t)$.

10. If $T = S(t')$ and $t' > t^*$ at numerous values of t', then the efficient tariff when the government wishes to increase the level of lobbying and tariff from t^* must lie between t^* and the *maximum* value of t'.

11. An interior maximum of social welfare is obtained when (7) is satisfied with equality (and the second-order conditions for maximization are satisfied).

12. Since marginal propensities to consume must add up to unity, we have $(1 - tp^* (\partial X_1/\partial 1)) = (p^* (\partial X_1/\partial I) + (\partial X_2/\partial I))$, and this expression is positive so long as good 2 is not inferior.

References

Bhagwati, J. N., 1959, Protection, real wages, and real incomes. *Economic Journal* 69: 733–44.

Bhagwati, J., and T. N. Srinivasan. 1979. On inferring resource allocational implications from DRC calculations in trade-distorted, small open economics. *Indian Economic Review* 14, no. 1 (April): 1–16.

———. 1980. Revenue-seeking: A generalization of the theory of tariffs. *Journal of Political Economy* 88, no. 6 (December): 1069–87.

Bhagwati, J., T. N. Srinivasan, and H. Wan, Jr. 1978. Value subtracted, negative shadow prices of factors in project evaluation and immiserizing growth: Three paradoxes in the presence of trade distortions. *Economic Journal* 88 (March): 121–25.

Brock, W. A., and S. P. Magee. 1978. The economics of special interest politics: The case of the tariff. *American Economic Review Papers and Proceedings* 68, no. 2 (May): 246–50.

Caves, R. E. 1976. Economic models of political choice: Canada's tariff structure. *Canadian Journal of Economics* 9, no. 2 (May): 278–300.

Cheh, J. 1974. United States concessions in the Kennedy Round and short-run labour adjustment costs. *Journal of International Economics* 4, no. 4 (November): 323–40.

Johnson, H. C. 1960. The cost of protection and the scientific tariff. *Journal of Political Economy* 68, no. 4 (August): 327–45.

Kemp, M. C., and C. Khang, C. 1975. A convexity property of the two-by-two model of production. *Journal of International Economics* 5: 255–61.

Pincus, J. J. 1975. Pressure groups and the pattern of tariffs. *Journal of Political Economy* 83, no. 4 (August): 757–78.

Srinivasan, T. N., and J. Bhagwati. 1978. Shadow prices for project evaluation in the presence of distortions: Effective rates of protection and domestic resource costs. *Journal of Political Economy* 86, no. 1: 96–116.

Comment   Robert E. Baldwin

The Feenstra-Bhagwati paper is an ingenious application of policymaking under second-best conditions. How, the authors ask, would the usual tariff-seeking analysis, whereby pressure groups continue to incur additional (and increasing) lobbying costs in order to increase a protective tariff until they equal the additional (and decreasing) real income benefits associated with these expenditures, be changed if the government in an effort to improve national welfare utilized the tariff proceeds to bribe the interest group into accepting a different tariff rate? Using a model in which the Stolper-Samuelson theorem holds and in which labor engages in lobbying in response to an initial decline in the international price of the labor-intensive import good, they show that the optimal compensation payment to labor by the government could result in this "efficient" tariff being either lower or higher than the optimum rent-seeking duty for labor in the absence of this form of government intervention.

While the use of tariff revenues to gain the acceptance of tariff changes is not common, the National Wool Act of 1954 is an example of such a policy. In the early 1950s producers of manufactured woolen products pressed for a reduction in the duty on raw wool in order to reduce the cost of one of their major inputs. The duty was reduced, but as compensation to United States wool producers the act permits them to receive up to 70 percent of the accumulated duties on wool and manufactured woolen products.

Let me make a few comments about some of the assumptions in the Feenstra-Bhagwati analysis. One concerns the supposition that capitalists, who lose as the tariff is increased, do not themselves engage in lobbying because the optimum rent-seeking duty and the "efficient" tariff are assumed to yield a lower domestic price for the import-competing good than the level prior to the initial international decline in the price of this good. While these price relationships seem reasonable, it may not be the case that capitalists fail to resist a decline in their real income simply because this income still remains above some initial level. It does not take long for income groups to develop a vested interest in maintaining economic benefits they have received. However, if the problem is posed as one where labor is resisting the full tariff cut agreed upon as part of a multilateral trade negotiation, it does make sense to suppose that the lobbying activity of the capitalists will be less than that of the workers.

Robert E. Baldwin is the F. W. Taussig Research Professor of Economics at the University of Wisconsin–Madison. Among his recent articles is "Welfare Effects on the United States of a Significant Multilateral Tariff Reduction" (with J. H. Mutti and J. D. Richardson), *Journal of International Economics*, August 1980. His study *The Political Economy of U.S. Import Policy* will be published in 1983.

A more significant assumption on the part of Feenstra and Bhagwati is that, subject to the ability of labor to secure the real income level associated with its optimal lobbying tariff, the government seeks to maximize social welfare. Since labor's real income is being held constant by utilizing the tariff proceeds as a labor subsidy, this means—as the authors note—that the government maximizes the welfare of the capitalists, even though they do not press for help by lobbying. The assumption that the government behaves in this manner seems somewhat inconsistent with a model that emphasizes the role of lobbying in determining policy. In such models the government is usually assumed to respond only to political pressues from common-interest groups and not to have a general welfare function of its own. When the government is assigned an independent role, it generally is the one of promoting the real income interests of those employed in the government. Thus the authors might justify in more detail why they believe that it is reasonable to assume that the government will promote the welfare interests of the capitalists. Furthermore under these assumed conditions they should also consider, as a possibly superior welfare-increasing policy to compensation, the use of the tariff proceeds by the government for informational purposes designed to counter the lobbying of labor.

If one assumes that only labor engages in lobbying and also drops the assumption that the government aims to maximize welfare subject to this lobbying, then it seems reasonable to suppose that labor will seek to improve its position not only by raising its wages but by obtaining the tariff proceeds directly as a subsidy. In this case the tariff revenue curve in figure 9.2 would be added to the benefits curve in that figure. The cost curve might also be increased if additional lobbying was required to obtain this subsidy. In any event, the optimal tariff under these assumptions could be either higher or lower than the equilibrium level when it is assumed these proceeds cannot be obtained directly by labor. Of course, one might go further and ask why labor does not seek as a subsidy some of the capitalists' extra income. One reason why most political models of this type specify lobbying benefits and cost functions for all income participants and all policy actions is to yield unique solutions for any type of lobbying activity and thus block this type of speculation.

A relevant international application of the Feenstra-Bhagwati model is to analyze the use of the windfall gains from quotas to bribe foreign producers into accepting export restraints. If a Cairnes-type model is utilized in which the incomes of all groups employed in a national industry move in the same direction in the short run, one can think of a domestic industry as lobbying for protection while the foreign industry counters with its own lobbying because of the adverse terms-of-trade consequences of tariff increases. The equilibrium tariff is the one where these opposing faces are balanced in the usual way with the tariff proceeds going to the domestic government for general revenue purposes. Suppose, however, that the domestic industry proposes a quota system whereby the windfall gains (the equivalent of the government's revenue under a tariff system) go to the foreign producers. This is what in fact happens under most voluntary export-constraint arrangements. Following the Feenstra-Bhagwati line of thought, foreign producers can be bribed by these windfall gains into accepting more stringent restrictions on their exports than they otherwise would have obtained. Both the domestic and foreign industry can, in other words, be made better off than under the adversarial tariff-seeking solution. However, consumers in the country imposing the restriction lose both because the domestic price rises and because tax revenues fall. It would be interesting to see the implications of this problem fully explored in terms of the Feenstra-Bhagwati model.

10   The Political Economy of Protectionism

Robert E. Baldwin

Although economic historians have traditionally studied international trade policies in both economic and political terms, it has only been within the last decade that trade economists have manifested much more than casual interest in this approach.[1] Over a dozen articles or papers have been written since 1974 in which trade economists have analyzed in quantitative terms the relationship between the level of protection (or a change in the level) afforded different industries or income classes and various political and economic characteristics of these sectors or groups that appear to influence the level of protection.[2] This greater attention to the political economy of protectionism is only one indication of the growing interest by economists in public choice—a subject that Mueller (1976) defines as the application of economics to political science. According to Mueller public choice developed as a separate field in response to the issues raised by Bergson (1938), Samuelson (1947), and Arrow (1951) in their pioneering work on social welfare and also in response to the explorations in the 1940s and 1950s of the conditions in which the free market mechanism fails to achieve a Pareto-optimum allocation of resources.

Robert E. Baldwin is the F. W. Taussig Research Professor of Economics at the University of Wisconsin–Madison. Among his recent articles is "Welfare Effects on the United States of a Significant Multilateral Tariff Reduction" (with J. H. Mutti and J. D. Richardson), *Journal of International Economics*, August 1980. His study *The Political Economy of U.S. Import Policy* will be published in 1983.

The author is grateful for the valuable comments of the discussants and other conference participants and especially for Jagdish Bhagwati's help in tightening up the paper. Thanks are due to the Office on Foreign Economic Research, United States Department of Labor, and the World Bank for financial support in undertaking the research underlying this paper.

10.1 Welfare Economics: Bergson, Samuelson, Arrow, et al.

A discussion of the political economy of trade policy can usefully begin by placing the subject in the framework established by Bergson and Samuelson for analyzing social welfare. The Bergson-Samuelson formulation of the social welfare function makes a clear-cut distinction between individual tastes or preferences for goods and services and individual values relating to general standards of equity or to other ethical judgments. These authors also assume that an individual's preferences for economic goods and services depend only upon his own consumption of these items and not upon what other individuals consume. Thus social welfare (W) is written as

$$W = W[U^1(X_1^1, \ldots, X_n^1; V_1^1, \ldots, V_m^1), \ldots$$
$$U^s(X_1^s, \ldots, X_n^s; V_1^s, \ldots, V_m^s)],$$

where the U terms represent ordinal utility measures for the s individuals, the X terms stand for the n commodities, and the V terms stand for the m productive services.

As Samuelson points out, the social welfare function characterizes some set of ethical beliefs that permits an unequivocal answer as to whether one configuration of the economic system is "better" than, "worse" than, or "indifferent" to any other.[3] Bergson also stresses that the social welfare function rests on ethical criteria.[4] Neither author analyzes in any detail the nature of the value judgments nor how the community selects a particular social welfare function. Bergson utilizes an egalitarian welfare function to indicate how a maximum welfare position would be determined, but he points out that any set of value propositions sufficient to evaluate all alternatives could be used. He states that the determination of prevailing values for a given community is a proper and necessary task for economists but does not pursue this topic at all himself.[5] With regard to the manner of selection of the welfare function, Bergson simply assumes—as Arrow notes—that there is a universally accepted ordering of different possible welfare distributions in any situation.[6]

The manner in which the social welfare function is used to determine a maximum social welfare point under a given set of economic circumstances is illustrated in figure 10.1[7]. Letting U^1 and U^2 be ordinal utility indices for individuals 1 and 2 (assumed for simplicity to be the entire community), suppose that the curve AA' represent the free trade utility-possibility function for the community with its given set of individual preferences, factor supplies, and technical production constraints. The necessary (but not sufficient) conditions for maximizing social welfare are the familiar Pareto-optimum conditions of production and exchange, and

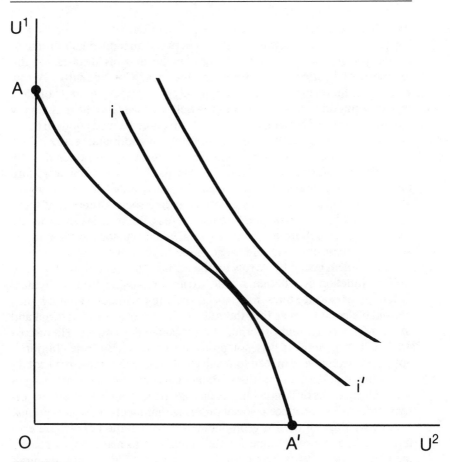

Fig. 10.1

these enable one to reduce the level of indeterminacy in the system to points along the utility-possibility frontier. Next, the social welfare function is depicted in the figure by means of a set of social indifference contours, along any one of which, e.g., ii', social welfare is constant. Since individuals are assumed to "count," the indifference contours cannot intersect and must slope downward, although their absolute slopes at any point are arbitrary. Obviously social welfare is maximized at the point of tangency between a social welfare contour and the utility-possibility curve. At the tangency point it is ethically judged that the marginal social utility of income (or of any commodity) is the same for the two individuals.

Arrow defines the social welfare function somewhat differently from Bergson and Samuelson. He first points out that the distinction between tastes and ethical values is by no means clear-cut.[8] To use his examples, there is little difference between the pleasure derived from one's own lawn and from one's neighbor's lawn or between an individual's dislike of having his grounds ruined by factory smoke and his distaste for the existence of heathenism in some distant area. Consequently, Arrow views each individual as ordering not only the various amounts of each type of commodity he may consume as well as of the labor he may supply but the amounts of both private and collectively consumed goods in every one else's hands. Each of these distributions of goods and services, i.e., each social state, is also ordered as directly represented rather than by using the notion of a utility function. He then defines a social welfare function as a process or rule which, for each individual ordering of alternative social states, gives a corresponding social ordering of these social states.[9] As Arrow points out, whereas Bergson seeks to locate social values in welfare judgments by individuals, he locates them in the actions taken through the rules society uses for making social decisions.[10]

The problem posed by Arrow on the basis of this definition of a social welfare function is whether a rule exists for passing from individual orderings of social states to a social ordering without violating such reasonable conditions as that the rule not be imposed or dictatorial and that it give a consistent ordering of all feasible alternatives. He discovered that in general it was not possible to find such a rule. Majority voting, for example, can lead to results that violate the transitivity condition. Only if at least a majority of individuals have the same ordering of social alternatives or if individual orderings are single-peaked will majority voting always produce a social ordering that meets these conditions.

An advantage of the Bergson-Samuelson formulation of welfare economics is that there is scope for the economist to make policy recommendations without it being necessary to inquire into a community's ethical standards or to know the process by which these standards are implemented. If a particular policy, e.g., free trade, gives a situation utility-possibility function entirely outside another policy, e.g., no trade, then the first policy will yield a point on a higher social welfare contour than the second policy no matter what the shape of the social welfare contours. Since, however, the implementation of a particular policy places the economy at some specific point on a situation utility-possibility function, redistributions of welfare along such a function must be permitted for this statement to have validity.

10.2 The Positive Theory of Trade Policy Determination

The contributions of Bergson, Samuelson, and Arrow prompted the developments that led, in particular, to the consideration of the related but distinct theory of public choice. In particular, the question was raised whether Pareto-efficient resource-allocational policies, delineated as such by economic analysis, would in fact be adopted under the political processes characterizing modern industrial democracies.

Writers pursuing the latter line of thought, e.g., Downs (1957) and Buchanan and Tullock (1962), postulate that voters and their elected representatives pursue their own self-interest in the political marketplace just as they do in the economic marketplace. The difference is that preferences are expressed by ballot box voting rather than dollar voting.

In applying this approach to trade policy, economists generally hypothesize producers and particular income groups to be the demanders of protectionism who seek to maximize the present value of the additional income they can obtain by reducing imports. Elected representatives (or the citizens themselves, if there is direct voting) are regarded as the suppliers of protection who also seek to maximize their own welfare. Under conditions of perfect competition in political markets this implies that they maximize their chances of election.

10.2.1 Perfect Markets

An important conclusion from this economic approach to political decision making is that Pareto-efficient policies will be implemented under majority rule provided that such conditions prevail as perfect information, no voting costs, and the absence of any costs of redistributing income.[11] Suppose, for example, that the foreign offer curve facing a country shifts outward and thereby enables the country to expand its consumption possibilities. In a vote between a tariff policy that restricts the consumption possibilities to its initial set and a free trade policy that enlarges this set, the latter policy will be selected, since it is possible to make a majority of voters (or even all voters) better off under the free trade policy than they are initially. However, in selecting a particular point among the many on the free trade utility-possibility frontier on the basis of majority rule, the cycling problem noted by Arrow can arise for the community. Each individual will order the alternative social states along this frontier on the basis of the utility he obtains from each. However, while individual preferences are transitive, majority voting will not in general yield transitive social preferences. If all points on the utility-possibility functions are to be considered, the only way out of the difficulty without abandoning majority rule is, as Arrow has shown, either to assume a universally-agreed-upon ordering of all welfare distributions (the Bergson approach) or at least to assume that a majority of voters possess identical orderings of these distributions. The latter approach means that the social welfare function is dictatorial; on the other hand, in accepting majority voting as the selection rule, the condition of nondictatorship loses its intrinsic desirability.[12]

10.2.2   Redistribution Limitations

Those who apply public choice theory to trade policy generally rule out the possibility of redistribution along a utility-possibility frontier. They assume in their analyses that the selection of a particular point on the frontier results from the operation of market forces as modified by trade taxes and as influenced by individual tastes and the prevailing distribution of productive factors.[13] This, for example, is the framework in which the Stolper-Samuelson (1941) theorem is sometimes utilized to account for protectionism in a capital-abundant economy. Since in the standard Heckscher-Ohlin-Samuelson trade model with two factors (capital and labor), two goods, and fixed trading terms a tariff will raise the real return to labor, protectionism will emerge if workers have more voting power than capitalists.[14]

But labor could always improve any position it attains under protectionism by permitting free trade and then redistributing income in its favor through lump-sum taxes that it could impose by majority voting. However, this possibility usually is not mentioned in discussing this application of economics to the politics of protection. Likewise, writers who analyze protection to particular industries and who assume that factors are industry-specific in the short run, generally do not introduce the possibility of free trade coupled with lump-sum redistribution to the factors in the industry as an option to be explained.

While most countries have some forms of automatic compensation to factors adversely affected by imports such as extended unemployment compensation, retraining payments, migration allowances, technical assistance, and governmental purchasing and scrapping of excess capital equipment, they usually do not fully compensate for the economic loss to these factors. Moreover, the measures are used to supplement protection from imports that takes the form of higher duties or quotas rather than to substitute for protectionism. Just why this is so is itself an important topic for investigation within a political economy framework. Some comments are made about this matter in the next section when discussing possible extensions of the usual analysis. The point here is simply that although the assumption made by previous writers in this field concerning limited redistribution possibilities may be consistent with the actual policies of most governments, it is a severe restriction upon first-best welfare analysis.

10.2.3   Information and Voting Costs

Besides generally ruling out the possibility of income redistribution within the context of free trade or protectionism, writers in the field also focus on the existence of various other imperfections in political markets that prevent a complete expression of the preferences of the population through the voting process. Information costs and costs of registering one's preferences through the voting process are two sources of such imperfections.

For example, in an environment of imperfect information some consumers may be unaware that the prices of an imported product and its domestic substitute have risen in response to a higher import duty. Moreover, if the increase in prices is modest compared with their budget outlays on the items, it may not be rational for these consumers to invest the time and funds to find out about the cause of the price rises in order to try to reverse these increases through the political process. Even if a consumer is aware of the reason for the price increases, he may find that the costs of registering his opposition through the political process are greater than his resultant loss in consumer welfare.

The existence of these types of costs together with the point that the welfare losses from protecting a particular industry are so widely dispersed that the loss to any one consumer is small were first emphasized by Downs (1957) as an explanation of why producers succeeded in obtaining protection from imports.

10.2.4   Elected Representatives and Political Parties

Another type of imperfection in political markets introduced in the literature on the subject concerns the fact that representative democracy with political parties prevails rather than direct democracy. If political markets operate perfectly, the actions of elected officials will merely reflect the wishes of the voters. For otherwise new candidates will enter the market and unseat existing representatives of the voters. However, the existence of imperfections that provide incumbents with special election advantages and make it very costly for new candidates to make their views widely known modifies this conclusion and increases the possibility that the wishes of a majority of the voters will not be carried out.

Brock and Magee (1974, 1980) have utilized game theory to analyze the manner in which one political party selects a particular trade policy and how a second party reacts to this choice. For example, they pose the problem of choosing preelection tariff positions by a protariff and a free-trade party in the following way. The protariff party maximizes its probability of election by increasing the level of protection it supports until the positive marginal effect on the party's election probability from the increased resources given by the protectionist lobby is just offset by the negative effect of lost voters and resource flows from free traders to the free-trade party. The free-trade party, on the other hand, chooses a position that minimizes the election chances of the protectionist party. Thus it will lower its tariff below the other party's tariff until the marginal positive effect on its election probability from resources and votes provided by free traders is just offset by the negative impact of increased funds flowing from the protectionist lobby to the protariff party. Assuming equilibrium is of the simple Cournot-Nash variety, they are able to derive such results as: (1) In the neighborhood of equilibrium, one party will become more protectionist when the second does, but the second party will adopt a more liberal position when the first party becomes more protectionist. (2) If the protectionist lobby becomes more powerful, it is not inevitable that both parties will become more protectionist; one of the parties may favor a lower tariff.

10.2.5   The Free-Rider and Externality Problems

Still another type of imperfection in the operation of political-economic markets emphasized by writers in this field, e.g., Olson (1965) and Pincus (1972, 1975), is the free-rider problem that is associated with the provision of a public good. A tariff (or the absence of one) has the characteristic of a public good in that a beneficiary from a tariff cannot be excluded from the benefits, even though he does not contribute to the costs of providing the tariff. For example, a firm in a protected industry benefits even if it does not contribute to the lobbying efforts required to secure the protection. Thus there is an incentive for each firm not to reveal its true preferences regarding its benefits in the hope that others will pay the lobbying costs. Olson argues that the voluntary formation of an effective lobbying group is more likely if the group is small and if the benefits are unevenly distributed, since under these circumstances the benefits to each individual member, or at least one member, increase.[15] Pincus adds that the costs of coordinating and monitoring a pressure group tend to reduce lobbying activity if an industry is widely dispersed geographically.

This framework has been applied to explain both why protectionism exists despite the fact that consumers represent a majority of voters as well as why some industries are more highly protected than others. Consumers are too numerous and widely dispersed for effective liberal-trade pressure groups representing their interests to be formed. While these factors generally do not prevent producers from organizing into pressure groups, one does expect that pressure groups will be more effective if the industries they represent are characterized by high levels of firm and geographic concentration. However, Olson notes a possible exception. Some groups provide both private and public goods and collect funds for organizing and lobbying from the sale of the private good. For example, a group may sell a magazine or journal that provides helpful technical information to its members. Consequently, even though the structure of an industry appears unfavorable for organizing into an effective pressure group, it may in fact be well organized for this reason.[16]

While a tariff has the public good characteristic that all producers in a protected industry benefit from the higher price no matter whether they do or do not contribute to the costs of obtaining protection, it lacks the characteristic of a pure public good that increases in benefits to one producer do not reduce the benefits to other producers. The producer benefits from protection mainly take the form of temporary rents, although expansion in the protected sector may also increase long-run returns to some factors. The distribution of these benefits among existing producers depends upon how rapidly and to what extent they respond on the supply side as well as on how fast new domestic competitors take advantage of the enhanced profit opportunities. In deciding how much to invest in lobbying activities, an individual producer must estimate the supply response of others as well as his own in order to be sure he earns at least the market rate on his rent-seeking investment. Even if there is only one producer, he must be concerned with the possibility that his lobbying investment will create profit opportunities so attractive that other firms will enter the market and prevent him from earning an acceptable return on his lobbying activities. In other words, just as a protective duty is no guarantee that individual entrepreneurs in an infant industry will undertake greater investments in acquiring technological knowledge, so too is the existence of net benefits from lobbying not a guarantee that the rent seeking will be undertaken.

This externality problem may in part explain why protectionist efforts over the last fifty years have usually focused on depressed industries. It is not rational for capitalists outside such an industry or even within the industry to invest in new productive capacity nor for outside workers to seek employment in the sector if a tariff increase occurs that still leaves the rate of return on investment and the wage rate below what they are generally. Those involved in such an industry know that the distribution of rents on existing physical and human capital in the industry is likely to be closely related to existing factor supplies and can be more certain of their return from such a tariff.

10.3   Modifying the Positive Theory of Trade Policy Determination: Social Values and Interpersonal Effects

The public choice theory of trade policy determination reviewed above is based on the assumptions that all individuals in the economy seek to maximize their welfare and that individual welfare depends only upon the goods and services a person consumes directly.

However, it is evident that considerations of equity and social justice may well affect policy choices. Thus the fact that low-income workers, including women and migrants, are substantially employed in textiles may account partly for the protection granted to this industry in some of the developed countries. The desire to protect the incomes of the under-privileged groups, whether defined by sex or citizenship or by regional location (e.g., depressed regions), can thus well provide an input into the tariff-making process, though, it must be stressed, this does not in itself explain the choice of tariff protection rather than other policy instruments in granting this element of redistribution to the concerned group.

Among the many studies of tariff making or tariff reduction that have stressed this issue, one may include Cheh (1974), Caves (1976), Helleiner (1977), and Anderson (1978). Corden (1974, p. 107) has suggested that societies may have a "conservative welfare function" which requires that trade policy should be implemented so as to avoid "any significant reductions in real incomes of any significant section of the community."[17]

If altruistic notions do contribute to protection, one may well ask what prompts such altruism. Arrow (1975) gives three reasons why an individual undertakes actions that are, or seem to be, expressions of altruism. First, the welfare of the individual may depend not only on the goods he consumes but also on the economic welfare of others. An altruistic relationship exists if the individual's welfare decreases when the welfare of others decreases.[18] As will be recalled, interpersonal relationships of this type are excluded from the Bergerson-Samuelson formulation of the social welfare function, though not from Arrow's. Second, not only may the individual derive satisfaction from seeing someone else's satisfaction increased, but also he may gain satisfaction from the fact that he himself has contributed to that satisfaction. Third, an individual may be motivated entirely by his own egotistic satisfaction, but "there is an implicit social contract that each performs duties for others in a way calculated to enhance the satisfaction of all"—an argument that implies enlightened self-interest.[19]

Of these reasons for altruistic behavior, the last may have particular relevance to protectionist policies. Thus it may be that an individual supports a tariff increase outside his own industry because he thinks this action will enhance his own chances of receiving tariff protection should his industry come under severe import competition in the future. It is this idea that serves as the basis for regarding tariffs as a type of insurance policy (see Corden 1974, pp. 320–21; Cassing 1980, pp. 396–97). Workers and capitalowners who are risk-adverse wish to avoid human and physical capital losses due to sudden and significant increases in imports that compete with the domestic products they produce. However, private markets to insure against this risk fail to exist, apparently for reasons of inadequate data or "moral hazard." The import relief legislation involving recommendations from the International Trade Commission can, for example, be viewed as a means of providing the desired insurance. However, if this view is adopted, one is left guessing why the implicit contractual behavior agreed upon by different industry groups chooses tariffs as the method of providing relief against import competition since this policy leaves consumers worse off and thereby reduces the scope of the implicit contractual arrangements embracing other groups with a political role.

Moreover, protection may well reflect broader goals, such as those analyzed by Johnson (1960) in his seminal analysis of the "scientific tariff" where he analyzed the optimal tariff structure to promote collective goals such as industrialization, self-sufficiency, "a way of life," and military preparedness.[20] While Johnson considers the question of optimal tariff structures to reflect these goals at minimal cost, the question as to whether protection or alternative policy interventions will be the least-cost policies to adopt in pursuit of such goals is explored in other papers by Johnson (1965) and Bhagwati and Srinivasan (1969).

That altruism, a Bergsonian approach, and the pure public-choice-theoretic solution can result in different tariff outcomes may now be simply illustrated. Thus, in figure 10.2, AB is the production possibility curve for goods X_1 and X_2. A shift in the terms of trade of this small, open 2×2 economy will shift production from P to P_0^*. The optimal solution, in Paretian economic terms, is then at P_0^* with zero tariff. It is also the pure public-choice-theoretic majority-rule solution under the ideal restrictions set out in section 10.2. But suppose now that there is an "altruistic," "empathetic" feeling toward labor in this model. And depict the real wages of labor in the lower RHS quadrant. There, as the production of X_1 (the $\underline{K}$-intensive good) falls with the imposition of successively higher tariffs which raise the relative price of good X_2, the real wages of labor rise à la the Stolper-Samuelson theorem. Therefore an "altruistic" tariff (t_A) may be depicted as that which brings production to P_A and real wages up from W_0 to W_A. On the other hand, one may envisage a government which instead maximizes a quasi-Bergson social welfare function such as that represented in the lower LHS quadrant. This social welfare function is defined directly on wage and rental incomes in the 2×2 model, rather than on the utilities of the wage and rental earners as in the classic Bergsonian social welfare function. The tangency of the social indifference contour with the wage-rental locus in the lower LHS quadrant then determines the corresponding production at P_B and the associated "Bergsonian" tariff rate t_B.[21]

10.4 Lobbying-determined Protection Reflecting Foregoing Considerations

The degree of protection resulting from the foregoing considerations can be formally analyzed along the lines of figure 10.3. Let $0t_0V$ be the "cost of lobbying" curve, reflecting the dollar cost of securing increasing levels of tariff protection by a lobby. Such a curve will reflect factors such as that the willingness of elected officials to grant additional protection to an industry is (1) inversely related after a point to the degree of protec-

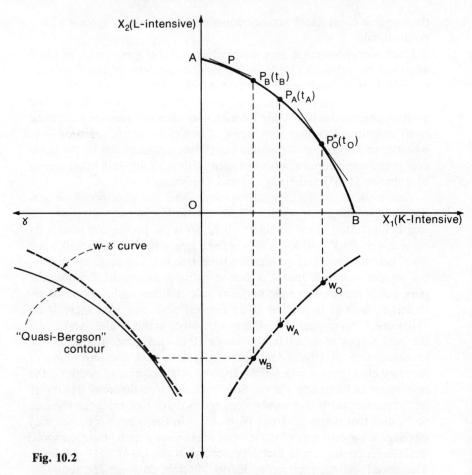

Fig. 10.2

tionism already given to the industry; (2) positively associated with the magnitude of producer lobbying expenditures (both of these relationships are part of the Brock-Magee model); and (3) positively correlated with the degree to which economic conditions in the industry match either the altruistic values or the social insurance desires of the voters. Not only are industry lobbying funds provided to candidates so that voters can be informed about how they have been, or will be, helped by the candidates, but also they are spent by an industry to convince voters that the industry's condition or cause of injury merits assistance on such grounds as fairness and equity. In other words, lobbying funds deployed by an industry will tend to reflect, in varying degrees, the diverse factors that have been discussed earlier in this paper. Reflecting the fact therefore that altruism may result in some protection at zero or negligible cost, the $0t_0V$ curve has the stretch $0t_0$ along the horizontal axis.

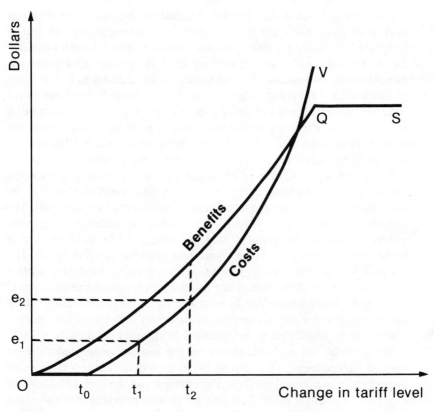

Fig. 10.3

The curve $0QS$ in figure 10.3, on the other hand, reflects the benefits from tariff protection. These are assumed to increase until they level out at Q with maximal protection implied by the prohibitive tariff.

The equilibrium, endogenous tariff then emerges in the usual profit-maximizing fashion. That is, the industry in question will select the particular lobbying-expenditure level at which the additional cost of an increment in the tariff, i.e., the marginal cost of a tariff increase, is just equal to the marginal revenue from the tariff increase. The expenditure level that maximizes the industry's net benefits is $0e_2$ in figure 10.3, and the associated tariff increase is $0t_2$.[22]

Other industries that may or may not be faced with a recent decline in the foreign import supply curve will have similarly shaped gross benefits curves indicating the increase in producer surplus associated with further increases in any existing tariffs and also similarly shaped voter-support curves indicating the highest duty increases obtainable by the industry at various expenditure levels. For many industries the voter-support curve may lie entirely above the benefits curve so that no duty change will be supported. Another possibility is that the voter curve, though intersecting the tariff-increase axis at a positive level, rises more rapidly than the benefit curve. In this case the best policy for the industry to follow is not to lobby at all.[23] It may also be the case that the voter-support curves for different industries are not independent of each voter. For example, if voters have recently supported tariff increases in other industries, the voter-support curve for the industry depicted in figure 10.3 may lie further to the left than if there had not been these increases.

The voter-support curve of an industry receiving protection may also rise over time (and thus lead to a lower optimal tariff increase for the industry) as voters learn from their experiences with a higher tariff. The industry may not live up to its promise to become internationally competitive again or the workers may not appear to be so deserving of assistance as voters learn more about them after the initial duty rise. It is for such reasons that import protection for a particular industry is often only temporary. But the model can also account for indefinite increases in protection. The information disbursed by an industry concerning why it deserves assistance may remain valid indefinitely in the minds of voters or else never be disproved by information from other sources.[24]

Many variations and extensions on the analysis presented thus far suggest themselves.[25] One would be to introduce various degrees of imperfection in political markets. For example, on the basis of his control of a party's political mechanisms or his greater previous political exposure, the incumbent may be able to obtain a higher duty for an industry than any alternative candidate who is given the same amount of campaign funds. In this case the official will share in the producer surplus generated by the tariff increase by becoming the recipient, say, of campaign contributions that reduce the need for the person to campaign as hard as would otherwise be necessary. Another modification would be to introduce interindustry differences in the ability to raise lobbying funds from firms and workers. Because of the free-rider problem, many industries, for example, may not be able to undertake the expenditures needed to maximize net benefits.

More broadly, investigations are needed concerning the different forms of assistance received by industries. Why is one industry helped by the imposition of quotas while another only receives tariff protection or perhaps extended unemployment insurance? Or why is one industry aided directly by subsidies in various forms and another indirectly by import protection? The reasons the political process does not yield the free trade solution coupled with income transfers to compensate individuals who lose under this policy must also be studied and empirically tested.

Although this last question is worthy in itself of a separate paper, a few economic and political reasons come immediately to mind. First, under the free trade–income subsidy approach, it would be necessary to set up a costly administrative mechanism both for determining just which firms and what workers are injured by cheaper imports as well as the extent of their income loss and for channeling the appropriate compensation to them. On the other hand, a tariff increase that in part offsets a decrease in import prices partially compensates injured individuals through the operation of the price system. However, the drawbacks of a tariff increase as a compensation means are that it provides extra income for those who may not be very seriously injured by the fall in import prices and does not help those who are too inefficient to remain in the industry with only a partial reversal of the price decline.

The unfavorable experience with actual income-compensating schemes (in contrast to the ideal lump-sum redistribution arrangements assumed in welfare economics) may help account for the failure of the free trade–income subsidy approach to be extensively implemented. For example, there is evidence suggesting that the special unemployment benefits extended to trade-displaced workers in the United States may make employers more willing to lay off workers and may encourage those who do lose their jobs to remain unemployed for longer periods than otherwise.[26] Such behavior tends to turn both government officials and the general public against this approach. The tariff-raising method also has the deficiency that firms may lay off workers and reduce their efficiency-increasing efforts in the expectation of receiving import protection, but such abuses are probably politically less transparent than those associated with direct income payments.

Gainers from free trade also may be reluctant to support income-compensating measures because they are unsure of the tax burden they will bear under these schemes. If, in response to a decrease in the price of an import good, a tariff is introduced that completely restores the initial price, a voter whose money income is unaffected by the change knows that he will be no worse off than before the price decline even if he does not receive any of the tariff proceeds. Voters who are risk-adverse may prefer this situation to free trade coupled with an uncertain redistribution scheme that could reduce their real income. Moreover, since it is extremely expensive to levy an income tax that captures part of the consumer surplus gains of just those who benefit from lower import prices, some voters might expect any income subsidy program to be financed through the progressive income tax system used to support most redistributive programs. Those who think they will lose on balance under this arrangement will tend to oppose the free trade–income subsidy approach. A politically appealing feature of increasing the tariff to restore in part the initial domestic price of the imported good is that those who gain from cheaper imports pay the costs of partially compensating those who are injured.

Finally, losers from trade liberalization are likely to oppose exclusive reliance on direct income redistribution. Direct income transfers clearly separate the subsidized and productive parts of one's income-receiving activities and tend to demean the recipients. Price-increasing schemes do not seem to be as objectionable to beneficiaries on this ground, since the subsidy element is less transparent. The greater transparency of tax-financed subsidies to voters is another likely reason for opposition to the free trade–income subsidy approach by those who are injured by free trade. Experience suggests that the duration of voter support for this compensation method is likely to be less than under the tariff-raising approach.

A political-economic analysis of import policy or any other public issue in which various second-best constraints are imposed does not, it should be stressed, mean that discussions of welfare-increasing policies are not longer relevant. Rent-seeking activities are themselves often regarded as a completely wasteful use of economic resources. However, in the political economy model outlined here where the absence of perfect information is a key assumption and where rent-seeking activities mainly take the form of informational expenditures (rather than, say, of income-redistributing bribes), the matter is not as clear-cut as this. Some of the information provided may be socially valuable from a benefit-cost viewpoint, even though the self-interest goal of an industry leads it to present the type of information that maximizes its likelihood of receiving protection.[27] Nevertheless, the general public is unlikely to obtain the particular set of information it would prefer to receive from any given level of informational outlays. Levying a tax on the industry's information expenditures and spending the proceeds on the type of information about the industry preferred by the general public would be an example of the kind of policy that could bring about a potential increase in welfare for the majority of voters, who are outside the industry.[28] Moreover, some industries that the community would want to assist if their economic conditions were better known may be unable to organize their members for the purpose of providing such information. As a result, the particular set of industries actually assisted may not be the ones that maximize the welfare of the voting majority for any given magnitude of information expenditures, even if the expenditures made in each industry are of the type desired by the public. Other areas of policy interest involve devising fiscal and institutional mechanisms for selecting and financing the volume of information expenditures that maximizes the community's welfare within the given set of constraints.

10.5   Empirical Results: A Review

The industry characteristics that have been used in empirical efforts to account for industry differences in tariff rates (or changes in these rates) can be divided into three groups: (1) those that indicate the ability and willingness of the productive factors employed in an industry to provide funds and other resources for lobbying efforts; (2) factors that reflect the willingness of the majority of voters and their elected representatives to grant protection; and (3) features that relate to the magnitude of the benefits obtained from different levels of (or increases in) protection.[29]

The first set of factors relate to the voter-support curve $0t_0V$ in figure 10.3, which indicates the tariff increases voters would support at various levels of lobbying expenditures. However, because of the free-rider problem associated with voluntary lobbying contributions, the feasible range of this curve for the particular industry may be such that the optimum tariff increase cannot be attained. As mentioned earlier, the ability to overcome the free-rider problem and form a common interest group (thus extending the range of the voter-support curve beyond only minimum expenditure levels) is supposedly positively correlated with the degree of industry concentration and negatively related both to the size of the industry in terms of number of firms and to the degree of geographic dispersion. In addition, as Olson (1979) points out, usually a lobbying organization is not formed immediately—or, if the organization already exists, resources are not forthcoming in significant amounts from the membership—upon the emergence of a new common interest for a group. A crisis or repeated series of crises may be necessary to shock the individuals in the group into establishing the organization or increasing their contributions to it. To capture this effect such variables as growth conditions and the level of (or, preferably, the change in) the import penetration ratio have been employed in various regression analyses. In general, the concentration ratio has not been significant in most studies. However, the number of firms, the import penetration ratio, and (especially) measures of growth perform better in the expected manner.

When an industry is subject to greater import competition, the relative change in producer income caused by a given decline as well as the ability of capitalists and workers to move into alternative productive lines may also affect the willingness of those in the industry to contribute to lobbying efforts. The first effect is usually measured by the share of value added in total output and the second by such variables as the average age of the workers, their average wages, an industry's specialization ratio, and the share of capital income in value added. The value-added ratio has turned out as expected in some studies, while among the measures of resource flexibility the average wages are almost always highly significant and the average age is significant in most instances. The other measures of resource flexibility do not perform as well. Still another variable influencing the absolute size of lobbying expenditures by an established pressure group is simply its size in terms of the total income of its members. This variable does not turn out to be significant in most regression analyses.

It should be noted that several of the variables affecting lobbying pressures by domestic producers also influence counterlobbying pressures by both foreign producers and domestic consumers. However, the assumption is usually made that the impact of domestic producers dominates that of the other two groups.

Aside from the ability of an industry to undertake lobbying efforts, the shape of the voter-support curve depends upon the willingness of voters and their elected officials to grant import protection. For example, if voters are particularly sympathetic toward low-income workers who suffer income losses and to those who have difficulty in adjusting to income losses, one would expect that tariff rates would be higher (or GATT–related tariff cuts less) in industries with relatively low wages, high proportions of unskilled workers, high average age of workers, etc. However, the higher the growth rate in these industries, the less favorable is the voter likely to be toward a given tariff increase in such industries. Because of attitudes of "fairness" on the part of voters, variables such as the level of import penetration as well as the particular reason for a sudden increase in imports, e.g., dumping, may also influence the shape of the voter-support curve. Voter views on whether an industry's decline jeopardizes some desirable national goal, e.g., national defense or foreign relations with an important foreign country, may also play a significant role in determining the nature of a voter-support curve.

A selfish reason why voters may resist tariff increases is the fear that foreign tariff retaliation will decrease output in the industries where they are employed. Thus one expects increased protection for a particular industry to be easier to obtain if only a few other industries are also pressing for import relief. Similarly, general tariff-cutting efforts by a government are likely to be easier to undertake if other governments are also cutting their import duties. If the majority of voters favor protectionism primarily for selfish, long-run insurance purposes, one would expect this policy to operate mainly in industries where average wages are near those of the voters as a whole on the grounds that these are more similar to the industry for which the average voter wants insurance, namely, his own industry.

The size of the industry in sales or employment terms is likely to affect the voter-support curve for several reasons. Each individual voter realizes, for example, that when the foreign import supply curve is completely elastic in an industry, the producer-surplus benefits obtained from a given import price rise are greater, the greater is the domestic industry's supply. He may also be more willing to grant this price increase, the larger the number of workers per dollar of increase in net benefits. On the other hand, the more significant the protected item is in his budget, the less ready is he likely to be to support increased duties. In addition, industry size influences the curve because of the voting strength of those employed in an industry itself, the magnitude of general tax revenues lost from the declining industry, and the existing degree of knowledge on the part of voters about the sector. The relations of other industries, as import suppliers or output users, to the particular industry under consideration should also be considered in the context of the preceding factors.

Among the variables included in the second group of factors influencing the shape of the voter-support curve, measures of human capital, such as average wages and the proportion of unskilled workers, perform the best and, indeed, seem to be the most significant variables in the various studies taken as a whole. Tests of different international policy variables are not numerous enough to generalize, but Caves (1976) did find some support for Canada's tariffs being related to their economic development goals. Fieleke (1976) on the other hand found that a national defense variable was not significant in accounting for the United States tariff structure. Industry size as measured by number of employees is significant in the expected manner in some of the studies.

Though not included thus far in any of the regression analyses, various factors relating the ability of elected officials to deviate from the preferences of the voters (and still get reelected) could also be included as influences on the shape of the curve indicating the support of decision makers for tariff increases.

The magnitude of the industry benefits from different levels of protection or increases in protective levels, i.e., the position of the producer benefits curve $0QS$ in figure 10.3, depends on the elasticity of the industry's short-run supply curve, the level of output from which tariff increases are being considered, and any other supply curve shifts due to factors other than the initial downward pressure on price. If, for example, productive factors are completely immobile in the short run, the short-run supply curve will be vertical and the benefits curve will therefore be steeper up to the tariff increase that restores the initial price. This will raise the equilibrium tariff level *ceteris paribus*.[30] As already noted, the degree of factor mobility can be measured by such variables as the average wages in an industry, the average age of its employees or, if one considers capital to be more immobile than labor, capital's income share, and the elasticity of substitution of labor for capital in other sectors.

Furthermore, the higher the degree of product specialization in the industry the more likely it is that a higher proportion of the factors in the industry will be immobile in the short run.

Since a given percentage increase in domestic supply in response to a 1 percent increase in price will increase producer surplus by a larger sum if the initial output level is large, the slope of the benefits curve is also related to the industry's output level. While short-run shifts in the domestic demand curve will not affect the short-run benefits of a given tariff increase in cases where the foreign supply curve is perfectly elastic, these shifts will have an independent price effect when this curve is less than perfectly elastic. An increasing demand curve will add to the short-run benefits of a given tariff increase. Still another factor of this type is the extent to which producers in an industry own comparable facilities abroad that export either back to the home country or to third countries. In the latter case the producers do not wish to set off tariff increases in their export markets.

As the preceding discussion indicates, it is difficult to find variables that enable one to discriminate among different hypotheses concerning the reason for interindustry differences in protectionism. Should, for example, the fact that protectionism is comparatively high in industries with comparatively low per worker levels of human capital be interpreted as support for the hypothesis that voters behave in an altruistic manner or for the hypothesis that, because of their poorer adjustment ability, low-income groups are more likely to overcome the free-rider problem that tends to limit lobbying efforts? Moreover, quite aside from interindustry differences in voter attitudes or in the free-rider problem, the equilibrium tariff increase after a given decline in the foreign supply curve will be greater if low levels of human capital are associated with inelastic short-run industry supply curves. One way in which the first two hypotheses might be disentangled would be to determine whether per capita lobbying resources, in terms of money, letter-writing efforts, and other measures of political pressures, on the part of low-wage workers are in fact greater than for high-wage workers in response to a given decline in income. Furthermore, it might be possible to separate the last hypothesis from the others by introducing measures of short-run supply elasticity as well as average wages into the regressions.

Most of the other variables mentioned also can be interpreted as affecting both curves in figure 10.3. The direction of their impact on tariff levels is generally the same, but again existing analyses do not enable one to discriminate among the underlying forces for which these variables serve as proxies. Yet, if one of the objectives of such investigations is to suggest policies or institutional changes that will increase welfare in the second-best world of trade-policy formation, the ability to make such distinctions is essential. The possibility of succeeding in this regard would seem to require greater efforts to determine the various separate relationships that make up a total model of the political economy of protectionism.

Notes

1. The most famous United States historical study along these lines is Taussig (1931). See also Schnattschneider (1935).
2. Several of the articles will be discussed in the text, while all are listed in the references at the end of the paper.
3. Samuelson (1947, p. 221).
4. Bergson (1968 reprint, p. 413).
5. Bergson (1968 reprint, p. 413).
6. Arrow (1963, p. 71).
7. Samuelson (1956, p. 15).
8. Arrow (1963, p. 18).
9. Arrow (1963, p. 23).
10. Arrow (1963, p. 106).
11. It has also been pointed out by Coase (1960) that with these conditions some market failures, e.g., certain externalities, will be corrected through private contracts without requiring any government intervention.
12. Arrow (1963, p. 74).
13. The only redistribution generally mentioned relates to the tariff proceeds, and this is not brought into a discussion of attracting additional votes.
14. If workers pursue their self-interest, they will raise tariffs to the levels that eliminate trade. In fact, they could even lobby for export subsidies.
15. See Brock and Magee (1974) for a modeling of some of Olson's concepts in terms of a noncooperative game.
16. One could say that, in these cases, the cost of lobbying is low because it is marginal to a public-good activity already in place.
17. However, the question of what is a "significant section" of the community here can depend, in a pluralistic democracy, on lobbying by the section itself, so that it is not clear that the explanation of protection provided by resort to such a notion as Corden's is truly independent of the kind of explanation resulting from public-choice theory based wholly on self-interest.
18. If the individual's welfare increases, the relationship is one of envy rather than altruism.
19. Arrow (1975, p. 17). Arrow is discussing the reasons why people give blood to individuals they do not personally know.
20. One of the hypotheses tested by Caves on Canadian data is that there is "a collective national preference for industrialization while also promoting prairie settlement and a national transportation system." Caves (1976, p. 279).
21. The diagram assumes the necessary convexities for an interior maximum, of course.
22. If the industry is initially in a tariff equilibrium position but the voters change their views and agree upon a general tariff-cutting rule under a GATT–sponsored trade negotiation, the point $0t_2$ can be interpreted as the tariff increment above the formula cut that minimizes the industry's losses relative to its initial income level.
23. If the absolute slope of the voter support curve is less at all points than the absolute slope of the non-horizontal portion of the benefits curve, a prohibitive duty will be imposed.

24. In the narrow self-interest model where voters are in effect tricked into permitting increased protectionism, it is much more likely that the protection to an industry will decline as voters gain experience from repeated "plays" of this political "game."

25. Lobbying-determined tariffs are analyzed, in explicit models, by Findlay and Wellisz (chapter 8) and Feenstra and Bhagwati (chapter 9) in this volume. In fact, Feenstra and Bhagwati develop benefits and costs curves much like those in figure 10.3.

26. See Richardson (chapter 12 here) and Neumann (1979).

27. The appropriability problem may prevent this information from being provided through the private market mechanism.

28. Since these voters would have the option to ask for the same type of information the industry would have furnished with the taxed funds, the ability to select a different information set provides the opportunity for a potential welfare increase.

29. Since the 1930s the average tariff level for dutiable manufactures has decreased very significantly in the industrial countries. For example, in the United States the ratio of duties collected to the value of dutiable imports declined from 59 percent in 1932 to 10 percent in 1970. Consequently, existing interindustry differences in tariff rates are closely related to the ability of industries to resist the general downward pressure on tariffs.

30. Presumably in the initial position the marginal benefits of a tariff increase are less than the lobbying expenditures needed to achieve the tariff increase.

References

Anderson, K. 1978. Politico-economic factors affecting structural change and adjustment. In C. Aislabie and C. Tisdell, eds., *The economics of structural change and adjustment*. Institute of Industrial Economics, Conference Series no. 5, University of Newcastle.

———. 1979. Toward an explanation of recent changes in Australian protectionism. Mimeographed.

Arrow, K. J. 1951. *Social choice and individual values*. New York: Wiley.

———. 1963. *Social choice and individual values*. 2d ed. New York: Wiley.

———. 1975. Gifts and exchange. In E. S. Phelps, ed., *Altruism, morality, and economic theory*. New York: Russell Sage Foundation.

Baldwin, R. E. 1976. The political economy of postwar U.S. trade policy. *Bulletin*, 1976–4, New York Graduate School of Business Administration, Center for the Study of Financial Institutions.

Bale, M. D. 1977. United States concessions in the Kennedy Round and short-run labor adjustment costs: Further evidence. *Journal of International Economics* 7, no. 2 (May): 145–48.

Bergson, A. 1938. A reformulation of certain aspects of welfare economics. *Quarterly Journal of Economics* 52 (February): 310–34. Reprinted in 1968 in Alfred N. Page, ed., *Utility theory: A book of readings*, pp. 402–22. New York: Wiley.

Bhagwati, J. N., and T. N. Srinivasan. 1969. Optimal intervention to achieve non-economic objectives. *Review of Economic Studies*, vol. 36 (January).

Brock, W. A., and S. P. Magee. 1974. An economic theory of politics: The case of tariffs. Mimeographed.

———. 1978. The economics of special interest politics: The case of tariffs. *American Economic Review* 68, no. 2 (May): 246–50.

———. 1980. Tariff formation in a democracy. In J. Black and B. Hindley, eds., *Current issues in commercial policy and diplomacy.* London. Macmillan.

Buchanan, J. M., and G. Tullock. 1962. *The calculus of consent.* Ann Arbor: University of Michigan Press.

Cassing, J. H. 1980. Alternatives to protectionism. In J. Leveson and J. W. Wheeler, eds., *Western economies in transition*, pp. 391–424. Boulder: Westview Press.

Caves, R. E. 1976. Economic models of political choice: Canada's tariff structure. *Canadian Journal of Economics* 9, no. 2 (May): 278–300.

Cheh, J. H. 1974. United States concessions in the Kennedy Round and short-run labor adjustment costs. *Journal of International Economics* 4: 323–40.

———. 1976. A note on tariffs, nontariff barriers, and labour protection in United States manufacturing industries. *Journal of Political Economics* 84: 398–94.

Coase, R. 1960. The problem of social costs. *Journal of Law and Economics* 3: 1–44.

Constantopoulos, M. 1974. Labour protection in Western Europe. *European Economic Review* 5: 313–18.

Corden, W. M. 1974. *Trade policy and economic welfare.* Oxford: Clarendon Press.

Downs, A. 1957. *An economic theory of democracy.* New York: Harper & Row.

Fieleke, N. 1976. The tariff structure for manufacturing industries in the United States: A test of some traditional explanations. *Columbia Journal of World Business* 11, no. 4 (Winter): 98–104.

Helleiner, G. K. 1977. The political economy of Canada's tariff structure: An alternative model. *Canadian Journal of Economics* 4, no. 2 (May): 318–26.

Johnson, H. G. 1960. The cost of protection and the scientific tariff. *Journal of Political Economics* 68, no. 4 (August): 327–45.

———. 1965. Optimal trade intervention in the presence of domestic distortions. In R. E. Caves, H. G. Johnson, and P. B. Kenen, eds., *Trade, growth, and the balance of payments.* Amsterdam: North-Holland.

Magee, S. 1976. Three simple tests of the Stolper-Samuelson theorem. December, Xeroxed.

Mayer, W. 1974. Short-run and long-run equilibrium for a small open economy. *Journal of Political Economics* 82, no. 5 (September/October): 955–67.

Mueller, D. C. 1976. Public choice: A survey. *Journal of Economic Literature* 14, no. 2 (June): 395–433.

Mussa, M. 1974. Tariffs and the distribution of income: The importance of factor specificity, substitutability, and intensity in the short and long-run. *Journal of Political Economics* 82, no. 6 (December): 1191–1203.

Neumann, G. R. 1979. Adjustment assistance for trade-displaced workers. In D. B. D. Denoon, ed., *The new international economic order: The U.S. response.* New York: New York University Press.

Olson, M. 1965. *The logic of collective action: Public goods and the theory of groups.* Cambridge, Mass.: Harvard University Press.

———. 1979. The political economy of comparative growth rates. Mimeographed.

Pincus, J. 1972. A positive theory of tariff formation applied to nineteenth century United States. Ph.D. thesis, Stanford University.

———. 1975. Pressure groups and the pattern of tariffs. *Journal of Political Economics* 83, no. 4 (August): 757–78.

Rawls, J. 1971. *A theory of social justice.* Cambridge, Mass.: Harvard University Press.

Ray, E. J. 1979. Tariff and nontariff barriers to trade in the U.S. and abroad. October, Xeroxed.

Riedel, J. 1977. Tariff concessions in the Kennedy Round and the structure of tariff protection in West Germany: An econometric assessment. *Journal of International Economics* 7, no. 2 (May): 133–43.

Samuelson, P. A. 1947. *Foundations of economic analysis,* chap. 8. Cambridge, Mass.: Harvard University Press.

———. 1956. Social indifference curves. *Quarterly Journal of Economics* 70, no. 1 (February): 1–22.

Schattschneider, E. E. 1935. *Politics, pressures, and the tariff: A study in free private enterprise in pressure politics, as shown in the 1929–1930 revision of the tariff.* New York: Prentice-Hall.

Stolper, W., and P. A. Samuelson. 1941. Protection and real wages. *Review of Economic Structure* 9, no. 1 (November): 58–73.

Taussig, F. W. 1931. *The tariff history of the United States.* Cambridge, Mass.: Harvard University Press.

Comment   Stephen P. Magee

Most blind men who have examined the elephant of political economy have come away with different impressions of the animal. My substantial

Stephen P. Magee is the McDermott Professor of Finance at the University of Texas at Austin. He is the author of *International Trade and Distortions in Factor Markets* (Marcel-Dekker, 1976) and *International Trade* (Addison-Wesley, 1980).

agreement with Baldwin's views leads me to worry that we are either both looking through a glass darkly or both specializing in the same corner of the beast. Since there are so many areas of agreement, this discussion will be limited to the few issues on which we disagree.

Baldwin is skeptical, and properly so, about the Downsian view that competitive markets plus efficient political bribing lead to Pareto optimality. He does a nice job of relaxing the rather restrictive assumptions of this model in the process of attempting to explain tariffs. He is overly optimistic, however, in his reintroduction of social values and interpersonal effects. The Corden "conservative welfare function," Arrow's "altruism," and the Phelps "generalized regard for human rights" models all culminate in the "insurance theory of tariffs." According to this view, government policy on protection provides an insurance policy for risk-averse economic agents. The result is back-door Downsianism: Pareto optimality somehow emerges from rent seeking by protectionist and free trade forces. To my way of thinking, this approach places excessive credence in the potential optimality of rent seeking. There are seven reasons why I believe that this "public welfare view of tariff setting" is a myth.

First, such a view can be defended by appeal to the Coase theorem. When applied to the tariff problem, the theorem asserts that with well-defined property rights, competitive rent seeking by pro- and antitariff forces will lead to Pareto optimality. The fallacy in this view is the failure to see that the legal rules of the game themselves are established by a rent-seeking process. If there are differential costs to groups in setting up the rules of the game, we will observe subsequent competition on issues such as protection resulting in one group in society gaining less than other groups give up.

Second, political markets in information are notoriously imperfect. Successful politicians are frequently those most capable of distorting the views of their opponents to voters: Lyndon Johnson's characterization of Goldwater and Richard Nixon's description of Richard McGovern are cases in point. The manifestation of this behavior in United States discussions of protectionism is illustrated by the protectionist appeal that "tariffs protect jobs." Protectionists do not advertise that tariffs in the United States protect lousy jobs at the expense of good jobs, just as free traders fail to mention that United States tariffs are progressive, benefiting low-wage labor.

Third, Baldwin feels that one failure of elected representatives is that they do not always act in the interest of voters. Though Baldwin discusses Arrow's impossibility theorem earlier, he should have mentioned it here since some patterns of underlying preferences make it impossible to determine the "interest of voters." A related point is that there are situations in which the more competitive the political system, the more likely the parties are to sell distortionary policies to well-organized interest groups. The proceeds of such sales are used to improve the party's chances of election (see Brock and Magee 1980).

Fourth, there are empirically indistinguishable alternatives to the insurance theory of tariffs as explanations of both old industries and industries with market power. The low opportunity costs of lobbying activity for low-wage labor and factors in markets with distortions suggest why we would see protection in these industries. Furthermore, the insurance theory is better applied to dumping laws than to tariffs. The theory would suggest that we should observe the rapid application of temporary protection to industries in which unanticipated changes have occurred in world prices. Unfortunately for the theory, (1) this occurrence is also explained by the low opportunity cost of lobbying for unemployed resources and (2) the protection is seldom temporary.

Fifth, the insurance model cannot explain why political markets appear to prefer voluntary export restraints by foreigners as first-best, quotas as second-best, tariffs as third-best, production subsidy as fourth-best, and labor subsidy as fifth-best when unexpected price changes cause wages to fall in certain sectors. Bhagwati (1971) showed that exactly the reverse ranking would hold if the system were operating on the basis of welfare efficiency. The view Brock and I have developed is that redistributive policies are the prices which clear political markets between competing groups. Each party selects policies which maximize its probability of election. In equilibrium, they will have balanced the marginal positive effects of the resources they collect against the negative general voter effect emanating from the general disaffection the distortionary policy generates. This means that each party will select a policy achieving redistribution which is the most indirect and difficult for the voters to understand.

Sixth, I think an underemphasized explanation of protection is that it protects distortionary rents which have been developed through local monopoly power. If the steel industry is imperfectly competitive and earns supernormal profits, labor unions attempt to force management to share these rents. The result is high wages, unionization, and barriers to entry in the factor market for this industry. When imports threaten to reduce the output of the domestic steel industry, the monopoly profits accruing to management and the distorted wage differentials earned by labor stimulate both factors to act in concert. The distortions reduce the mobility of factors in as well as out of the industry. This generates Cairnesian-type lobbying behavior rather than the more traditional Stolper-Samuelson lobbying. Stolper and Samuelson suggest that all capital would be, say, for free trade while all labor would be for protection (or vice versa): their main point is that some labor should not be for protection and other labor for free trade. An empirical test of the Cairnesian versus the Stolper-Samuelson approach indicates that nineteen out of twenty-one industries lobbying on the President's trade bill in 1973 followed the Cairnesian approach (Magee 1980*a*). In a two-factor world, if we plot the positions of capital and labor in a 2 × 2 table, we should find all of the observations in the diagonal cells if the world behaves in a Cairnesian (noncompeting group) fashion. If the Stolper-Samuelson model is correct, all the observations would be in one of the two off-diagonal cells. Notice in figure C10.1 that nineteen of the twenty-one industries studied fell along the diagonal, which rejects the Stolper-Samuelson model.

Seventh (and finally), competitive political markets show considerably more concern over redistribution than over the social welfare issues. What is best for society is much less important than which groups in society can most effectively channel their desire for larger amounts of income into effective political clout. Analysis of United States tariffs on directly competitive imports in 1971 indicates that the social costs are only about 7 percent of the consumer loss. Furthermore, when the stakes are high on both sides (for free traders and protectionists) and when elections are close, large amounts of resources can be channeled into rent seeking with considerable loss (see Magee 1980*b*).

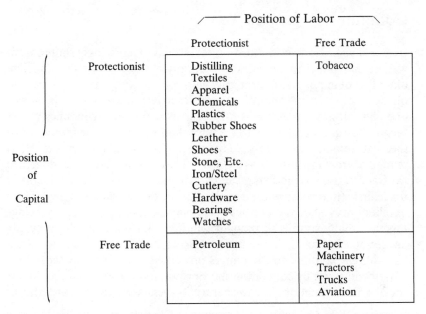

Fig. C10.1   A classification of twenty-one United States industries according to the political preferences of capital and labor. Source: Magee (1980*a*).

To summarize, the issue in competitive rent seeking is whether virtue and optimality emerge or whether the economy is shoved toward a black hole. While some may argue that the horse race is a close one, I'll put my money on the sow's ear over the silk purse.

References

Bhagwati, J. N. 1971. The generalized theory of distortions and welfare. In J. N. Bhagwati et al., eds., *Trade, balance of payments, and growth*, pp. 69–90. Amsterdam: North-Holland.

Brock, W. A., and S. P. Magee. 1978. The economics of special interest politics: The case of the tariff. *American Economic Review Papers and Proceedings* 68 (May): 246–50.

————. 1980. Tariff formation in a democracy. In J. Black and B. Hindley, *Current issues in international commercial policy and diplomacy*, pp. 1–9. London: Macmillan.

Magee, S. P. 1980a. Three simple tests of the Stolper-Samuelson theorem. In P. Oppenheimer, *Issues in international economics*, pp. 138–53. London: Routledge & Kegan Paul.

————. 1980b. The black-hole theory of competitive rent seeking. Department of Finance, University of Texas at Austin, mimeographed.

Comment   Stanislaw Wellisz

In recent years trade economists' interests have increasingly shifted from welfare economics to the political economy of trade and protection. The older line of inquiry dealt primarily with comparative statics and focused on the first best, while admitting obstacles to its achievement.[1] The newer one concentrates on adjustment processes and is the economics of the second best par excellence. More important perhaps is the treatment of the institutional framework. Trade economists (Marxians excepted) tended to treat institutions as a datum. They now attempt to endogenize the trade regime by modeling the political process. Baldwin, who himself made important contributions to the welfare discussion,[2] now gives us an excellent survey of the political economy of trade. The survey brings together many strands of thought, clarifies difficult issues (I especially appreciate the lucid interpretation of Brock and Magee), and provides a valuable background to the papers presented at this conference.

Baldwin starts by comparing the Bergson-Samuelson with the Arrow social welfare function. The former treats social welfare as an ordering of

Stanislaw Wellisz is professor of economics at Columbia University. He has made contributions to developmental theory, the theory of organization of the firm, and international economics (jointly with Ronald Findlay). His publications include *The Economics of the Soviet Bloc* (New York: McGraw-Hill).

individual utilities performed by a grand ranker with his own preferences. The latter views social welfare as a mapping from individual to aggregate preferences. The inherent difficulties of these formulations need not detain us here. It may be worthwhile to point out, however, that the former corresponds to the conception of the government as a guardian of public interest, whereas under the latter the government is merely an executor of the resultant of individual or collective pressures.

The distinction between the two concepts of the social welfare function helps clarify some of the models discussed by Baldwin. Thus we may pose ethical questions to a Bergson-Samuelson type of government, but not to one of the Arrow type; conversely, we may ask how voting, lobbying, or for that matter the use of force explains the actions of the latter, but not of the former. But too much discussion of the nature of the social welfare function is counterproductive. It is idle to speculate why some interests helped by changes in trade patterns favor redistribution in favor of those who are hurt by the change. Those willing to give might be genuinely altruistic, or the poverty of others might constitute for them a negative externality, or they might follow an insurance principle (their "altruism" will be reciprocated in case of need), or maybe they think that if they do not yield a little voluntarily, more will be taken from them by force. Clearly, speculation as to the motives does not help our understanding or ability to predict the outcome.

The most significant progress made by the political economists of trade does not result from speculation about the nature of welfare functions, but from the consideration of problems affecting specific interest groups. The familiar 2 × 2 model tells us that if changes in trade patterns help one factor (such as capital), they are likely to hurt another (such as labor). Such a broad formulation throws little light on the pattern of interest groups in a world in which there is human as well as physical capital and where, in the short run, either type of capital may be highly specific. The new analysis helps us understand why, often, capital, management, and labor engaged in a given industry join forces in lobbying for or against protection. In the long run United States capital (or is it labor?) will benefit from increased foreign car competition. Right now the owners of specific capital employed in that industry, which means the stockholders, and various kinds of labor, including management and union leaders, are hurt: owners of specific factors *do* unite.

By the same token economists have retreated from policy descriptions derived from analytically illuminating, but overly simplified, models. Thus the maximization of social welfare subject to the constraint that employment of a factor be maintained on a specific level (or, by the same token, that the income of a specific factor be maintained on a given level) leads to the conclusion that a tax-cum-subsidy scheme is superior to tariff protection.[3] Now that the United States government is taking such direct

292 Robert E. Baldwin

compensatory steps (many other governments have done so before, and failed) we begin to realize how difficult it is to determine in practice who is hurt by changes in trade patterns.

Direct subsidization leads to a host of difficulties which can be broadly subsumed under the moral hazard label. The reliance on old-fashioned trade restraints, for all the inefficiencies they create, at least avoids that difficulty.

For all the progress we have made, our knowledge of the political economy of trade is still in its infancy. The observed pattern of trade restraints is compatible with any number of hypotheses concerning the nature of political processes. The reality, which has so long eluded the analysis of political scientists, has yet to yield its secrets to the investigation of economists armed with more powerful analytic tools. Likewise, our understanding of specific restrictive measures is also rather weak. When confronted with the question, why tariffs, or why quotas, or why voluntary restrictions, we beat a hasty retreat from analytic to common-sense explanations. Yet if we hope to improve policy—and, after all, we are all moralists at heart—we should have a clear understanding of the factors dictating the current practice.

Baldwin's survey is doubly valuable: it shows what we have accomplished and what is yet to be done. We may be humbled by how little we have accomplished, but, unlike Alexander, we need not despair that nothing is left to conquer.

Notes

1. For a classic statement, see Samuelson (1962).
2. In particular, see Baldwin (1952, 1953–54).
3. For an elegant proof of such propositions, see Bhagwati and Srinivasan (1969).

References

Baldwin, R. E. 1952. The new welfare economics and gains in international trade. *Quarterly Journal of Economics* 65: 91–101.
———. 1953–54. A comparison of welfare criteria. *Review of Economic Studies* 21: 154–61.
Bhagwati, J. N., and T. N. Srinivasan. 1969. Optimal intervention to achieve non-economic objectives. *Review of Economic Studies* 36: 27–38.
Samuelson, P. A. 1962. The gains from international trade once again. *Economic Journal* 72 (December): 820–29.

III. Adjustment Processes, Assistance Policies, and Political Response: Some Empirical Realities

11 Adjustment in Process: A Lancashire Town

Ronald P. Dore

This paper is an interim report from a field study. It concerns the structure of industry in the former textile town of Blackburn: how, why, and in what manner are textiles going downhill? What is going uphill, and why?

The focus of the research is on one particular kind of adjustment problem—that arising from the dynamics of trade between the NICs (and subsequent generations of NICs) and OICs. The assumptions, positive and normative, on which the investigation is based are as follows:

1. As in the Bhagwati paper (chapter 6), which takes the same focus, there are assumed to be in the OICs (*A*) one set of (manufacturing) industries which are losing domestic markets to imports because the NICs' potential comparative advantage from differential wage rates is being increasingly realized as the NICs learn by doing (*and* by studying); these are industries well advanced in the product cycle, where learning by doing and studying is easier; (*B*) another "Schumpeterian" set (mostly manufacturing, some services) at an earlier stage of the product cycle in which the OICs retain comparative advantage in international trade *and* where productivity growth is more rapid and hence from whose expansion the OICs have most to gain in terms of growth in per capita national income (NI); as well as (*C*) an intermediate range of industries not clearly in either category, including, of course, poodle clipping and discos and retailing and emergency wards which provide non-internationally traded goods and services.

Ronald P. Dore is a Fellow of the Institute of Development Studies at the University of Sussex and a distinguished sociologist. Most of his work has been on Japanese society and comparative patterns of development. He is the author of *British Factory–Japanese Factory* (Berkeley and Los Angeles: University of California Press, 1973).

Much of the information in this paper was collected by the author's collaborators, Geoffrey Shepherd, Gillian McHugh, and Jill Eaton, though they deserve the usual absolution from any responsibility for any use of it.

2. It is assumed that the sort of dynamic change which would take place in the OICs in the absence of any market distortions except trade union protection of wage levels would be roughly: Increasing import penetration in the domestic markets of A industries leads to the following: (a) employment declines (wages do not drop) in OIC A industries; (b) a consumer surplus is generated in OICs from the purchase of cheaper imports; (c) demand in the exporting NICs increases for imports of the OICs' B industries; (d) the consumer surplus and the NIC demand both stimulate expansion in B and C industries, which absorb the labor released from the A industries; (e) the increased exports of OIC B industries to NICs balances the external accounts to pay for increased imports.

3. Some such outcome is assumed to be desirable. More specifically, for all the reasons about shared interests in world stability and prosperity set out in the Brandt (1980) report, we assume that the policy objectives of OIC governments should *also* give very positive weighting to the welfare gains accruing to the NICs from this process.

4. But to ask that, in order to achieve this desirable outcome, market forces should be let rip is to ask for the moon. Most modern societies do not work like that. In Europe at least, in Japan, and increasingly in the United States, the political clout of the interest groups who lose in the process of writing off the A industries is too great to let it happen.

5. The only way to move toward this desirable outcome therefore is to buy off the opposition.

6. One can also (Diamond's debate, beginning in section 5.5) find arguments from justice for doing so on the following lines: Current world norms concerning what citizens have a right to demand of governments have come to include the right to the protection of jobs against import competition. The entrepreneur who goes bankrupt or the worker who loses his job because the government fails to offer such protection has, on this argument, a claim to more consideration than someone who reaches the same plight through his own inefficiency.

7. But how best to provide the compensation? How will such compensation best (a) provide an inducement not to resist the run-down of the A industries, (b) produce the least frictional hurt from that run-down, with (c) the most just graduation of hurt to compensation and (d) at the same time optimizing distribution of the incremental flow of capital and labor, respectively, as between the B and C industries? The best way to work toward an answer to those questions, we thought, was by talking to people currently affected by the process. Our specific questions are:

—When a textile entrepreneur is faced (not just because of import competition but because of any noncyclical secular change) with a declining market and the prospect of nonviability, what factors enter into his choice between closing down, rationalizing to cut costs and stay competitive with the same products, or changing his product mix? In particular, how far do his relations with his workers and with his workers' unions constrain those decisions?

—Assuming that he would see any one of those three alternatives as inferior to getting government protection through the exercise of "voice," what systematic factors affect his likely success in doing so?

—Some enterprises retain their market shares and remain profitable even in the face of import competition; what are the specific products, or processes, or managing or marketing styles, which differentiate these firms from those that go under?

—What are the differences between the small family firm and the large corporation in these various respects?

—Who suffers from an industry's decline, and in what way and how much? How easily are people's skills and capital assets redeployed? What material and psychic costs do people incur in getting new jobs and perhaps homes? What are the secondary effects on commerce and services in towns where a contracting industry is concentrated?

—What are the new enterprises that expand employment as the A industry contracts? Are there any observable "phoenix" micromechanisms whereby the new firms arise directly from the ashes of the old, directly utilizing resources released by the decline of the old (which might give clues as to useful types of state intervention)?

For a variety of reasons fairly obvious from the nature of the questions (including, apropos of entrepreneurs' decision making, the hypothesis that local factors, not just the state of national markets, probably enter into their calculations) the study concentrates on the weaving industry in a single town, Blackburn.

11.1   Recent Trends

Textiles in Blackburn have been in steady decline since the days, at the beginning of the century, when Lancashire supplied the home market before breakfast and spent the rest of the day clothing the remainder of the empire. In the town itself the 140 weaving mills of the early 1930s have contracted to a mere dozen, with another dozen in the outskirts, but in the same travel-to-work area. Textiles, having accounted for more than half of total employment half a century ago, made up 12 percent of total employment and 23 percent of employment in manufacturing in 1973 (Blackburn travel-to-work area as a whole), 10 percent and 20 percent, respectively, in 1976, and doubtless even less today. Close to 15 percent of the jobs remaining in weaving in November 1979 were lost in the following eight months, and the number of unemployed former textile workers rose from 225 to 824. This acceleration of decline was brought about not by competition from Third World countries (which is held steady by the MFA) but by the general recession sharply exacerbated by a combination of overvalued pound, high interest rates, and stronger competition from the European periphery (Rumania, Turkey, Greece, Portugal) less restrained by quota restrictions and aided by taste changes. (Foreign producers responded more rapidly to the growing demand for denims and corduroys: new competitors snatch new markets more easily than they erode old ones.)

Firms which have recently closed or undergone major, reduced-scale reorganization include the following:

1. A velvet manufacturer (155 employees, branch of a French, medium-sized enterprise) producing 90 cm widths, losing its markets to German competitors producing the 150 cm widths preferred by garment makers. Is marking time with one-day-a-week working pending decisions about reequipment.

2. A plant (430 employees) of large corporation A specializing in woven mattress ticking made on Jacquard looms. Progressively lost markets to products of a newer, cheaper, stitch-bonded process. Has reequipped to produce polyester-cotton sheeting for markets now rapidly being invaded by United States imports.

3. A family firm (200 employees) weaving cotton-synthetic mixes for outer garments in what is claimed to be temporary trouble because of (a) some reduction of orders due to recession and (b) some delayed purchases due to converters' unwillingness to hold stocks at a time of high interest rates. But the owners have recently floated a new merchanting enterprise to import cloth for sale to converters and garment makers.

4. A plant (850 employees) of large corporation A specializing in crease-resistent cotton-synthetic mixes for garments with their own brand-named cloth. In trouble for five or six years because of fashion switch to denims, and imports of ready-made suitings chiefly from Portugal, Rumania, and the United States. A reconstruction plan undertaken in 1978 involving reequipment and new ventures in women's wear foundered in 1979. Factory closed.

5. A former family firm (130 employees) taken over in 1963 by large corporation B, but run as an independent unit by former owner. Specialized in curtain fabrics woven on Jacquard looms. Like 2 above, faced with gradually narrowing markets as a result of competition from stitch-bonded prints. Closed and remaining business transferred to sister mill in Yorkshire, 1980.

6. A former family firm (80 employees) acquired some time ago by a medium-sized Manchester firm of converters and garment makers. Wove a variety of cloth, mainly industrial, on 1890-vintage Lancashire looms driven on direct drive by an even older steam engine. Had barely survived in recent years, in spite of import competition driving down prices, by virtue of lower than average wages, refusal to countenance any major repair and upkeep expenditure, and assistance from government tempo-

rary employment subsidy. Ending of the subsidy and imminent need for several major items of capital expenditure (new pirn winders, major repair to steam engine) precipitated closure 1979.

What have we so far learned from our interviews concerning the determinants of the choice between rationalizing, diversifying, or closing?

11.2 The Rationalizing Option: General

For the family firms, the time for choice between the "hanging-on" option 6 above and the "fight-back" option 3 is long since past. No one would now put large infusions of capital into Mill 6: it could survive as long as it did only because all its fixed assets had long been written down to zero and it had to cover only (day shift) wages, material costs, and interest on working capital. Mill 3 started reequipping with modern shuttleless looms, exploited by three-shift working, in the 1960s when prospects were better: it has been able to reequip with later vintages every four or five years (*a*) because it had good secondhand machines to sell and (*b*) because of the liberal capital depreciation allowance system available to British firms generally (for machinery, not buildings), which permits the entrepreneur to choose his own pattern of depreciation—even 100 percent allowances in the first year with any resulting loss making it possible to claim tax refunds on any profits of the preceeding three years.

Other ingredients of Mill 3's survival strategy were:

a) Improved marketing, concentrating on flexibly picking up (albeit small) orders for new or difficult types of cloth of the kind it is not worth ordering, or not possible to order, from a distant foreign producer; capitalizing also, where possible, on converters' and garment makers' buy-British patriotism (one major retail chain uses its buy-British patriotism as an element in its advertising), and on their prudent concern to keep some local suppliers available in case the Suez Canal blows up.

b) Improved labor productivity—most recently in the case of Mill 3 by the importation of a Pakistani-Swiss production engineer (borrowed from the machine suppliers) who by a combination of machine debugging, work reorganization, and task analysis provided the rationale for reduced manning (which still, according to the management's not disinterested calculations, leaves them 15 to 30 percent overmanned as far as overlookers were concerned as compared with European firms using identical machines). This was accepted after much bargaining between the workers, union, and management in return for increases in wages (partly in the form of a productivity bonus) and a compromise settlement over the management's demand, apropos of the skilled men, that it, rather than the unions and workers, should decide which workers might stay and which go. This made Mill 3's wages the highest in the district—for knotters, for example, 36 percent above the wages of the lowest-wage firm among the thirty-seven in the district covered by the relevant union branch (£94.71 and £69.40 per week).

In inflationary periods, of course, wage leaders which become wage leaders in order to get their work force to accept changes they would otherwise resist are able to slip back in succeeding years by lesser increases, though Mill 3's management believes that its ability to select efficient workers and to demand efficient performance depends on its reputation as a high-wage mill.

11.3 The Rationalization Option: Wage Cuts

Actual money wage cuts seem never to be part of a rationalization policy (except that in the case of Mill 1, when the mill went onto one-day-a-week short time, laying off the manual workers at 75 percent of regular wages paid for by a government short-time working subsidy, skilled workers, employed under guaranteed-salary staff conditions, agreed to take a 10 percent cut). Real wages can be eroded over time, however, by failure to compensate fully for inflation. The norm-setting wage agreement between the national (in effect Lancashire) Federation and the Textile Employers Association (and the similar agreement between the Employers' Association and the Overlookers who preserve their superior craft standing by remaining outside the Federation) provides for general increases. The agreement for a 14 percent increase in the 1980 round (at a time when consumer price inflation was approaching 20 percent) seems to have been generally implemented. But this represented an increase on wage structures which have come to vary from mill to mill as a result of ad hoc bargains negotiated by the district secretaries (full-time union men and women) of the respective craft unions—the Weavers, the Overlookers, the Knotters, the Tapers, and the Warehousemen. Even for the craft skills with fixed time payments, the high-wage firms may pay 40 percent more than the lowest, and for weavers in particular the complexities of the piecework systems used, weighting a basic "x pence per 1,000 picks" principle by a variety of adjustments for types of cloth, do not allow an easy *ex ante* comparison of wages when rates are fixed—hence the even greater variety of *ex post* wage packets.

The scope for cutting real wages, however, is limited. Mills 4 and 6, especially the "hanging-on" Mill 6, have been low-wage firms in recent years. Both were in small outlying communities on the town's outskirts with no alternative employers nearby, and they were able to retain such workers as they did retain thanks to a strong walk-to-work preference, and in the case of Mill 6 in part by the persistence of noncontractual managerial-discretionary elements in the wage. As the former manager explained:

Some of the cloth would be slower weaving—coarse counts, say, with a lot of changes of pirn, so you'd go to the weaver and you'd say: "Do this one for me love, and I'll see you right at the end of the week." And she'd say: "Oh, you will, will you. How much you going to give me, then?" And I'd say, "Oh threppence!". "I'll see you dead first," she'd say, but she'd do it and then, say, you'd slip an extra three quid into the wage at the end of the week.

The jocular exchange serves as a substitute for contractual bargaining, preserving the manager's discretionary authority, but making allowance—at the verbal level—for the worker's egalitarian pride. It also inhibits exchange of information by workers about their wage levels and reduces wage predictability.

The low-wage firms did, however, suffer from a shortage of skilled workers. The inability to fill overlooker vacancies meant that Mill 6 was operating only 140 of its 288 working looms for its final half year. (Several Blackburn overlookers left the industry for engineering in that period: four, from Mill 4, to work in textiles in Sudan.) Managers at Mill 4, the other low-wage firm (larger and with much more rationalized, impersonal wage systems), also complained that the Overlookers' Union would not help them to fill vacancies, and complained further of the low quality of their weaver labor and of high turnover (47 percent in the twelve months preceding closure) and high absenteeism (12 percent). This they ascribed largely to the fact that the sickly smell of impending doom has attended the textile industry for so long that few young people have been attracted into it except reluctantly through family connections, because of next-door convenience, or because they could not find better jobs. In the larger mills there were frequent complaints of sloppy work, bad timekeeping, absenteeism, "leaving as soon as we've finally got them trained to a reasonable standard," losing orders because "we just couldn't meet the Swedish quality requirements for the aircraft blinds: you can't get workers to take that much trouble." In the smaller mills, where such complaints gave way to praise for "a fine lot of workers," the average age was relatively high. (Of the total 454 ex-textile workers unemployed in the Blackburn area in February 1980, 40 percent were over forty.)

11.4   The Rationalization Option: Immigrants

The "Bhagwati option"—survival by importing immigrant labor—is not necessary for Blackburn employers since the immigrants are already there. A good many, from Pakistan, India, and Bangladesh, have been there for twenty years. They do not seem to represent a low-wage alternative work force since they are paid union rates and there are no segregated jobs—i.e., no job rates which apply only to Asians let alone to all Asians. However, in marginal matters of interpretations of rates, willingness to accept cuts in conventionalized overtime working, etc., their vulnerability may make them a cost advantage. (As a community relations official put it, "They are a very accepting community—not looking for trouble: easily satisfied with the treatment dished out to them.") And they do clearly represent a low-wage alternative in one respect. They predominate on the (permanent) night shift of many factories, and it is generally agreed that even with current (7 percent) unemployment levels in Blackburn it would be impossible to man the night shift without them. This is spoken of as if it were not a question of wages, but of work attitudes: native born are "not that desperate for money that they are willing to work nights." More realistically one might say that the night shift premium (currently 25 to 30 percent depending on the factory) would have had to have been bid up to some considerable degree to attract suitable workers from other industries, certainly five years ago when unemployment rates were 2 to 3 percent, and perhaps even now when they are much higher.

The proportion of Asian workers varies widely between factories for reasons which seem wholly idiosyncratic and largely to have to do with the levels of racial prejudice of managers or key white workers, the success of early Asian employees in establishing rapport with supervisors and bringing in friends, etc. No systematic correlation with any economic parameters has been discerned.

11.5   The Rationalization Option: Labor Flexibility

Differences between types of looms, of yarn used, and of type of weave so much affect the volume and structure of minimally necessary tasks that it is difficult to compare manning ratios from mill to mill, but it is our impression that there exists a considerable difference between the most tightly and the most loosely manned firms. Tight manning seems often to be the result of improvisation to cover unfilled vacancies rather than of deliberate rationalization. Production planning to avoid peak bunching of some key tasks ("gating" new beams, knotting the ends, etc.) on several looms at once is technically difficult to do effectively, and the alternative of comfortable staffing to take care of peaks even though some workers are often less than fully employed has obvious attractions.

Other limits to the ease with which productivity levels can be raised by reducing manning include (a) indivisibilities and (b) skill demarcations. As for the first, the number of looms per weaver is difficult to increase marginally because of physical layout. Where the looms are banked in rows of ten, it is possible to go from ten per weaver to fifteen per weaver (if a change in the type of loom use could justify such a large jump), but to go from ten to twelve or thirteen causes problems. In Mill 2 with the switch from Jacquard multicolor weaving to simpler sheeting materials which justified a shift from ten to eighteen looms per weaver, the whole factory layout had to be altered.

Skill demarcations are described as less of a problem than they used to be. The trades with traditional apprenticeship schemes—overlookers, beamers, tapers, and sizers—were traditionally jealously protective of their status as skilled "time-served" men. Their unions would not allow managers to promote, for example, weavers to such jobs even though they had informally acquired adequate competence. This is now largely a thing of the past: the sense of a shared interest in keeping ailing firms afloat—and the sense that most *are* ailing—combined with the steady increase in the number of skilled men who prefer exit to voice, has much reduced these difficulties.

Nevertheless, in a very traditional industry, even small measures of work intensification—in one instance expecting weavers to do their own creeling (linking up the cones of thread to feed the automatic pirn-winders)—meet with disgruntled resistance, and compliance usually has to be "bought." When Mill 2 went over to sheeting with eighteen looms per weaver, groups of workers were sent to another of the firm's mills where the system was already in operation to observe its working. A number of meetings were held, culminating in a mass meeting addressed by the group managing director. The workers finally agreed to a six-month trial period during which they were guaranteed as a minimum their average earnings of the previous six months.

"Negotiation costs" thus remain a not negligible factor in entrepreneurial decision making, but they need not be too high for managers with the right approach. One mill in the outskirts had achieved an effective piece of rationalization not yet found elsewhere. A single group of workers rotated (both within and between shifts) between weaving and cloth-inspecting jobs. The mill was, significantly, part of a larger group with a profit-sharing scheme and an intricate system of councils which ensured a form of managerial accountability to the rank-and-file "partners"—the firm's employees—and this gave a special character to manager-worker relations. For example, one possible problem of the new work arrangement—that weavers might subsequently have to inspect their own cloth—was solved by the "moral incentive" device of getting them to sign the tickets which accompanied the cloth out of the factory. As the recession deepened in the summer of 1980 this was one of the few mills still working at capacity, though how far this can be attributed to its "high trust" labor management policy, how much to its vertical integration with a chain of department stores or to the strength of its relatively up-market product lines, we were unable to judge.

11.6   The Rationalization Option: The Multiplant Corporation

In appearance and ethos, there was more than a half-century jump from Mill 6 with its mid-nineteenth-century steam engine, leaky water lodge, and 1890s looms in tumbledown premises, to multinational *A*'s Mill 4 with its carpeted reception area complete with pretty receptionist, tropical fish tank, leather armchairs, and coffee table magazines—*and* its expensive reequipment program only a year ahead of its decision to close. The differences are particularly important, given the high degree of ownership concentration in the United Kingdom textile industry.[1] The ability to concentrate financial resources at strategic points, probably also access to finance on favorable terms (and the security of knowing that British governments in the 1970s do not allow firms with 30,000 workers to go bankrupt), makes for a relatively bold approach to capital investment schemes—with a little bit left over for a fish tank to emphasize the break with Protestant ethic-type penny-pinching asceticism.

The large corporations can also take closure decisions with greater ruthlessness and at an earlier stage in the decline process than in the case of a family firm. The board which takes the decision (and which may well do so against the strenuous pleadings of the mill manager) does not have its financial vision much obscured by ties of local sentiment. Second, the remaining business and much of the still valuable equipment—those grounds of tenuous optimism which prompt the family firm owner to hold on in hopes of something turning up—can be transferred to another plant of the same firm. This happened with both Mills 4 and 5, each of which had counterparts within their respective grousp. Courtaulds, the group which owned Mill 5, indeed, was reported in July 1980 to have closed 50 of its 350 plants and made 12,000 workers redundant in the preceding year. Its chairman declared his intention to give full priority to the development of nontextile interests (including paint, plastics, packaging, etc.), to concentrate resources on the strongest businesses, rather than to "squander them in areas of long-term weakness" (*Guardian*, 25 July 1980).

Hearsay explanations of why Mills 4 and 5 were closed rather than other plants within the group did not suggest that rigorous performance analyses played a major role. In one case the counterpart had been acquired by the group only two years before for a considerable sum, and "the shareholders would have started asking awkward questions if we closed that down, although it was probably the less efficient of the two." In the other case, the two main factors were said to be, first, that the closed mill was in a newer, more marketable building; second, that the survivor mill to which most of its business was transferred was fairly close to another mill of the group and so could share certain management services.

11.7   The Rationalization Option: Management Quality

One does not get the impression that managers either of the smaller firms or of the plants owned by multinationals are much given to the techniques of scientific management. Professional competences appear to be narrow and practical, and not much accompanied by an analytical grasp of the state of the industry or the economy as a whole. If these impressions are correct, the explanation is fairly obvious. The declining star of the textile industry has not for several decades held much glitter for the high flyer. University graduates are rare in textile management. Perhaps the major exception as a route for talent into the industry has been some of the top management of the larger groups who have come into the industry via chemicals and synthetics, but even in those groups a large proportion of middle management entered the industry via family firms which were subsequently taken over.

11.8   The Diversification Option

Courtaulds is exceptional in its shift of emphasis away from textiles. Almost universally among textile managers mention of Kanebō, the Japanese textile firm that has diversified into cosmetics, and the question, Is that possible here? produces dismissive answers. A senior manager of another of the big three groups:

> We've never regarded ourselves as being anything but experts in textiles. From time to time we've acquired other businesses incidentally, as part of takeovers—an animal feed stuffs business recently—but we've always sold it off.

The manager of the curtain-weaving mill now losing out to the new stitch-bonded process:

> No. We never thought of going into the stitch-bonded business ourselves. You say we'd have the advantage of knowing the markets, having the connections. But its not our trade to be doing that sort of thing. We'd have to turn ourselves into converters. It's like asking Wedgewoods to make plastic cups. That's ICI's job.

A parochial traditionalism is as responsible for this lack of hubris—or down-with-the-ship captain's pride—as a realistic appraisal of their own capacities. "See that row of houses over there! My great-great grandfather built those in the 1850s—with inside bathroom too." And as for parochialism, hear the same man's eloquence about the hopeless peripherality of Blackburn: to be sure he can get up at six and be in Frankfurt by ten, but that's not the same as being *in* the German heartland of Europe where everything is happening.

Only two cases of diversification out of weaving have come our way in Blackburn. Mill 1 established a small knitting business in the later 1960s when it seemed that knitters were taking markets away from the looms. Another firm's machine room developed a capacity for producing plastic extruders, and the firm has gone over to making fine-mesh plastic net by methods which won it a recent prize for innovation.

Even within weaving, specialization was traditionally extreme: "A firm that did cloth for men's trousers would never touch the women's trousers business." Now, however, most firms have had to accept that degree of versatility to survive. The converters are said also to have become more sharply contractual in their business attitudes, more willing to drop a regular supplier in favor of a new one if the price is right. (But this is the first round of hearsay, not yet cross-checked into a coherent story.)

11.9   The Closure Option: Labor Relations

We have not met a single person in Lancashire who does not think that it is wicked of the governments of Britain and the European Community (EC) to deny textile firms protection and so force them into closure. Everyone concerned will always lobby for protection rather than face closure. We have seen, however, some of the reasons why the preference gap between the two alternatives—the degree of desperation with which closure would be evaded—is likely to be different, for example, as between a family firm and a large corporation. It is a matter of some interest—in view of what is generally considered to be a major source of rigidities in the OIC economies—to ask how far the determination to avoid closure is enhanced by humane concern for the workers employed, as against the psychic or monetary cost of dealing with attack from workers threatened with redundancy or their unions, as against the cost of the consequent effects on the morale of the workers left behind.

As for sentiment, it is probably stronger in this industry than in many others precisely because of the characteristics of managers mentioned above: a good many of those in managerial positions began as office boys at fourteen or apprentices at sixteen, or were the heirs of family firms sent to serve their time as apprentices with some of the men whose masters they were destined to become. It is doubtful, however, if such sentiments play anything but a fleeting marginal role in decisions about closure.

But what about the prospect of public uproar, of having the mill invaded by angry workers determined to sit in until the closure decision is reversed, the prospect of bad publicity, much nervous strain, possibly damage to assets, or the cost of legal action?

Such events are commonly reported in the press from other industries, but there is little evidence that concern about worker or union reactions of this type enters even marginally into calculations about closure in the textile industry. Militancy is not the textile unions' style. "It's not a question of them and us, really. It's how we can keep the industry alive," said one union official. "The employers do their best, and they're very good really, though we have our little tiffs with them from time to time. But by and large we've the best of relations with the Employers Association"—a view that is generally echoed on the other side. When Mill 4 was closed, the unions succeeded in extracting from the firm an additional *ex gratia* payment to redundant workers of half a week's salary per year of service (on top of the statutory entitlement of half to one and a half week's pay per year of service—depending on age—up to a maximum of thirty weeks' pay). This was spoken of by the unions as markedly generous, but the resultant sum—in total, say, £2,500 for a fifty-year-old weaver with twenty years' service—is far below the sums demanded and received by the militant unions in shipbuilding and steel. A number of reasons explain this quiescence.

1. The generally small size of plant. Five thousand workers with 12,000 votes have a much bigger chance of attracting government intervention, even than the 850 workers of Mill 4.

2. The nature of the union membership—older, more female, more immigrant.

3. The fatalism induced by long years of steady decline. There is a great deal of bitterness about the treatment given to textile workers in comparison with others. "Take steel workers or car workers. Why is it they get £5,000—even £15,000—whereas for us the absolute top limit's under £3,000. They've been kicking textiles in the teeth ever since I've been in it. But if the textile unions behaved the same way as the car unions, they'd just shut the whole industry down. How much British industry is there invested in Hong Kong, for instance? British titled people, too. All Tories of course."

4. Textile workers have lived with the prospect of redundancy so long that redundancy has become part of their accepted scheme of things, and the redundancy payment has been incorporated into their life-planning process. For many people who have lived frugal lives on weekly incomes, a lump-sum payment though not a large one in comparison with other industries—three times, say, the cost of a holiday on the Costa Brava that you save up for for a whole year—is not negligible. Women in their fifties with a long record of hard work and dependability have not been too afraid of being unable to find something to fill in the few years till their pension starts, and may even begin to fear that they will be "cheated of their redundancy" if the firm fails to collapse before they reach sixty.

5. Long years of cooperation between unions and employers in their shared common interest of lobbying for protection have created a steady

pattern of cooperation. Employers were particularly willing to make accommodations in order to secure that cooperation during the periods of Labour Party rule when the voice of the unions carried more weight.

6. One consequence of cooperation between unions and management is the automatic check off of union dues. This eliminates the weekly due-collecting need for contact between union member and official and thus reduces information flow and the sort of reverberatory process whereby grievances articulated become magnified.

7. With steadily declining membership the (very very modest) salaries and expenses of full-time officials are less and less covered by current subscriptions, more and more dependent on interest from the funds accumulated in the days when membership was much larger. A strike which ran down those funds would mean the end of some of the smaller unions.

11.10   Who Suffers How Much?

Our interviews with former textile employees are not yet extensive enough to support any very meaningful generalizations; only a few tentative ones are possible.

First, some samples of the individual cases:

1. Fifty-year-old widow, weaver, and lately warper (making up warp beams). Altogether she has had fourteen jobs, from four of which she has been made redundant (the last at Mill 5), mostly as a weaver or warper, but with occasional spells as a machinist outside textiles and two spells at home during the infancy of her two children. After thirteen weeks of unemployment she is waiting for a response to a job application (via the government Job Centre) to the local Ordnance Factory—which would pay her more than her previous job. Through personal connections she has had two opportunities to work as a warper in surviving mills. In one the pay was not good enough. The other was a mill she "didn't fancy": it had a bad reputation.

2. Former general manager of Mill 6. Started as an office boy, then chief clerk in a weaving firm which offered him the chance to do (practical) management training—part-time study for textile diploma plus varied work experience including a spell with a machinery manufacturer. In his subsequent career has had six mills collapse under him. Lives in a modest terraced house, talks with enormous enthusiasm about the technicalities of his job (dashes to the kitchen to snip a square from his wife's kitchen towel to help explain the construction of terry toweling) as of the steam engine, the running of which he had to combine with his general managership for the last six months of the mill's life, the driver having been incapacitated by illness. Had heard of a weaving manager's job going in the Philippines, but could not leave aged parent. After thirty

weeks of job hunting sought refuge from a growing sense of uselessness in a job as hospital orderly.

3. Fifty-five-year-old widow, weaver. Has had only two jobs, each for twenty years; the last in Mill 6. No easy substitute available for that last job since she was allowed to come home during the day (a stone's throw from the mill) to care for her bedridden mother and (only recently died) bedridden husband. Regrets losing the lively life of the mill, but has decided not to work: her widow's pension, her mother's old-age pension, a disabled person's attendant allowance and rate rebate provide enough to live on.

4. Twenty-six-year-old Pakistan-born, English-educated male weaver, made redundant at a Blackburn mill. Applied for a job at a local electronics firms early in the sixty-day-notice period and was finally offered one by the firm in the second week of unemployment.

5. Forty-eight-year-old former creeler—her ninth job interspersed with intervals for bearing four children. Earlier jobs had included that of machinist at the local Ordnance Factory: she applied to return (after a ten-year interval) and was taken on as an inspector after six weeks' unemployment.

6. Sixty-one-year-old works manager of a mill on the outskirts of Blackburn which closed early in 1979. In the ensuing six months he was privately offered one mill managing job but refused it because it involved working the two to ten shift at an ordinary day rate. He applied for another advertised job without success and finally, after six months, was offered via the government Employment Agency the job of deputy manager at a skill training center for "difficult" youths. Has been developing a small private brush-making workshop as a sideline.

7. Thirty-year-old man, started career as glassworks boy at age fifteen, became an overlooker's apprentice, and after qualifying as a skilled man (supervisor, setter, and maintainer of looms) continued through a series of five part-time-study technical diplomas and a series of promotions to a works manager position, his fourth job in the textile industry. After some years of desultory and steadily more intensive "looking around" for prospects of getting out of an obviously declining industry, he was offered, largely through sports club associations, a job as a brewery salesman. He now has less responsibility, fewer and more gentlemanly hours for more money, and a company car. The mill he left has not yet closed.

How much can one generalize?

First, we need not grieve too much for the owners of capital who at the very worst have reasonably valuable land to sell, possibly a useful mill site, and machinery (though one admittedly manager rather than owner claimed that he would rather take £40 a ton for scrap than add to the capacity of Third World producers).

Second, the managers of firms within the larger groups are also reasonably well cared for. One of the group's management services division was said to have 322 executives at the end of 1979 whom it was trying to place within the group on the assumption that they would—with considerable financial assistance—be prepared to move to another part of the country. A high proportion of these were expected, in fact, to move out of the company, leaving only those the group proposed to promote in order to keep and (probably a larger number of) those who had so few alternatives that they were prepared eventually to accept a sideways or downward shuffle.

Many managers and skilled supervisory staff of the smaller companies, however, just lose their jobs—and often have considerable difficulty in finding alternatives. The alternatives they do find tend to give little satisfaction and to utilize not their very considerable technical or marketing skills, but only their "leadership" ability to give orders with some confidence that they will be obeyed.

The few younger skilled workers—e.g., overlookers—still in the industry have hitherto had little difficulty in finding other jobs, which often give them higher incomes—some in engineering by virtue of the intelligence and responsible work attitudes which got them their apprenticeship in the first place and were reinforced by their subsequent skilled-man status. The deepening of the recession in mid-1980 was clearly reducing opportunities, however.

Weavers and other nonapprenticeship ("semiskilled") workers probably have had and continue to have the greatest difficulty in finding work, particularly in recent months, though a few years ago at unemployment levels of three percent or less they seem soon to have been absorbed. Older workers are not at a particular disadvantage in this market; the general opinion of employers is that they are more dependable. (Erosion of the work ethic? More family ties than younger people? Later cohorts of semiskilled workers recruited from further down some putative general ability range?) A proportion of the women workers are marginal to the labor force: they work for supplementary family income and are noncontributors to unemployment insurance, not averse to taking several weeks holiday between jobs, and reliant on the grapevine for news of alternative employment. The Job Centre—the state employment agency—registers all claimants of unemployment insurance plus nonclaimant job seekers who bother to turn to it for advice and news of vacancies (or retraining schemes of job search schemes—travel subsidies to follow up vacancies in other districts. etc.). In November 1979, the ex-textile workers on the books were 225 men and 49 women; in February 1980, 384 men and 104 women. In the latest employment census available (June 1976; the June 1977 figures were not to be available until May 1980!) women made up 35 percent of the textile labor force. On the assumption that their proportion among actual job losers was similar they were greatly underrepresented in the Job Centre–registered unemployed. They should have been 121 not 49 in November, 207 not 104 in February.

Asians among the latter group face particular difficulties in seeking jobs, from prejudice, from actual communications difficulty in environments where they may not have learned the particular vocabulary, and from diffidence about trying to break into occupations or firms in which Asians have not yet established a foothold. Their unemployment rate in a 1977 survey, at a time when the general unemployment rate was 6.5 percent, was 26 percent among heads of households and 21 percent for the whole labor force. A certain amount of outwork by their wives for the garment industry somewhat eases their families' financial situation.

So also, of course, does the availability of unemployment benefit and supplementary benefit, as well as drawings from the earnings-related contributory scheme, ease their load. The financial plight of the unemployed is very different from that documented for Blackburn by the Pilgrim Trust in the 1930s (Pilgrim Trust 1938). Whether that also mitigates the psychological effects is less certain. One overlooker describing his five weeks' unemployment (which ended in his getting another overlooker's job) spoke of his loss of confidence, his growing sense that nobody would want him anymore. But he found some consolation, at least, in the fact that he had enough money to do some photography and print his own color enlargements.

Job-search areas are usually very narrow for the Blackburn born. Moving house is considered an extreme measure, and a journey to work of more than a mile and a half is frequently seen as a great hardship. The immigrants are a good deal more mobile, but depend on their community grapevine rather than the government information service. A number of Asians were said, for instance, to have gone to work in Danish hotels through personal connections.

11.11   Secondary Losers

With only 10 percent of the labor force in textiles, the contribution of the loss of jobs in that industry to the increase in total Blackburn unemployment (the monthly rate rose from 1.8 to 2.3 percent in 1974 to 6.1–6.8 percent in 1979) has been relatively small. There is consequently little awareness any longer of textile decline as *the* central problem of the Blackburn economy. The local community relations officers (particularly concerned with the hard-hit Asian community) and a borough councillor or two will join the textile employers and unions in delegations to the Department of Trade to demand protection, but the plight of the textile industry is not a dominant theme of borough council meetings, nor do changes in the consumer market stemming from textile fluctuations appear to have entered into the calculations, e.g., of the chain store which recently opened a new up-market department store in the redeveloped city center.

11.12   The Lobby for Protection

The actual pattern of losses to individuals described above does not seem very directly to affect the strength of the protectionist lobby. Lobbies, petitions, protests are organized chiefly by the Textile Employers Association and the unions. In terms of personal motivation, they are threatened not by any immediate loss of job (such as might be made up for by compensation schemes) but by a *slow dwindling* of their raison d'être and resource base. The Employers Association may have to dispense with a part-time secretary as a quid pro quo for getting its remaining members to pay increased dues. The knotter's secretary hardly feels he can ask his hard-pressed committee to increase his £2 a week car allowance in line with inflation. Only the unions whose investments cover a large part of current outgoings are free from such pressure.

11.13   Whither Do Resources Move?

Former mills still provide (£2–3 per square foot) factory space, and its availability has been a decisive factor in inducing the start-up of some of the small enterprises that have begun business in the last five years, though almost equally cheap (subsidized) sites on industrial estates have been an available alternative for a large number.

Another example of direct transfers: a nest of four firms (manufacturing fine-tolerance deep-drawn pressings, electronic machine utilization recorders, prototype printed circuits, and importing and customizing visual display units) was started out of capital gained by selling a family textile firm to one of the large groups, out of managerial experience gained within that same group, and partly out of a market for automatic loom-monitoring equipment, knowledge of which had come from that experience.

Such examples are rare, however. Our sample of new or expanded firms is as yet small and unsystematic, permitting few generalizations, since information about the total population (and hence about the representativeness of the firms we have found on a street-by-street research basis) is hard to come by. Three of the fourteen new firms are utilizing relatively new technologies (the pressings, monitoring equipment, and printed circuit firms just quoted). Three adapt imports from technologically superior foreign sources for the British market (computer visual displays, municipal service and heavy agricultural vehicles—some of the latter from a domestically produced base, and a furniture foam cutter).

One, a carpet tufter, is in an industry of which there is an expanding concentration in Blackburn—carpet making and tufting machine manufacture—serving a market with higher income elasticities than textiles. Two—a larger do-it-yourself supermarket and a furniture wholesale-retail business—were specifically attracted by large, cheap areas of space in old mills. Others—a jobbing steel fabricator, a department store, a firm making small electric motors and transformers, one making parts for commercial vehicle air brakes, and one making plastic blow mouldings— might have been located anywhere and owe their location to a variety of personal and idiosyncratic factors.

As for overall shifts in employment, recent figures are not yet available, but the 1973–76 figures reflect the familiar story of the deindustrialisation of Britain. Employment as a whole fell from 98 to 93 percent of a roughly constant labor force, but the decline in manufacturing employment was 9 percent rather than 5 percent. Increases took place in services (both "miscellaneous" and "professional and scientific" services, but with distribution stable and government services falling slightly in absolute numbers—though not in percentage of the employed) and in a small number of minor manufacturing branches: paper, printing, and publishing; timber and furniture; food, drink, and tobacco.

Nearly all these firms have benefited from one or other of the following:

—Twenty percent grants toward capital equipment by virtue of the fact that Blackburn was an Intermediate Development Area.

—A regional employment premium, partial subsidization of new workers for an initial period (until 1977 only).

—Small industries employment premium, a similar scheme for small businesses only (after 1977).

—Assistance in finding, or improving, premises or rent subsidies, from the local authority, the regional Development Association, or the Industrial Estates Corporation whose brand new industrial estate premises are rented at not very much more per square foot than old mills.

—An equity contribution from the National Research Development Corporation (in the case of the electronics firm).

None of them, however, was prepared to ascribe a very large role in their scheme of things to such assistance. One claimed to have refused to bother with the £600 he would have been entitled to as employment premium for his five-worker establishment on the grounds that it was not worth the paperwork and the dealing with intrusive officials.

11.14   Adjustment Assistance

The British cotton textile industry has once had a comprehensive reorganization scheme (1959) which involved incentives for scrapping and exit—but combined them with subsidies for reequipment and process and product innovation. The result, as documented by Miles (1968) and summarized by Wolf (1979), was that the reequipment substantially compensated for the scrapping, the productivity increases and product innovation were insufficient to restore competitiveness, and the taste for protection grew on what had fed it. Import restrictions grew and have become a permanent feature. Few in Lancashire really expect the MFA to be allowed to lapse in accordance with the promises at its signing.

Recently the textile industry has benefited from two additional forms of protective subsidy, both general measures not specifically aimed at textiles. The Temporary Employment Subsidy was a measure for firms facing unprofitability owing to temporary trading conditions. They could claim a wage subsidy for a limited—but renewable—period. This gave firms every incentive to sustain production levels and compete by cutting prices, an effect which brought strong complaints of unfair subsidization from Europe. Overmanning was also encouraged, which conventionalized labor practices that had to be "bought out" when business started again in earnest. In April 1979, as a result of criticism, the scheme was replaced by the Short Time Working Subsidy, which paid up to 75 percent of wages for days not worked by firms which cut back production by moving to short-time working if it could be shown that the alternative was large-scale redundancy. This was free of some of the disadvantages of the earlier scheme.

The industry's own demands for "adjustment" are, of course, at best for "temporary" protection while it restores competitive profitability, at worst for permanent support.

The political effectiveness of these demands is there for all to see. The question is whether less undesirable adjustment measures (undesirable from the value assumptions taken in this paper) would reduce the strength and political effectiveness of the demand for the existing type of measures.

Wolf (1979) discusses the effect of genuinely temporary protection in inducing greater capital intensiveness which may restore competitiveness, thereby maintaining production levels but with considerably reduced employment—an outcome which he disapproves of on normative assumptions similar to those adopted here; i.e., it leads neither to the preservation of OIC jobs nor to the increase in NIC exports. If, however, it genuinely does lead to very considerable productivity increases through product and process innovation and so restores competitiveness—if, that is to say in terms of our earlier classification, an A industry is transformed by a new round of innovation into a B industry—it is hard to object to the process. (Though one might wonder what the NICs would do if all the A industries could be rescued for the B category in this way.) In practice, however, although something of this kind may well have happened in parts of the Japanese and German textile industries, and in isolated firms even in Britain, the evidence that it has been or could be a general phenomenon is lacking. The loss of jobs through increased capital intensiveness is easy to document; the actual restoration of competitive profitability much less so since protection measures for a fixed term have generally turned out to be anything but nonrenewable.

A form of temporary protection for an import-threatened industry which might have better results is a degressive tariff tapering to zero in a fixed term of years, the revenue proceeds of which are used only to pay for scrapping and exit compensation—for the same product lines as the tariff applies to—not for reequipment of firms which elect to stay in the business. With a degressive tariff, the slide gets established at levels at which it still holds off imports. By the time it ceases to do so and the threat increases, the degressive slide has an established legitimacy and it is hard for protesters to choose any rational point at which to cry halt. If the compensation amounts—perhaps with guaranteed minima backed by government revenue—were to vary with tariff revenue income, this would encourage early exit and create an interest group directly concerned with maximizing imports. One of the principles implicit in such a measure is already embodied in the MFA's provisions for an annual increase in quotas from Third World producers.

Most of the adjustment measures discussed above are aimed at firms or workers. We have seen that the real losers whom nobody thinks of compensating (the full-time paid organizers of the successful lobbies!) are the officials of the textile associations and unions. Why should these associations and unions not also be compensated for lost membership fees?

How much of the compensation should go to the owners of capital, how much to the workers? Take first the political argument: which is it more necessary to bribe? In the British textile industry, as we have seen, worker resistance to closure is not a significant factor in affecting managerial closure decisions, and union officials have their own reasons, not just (perhaps not primarily) their members' reasons for wholehearted lobbying for protection. The conclusion would seem to be that for textiles (not perhaps for steel or shipbuilding with more militant unions) the employers need sweetening the more. In equity terms, the case for providing either party with compensation over and above that which is afforded by the country's economic institutions to those made redundant or going into liquidation from any other industry depends on one's assessment of how far, given prevailing standards of the levels of security and comfort governments ought to guarantee their citizens, owners and workers in import-threatened industries can be deemed to have a presumptive "right" to expect protection.

Supposing compensation is to be paid to the losers, are there any devices which might increase the likelihood that the compensation paid is used to stimulate the growth of employment capacity in the *B* and *C* industries and export capacity in the *B* industries? (Again, there is no reason in equity why the measures—in Britain the considerable array of measures, see those listed above for firms, plus retraining schemes, job-search travel schemes, home removal schemes for workers—which are generally available to promote these purposes should be available only to, or preferentially to, those coming out of import-threatened industries. The proposition is: supposing considerable sums are going to be paid in compensation anyway, can they also be diverted to this purpose without losing their compensating ([bribery] function?)

Two possible devices exist. First, if exit compensation is paid to a firm which gets out of a threatened industry, an additional premium could be paid if, instead of closing, it retains the firm's identity and premises and at least some of its work force and switches to production of a new product. If the society concerned is one like Japan where there is a belief in the ability of government officials to pick winners, the premiums might be graduated to the desirability of the industry entered.

Second, redundant workers might be given a reemployment voucher. They give this to anyone who offers them a job, and their new employer can use each voucher as collateral for a capital equipment loan of £x. If the employee is still with the same outfit after, say, twelve months, the voucher can then be cashed in, by the employer for y percent of £x. The worker's compensation is in the form of enhanced reemployment chances, but he might also be given a delayed cash compensation at the end of twelve months, if only to deter him from trying to profit directly from his ability to confer financial benefits on an employer by claiming his "cut." Doubtless there are innumerable snags in this process, over and above the difficulties of administrative verification. One obvious one is in terms of the distinction between the *B* category, technological frontier, "Schumpeterian" industries and the *C* category, service, transport, construction, etc., industries. The reemployment voucher scheme attaches fixed sums of capital to workers, whereas it is to more capital-intensive *B* industries that one would wish to direct more capital, and more labor-intensive *C* industries more labor.

11.15 Conclusions

The conclusions of what is primarily an attempt to describe the state of a declining industry over one six-month period cannot do much more than arbitrarily single out a few points for emphasis.

A matured decline such as that of the British textile industry (steadily downhill for five decades) has certain particular features of its own in terms of the nature of its recruits, the degree of ingrained pessimism, etc., which distinguish it from greener candidates for decline. The large corporation does seem to respond more rapidly to signals betraying long-term trends than do family firms. An industry as tradition-bound as textiles does find diversification extremely difficult and uncongenial. It is hard to identify any factors which would enable some of the more innovative textile firms to stay internationally competitive without government protection, except converters' and industrial users' preference for a reserve of fallback local supplies, ability to produce certain specialized lines, and, in a few cases, art design superiority. (The possibility that the British industry is more "hopeless" in these respects than the industry of other OICs—and the implications this has for intra–OECD adjustment policies—will be one focus of the Britain-Japan-France comparison that we hope to develop at a later stage of our research.) Particular closure decisions are not much affected by worker resistance, though unions are important elements in the organization of protectionist lobbies, and in any schemes for adjustment compensation the separate claims of unions and employers' associations should be considered. There is room for experiment in linking compensation on one hand with degressive tariffs and on the other with the promotion of a better industrial structure through the channeling of investments and employment creation.

Notes

1. Two-fifths of textile employment was in the three largest firms and nearly two-thirds in the largest ten (24 percent and 32 percent in France, which had the next highest degree of concentration) (Shepherd 1980).

References

Brandt, W., et al. 1980. *Programme for survival*. London: Pan Books.
Miles, C. 1968. *Lancashire textiles: A case study of industrial change.* Cambridge: Cambridge University Press.
Pilgrim Trust. 1938. *Men without work: A report made to the Pilgrim Trust.* Cambridge: Cambridge University Press.
Shepherd, G. 1980. How have the industrialized countries addressed the problem of adjustment? Paper for Conference on International Trade in Textiles and Clothing under the Multi-Fibre Agreement, organized by the International Chamber of Trade, Paris, and the Trade Policy Research Institute, London, held in Brussels.
Wolf, M. 1979. *Adjustment policies and problems in developed countries.* World Bank Staff Working Paper no. 349.

Comment   J. David Richardson

This is a refreshing and transparent paper, full of apt anecdotes that should suggest new themes for analytical and empirical research, and instruct policy historians and reformers. The virtue of a survey-based, representatively anecdotal approach is that it avoids the fallacy of *de*composition—generalizing from the aggregative to the particular—that tempts us so often as economists. The disadvantage of such an approach is that its domain of application may be quite narrow. To illustrate by one caveat: the textile industry in Blackburn, Lancashire, seems to have passed beyond decline into a moribund state; the United States textile industry, by contrast, is more accurately described as "threatened," and parts of it are positively healthy. Certain features of the British industry might not therefore be generally characteristic of other nations' counterparts—among others, its muted political activism and its resigned, fatalistic employees.

A number of findings in Professor Dore's paper deserve highlighting and comment. The first is the remarkable length of the adjustment process. The Blackburn industry has been losing out to foreign competition for roughly fifty years. This is "too long" by any sensible normative measure I can imagine because it spans several generations of workers, most of whom would have taken their first job in a clearly declining industry with their eyes open to its state. This raises the question of how other members of a society (or the government) should weigh their demands for compensation—did not they have adequate warning? Or would not adjustment costs have been fairly small for a government program that *dis*couraged new investment and new hires in such an industry (especially of the young)? Dore is attracted to government programs like this that promote exit and scrapping, and I would subscribe to his opinion.

Such programs can presumably be made politically feasible by liberal employment of carrots (exit bribes) rather than sticks (entry barriers). A degressive tariff with revenues earmarked for exit carrots in the same industry is an appealing illustration suggested by Dore, an illustration bolstered by several examples of Blackburn people whose impending redundancy payments affected their labor market behavior in a desirable way.

This discussion raises a generalization that is implicit in many of Dore's cases. Compensation schemes have their own efficiency and equity effects—effects that do not generally restore the allocation and distribution that existed before the initial shock. Some of these are favorable on

J. David Richardson is professor of economics at the University of Wisconsin–Madison, research associate of the National Bureau of Economic Research, and author or editor of three books and numerous contributions to professional journals and published collections of papers.

standard economic grounds: Dore's degressive tariff is an equity-motivated bribe that also aids the adjustment process. Others are not so favorable: do not the losers from the effects of compensation schemes have a right to compensation? . . . and then by precedent the losers from the compensation scheme to compensate the losers from the compensation scheme? . . . and then . . . and then . . . in an endless and inefficient sequence of resource diversion away from production and toward suing-for-injury.

Several other thought-provoking findings concern differences in motivation and personality of textile workers and managers. The most dynamic of the group seemed to be those in Romania, Turkey, Greece, and Portugal who, to illustrate, "responded more rapidly to the growing demand for denims and corduroys." Presumably they were among the most ambitious and skilled workers in their society, and were attracted by a share of the rents being generated in the rapidly growing textile industries of the European periphery. Least dynamic were the workers and managers who remained in Blackburn and who worked for smaller, family-run companies. They had the most severe burdens of adjustment, but they also had strong family ties to the area, a pronounced "walk-to-work preference," and an aversion to working the night shift. One cynically wonders to what degree they may have been chronic under-achievers, less deserving of compensation than in need of exhortation, counseling, and willingness to be reconciled with the consequences of their own nonpecuniary choices. In between these extremes fall British workers and managers of larger, publicly owned, multiplant companies who seemed ready to move both geographically and with respect to the type of job taken. Their adjustment burdens seemed relatively minor, and hence also their need for compensation and government assistance in adjusting. Verifying and explaining such behavioral differences strikes me as a fruitful area for careful sociological and economic research. So does doing the same for family-owned versus publicly owned firms, small versus large, multiplant versus single-plant, etc.

Professor Dore's behavioral differences reinforced my own predilection that multiplant, multidivisional firms have the institutional potential to arrange efficient intrafirm adjustment and generous compensation for their own displaced employees. That no such "private-insurance adjustment assistance" is practiced on any large scale to my knowledge I ascribe to the relatively recent advent of government programs along such lines. As experience with official programs sours, I predict increased employee demands for firm-level adjustment assistance provisions in negotiated contracts, and increasing corporate willingness to oblige as long as parallel contract provisions alleviate moral hazard problems that may develop.

I would differ with Dore in a few places, for example, with his implicit approval of government programs to encourage diversification by firms being pressured by imports. Diversification in this paper denotes shifting of a firm's efforts toward new product lines. The problem with this is that it can indenture workers and managers to an institutional shell that was revealed by the market already to be comparatively unsuccessful. (If it had been a successful firm, diversification would presumably have been profitable for it without government encouragement.) There seem to be few economic reasons for preserving institutions, especially unsuccessful ones, in contrast to preserving the skills and well-being of individuals. So it is arguably more efficient on economic grounds to allow firms to die rather than to diversify, after which diversification does take place, but individual-by-individual diversification by employees of the dead firm—into new skills, new responsibilities, and relatively more successful institutional shells (firms). The upshot of this argument is of course to cast doubt on the wisdom of all government programs aimed at the survival of firms rather than their exit. It also forces me to demur at Dore's (tongue-in-cheek?) suggestion that textile associations and unions need institution-preserving compensation, too.

Finally, I was surprised at how easy was the typical adjustment of most individuals and firms profiled—even in the absence of government assistance. Many workers switched industries and acquired new skills without official assistance or protracted periods of unemployment, even those who seemed least ambitious, skilled, and mobile. Some workers even switched countries, moving to comparable or better positions in the Sudanese and Philippine textile industries. And while firms took advantage of government assistance when offered, "None of them...was prepared to ascribe a very large role in their scheme of things to such assistance." Indeed, it does only a little violence to this excellent paper to characterize it as documenting a history of gradually successful private adjustment and questionably successful official efforts to ease that adjustment.

12 Trade Adjustment Assistance under the United States Trade Act of 1974: An Analytical Examination and Worker Survey

J. David Richardson

12.1 Introduction and Overview

Since 1962 United States workers and firms suffering transitional injury due to international trade have been able to benefit from a program of "adjustment assistance." The goals of trade adjustment assistance (TAA) have been to ease transition, compensate injury, and bleed political pressure for protectionism.

Section 12.2 of the paper outlines the economic principles underlying these goals, and their shifting historical importance. Sections 12.3 and 12.4 discuss the personal characteristics of a representative sample of worker recipients of TAA in 1976, and their labor market success in several subsequent years. Their experience is compared to that of a matched sample of workers receiving standard unemployment insurance (UI). Comparisons in section 12.3 focus on differences in mean characteristics and experience between the TAA and UI samples, controlling only for whether workers returned eventually to the firm from which they

J. David Richardson is professor of economics at the University of Wisconsin–Madison, research associate of the National Bureau of Economic Research, and author or editor of three books and numerous contributions to professional journals and published collections of papers.

The author wishes to credit Steve Parker for valuable commentary and research assistance, and Walter Corson and Walter Nicholson for stimulating interaction and patient responses to endless questions. He is grateful to C. Michael Aho, Robert E. Baldwin, Robert W. Gillespie, Rachel McCulloch, Allen Proctor, Steven Symansky, Martin Wolf, and participants in seminars at Wisconsin, Illinois, and Tufts. Financial support from the Institute for Research on Poverty at the University of Wisconsin–Madison is gratefully acknowledged. The survey on which the empirical work is based was conducted by Mathematica Policy Research, Inc. (Princeton, New Jersey), under contract (J9K70010) to the United States Department of Labor, Bureau of International Labor Affairs, Office of Foreign Economic Research. Opinions and interpretations expressed herein are the author's, and should not be taken to represent those of any of the individuals or institutions named above.

322   J. David Richardson

were initially separated. Comparisons in section 12.4 focus on differences
between the TAA and UI samples in their ability to recover lost employment and income, using a regression approach that in principle controls
for all relevant variables, and not for just one.

The most important conclusions of the research are the following. (1)
The majority of TAA recipients in 1976 were not permanently displaced,
but returned eventually to their former employers. By contrast, a far
greater proportion of UI recipients suffered permanent displacement. (2)
Workers receiving TAA had higher incomes on average than their counterparts who received only UI. The incomes of the former furthermore
fell less frequently below the poverty line. (3) TAA recipients nevertheless experienced more frequent and enduring transitional unemployment
than did UI recipients, and did not return to their former income level as
rapidly. (4) The reasons for conclusion (3) were unclear. In particular, it
could not readily be explained by differences between the TAA and UI
samples in permanence of layoff, generosity of program benefits, age,
experience, industry, affluence, economic environment, socioeconomic
status, or behavioral responses to any of these variables.

Conclusions (1) and (2) are at variance with most previous work on
TAA. Conclusion (3) is not, but the traditional explanations for it are
those that conclusion (4) rules out.

12.2 Historical and Economic Underpinnings of
United States Trade Adjustment Assistance

12.2.1 Economic Underpinnings

United States trade adjustment assistance (TAA) can be historically
explained as alleviating three problems that relate to international trade
liberalization. The first is a problem of distributional equity, reflected in
protectionist political pressure, and the second, of allocative efficiency,
reflected in much economic commentary.[1] Political economy plays an
important role in its most recent justification—it is now frequently defended as a bribe necessary to avoid disastrous deliberalizing trade wars.

1. *Distributional equity.* Except in ideal worlds, there are always gainers and losers from trade liberalization. To design and carry out practical
mechanisms whereby *every* loser was fully compensated (and more)
would require a mammoth diversion of any nation's resources from
wealth-producing to wealth-transferring activity. Yet in the absence of
such mechanisms, there may be instances in which trade liberalization is
rejected or reversed because it undermines a society's sense of equity or
because its rejection creates an implicit contractual claim to comparable
protection (insurance) in similar circumstances by those who sacrifice

their gains from trade liberalization voluntarily (in order to inherit such insurance).[2] Once one grants either such altruism or such implicit social contracting, there exists the possibility of a social consensus that the moderately increased satisfaction of the many from trade liberalization could be judged insignificant compared to the dramatic unhappiness imposed on the few.[3]

Partial compensation is of course one compromise position between no compensation and maintenance of the status quo. It seems reasonable to insist that government policies like trade liberalization, undertaken in the name of the whole society, should not burden any one part of it excessively.

2. *Allocative efficiency.* Furthermore, the kind of losses that trade liberalization can cause are in part *social* losses. In the face of contractually determined, downwardly rigid rates of increase[4] in wages, rents, borrowing costs, and dividends, trade liberalization that discourages domestic demand for import substitutes may cause temporary layoffs and idling of productive land and equipment. Dislocated labor and resources are made involuntarily unproductive until they can be reabsorbed.[5] And even then, their productivity may remain temporarily below par if labor must be retrained and if resources must be retooled, refurbished, and relocated—often by labor and resources that are themselves diverted from other productive activity. The national efficiency cost of this adjustment process is measured by the value of goods which could have been produced, but were not, because of temporary unemployment, under-utilization, and diversion of resources.[6] (And there may also be very real subjective and psychic costs to those unemployed that affect their future productivity unfavorably and permanently.)

Both of these concerns can be seen underlying the United States political/economic/philosophical concept of "injury" that was prominently stressed in the Trade Agreements Act of 1934.[7] The belief is that trade liberalization should be abandoned if it involves undue economic injury to United States firms or labor groups. That rule was formalized in the late 1940s by the "escape-clause" provisions of United States trade legislation, and also by Article XIX of the General Agreement on Tariffs and Trade (GATT). Governments could "escape" from trade concessions that caused undue injury by restoring their previous trade barriers or acceptable substitutes. The domestic income distribution would presumably return toward the desired status quo. And wasteful unemployment of labor and resources would be discouraged.

Invoking the escape clause, however, appeared to many commentators to be a costly way to avoid undesirable dislocation. It essentially surrendered all resource-reallocation and standard-of-living gains that had come from trade concession in the name of avoiding inequity and dislocation, thereby throwing out the baby with the bath water. Furthermore, under the rules of the GATT, recourse to the escape clause allowed trading partners to be compensated[8] through retaliation—which could sometimes impose unexpectedly severe injury on the United States exportables sector. Finally, the United States escape clause made other nations less willing to embark on significant multilateral liberalization, since they could not be certain of just how permanent United States concessions would be (Metzger 1971, p. 324).

In practice, the escape clause was simply infeasible as a tool for avoiding inequity and dislocation while pursuing expanded national purchasing power through trade. Between 1947 and 1962, the United States Tariff Commission found injury in thirty-three `escape-clause cases brought before it and split evenly in eight more. Of the forty-one, the President invoked the escape clause in fifteen and refused to do so in 26, presumably with an eye to foreign reaction and retaliation. In the fifteen, at least some beneficial trade liberalization was abandoned. In the twenty-six, at least some undesirable injury was left unrequited.

To several commissions and commentators in the 1950s, this Hobson's choice was neither intrinsic nor inevitable.[9] Most explored and recommended alternative ideas that later became embodied in trade adjustment assistance: (1) directly targeted financial support to compensate both dislocated labor and firms; and (2) encouragement to both labor and firms to reorient quickly their skills, resources, and enterprise toward expanding buoyant industries (such as exportables) where their productivity would be enhanced in the long run. It was hoped that the former aspect would ease distributional inequities from trade liberalization, and thereby remove political obstacles to it. It was hoped that the latter aspect would reduce the duration of inefficient, involuntary unproductivity for resources moving among sectors, and thereby reduce the economic cost of trade liberalization. Neither aspect, of course, would force the United States to forego beneficial trade concessions. And neither would provoke foreign anger, retaliation, or reluctance to bargain. Administrative resource costs of each kind of compensation would probably have seemed comparable—some government agency would have to investigate and recommend in each case, and the executive branch would have to approve or deny the recommendation. For all dimensions taken together, therefore, trade adjustment assistance seemed in principle to dominate escape-clause relief.

3. *Bribes*. In recent years, the issue underlying trade adjustment assistance has changed from "how much trade liberalization?" to "how much protection?" As a result, TAA is frequently defended from a new point of view that springs from political economy. It is argued that if TAA were not available, the political forces for increased protection would domi-

nate, imposing large social costs through inefficiencies that would increase exponentially as trade barriers rose. TAA still assists and adjusts *ex post*. But now it also bribes *ex ante* those coalitions of losers from trade that would destroy a socially beneficial status quo in the absence of TAA. In its new role, then, TAA has additional distributive and allocative effects: it compensates groups with credible threats to do social harm and avoids the allocative inefficiencies that are the instruments of that potential harm.

12.2.2   The Program under the Trade Expansion Act of 1962

The Kennedy administration was prodded by attitudes both at home and abroad to propose trade adjustment assistance formally in 1962. Kennedy very much wanted significant multilateral tariff cuts to assure United States access to the burgeoning European Common Market. To gain the same commitment from European nations, he proposed significant tightening of the criteria for escape-clause relief, so as to reassure them of the permanency of United States concessions. To reassure Congress about this tightening and to gain congressional authority for substantial tariff cuts, he proposed TAA as the preferable way of relieving any United States injury. A cautious Congress incorporated a carefully circumscribed program[10] into the Trade Expansion Act of 1962.

The most important distributional assistance provisions of this early TAA program were

—for labor: supplements to unemployment insurance (UI) payments to replace 65 percent of normal income for up to one year,[11] and up to a year and a half for workers who were over sixty or being retrained, as long as such payments did not exceed the maximum income-support level of 65 percent of the average weekly manufacturing wage;

—for firms: special tax privileges that enabled them to increase after-tax profits.

The most important provisions that were designed to reduce inefficiency by speeding adjustment included

—for labor affected (or threatened) by trade liberalization: (1) special encouragement to take part in existing training, counseling, and job-placement programs (but no special programs); and (2) relocation allowances covering family moving expenses to a new job elsewhere;

—for firms affected (or threatened) by trade liberalization: low-interest loans or loan guarantees for modernization or retooling of plants and equipment and for acquisition of working capital; free technical consultation on adapting to change, and on sales outlooks and forecasts.

In practice, trade adjustment assistance under this legislation was initially nonexistent. The support of organized labor for the United States program quickly dried up as seven years went by with significant import growth but without a single approval of *any* adjustment assistance case. (Six cases were turned down.) Adjustment assistance, in the eyes of most labor spokespersons, was a cruel hoax.

What created this dormancy was a combination of stringent criteria for eligibility and strict interpretation of the criteria by the Tariff Commission officials responsible for ruling on each case. To be approved for adjustment assistance benefits, petitioners had to prove not only that they had been injured by United States trade liberalization, but that it had been the *major* cause of their injury. "Major" was initially interpreted to mean "single most important." That conservative interpretation made approval almost impossible—labor and management are continually buffeted by a myriad of other important shocks in addition to trade liberalization.

Furthermore, the process of applying for adjustment assistance was a bureaucratic nightmare. It not only diverted the services of company and union officials, but also required lawyers in preparation of "the case," and finally involved considerable time. Each case had to be determined within roughly eight months, but coupled with other lags and delays, it could sometimes take more than two years to receive the first adjustment assistance payments—even when the case was approved.[12] There is no doubt that many firms and labor groups simply were unwilling to apply. Even approval would have been unprofitable. For them, adjustment assistance might just as well not have been available.

The Nixon administration brought a shift toward less strict interpretations in the early 1970s and revived United States adjustment assistance. Both applications and approvals accelerated. Legislative revision of the adjustment assistance program under the Trade Act of 1974 made an even more dramatic impact, as revealed in table 12.1. Most dramatic of all is the increase in petitions and projected outlays brought on by the auto-centered recession of 1979–80. These are not reflected in the table but have been estimated to require an *extra* $1 billion of outlays in fiscal 1980 and $0.4 billion in fiscal 1981 (*Washington Star*, 3 April 1980). A total of 859 petitions for TAA were filed during the first three months of 1980 alone (Rosen 1980, p. 2)!

12.2.3   The Program under the Trade Act of 1974

Under the Trade Act of 1974, the number of workers certified eligible for TAA benefits quickly rose to more than ten times its annual average under even the liberal administration of the former program. And budget outlays mushroomed comparably.

Statutory changes that made adjustment assistance more attractive included (1) raising labor's potential income support with TAA supplements to 70 percent of normal income, as long as this did not exceed 100 percent (raised from 65 percent) of the average weekly manufacturing wage; (2) requiring that labor cases be determined in two, not eight, months, by the secretary of labor, and not by the slow-moving, quasi-judicial International Trade Commission (née the Tariff Commission); (3) providing separate funds out of tariff revenues for retraining trade-displaced workers; and (4) allowing reimbursement for a portion of job-search expenses.

But by far the most important statutory changes related to eligibility. First, adjustment assistance was made potentially available to firms and labor injured by imports for *any* reason, whether because of government trade concessions or not. And second, imports needed only to contribute importantly to the injury, not be its major cause.

While the second change is laudable from the point of view of equity (and perhaps efficiency), the first raises awkward questions regarding a distributional defense of TAA—that policy for the national interest not impose excessive burdens on any citizen. Why, for example, should workers be compensated at higher than UI levels for market-determined injury just because the markets are international? Is it economically defensible that the United States compensate domestic producers who are in an extreme case lazy or slow to adopt technological advances, thereby losing competitiveness to foreigners? Compensation for such injury *is* possible under the new adjustment assistance program. The increasingly familiar answer is that "political reality" dictates such compensation as a supernormal bribe to mollify protectionists. But the potential conflict between this rationale and a society's distributional goals is apparent. Such bribes may create inequities rather than curing them. And they clearly distort market signals and incentives.[13]

A second answer might begin with the observation that most foreign governments are committed to aiding industries that suffer structural dislocation and adjustment problems from any source, including the market.[14] In the light of this, protectionist changes in United States adjustment assistance can perhaps be defended as defensive, equalizing retaliation to foreign beggar-your-neighbor policies with adverse consequence for the United States income distribution.

A general impression of the 1974 program in practice is that its assistance (equity) provisions have been considerably more successful than its adjustment (efficiency) provisions. And success for one is not necessarily unrelated to failure for the other. Insufficient attention has been drawn to the intrinsic incompatibility of "assistance" and "adjustment" programs as presently structured: one of the surest ways to bring about adjustment would be to provide no assistance, and assistance that compensated for every burden would leave no incentive to adjust. One of the surprising conclusions of the worker survey reported on in subsequent sections was the large number of TAA–supported workers who returned not only to

Table 12.1   The History of United States Adjustment Assistance

	Adjustment Assistance for Labor					Firm Adjustment Assistance		
	Cases Approved	Cases Denied	Number of Workers in Cases Approved	Number of Workers in Cases Denied	Dollar Outlays (millions)	Cases Approved	Cases Denied	Dollar Outlays (millions)
Under the Trade Expansion Act of 1962								
1962–72[1]	56	80	23,519	27,632	n.a.	6	15	n.a.
1972–75[2]	54	91	30,380	39,799	n.a.	22	n.a.	n.a.
Total	110	171	53,899	67,431	75.6	28	n.a.	45.3
Under the Trade Act of 1974								
1975[3]	123	112	51,261	56,887	n.a.	13	1	3.5
1976	428	442	131,765	177,889	162.5	25	3	14.4
1977	413	612	107,674	99,624	151.7	116	3	24.3
1978	844	1,010	126,403	−65,179[4]	280.0+	129	1	72.2
1979[5]	710	957	165,123	63,189[6]	270.0[7]	n.a.	n.a.	n.a.

Sources: United States House of Representatives, Hearings before the Subcommittee on Foreign Economic Policy of the Committee on Foreign Affairs, Ninety-Second Congress, Second Session, 24–26 April, 9–11, 17 May 1972, entitled *Trade Adjustment Assistance* (Washington, 1972), p. 49; President of the United States, *Twentieth Annual Report on the Trade Agreements Program—1975*, pp. 47–50; *Twenty-First Annual Report on the Trade Agreements Program—1976*, pp. 56–59, 74; *Twenty-Second Annual Report on the Trade Agreements Program—1977*, pp. 65–70, 118; *Twenty-Third Annual Report on the Trade Agreements Program—1978*, pp. 92–93, 163–66; United States Department of Labor (1979) table entitled "Cumulative Program Activity."

Note: n.a. = not available.

[1]October 1962, when the Trade Expansion Act took effect, through February 1972.

[2]March 1972 through March 1975, when the Trade Expansion Act was superseded by the Trade Act of 1974.

[3]The nine months from April to December.

[4]The cumulated total of workers denied adjustment assistance unaccountably *falls* from the 22d to the 23d *Annual Report on the Trade Agreements Program* (see sources above). Three industries account for almost all the decline:

	Workers Denied Trade Adjustment Assistance	
	4/3/75 – 12/31/77	4/3/75 – 12/31/78
Total	334,404	269,221
Fabricated Metal Products (SIC 34)	40,308	9,305
Electrical Machinery (SIC 36)	26,056	16,194
Transportation Equipment (SIC 37)	135,635	64,438

[5]First eleven months of 1979 except for dollar outlays, which are for the calendar year.

[6]332,410 less 269,221 (see note 4 above).

[7]*Washington Post*, 10 April 1980.

their former industry, but to their former firm (roughly three out of every five), and even to their former job.[15] Generous TAA benefits may even have brought about a perverse expansion of the number of workers needing to be compensated—if it made employers more willing to lay them off.[16] Once a worker is certified eligible for TAA benefits, that eligibility is automatically activated for all layoffs covered by the petition in the subsequent two years.

On the basis of the survey of 1976 recipients that is described below, adjustment aspects of the 1974 program—training, counseling, job-search, and relocation allowances—were neglected about as much under the 1974 program as earlier. Less than 10 percent of TAA recipients took advantage of available employment services, and published figures on cumulated experience are even more discouraging (United States Department of Labor 1979). Only 1 out of every 30 TAA recipients from 1975 through 1979 (November) entered training; only 1 out of roughly 200 received a job-search allowance; and only 1 out of roughly 350 received a relocation allowance.[17]

Distributional goals and realizations are by contrast much more consistent. Combined UI and TAA payments replaced 76 percent of after-tax income on average for as long as the eligibility of workers surveyed lasted. Nevertheless, the survey reveals that workers who are permanently displaced by trade seem to suffer a large income sacrifice even three or four years after displacement (10 percent lower incomes for men than in their former job, compared to 20 percent *higher* incomes for comparable UI recipients; 5 percent lower for women, compared to 16 percent *higher*). And it seems there still remained substantial unpredictability and unduly long delays in the process of petition, certification, and delivery of benefits. Despite the attempt to streamline the process, the first TAA payment was still generally received more than a year after the separation that justified it.[18] Lump-sum payments were still received by almost four out of five surveyed TAA recipients, and delays in payments during the first year after separation caused workers' income losses to be more than 50 percent higher than if TAA payments had been made "as earned."

12.3   TAA Experience under the Trade Act of 1974: Means and Cross-Tabulations from a Comparative Survey of Workers

Describing the beneficiaries of the program, including the stability, level, and growth of their income, is more important for TAA than for many other government programs because of its distributional and political justifications. Sensible assessments of the program must identify whether those who are aided are in fact "deserving" by some measure of equity or political muscle. And such assessments should attempt to measure the extent to which program benefits offset injury.[19] How the "deserving" are defined—whether as poor, old, ambitious, productive, politically powerful, or some combination—will not concern us here.

We will characterize workers receiving TAA, and not firms. In this section we do so by comparing them one-dimensionally and two-dimensionally to a sample of peers, focusing on unconditional mean differences or else controlling for one other variable via cross-tabulations. In the next section we compare TAA recipients to their peers multidimensionally, controlling when feasible for all variables that are alleged to cause different worker experience via regression analysis.

12.3.1   A Recent Survey

The most recent survey of worker recipients of TAA was commissioned by the United States Department of Labor and is summarized in Corson et al. (1979).[20] Sample design and survey methods are described at length in appendixes A and B of that report.

Interviews were carried out from November 1978 through February 1979, virtually all of them in person, under the supervision of Mathematica Policy Research, Inc. (Princeton, New Jersey). Interviewees had received first TAA payments in 1976, and the survey sample was designed to represent the population of 1976 TAA recipients. Eighty-four percent of those interviewed were separated from their employer in late 1974 or 1975; 16 percent were separated in 1976. For comparison purposes, a smaller sample of UI recipients (not receiving TAA) was selected from the same state unemployment offices that administered benefits to TAA recipients.[21] The interview form was pretested and modified accordingly. Interviewers were trained and continually supervised. Interview data were cross-checked through subsequent calls and visits by supervisors. The response rate among TAA recipients was 70 percent, and among UI recipients 54 percent. A few known characteristics of nonrespondents (from state unemployment office records) were compared to characteristics of respondents. These suggested little nonresponse bias and no particular reason for believing that biases which remained affected one group unduly compared to the other. The ultimate survey sample consisted of

—963 TAA recipients,
—538 UI recipients.

The TAA sample was stratified by industry, represented in the same proportions that characterized the industry source of 1976 TAA payments. Columns (1) and (2) of table 12.2 describe the interindustry manufacturing distribution of workers in the survey (only one worker interviewed was in a nonmanufacturing industry) and in the corresponding national population of TAA recipients. Column (3) suggests that the distribution has some claim to generality, having not changed signifi-

Table 12.2   Percentage Distribution of TAA and UI Recipients in
Manufacturing, by Industry

	TAA Recipients			UI Recipients
	1976 Survey Sample (1)	1976 National Population (2)	1975–80[1] National Population (3)	1976 Survey Sample (4)
Footwear	7.7	8.4	10.3	0.4
Apparel and other nondurables	30.3	25.7	22.5 plus[2]	22.8
Automobiles	23.7	28.7	22.6	12.7
Steel	20.6	18.1	18.9	19.2
Other durables	17.7	19.1	11.8 plus[2]	44.9

Sources: Column (2) from Corson et al. (1979, p. 192); columns (1) and (4) from data tape underlying Corson et al. (1979); column (3) from Rosen (1980, p. 3).
[1]From the start of the program through the first three months of 1980 only.
[2]13.3 percent of TAA recipients are unaccounted for in the source cited above.

cantly during the first five years of the new program. In late 1979 and early 1980, however, the auto industry's share of TAA certifications mushroomed. Column (4) describes the matched UI sample in the survey.

Interviews were conducted in seven states, three chosen for the high proportion of TAA payments being made there (Ohio, Pennsylvania, and New York), and four chosen randomly (California, Indiana, Massachusetts, and Virginia) from a set of four industry groupings, with the probability of selection being proportional to the number of TAA payments in each state. Sixty-five percent of the national population of TAA recipients resided in those seven states. Equal numbers of interviews were conducted at each of ten locations within each state. The locations were chosen from a random sample of TAA petitions classified by industry and weighted by the number of workers each petition covered. The locations ultimately selected reflected a significant variety of labor market conditions.

As this was the first comprehensive survey of worker experience under the Trade Act of 1974, some differences from previous surveys are due to the changes in the TAA program from the Trade Expansion Act of 1962. Chief among them is the dramatic increase in recourse to TAA, due largely to the easing of the eligibility criteria. As a result there is some reason to believe that this survey is more representative and more reliable than prior ones because of the larger pool of TAA recipients to sample and because of the reduction in any systematic bias (for example, against small petitioners) caused by excessive petition costs under the old program.

On the other hand, there are subtle differences between this survey and previous ones that arise because of changes in eligibility requirements. Because imports need now be only an important cause of injury and not the major cause, it is almost certain that workers in the current survey will be less injured by trade on average than workers in previous surveys. On the other hand, because TAA can now legally be awarded because of trade-related injury for *any* reason, whether due to prior government trade concessions or not, the current survey is probably more representative than earlier ones of workers displaced by imports as a whole, rather than just that portion of imports on which the government negotiated liberalization.

12.3.2   Characterizing TAA Recipients

The most important information in evaluating the TAA program concerns the characteristics and experience of workers receiving TAA. Some of these characteristics and experiences in our sample confirmed widespread impressions; many did not. Some are well known from previous surveys; others have received little notice.

It is known, for example, but underemphasized, that almost all recipients of TAA work in manufacturing industries. Hence their peers are most accurately other manufacturing workers, not United States labor at large. It is also well known that TAA recipients are more concentrated than their peers in footwear and apparel, as table 12.2 reveals. It is less well known that the auto industry is the source of a much higher proportion of TAA recipients than of their peers—even as early as 1976. These industry differences between the TAA and UI samples can be argued to be the sole source of differences between beneficiaries of TAA and others, without any reference to international trade. But this observation begs the question of what caused the industry differences—to which a sensible answer is international trade.

Among the most important findings of this survey is that TAA recipients were much more likely than UI recipients to experience temporary unemployment or reduced hours, as revealed in table 12.3. They were only barely more likely than UI recipients to have worked for a company that closed down, and much less likely to have changed their industry or occupation between separation and the interview, roughly three years later. For TAA recipients, worker experience differed significantly among those on permanent layoff, those on temporary layoff, and those on reduced hours. Workers on temporary layoff made up the majority of the TAA caseload. Since most previous commentary on TAA has focused on permanently displaced workers, it is useful here to describe the connection between temporary worker displacements, international trade, and the TAA program.

Table 12.3   Percentage Distribution of Surveyed TAA and UI Recipients (1976),
                    by Type of Separation and Adjustment

	TAA Recipients	UI Recipients
Type of Separation		
Permanent	25.2	56.8
Temporary	58.2	39.9
Reduced-hours[1]	16.6	3.3
Adjustment		
Company closed down	16.0	15.2
Changed industry	15.6	31.2
Permanently displaced	67.5	68.0
Changed occupation	25.1	39.1
Permanently displaced	54.0	60.8

Source: Corson et al. (1979, pp. vi, 38, 42, 68).
[1]The average reduction was from forty-one hours per week to twenty-three hours per week, and the average spell of reduced-hours employment lasted fifty-six weeks.

Temporarily displaced workers have both unique advantages and unique problems when compared to the permanently displaced workers usually visualized as being primary recipients of TAA. Relative to permanently displaced workers, the duration of trade-related dislocations for those temporarily displaced is likely to be short, and their income loss only moderate. But if such short spells of unemployment occur more frequently because of trade, workers who are prone to temporary displacement may still suffer disproportionately from unpredictable and uncertain income streams.[22] Compensation for such volatile incomes and job prospects might be an important justification for paying temporarily displaced workers. No clear adjustment (efficiency) motive exists for TAA in this case because it is not obvious that the workers should leave the industry on economic grounds.

But why should trade increase the volatility of worker incomes in import-competing industries? There seem to be a number of reasons. First, in industries such as steel, dumping is widespread and unpredictable, causing United States business to sag notably some years (even quarters) and rebound in others. Second, speculative import purchases may take place when dollar depreciation threatens, and then may be offset subsequent to dollar depreciation by abnormally low import purchases. Domestic business can be correspondingly slack, then prosperous,[23] depending on product durability, substitution patterns, and buyer loyalty to competing varieties. Employment in domestic industries can thus be correspondingly slack, then prosperous. The auto industry seems to be a good candidate for sensitivity to exchange-rate-related demand fluctuations. And speculation based on changes in orderly marketing agreements can have similar effects.

But does TAA cause some temporary unemployment while alleviating its burdens? An unanswered question is whether the liberal availability of TAA supplements to standard unemployment insurance increases incentives that encourage employers to lay off workers temporarily (because such workers are better accommodated), as discussed above. If so, any such additional workers will be worse off because their TAA payments do not match their straight salary. And there may be some cost to the economy as a whole if the temporary nature of a worker's dislocation inhibits job search and if TAA keeps workers affiliated with a declining industry when more productive positions are available elsewhere.

Similar questions arise with respect to the availability of TAA for workers placed on reduced hours by their employers. Presumably employers use the option of reducing or increasing hours for the same reasons they use temporary layoffs. And fluctuations in hours may be related to trade in the same way as temporary layoffs. But once again, to the extent that TAA availability for reduced hours encourages employer recourse to them, it increases the need for compensation while simultaneously satisfying it. TAA availability may again undermine any adjustment goals of the program by indenturing workers to a declining industry and discouraging their job search. From an efficiency perspective, it is clearly better to have half as many workers full-time (with the remainder in other jobs) than the historical work force all working half-time.

Some findings from the present survey confirm common beliefs about TAA recipients, whether permanently, temporarily, or partially dislocated. Table 12.4 reveals that they are somewhat older, less educated, more stable in their employment history, and more likely to be union members, female, minority status, married, and the head of a household than the average unemployed worker.[24]

But they are not likely to be poorer. Fewer fall below the poverty line. And their predislocation incomes (principally for men) exceed the incomes of their peers, as do household incomes. This finding seems to preclude any relative-income, "progressive" motivation for maintaining TAA benefits that are more attractive than UI benefits.

The conventional belief that trade-displaced workers face more difficult short-run adjustment problems than a typical unemployed worker does seem to be borne out in table 12.5, especially for those who are permanently laid off. The duration of their initial unemployment spell is longer than for UI recipients, and the incidence of recurrent separations is slightly more frequent. Those TAA recipients never recalled to their previous job between separation and interview spend a larger proportion of weeks unemployed, and are more likely to be out of the labor force than their UI counterparts. The latter finding may reflect retirement or discouragement more than anything else, since TAA recipients were

Table 12.4   Distribution of Surveyed TAA and UI Recipients (1976), by Personal and Preseparation Job/Income Characteristics

	TAA Recipients	UI Recipients
Personal characteristics		
Mean age in years[1]	39.9	35.9
Mean years of education[2]	10.4	11.4
Percent that had vocational or technical schooling[2]	24.8	27.6
Percent female	38.5	35.5
Percent minority	20.9	19.7
Percent married[2]	79.0	68.1
Percent head of household[2]	94.5	87.7
Preseparation job/income characteristics		
Mean years tenure	11.8	7.8
Percent quit or fired (not laid off)	1.1	6.8
Percent in union[3]	81.3	65.8
Mean annual income of recipient[4]	$11,080	$9,820
Mean annual income of spouse[4]	$2,690	$2,820
Percent of households with income below poverty line[4]	1.9	3.7

Source: Corson et al. (1979, pp. 17, 21, 28, 38).
[1]At separation date.
[2]At interview date.
[3]At separation date, not including workers on reduced hours in the base.
[4]In year before separation, 1975 dollars.

relatively less likely to receive training. There is, of course, a potential causality problem in these findings. Comparatively generous TAA benefits may have encouraged workers to take longer to locate a new job and hence increased their measured unemployment spells at first. This could be true despite the lumpiness and unpredictability of TAA payments.

By the interview date, roughly three to three and a half years after initial layoff, most differences in the adjustment burdens of TAA recipients and typical unemployed workers disappeared. TAA recipients are actually less likely to be unemployed or out of the labor force (barely) than others. But those who have not returned to their earlier jobs are likely to have experienced a significantly greater decline in income than the average reemployed worker (and even the temporarily displaced TAA recipients suffer a small relative decline). They might have been presumed to lose rents on accumulated on-the-job skills that are probably greater than those of the average unemployed worker, since TAA recipients have a longer and more stable work history. They may also have lost some rents that are unrelated to skill and a function of their former industry's political pressure for protection against imports.

Some of these findings are surprising in the light of previous surveys of TAA recipients (see note 12). Part of the explanation can be found in the

Table 12.5   Distribution of Surveyed TAA and UI Recipients (1976), by Job Market Experience between Separation and Interview

	TAA Recipients	UI Recipients
Between separation and interview		
Mean weeks of first unemployment spell		
after separation	21.9	21.9
Permanently displaced	41.8	32.8
Temporarily displaced	17.4	16.3
Percent of weeks unemployed	18.4	20.9
Never recalled	28.0	25.4
Recalled at least once	15.6	18.0
Percent of weeks out of the labor force	8.3	9.9
Never recalled	26.3	20.5
Recalled at least once	3.0	3.1
Percent of weeks employed	73.8	69.5
Never recalled	46.0	54.6
Recalled at least once	82.0	79.2
At interview		
Percent unemployed	7.2	11.6
Percent out of labor force	11.9	12.0
Percent employed	80.9	76.4
Ratio of mean weekly wages: interview		
job to preseparation job[1]		
Permanently displaced	0.92	1.18
Temporarily displaced	1.22	1.25

Source: Corson et al. (1979, pp. 48, 58, 59, 64, 65, 69).
[1]1975 dollars.

rapidly shifting industrial incidence of injury from trade in the early 1970s. The relative importance of the footwear industry and the electronics industry declined in successful TAA petitions; the relative importance of apparel, autos, and steel increased (apparel has since declined and footwear has risen again, according to table 12.2). This altered worker characteristics among TAA recipients because skill mix, ethnic concentration, job stability, and average wages differ substantially from industry to industry. And it was to be expected to the extent that cumulative and ongoing competitive pressures (many from newly industrializing countries) reduce the industrial importance of declining United States industries such as footwear and textiles by causing marginal firms to fail.

12.3.3   The Sample as a Reflection of the Effects of Both Trade and TAA

It would have been valuable to be able to measure *separately* the effects of import competition on workers and the effects of the TAA program itself (see note 19). No continuous measure of the former was employed besides the certainty that trade had been an "important" cause of dislocation, as prescribed by the legislation embodying certification

requirements.[25] It was impossible to know just how important trade alone
had been in altering wages and working conditions before and after TAA
receipt. The survey measured mixed effects of both trade and TAA on
wages and working conditions. Since TAA in many aspects is designed to
offset the impact of trade on United States workers, it seems likely that
the survey and the analysis below understate both the (presumably
unfavorable) effects of import competition on some United States workers and the (presumably favorable) effects of TAA. They do, however,
probably reflect the net effect of both forces with considerably more
accuracy. One test of the success of TAA in achieving its distributional
goals would be that these net effects are small.

Measuring the impact of trade alone on workers is a difficult task. Yet it
is done subjectively every day in administrative determination of certification. A valuable complement to surveys like the one summarized
would be research on the certification process itself. What economic and
other variables underlie decisions to approve or disapprove a TAA
petition? Can one determine a set of variables and the weights attached to
them that predict the yes/no decision on the petition with some
accuracy?[26] If so, one could use those same variables and weights to
measure the severity of workers' injury from trade. One might also be
able to explore the budgetary and performance implications of changing
the weights attached to the criteria underlying certification, as is implicitly proposed whenever TAA is legislatively reconsidered.

12.4 TAA Experience under the Trade Act of 1974: Job and Income Recovery in a Regression Approach

One- and two-dimensional comparisons of TAA and UI recipients are
sometimes misleading. Many comparisons in section 12.3 are explained
not so much by TAA/UI differences in programs, labor markets, or
competitive pressures as by TAA/UI differences in age, experience,
industry mix, etc. Cross-sectional multiple regression provides a useful
way to control for less important sample differences among workers while
focusing on those that are most interesting.

Tables 12.6 and 12.7 provide examples of such regressions, each vector
of estimated coefficients being displayed in a column. The dependent
variable explained in table 12.6 reflects medium-term employment recovery after initial separation—it is the percentage of weeks employed in the
three to three and a half years between initial separation and interview.[27]
The dependent variable explained in table 12.7 reflects medium-term
income recovery in the same period—it is the log of the weekly wage (in
1975 dollars) of each individual in his or her job at the interview date,
given (as an independent variable) his or her weekly wage (in 1975
dollars) before separation.[28]

Table 12.6   Job Recovery Regressions: Determinants of Percentage of Weeks Worked between Separation and Interview

Table Entries Give Extra percentage of weeks worked . . .	Entire Sample	All UI Recipients	All TAA Recipients	Permanently Displaced UI Recipients	Permanently Displaced TAA Recipients
SAMPLE IDENTIFIERS					
. . . if individual *received trade adjustment assistance*	−4.56 (2.40) .06	—	—	—	—
. . . if individual *experienced temporary separation*	21.34 (2.01) .00	19.33 (4.40) .00	23.66 (2.40) .00	—	—
ADMINISTRATION OF BENEFITS AND SEPARATION					
. . . for each extra percent of after-tax income before separation that UI and TAA benefits *replaced* during *first spell* of unemployment[1]	−0.0481 (0.0480) .32	0.0821 (0.140) .56	−0.0538 (0.0518) .30	0.156 (0.236) .51	0.215 (0.124) .09
. . . for each extra percent of after-tax income before separation that UI and TAA benefits *replaced* during *all spells* of unemployment[1]	0.0122 (0.00957) .20	−0.00433 (0.0355) .90	0.0212 (0.00974) .03	−0.0155 (0.0510) .76	0.0152 (0.0145) .30
. . . for every week of official employer *notification* prior to separation, or of *"suspected job loss"* prior to notification	0.0400 (0.0641) .53	0.0685 (0.120) .57	0.0527 (0.0838) .53	0.0620 (0.187) .74	0.226 (0.210) .28
ECONOMIC ENVIRONMENT					
. . . if recipient was a *union* member in the preseparation job	−4.67 (2.32) .04	−3.97 (4.80) .41	−5.94 (2.85) .04	−4.63 (7.36) .53	−7.31 (7.29) .32

Table 12.6   Continued

Table Entries Give Extra percentage of weeks worked . . .	Entire Sample	All UI Recipients	All TAA Recipients	Permanently Displaced UI Recipients	Permanently Displaced TAA Recipients
. . . if the recipient's company *closed* down	4.19 (2.35) .07	7.75 (5.82) .19	5.54 (2.66) .04	0.373 (14.43) .98	4.74 (7.44) .53
. . . for each extra percent of labor force *unemployed* in state and industry group	0.216 (0.261) .41	0.264 (0.602) .66	0.199 (0.292) .49	0.215 (1.31) .87	0.319 (0.793) .69
Industry					
. . . if individual worked in the *apparel* industry rather than durables (less autos, steel)	14.27 (3.37) .00	15.66 (9.35) .10	15.67 (3.72) .00	17.07 16.62 .31	24.80 (9.45) .01
. . . if individual worked in the *footwear* industry rather than durables (less autos, steel)	6.67 (4.63) .15	No observations	8.33 (4.76) .08	No observations	15.09 (10.51) .16
. . . if individual worked in *other nondurables* industries rather than durables (less autos, steel)	−9.38 (4.34) .03	−11.80 (5.47) .03	No observations	−13.35 (9.36) .16	No observations
. . . if individual worked in the *auto* industry rather than durables (less steel)	−0.0268 (2.50) .99	0.534 (5.68) .93	1.96 (2.88) .50	−7.13 (15.05) .64	33.61 (9.93) .00
. . . if individual worked in the *steel* industry rather than durables (less autos)	0.216 (2.41) .93	0.750 (5.14) .88	0.249 (2.80) .93	3.38 (10.24) .74	0.387 (11.54) .97

AGE, EDUCATION AND EXPERIENCE

... for each year (X) of age²	1.20	−3.00	2.99	−4.74	6.86
	(0.826)	(2.05)	(0.945)	(4.14)	(2.13)
	.05	.15	.00	.26	.00
	−0.0326X	+0.0561X	−0.0714X	+0.134X	−0.117X
	(0.0199)	(0.0510)	(0.0224)	(0.118)	(0.0510)
	.10	.27	.00	.26	.00
age at maximum/minimum value of dependent variable³	36.8	53.5	41.9	35.4	58.6
... for each year of education	0.311	1.35	−0.170	1.49	−0.441
	(0.397)	(0.876)	(0.461)	(1.56)	(0.965)
	.74	.16	.25	.35	.65
... for each year (X) of experience in the labor force²	−0.182	1.85	−0.78	0.607	−2.99
	(0.548)	(1.31)	(.621)	(2.51)	(1.51)
	.74	.16	.25	.81	.05
	+0.0102X	−0.0324X	+0.0212X	−0.0442X	+0.107X
	(0.0214)	(0.0518)	(0.0240)	(0.111)	(0.0553)
	.63	.53	.38	.69	.06
labor force experience at maximum/minimum value of dependent variable³	17.8	57.1	33.9	13.7	27.9
... for each year (X) of experience in the preseparation job²	0.408	−0.184	0.290	−0.161	0.835
	(0.294)	(0.603)	(0.385)	(1.21)	(1.04)
	.17	.76	.45	.89	.42
	−0.0147X	−0.00832X	−0.000255X	0.00458X	−0.0288X
	(0.0160)	(0.0272)	(0.0228)	(0.0294)	(0.0580)
	.36	.76	.98	.94	.62
... job experience at maximum/minimum value of dependent variable³	27.8	0[4]	>60[4]	35.2	29.0

Table 12.6   Continued

TABLE ENTRIES GIVE Extra percentage of weeks worked . . .	Entire Sample	All UI Recipients	All TAA Recipients	Permanently Displaced UI Recipients	Permanently Displaced TAA Recipients
SEX/MARRIAGE STATUS					
. . . if *married male* rather than unmarried male	3.54 (2.44) .15	1.68 (4.96) .76	3.71 (2.82) .19	4.05 (9.77) .68	8.48 (8.51) .32
. . . if *married female* rather than unmarried male	−8.49 (3.50)	−11.93 (7.72)	−5.48 (4.00)	−12.28 (14.48)	−7.01 (9.85)
. . . if *unmarried female* rather than unmarried male	−2.70 (3.67) .46	−12.93 (7.72) .10	−2.95 (4.36) .50	−9.81 (12.40) .43	−11.25 (10.79) .30
SOCIOECONOMIC STATUS					
. . . if *black*	−3.18 (2.37) .18	−2.32 (6.13) .71	−2.10 (2.64) .43	−1.61 (33.46) .96	−21.72 (6.66) .00
. . . if *Hispanic*	−5.07 (3.63) .16	−7.40 (7.67) .34	−5.27 (4.22) .21	−11.23 (14.10) .43	−12.99 (9.37) .17
. . . if *disabled*	−18.21 (7.38) .01	−59.62 (17.11) .00	−3.65 (8.42) .66	−53.31 (23.70) .03	11.74 (15.90) .46
INCOME POTENTIAL, ASPIRATION, AND MOBILITY					
. . . for each extra $100 of weekly *recipient income* before separation[1]	−0.311 (1.38) .82	−4.66 (3.79) .22	1.46 (1.49) .33	1.28 (6.28) .84	1.57 (3.28) .63

	(1)	(2)	(3)	(4)	(5)
... for each extra $100 of weekly income of *other household members* before separation[1]	0.932 (0.706) .19	2.32 (1.30) .08	0.211 (0.891) .81	2.19 (1.97) .27	-4.41 (2.66) .10
... if recipient was working a *second job* at time of separation	9.23 (4.81) .06	4.08 (8.73) .64	8.04 (6.22) .20	11.87 (20.35) .56	3.10 (13.01) .82
... if recipient expressed *willingness to move* to another area to find suitable job	-3.86 (2.07) .06	-5.33 (4.39) .23	-3.50 (2.39) .14	-6.74 (7.82) .39	5.13 (5.60) .36
CONSTANT	45.47	102.42	10.17	116.75	-58.37
R^2	0.304	0.408	0.323	0.393	0.411
CALCULATED F (significance level)	8.12(.00)	2.90(.00)	6.70(.00)	1.09(.39)	1.95(.01)
NUMBER OF OBSERVATIONS	589	152	437	76	107
DEGREES OF FREEDOM	558	122	407	47	78

Note: Each column of the table represents one regression. Each entry gives the regression coefficient, its standard error (in parentheses), and the significance level of the regression coefficient on the hypothesis that its value was zero.

[1] All nominal magnitudes deflated or inflated to 1975 dollars.

[2] Each regression includes the relevant independent variable (X) and its squared value. Each table entry records the marginal effect of the independent variable on the dependent variable, a derivative that varies with the value of X itself. The upper coefficient is that attached to the linear term (standard error in parentheses), and the lower coefficient is twice that attached to the squared term (twice the standard error in parentheses).

[3] Each table entry is that value of X (see note 2) for which weeks worked (table 12.6) or weekly income (table 12.7) is at a maximum or minimum value.

[4] Estimated maximum or minimum value of dependent variable takes place at infeasible values of X (see note 2).

Table 12.7   Income Recovery Regressions: Determinants of Weekly Income (log) in Job at Interview

TABLE ENTRIES GIVE Extra percentage of income earned . . .	Entire Sample	All UI Recipients	All TAA Recipients	Permanently Displaced UI Recipients	Permanently Displaced TAA Recipients
SAMPLE INDENTIFIERS					
. . . if individual *received trade adjustment assistance*	−0.831 (0.375) .03	—	—	—	—
. . . if individual *experienced temporary separation*	3.09 (0.312) .00	4.16 (0.625) .00	2.99 (0.370) .00	—	—
ADMINISTRATION OF BENEFITS AND SEPARATION					
. . . for each extra percent of after-tax income before separation that UI and TAA benefits *replaced* during *first spell* of unemployment[1]	0.00527 (0.00738) .48	0.0235 (0.0200) .24	0.00815 (0.00795) .31	0.0501 (0.0386) .20	0.0212 (0.0218) .33
. . . for each extra percent of after-tax income before separation that UI and TAA benefits *replaced* during *all spells* of unemployment[1]	0.00144 (0.00148) .33	−0.00485 (0.00504) .34	0.00322 (0.00151) .03	−0.00868 (0.00822) .30	0.00274 (0.00258) .29
. . . for every week of official employer *notification* prior to separation, or of *"suspected job loss"* prior to notification	0.0189 (0.00992) .06	0.0468 (0.0168) .01	0.0165 (0.0129) .20	0.0874 (0.0296) .00	0.0126 (0.0378) .74
ECONOMIC ENVIRONMENT					
. . . if recipient was a *union* member in the preseparation job	−0.259 (0.360) .47	−3.20 (0.680) .00	0.809 (0.439) .07	−4.52 (1.19) .00	0.113 (1.29) .93

. . . if the recipient's company *closed* down	0.429 (0.362) .24	−1.49 (0.822) .07	0.880 (0.409) .03	−2.46 (2.29) .29	1.06 (1.31) .42
. . . for each extra percent of labor force *unemployed* in state and industry group	−0.0177 (0.0402) .66	−0.00474 (0.0850) .96	−0.000795 (0.0450) .99	−0.148 (0.208) .48	0.0900 (0.140) .52
INDUSTRY					
. . . if individual worked in the *apparel* industry rather than durables (less autos, steel)	1.48 (0.521) .00	1.86 (1.32) .16	0.887 (0.573) .12	5.46 (2.63) .04	1.15 (1.59) .47
. . . if individual worked in the *footwear* industry rather than durables (less autos, steel)	1.81 0.714 .01	No observations	1.87 (0.736) .01	No observations	0.128 (1.82) .94
. . . if individual worked in *other nondurables* industries rather than durables (less autos, steel)	0.197 (0.669) .77	0.935 (0.770) .23	No observations	2.18 (1.50) .15	No observations
. . . if individual worked in the *auto* industry rather than durables (less steel)	1.04 (0.387) .01	1.32 (0.796) .10	0.848 (0.445) .06	3.50 (2.39) .15	3.53 (1.81) .05
. . . if individual worked in the *steel* industry rather than durables (less autos)	0.971 (0.372) .01	1.29 (0.725) .08	0.940 (0.433) .03	2.92 (1.63) .08	0.719 (2.05) .73
AGE, EDUCATION, AND EXPERIENCE					
. . . for each year (X) of *age*	0.123 (0.127) .33	−0.248 (0.286) .39	0.183 (0.146) .21	−0.478 (0.653) .47	0.806 (0.376) .04
age^2	−0.00381X (0.00306) .22	0.00494X (0.00715) .49	−0.00532X (0.00345) .12	0.0107X (0.0187) .57	−0.0232X (.00898) .01

Table 12.7 Continued

TABLE ENTRIES GIVE Extra percentage of income earned . . .	Entire Sample	All UI Recipients	All TAA Recipients	Permanently Displaced UI Recipients	Permanently Displaced TAA Recipients
age at maximum/minimum value of dependent variable[3]	32.2	50.2	34.4	28.1	35.7
. . . for each year of *education*	0.0886 (0.0608) .15	0.123 (0.124) .32	0.0385 (0.0703) .59	0.0166 (0.255) .95	0.0968 (0.169) .57
. . . for each year (X) of *experience in the labor force*[2]	0.0335 (0.0846) .69	0.00335 (0.184) .99	0.130 (0.0956) .18	0.0339 (0.396) .93	−0.0770 (0.266) .77
	−0.00165X (0.00330) .62	.000231X (.00728) .97	−0.00570X 0.00369 .12	−0.00508X (0.0175) .77	0.00559X (0.00978) .57
labor force experience at maximum/minimum value of dependent variable[3]	20.3	0[4]	22.8	6.7	13.1
. . . for each year (X) of *experience in the preseparation job*[2]	−0.0179 (0.0454) .69	0.137 (0.0849) .11	−0.0902 (0.0592) .13	−0.129 (0.193) .51	−0.0500 (0.183) .79
	−0.000116X (0.00247) .96	−0.00626X (0.00382) .11	0.00436X (0.00352) .22	0.00393X (0.00468) .41	0.00211X (0.010) .84
job experience at maximum/minimum value of dependent variable[3]	0[4]	21.9	20.7	32.8	23.7

SEX/MARRIAGE STATUS

... if *married male* rather than unmarried male	0.615 (0.376) .10	-1.11 (0.699) .12	1.15 (0.434) .01	-1.27 (1.55) .42	3.58 (1.51) .02
... if *married female* rather than unmarried male	-0.353 (0.592)	-2.32 (1.10)	0.738 (0.629)	-3.13 (2.34)	1.99 (1.89)
... if *unmarried female* rather than unmarried male	-0.717 (0.575) .21	-2.59 (1.11) .02	0.0151 (0.681) .99	-2.43 (2.03) .24	1.94 (1.89) .31

SOCIOECONOMIC STATUS

... if *black*	0.0755 (0.366) .84	-0.112 (0.866) .90	0.162 (0.408) .69	-9.09 (5.31) .09	-1.51 (1.20) .21
... if *Hispanic*	-0.542 (0.560) .33	-2.48 (1.08) .02	-0.0779 (0.651) .90	-4.22 (2.23) .06	0.668 (1.64) .69
... if *disabled*	-5.22 (1.14) .00	-7.52 (2.43) .00	-4.50 (1.30) .00	-4.18 (3.84) .28	-3.97 (2.83) .16

INCOME POTENTIAL, ASPIRATION, AND MOBILITY

... for every extra percent of weekly *recipient income* before separation[1]	0.655 (0.536) .22	0.982 (1.07) .36	1.40 (0.637) .03	2.92 (2.00) .15	-0.166 (1.68) .92
... for every extra percent of weekly *income of other household members* before separation[1]	0.153 (0.329) .64	0.657 (0.590) .27	-0.226 (0.397) .57	0.301 (1.06) .78	0.274 (1.29) .83

Table 12.7   Continued

TABLE ENTRIES GIVE Extra percentage of income earned . . .	Entire Sample	All UI Recipients	All TAA Recipients	Permanently Displaced UI Recipients	Permanently Displaced TAA Recipients
. . . if recipient was working a *second job* at time of separation	0.938 (0.742) .21	0.0198 (1.23) .99	0.427 (0.955) .65	3.77 (3.21) .25	−0.420 (2.30) .86
. . . if recipient expressed *willingness to move* to another area to find suitable job	0.602 (0.319) .06	−0.169 (0.620) .79	0.981 (0.368) .01	0.181 (1.24) .89	2.56 (0.988) .01
CONSTANT	2.61	10.63	2.37	15.50	−13.33
R^2	0.33	0.51	0.37	0.56	0.48
CALCULATED F (significance level)	9.20(.00)	4.33(.00)	8.14(.00)	2.17(.01)	2.55(.00)
NUMBER OF OBSERVATIONS	589	152	437	76	107
DEGREES OF FREEDOM	558	122	407	47	78

Note: Each column of the table represents one regression. Each entry gives the regression coefficient, its standard error (in parentheses), and the significance level of the regression coefficient on the hypothesis that its value was zero.

[1] All nominal magnitudes deflated or inflated to 1975 dollars.

[2] Each regression includes the relevant independent variable (X) and its squared value. Each table entry records the marginal effect of the independent variable on the dependent variable, a derivative that varies with the value of X itself. The upper coefficient is that attached to the linear term (standard error in parentheses), and the lower coefficient is twice that attached to the squared term (twice the standard error in parentheses).

[3] Each table entry is that value of X (see note 2) for which weeks worked (table 12.6) or weekly income (table 12.7) is at a maximum or minimum value.

[4] Estimated maximum or minimum value of dependent variable takes place at infeasible values of X (see note 2).

Employment and income recovery were selected for emphasis in this section because they are thought to be the most important ways in which trade-displaced workers would suffer compared to others in the absence of the TAA program. The upper left entry in each table suggests that even with the TAA program, though, trade-displaced workers have less favorable experience than others. A TAA recipient who was identical to a UI recipient in age, experience, industry, socioeconomic status, etc.— and even in the proportion of preseparation income replaced by UI/TAA payments—would nevertheless have worked 4.56 percent fewer weeks over the three-year period, and be earning almost 1 percent (0.831) less per week, than the otherwise comparable UI recipient.

The direction of these differences squares well with intuition, although it is not clear what variables that are excluded from the regression might account for it. But neither the direction nor quantitative size of these differences squares with the one- and two-dimensional comparisons of table 12.5—an anomaly that reveals the advantage of a regression-based approach that holds all other things comparable (*ceteris paribus*). The left-hand regressions of tables 12.6 and 12.7 suggest that the comparative employment recovery of TAA recipients was less favorable than suggested by table 12.5 and that their comparative income recovery was much less *un*favorable.

The left-hand regressions of tables 12.6 and 12.7 were run over a subsample of both UI and TAA recipients.[29] But such a regression forces the responses of each group to control variables to have the same magnitude. One might hypothesize to the contrary that trade-displaced workers have quantitatively different responses because trade dislocation is somehow different from dislocations for other reasons. For example, one could argue that TAA recipients might be more responsive to advance notification than others because of their firm's more precarious market position. Or TAA recipients might be less successful per dollar of income support because they typically have had less experience than others in job search.

Columns (2) and (3) of the tables permit such differential responsiveness by allowing regression coefficients to differ between a UI sample of workers and a TAA sample, as do columns (4) and (5) for further subsamples of permanently displaced UI and TAA recipients.[30] The results do not strongly support the hypothesis of differential responsiveness. The complementary hypothesis that the regression over the UI sample (column [2]) is the same as that over the TAA sample (column [3]) could be definitively rejected only for wage recovery.[31] The hypothesis of identical responsiveness of permanently displaced UI recipients (column [4]) and TAA recipients (column [5]) was never rejected.[32] The appropriate conclusion seems to be that although trade-displaced workers and others do differ in job and income recovery as summarized above, this difference is due primarily to unidentified variables. Their employment/income experience might otherwise be largely determined by the same conventional list of variables in a quantitatively similar way.

No attempt was made to test more subtle hypotheses, specifically that, while responses were comparable to most independent variables, the two groups of workers responded differently to one or more. Along these lines, there is at least some suggestion in columns (2)–(5) of table 12.7 that wage recovery among UI recipients, but not among TAA recipients, was hurt by being married, female, Hispanic, unionized, or an employee of a company that closed.[33] Among TAA recipients, by contrast, wage recovery seemed importantly and positively determined by their willingness to move geographically, whereas that of UI recipients was not.

Most previous research has focused on workers who are permanently displaced by trade, and the regressions corresponding to this focus are in the right-hand column of each table. Some of the more interesting findings are summarized below. But caution in generalizing is strongly encouraged given the small size of the worker sample (107).

12.4.1   For Permanently Displaced TAA Recipients

1. The larger the proportion of preseparation wages that UI and TAA benefits replaced, especially at the beginning of unemployment experience, the larger the proportion of weeks employed in the subsequent three or three and a half years, and the stronger the income recovery path. The latter finding is familiar; the former much less so. While the former is quantitatively tiny and questionably significant, it suggests a possibility worthy of further investigation. It is well established that generous benefits lengthen first spells of unemployment.[34] Yet they may also thereby reduce the incidence and duration of subsequent spells by increasing the "efficiency" of initial job search. The first job taken after separation may more likely be a "good match."

2. Advance notification of an impending separation had a small and positive influence on job and income recovery, but the coefficients are not very significant by conventional standards.

3. TAA recipients in apparel, footwear, and the auto industry had much more favorable employment experience than TAA recipients in other industries (from seven to seventeen weeks per year more work). It is hard to account for this finding. One might sensibly have conjectured exactly the opposite, especially in apparel and footwear, since industry variables in the regressions might have been supposed to measure the interindustry intensity of import competition on workers. Perhaps in 1976 displaced garment and shoe workers were sufficiently protected by orderly marketing agreements at the product level that their job recovery was faster than elsewhere despite the long decline of their industries.

4. TAA recipients in the auto industry had much more favorable income recovery than TAA recipients in other industries (3.5 percent more *growth* in the weekly wage given what it used to be).

5. Rather than being a liability, the combination of greater age and labor force experience was favorable to employment recovery. Compared to an otherwise identical forty-year-old TAA recipient with twenty years of labor force participation, a fifty-year-old with thirty years of participation worked six and one-half weeks per year more between separation and interview, and a thirty-year-old with ten years of participation worked seven weeks per year less.

6. The combination of greater age and labor force experience was favorable to income recovery only up to a critical level, represented by persons in their mid-thirties with thirteen years of labor force participation. Compared to them, fifty-year-old workers with thirty years of participation recovered 2 percent less of their prior income stream.

7. Being black or Hispanic impeded job recovery, and being black or disabled impeded income recovery.

8. Job recovery was inversely related to labor market incomes of other members of a household, and the quantitative response was surprisingly large (more than two weeks less work per year by the TAA recipient for every $100 of other family income).

9. The incomes of those workers who expressed willingness to pull up stakes and move to find suitable employment were 2.5 percent higher than the incomes of those who were not willing, whether or not a move actually took place.

It bears repeating that these nine conclusions are for permanently displaced TAA recipients only, representing less than one-quarter of the TAA sample. Similar studies might profitably be carried out for temporarily displaced TAA recipients, although intuition regarding their experience is much less well developed. Finally, a great deal more work needs to be done along these lines before any assessment can be made of the robustness of the conclusions of this paper.

Notes

1. Section 12.2 is an expansion of parts of my contribution to Corson et al. (1979).

2. Chapter 10 by Baldwin is an expansion and illustration of these points. Cordes and Weisbrod (1979) identify rejection or reversal each as a form of implicit compensation, while classifying and evaluating other means of indirect compensation.

3. A public opinion survey summarized in Laudicina (1973, pp. 51–57) reveals that the most persuasive reason for opposing free trade was that "free trade would put some American laborers out of work because their jobs can be done by foreign labor at much lower cost." Thirty-four percent of the sample said they would "basically oppose" free trade. But only 15 percent would continue to "basically oppose" it "if American workers

who lost their jobs because of free trade did not suffer any personal financial loss and were retrained in jobs equal to or better than their old ones." The survey is also summarized in Frank (1973, appendix B).

4. In an inflationary environment, not only factor prices themselves, but their rates of increase over time may be temporarily rigid. Rigid rates of increase that are embodied in existing contracts presumably average near the sum of expected rates of inflation and productivity growth.

5. Characterizing dislocation as "involuntary" is controversial, as are therefore the "social" costs that rest on that characterization. The economics of optimal contracts suggests that labor and other factor suppliers may be influenced by uncertainty and subjective attitudes toward risk to *choose* (optimally from their viewpoint) rigid-price or rigid-rate-of-change contracts and (optimally again) to accept the consequent quantity adjustments to their employment and utilization rates. For similar reasons, producers may *choose* to contract for product price rigidity, and may find the offer of fixed-schedule contracts for factor prices more supportive of their goals in the face of uncertainty than flexible-price contracts. When rigid factor and product prices are optimally chosen in this fashion, it is not clear that there is any social cost to the resulting periodic unemployment and excess capacity. In this case, then, the principal defense of TAA must be on grounds of distributional equity.

6. Efforts to calculate these costs empirically have been made by Magee (1972), Cline et al. (1978), and Baldwin, Mutti, and Richardson (1980).

7. Metzger (1971, pp. 319–26) is a useful brief history of the concept and its reference to TAA.

8. Two "needs" for compensation invariably arise in trade policy: the need for domestic losers to be compensated by domestic gainers, and the need for foreign losers to be likewise compensated. In both cases, once the merit of compensation is granted, the key problem is finding the most efficient (or least inefficient) scheme for carrying it out. See Cordes and Weisbrod (1979). Also Bhagwati (1976, 1977) has a detailed theoretical and policy-related analysis of GATT Article XIX, suggesting specifically how it may be modified to account explicitly for the losses to the exporting countries from the invoking of market-disruption-related import restraints.

9. Frank and Levinson (1978, pp. 2–3) cite a number of examples, including an influential article by Clair Wilcox (1950); the "Bell Report" (United States Public Advisory Board for Mutual Security 1953); and the well-publicized 1954 ideas of David McDonald, president of the United Steelworkers of America in the "Randall Report" (United States Commission on Foreign Economic Policy 1954). For eight years following McDonald's proposal, congressional bills were introduced that codified the idea of trade adjustment assistance. But no hearings were ever held, even during consideration of the 1955 and 1958 extensions of the Trade Agreements Act (Metzger 1971, p. 323).

10. Congressional caution was due largely to the unprecedented nature of the program. The early 1960s also marks the beginning of a similar program to assist Americans dislocated by military base closings and to help them adjust. These years also saw passage of labor "adjustment" legislation such as the Manpower Development and Training Act (1962) and the Economic Opportunity Act (1964). On these parallel programs to TAA, see Frank and Levinson (1978, chapters 6 and 7). Trade adjustment assistance was also a temporary feature of the Canadian-American Auto Agreement and is summarized briefly by Fooks (1971, p. 352) and Jonish (1970).

11. One might argue that normal unemployment insurance would have been sufficient. But that would give no weight to the social-choice motivation for compensating this injury. Workers dislocated because of trade liberalization are paying a personal price for a policy deemed socially profitable. On the other hand, workers dislocated because of similar socially profitable policies such as deregulation, environmental control, and occupational safety and health standards receive no compensation beyond UI.

12. Bale (1973) reports an average delay of 13 months between separation and receipt of the first adjustment assistance check. McCarthy (1975a, p. 8) reports an average delay of 19.4 months for a sample of dislocated New England shoe workers. Other studies of worker and firm experience under the initial United States TAA program include McCarthy (1975b, c), Neumann (1978), and Neumann et al. (1976). Studies of worker experience under the most recent TAA program include Corson et al. (1979) and Jacobson (1979). Studies of worker and firm experience under both programs include numerous General Accounting Office reports, Frank and Levinson (1978), and Bale (1979).

13. Alan Deardorff has argued that one should not overemphasize the severing of TAA's link to trade concessions under the 1974 act. TAA is still linked to government trade policy to the extent that if it were not there, then increasingly protectionist trade barriers would substitute for it. One can view the United States government thus as using TAA in the familiar historical way to facilitate "concessions" on *potential* trade barriers (that is, to reject recourse to them).

14. Recent summaries of foreign adjustment assistance programs, some trade-related and some not, exist in Frank and Levinson (1978, chapter 9), Weisz (1978, part 3 and appendixes B and C), and United States General Accounting Office (1979). Baldwin and Bale (1980) contains a useful summary of Canadian adjustment assistance programs, and on these see also Jenkins et al. (1978).

15. This accords well with McCarthy's (1975c, p. 63) finding that roughly two out of three reemployed Massachusetts shoe workers who received TAA benefits under the 1962 program remained in the shoe industry. By contrast Neumann et al. (1976, pp. 3–19, 22) found that only about one in five reemployed TAA recipients remained in their former industry.

16. Employers do not pay any supplemental financial penalty for laying off workers who will be supported by TAA supplements to UI. Yet they may take advantage of the fact that comparatively generous TAA benefits make workers less resistant to layoffs. On the possible implications of these matters for temporary unemployment, see Feldstein (1975, 1976, 1978).

17. Use of these adjustment services has increased markedly among recent TAA recipients, however (information provided by C. Michael Aho).

18. Fourteen months on average from the survey, which applied to 1976. The average lag betweeen separation and application was half of the total. Considerable improvement in this aspect of performance has taken place in 1979 and 1980, however. See Rosen (1980, p. 4).

19. As described below, this aspect of any assessment is methodologically difficult. In principle, TAA benefits are paid whenever trade-related injury is documented and are not paid when no injury is present. Thus, in principle, one can observe instances only of simultaneous injury and benefit or of the absence of both. That is, one can detect only the net influence of injury and benefits. Short of social experimentation in which some economic agents experience either the injury or the benefits but not both, there seem to be only very subtle, uncertain ways of quantitatively assessing the scope of injury alone, the impact of benefits alone, or the "extent to which program benefits offset injury." A careful attempt is Jacobson (1979).

20. Previous surveys are referenced in note 12 above.

21. For reasons described in Corson et al. (1979, pp. 195–98), the UI sample was not matched precisely to the TAA sample with respect to either industry (see below) or time of separation. Only 65 percent of the UI sample left their jobs in late 1974 or 1975. Several comparison groups other than comparably located UI recipients were considered, yet seemed like inferior choices for reasons described in Corson et al. (1979, pp. 191–96).

22. This possibility rests on the assumption that wages and other provisions of contracts do *not* vary to offset the unpredictable and uncertain income streams. If contract terms do take account of this uncertainty, then there would seem to be no reason to believe that the

uncertainty produces suffering over the long run, and no case for compensation. See note 5 above. This possibility notwithstanding, uncertainty is precisely the reason why many policymakers subscribe to the need to compensate nations (analogously to workers) for volatile export earnings through the IMF's Compensatory Financing Facility and the EC's STABEX. These are self-financing loan programs, however, which raises the question of whether the TAA program should include concessionary (but repayable) loans for certain purposes.

23. The opposite phenomenon occurs when dollar appreciation is expected, and then actually takes place.

24. All comparisons are to unemployed manufacturing workers who receive UI payments. Such comparisons must be treated with caution, however, because of their one-dimensional nature. Pro-TAA commentary, for example, tempts one to think of recipients as especially "deserving" because they are *both* older and less educated. It is probably more accurate to think of them as less educated *because* they are older. Similarly, age may explain marital status, and both explain stability. Industry mix may explain minority status. Structural expansions of the regression analysis outlined in the next section of the paper could in principle control for such internal causality.

25. The same problem exists for Jacobson (1979) and is discussed by him. The technical counterpart to this statement is that the variable TAA (1 for TAA recipients, 0 for UI recipients) which underlies all the tabulations and regressions in this paper measures the influence on workers of both injury from trade and TAA itself. Tabular information on TAA recipients and regression coefficients therefore reflect the frequently offsetting influences of injury and its policy relief.

26. See Baldwin (1976) for an attempt to do this with congressional voting patterns on commercial policy.

27. Because it is a percentage, the dependent variable is truncated (limited). Ordinary-least-squares regressions such as those summarized below may thus be inferior to those run to explain a logit transformation of the percentage of weeks worked.

28. The presence of past wages in the regression is what allows the coefficients to be interpreted as "income recovery coefficients." Each can be taken to record the impact of the relevant variable on the individual's *change* in weekly wage between separation and interview, given the preseparation wage. This can be most easily seen by subtracting the (log of) preseparation weekly wages from both sides of the regression equation.

Other dependent variables could be examined in the same fashion to discern other differences in TAA and UI experience, e.g., labor force participation, search behavior (measured, say, by the number of job contacts), and adjustment to initial separation.

More precise descriptions of independent variables than provided in tables 12.6 and 12.7 are available from the author.

29. A total of 912 workers were excluded from the regression subsample because of missing or inconsistent data on some of the variables. Details are available from the author.

30. Of the 152 UI recipients in the sample underlying column (2), half were working for the same employer at the interview as when they were separated. Of the 437 TAA recipients in the sample underlying column (3), 76 percent were only temporarily displaced in this fashion.

31. The calculated value of the relevant F statistic was 2.22, versus critical values of 1.46 for a 5 percent significance level and 1.70 for a 1 percent significance level. In the employment recovery regressions of table 12.6, the calculated F statistic was 1.48.

32. The calculated values of the relevant F statistics for tables 12.6 and 12.7 were 1.08 and 1.42, respectively, compared again to critical values of 1.46 (5 percent significance) and 1.70 (1 percent significance). Note that the job recovery regression run over the permanently displaced UI sample was not itself significant at conventional levels.

33. All these relationships appeal to intuition except that between marriage and wage recovery. The negative impact of unionism in the former job is sensible if union members

are paid more than others, other things being comparable, since some union members will be forced to take subsequent jobs that are not unionized.

34. Hamermesh (1977) provides a summary.

References

Baldwin, R. E. 1976. The political economy of postwar U.S. trade policy. *Bulletin*, 1976–4, New York University Graduate School of Business Administration, Center for the Study of Financial Institutions.

Baldwin, R. E., and M. D. Bale. 1980. North American responses to imports from new industrial countries. Paper presented at Conference on Old and New Industrial Countries, University of Sussex, England, 6–8 January.

Baldwin, R. E., J. H. Mutti, and J. D. Richardson. 1980. Welfare effects on the United States of a significant multilateral tariff reduction. *Journal of International Economics* 10 (August): 405–23.

Bale, M. D. 1973. Adjustment to freer trade: An analysis of the adjustment assistance provisions of the Trade Expansion Act of 1962. Ph.D. thesis, University of Wisconsin, and Report no. DLMA 91–55–73–05–1 of the National Technical Information Service (Springfield, Virginia).

———. 1979. Adjustment assistance: Dealing with import-displaced workers. In Walter Adams et al., *Tariffs, quotas, and trade: The politics of protectionism*. San Francisco: Institute for Contemporary Studes.

Bhagwati, J. N. 1976. Market disruption, export market disruption, compensation, and GATT reform. *World Development* 4 (December): 989–1020.

———. 1977. Market disruption, export market disruption, compensation, and GATT reform. In J. Bhagwati, ed., *The new international economic order: The North-South debate*, pp. 159–91. Cambridge, Mass.: MIT Press.

Cline, W. R.; N. Kawanabe; T. O. M. Kronsjo; and T. Williams. 1978. *Trade negotiations in the Kennedy Round*. Washington: Brookings Institution.

Cordes, J. J., and B. A. Weisbrod. 1979. Compensation for economic change when lump sum transfers are not possible: A framework for evaluating alternatives. Processed.

Corson, W., and W. Nicholson. 1980. Trade adjustment assistance for workers: Results of a survey of recipients under the Trade Act of 1974. Processed.

Corson, W.; W. Nicholson; D. Richardson; and A. Vayda. 1979. *Final report: Survey of trade adjustment assistance recipients.* A final contract (J9K70010) report by Mathematica Policy Research, Inc. (Princeton, New Jersey), to the United States Department of Labor, Bureau of International Labor Affairs, Office of Foreign Economic Research, December.

Dewald, W. G., ed. 1978. *The impact of international trade and investment on employment.* Washington: Government Printing Office for the United States Department of Labor.

Feldstein, M. S. 1975. The importance of temporary lay-offs: An empirical analysis. *Brookings Papers on Economic Activity* 1975, no. 3: 725–45.

———. 1976. Temporary lay-offs in the theory of unemployment. *Journal of Political Economy* 84 (October): 937–57.

———. 1978. The effect of unemployment insurance on temporary lay-off employment. *American Economic Review* 68 (December): 834–46.

Fooks, M. M. 1971. Trade adjustment assistance. In United States Commission on International Trade and Investment (the "Williams Commission Report") (1971).

Frank, C. R., Jr. 1973. Adjustment assistance: American jobs and trade with the developing countries. Washington: Overseas Development Council Development Paper 13, June.

Frank, C. R., Jr., with the assistance of Stephanie Levinson. 1978. *Foreign trade and domestic aid.* Washington: Brookings Institution.

Hamermesh, D. S. 1977. *Jobless pay and the economy.* Baltimore: Johns Hopkins University Press.

Jacobson, L. 1979. The earnings and compensation of workers receiving trade adjustment assistance. Processed, December.

Jenkins, G. P.; G. Glenday; J. C. Evans; and C. Montmarquette. 1978. *Trade adjustment assistance: The costs of adjustment and policy proposals.* Contract (93/810–936–3) report by Econanalysis Incorporated to the Department of Industry, Trade, and Commerce, Canada, June.

Jonish, J. 1970. Adjustment assistance experience under the U.S.–Canadian automotive agreement. *Industrial and Labor Relations Review* 23 (July): 557.

Laudicina, P. 1973. *World poverty and development: A survey of American opinion.* Washington: Overseas Development Council Monograph 8.

Magee, S. P. 1972. The welfare effects of restrictions on U.S. trade. *Brookings Papers on Economic Activity* 3: 645–707.

McCarthy, J. E. 1975a. Adjustment to import competition. *New England Economic Review,* July/August, pp. 3–15.

———. 1975b. Contrasting experiences with trade adjustment assistance. *Monthly Labor Review,* June.

————. 1975c. *Trade adjustment assistance: A case study of the shoe industry in Massachusetts*. Boston: Federal Reserve Bank of Boston Research Report no. 58.

Metzger, S. D. 1971. Adjustment assistance. In United States Commission on International Trade and Investment (the "Williams Commission Report") (1971).

Neumann, G. R. 1978. The direct labor-market effects of the trade adjustment assistance program. In Dewald, ed. (1978).

Neumann, G. R.; M. V. Lewis; and G. P. Glyde; with the assistance of S. H. Sheingold. 1976. *The evaluation of the trade adjustment assistance program*. Processed, September.

Rosen, H. 1980. TAA-administrative information. Processed, May.

United States Commission on Foreign Economic Policy (the "Randall Commission"). 1954. *Report to the President and the Congress*. Washington: Government Printing Office.

United States Commission on International Trade and Investment (the "Williams Commission"). 1971. *United States international economic policy in an interdependent world*. Compendium of Papers, vol. 1. Washington: Government Printing Office.

United States Department of Labor. 1979. Management information report: Worker adjustment assistance under the Trade Act of 1974. Bureau of International Labor Affairs, Office of Trade Adjustment Assistance. Processed, 30 November.

United States General Accounting Office. *Considerations for adjustment assistance under the 1974 Trade Act: A summary of techniques used in other countries*. Report to the Congress, the Comptroller General, January.

United States Public Advisory Board for Mutual Security (the "Bell Commission"). 1953. *A trade and tariff policy in the national interest*. Washington: Government Printing Office.

Weisz, M. 1978. *Strategies for adjustment assistance: Experience in the U.S. and abroad and implications for future U.S. programs*. Paper presented at United States Department of Labor Conference on the Employment Effects of International Trade, 15 November.

Wilcox, C. 1950. Relief for victims of tariff cuts. *American Economic Review* 40 (December): 884–89.

Comment   C. Michael Aho

Richardson's paper provides an excellent summary and extension of the findings of a research contract done for my office by Mathematica Policy Research (Corson et al. 1979). He was one of the authors of that report, which was a useful, if not definitive, analysis of the workings of the trade adjustment assistance (TAA) program.

The Mathematica survey summarized by Richardson indicates that TAA recipients fall into three distinct categories—temporary layoffs, permanent separations, and partial separations. By far, the largest group was temporary layoffs (58 percent), followed by permanent separations (25 percent) and partial separations (17 percent). TAA recipients were older and less educated, and had higher earnings prior to separation than did other workers. Partly because of these factors, the study found that those TAA recipients who changed employers had substantial earnings losses for prolonged periods of time. These individuals suffered greater losses than did other permanent displacements.

Thus, while TAA recipients on average conformed with a priori expectations, the distribution of TAA payments raises serious equity questions. Further, since the permanent separations suffered more in terms of earnings losses, the survey revealed not only that the benefits may be inequitably distributed, but also that the adjustment services were not helping job changers to secure employment at an income level comparable to that from their former job.

As for the econometric analysis, the results obtained by Richardson are similar to those included in the Mathematica report except he used weeks worked between separation and interview instead of unemployment duration and weekly income at interview instead of earnings differentials. The survey collected a wealth of data and provided observations on most individual characteristics and labor market outcomes which ideally would be needed for a statistical analysis. For this reason, there is a temptation to include most of these variables in regressions as Richardson has done. However, this makes the results difficult to read and interpret. It can be argued that each regression includes too many variables. For example, two explanatory variables are included simultaneously to measure advance notice: weeks of official employer notification prior to separation and weeks of suspected job loss prior to official employer notification. It would have been better to run, alternatively, the first measure, official

C. Michael Aho is director of the Office of Foreign Economic Research at the Department of Labor. He directed and coauthored the review of *U.S. International Competitiveness* (Washington: Government Printing Office, 1980) and has authored several papers on international trade and adjustment.

These comments are the author's personal observations and do not necessarily reflect the views of the Department of Labor.

weeks, and then the first plus the second, suspected weeks plus official weeks. There is no reason to expect separate, independent effects from these two variables.

Similarly, in the wage equations, for example, it is incorrect to include "reservation income" as an independent variable, along with all the other variables that may affect subsequent wages through reservation income. A more selective strategy for choosing regression variables would have strengthened the analysis.

Although Richardson displays separate results for the entire sample, all TAA recipients, all UI recipients, permanently displaced TAA recipients, and permanently displaced UI recipients, and he stresses the wide differences between groups, he does not take advantage of the separation to conduct tests for significant differences between the equations. If analysis of covariance techniques had been used, one suspects a test of the overall regressions would lead to a rejection of the null hypothesis that they were drawn from the same sample. It would have been of even more interest to see if and to what extent the coefficients of the outcome variables differed for TAA and UI recipients and between the permanently displaced receiving TAA and those receiving UI.

However, even if an analysis of covariance had been conducted on a smaller number of variables, the issue of the proper control group would still remain. The sample of UI recipients in manufacturing is not an adequate control group for testing many of the more interesting hypotheses. Ideally, a larger sample, representative of manufacturing workers drawn from the same industries, would allow for tests of significant differences in labor market response and outcomes between the TAA population and other unemployed workers. The same industrial composition is important because the occupational mix and labor market outcomes are industry-specific. Jacobson (1978), for example, has shown how earnings losses are industry-specific.

Finally, it should be stressed that the survey was retrospective—workers were interviewed over three years after the layoff—and it was a survey. Richardson claims (section 12.3.1) that a check of "known characteristics of nonrespondents . . . suggested little nonresponse bias," but it was not tested for explicitly. In California, for example, the response rate was only 48 percent for TAA and 31 percent for UI recipients. No systematic effort was made to determine why response was so poor or, more importantly, what were the characteristics of nonrespondents.

Before raising research and policy issues which follow from Richardson's detailed statistical analysis, I would like to put the program in a different perspective—to set it in the political environment where trade policy decisions are made. The political case for some sort of compensation and adjustment program, like TAA, is that those who are most likely to be hurt by a freer trade policy frequently have the political power to block efforts to ease trade restrictions unless there exists some mechanism to compensate the "losers" for the costs (primarily earnings losses) of adjusting to a policy of freer trade.

The United States trade adjustment assistance program is scheduled to expire in September 1982 unless extended by the Congress. The program is currently mired in controversy because of budget overruns and perceived inequities and inefficiencies in the delivery of benefits and services, and will be the subject of an intense review over the next eighteen to twenty-four months. What has thus far been overlooked in the debate surrounding the program is the benefits from trade liberalization made possible as a result of the program's adoption. There are three distinct benefits. First, adoption of a liberalized TAA program was essential for the ability to engage in the recent Tokyo Round of the multilateral trade negotiations (MTN). Second, the existence of TAA gives the President and Congress an intermediate policy option between trade restrictions and no import relief. By providing some relief to displaced workers, TAA makes it easier politically to facilitate expanded trade opportunities. Finally, to the extent the program keeps down trade barriers or enables them to be reduced, it not only increases the economic welfare of the United States, but that of our trading partners as well.

The TAA program was an important precondition for legislative authority for United States participation in the Tokyo Round. In this political context, it is useful to compare the welfare gains from the MTN tariff cuts with the costs of the TAA program.[1]

Estimates of the annual static United States welfare gains from the MTN tariff reductions range from about $130 to about $770 million annually (Aho and Bayard 1980). These estimates pertain only to the effects of the tariff cuts, which were a relatively small part of the Tokyo Round. Most of the emphasis in the MTN was on drafting codes of conduct on nontariff barriers. These nontariff codes are expected to significantly reduce many nontariff barriers. Finally, the estimates are static. It has been argued that the potential dynamic gains are several times the size of the static gains. Given all of these factors, the welfare gains from the MTN could be several times the static estimates of $130–$770 million.

The administrative costs of the TAA program since its inception in 1975 have been in the range of $3–$5 million, and the beneficiary payments have until this year been less than $300 million. Thus even the sum of administrative costs and payments to workers is less than the annual static welfare gains from the MTN tariff cuts, at least until recently. (Only the administrative costs should be used for welfare comparisons.)

On the whole, TAA looks like a fairly good investment. A broader view of the MTN would incorporate the welfare impact of the MTN codes, the growth in trade, and other dynamic effects. This broader view would also include the opportunity cost of the MTN, not in terms of the status quo, but in terms of the likelihood that trade restrictions would have actually increased in the absence of the MTN. Taken together, these broader (and less easily quantifiable) welfare considerations suggest that the costs of the TAA program are probably significantly less than the gains from the MTN.

Even trade restrictions in selected industries can have significant consumer and welfare costs when compared with the administrative costs and benefit levels of the TAA program. T. Bayard and I compared the costs of TAA with welfare and consumer cost estimates for four industries where import relief was recommended recently by the International Trade Commission (stainless steel, leather-wearing apparel, and copper) or considered by the administration (autos) (Aho and Bayard 1980). In each case the President rejected relief and recommended that expedited adjustment assistance be granted instead.

In the case of autos, the annual welfare costs of restricting Japanese imports to 1979 levels (an estimated reduction of 250,000 units) would range from $25 to $40 million. The consumer costs estimates range from $1 to $2 billion annually.

In announcing his decision, the President noted that "between this fiscal year and the next, we are budgeting over a billion dollars extra to provide trade adjustment assistance to tide the auto workers over until new jobs can be provided for them." Thus, to the extent the existence of the TAA program makes it easier politically for the President to deny import restrictions, the program has beneficial impacts which are often ignored in narrow examinations of the efficiency consequences of increased benefits to displaced workers.

Although I have been approaching this in terms of a political and economic cost-benefit analysis for the United States, I hasten to point out that liberalized trade has benefits for the other nations of the world which are not accounted for in the calculations above. Although they do not vote in United States elections, foreign workers and producers in export industries should be in favor of a worker adjustment assistance program in the United States because the alternative, increased incentives to restrict trade, can have adverse effects on their employment and earnings.

This highlights an aspect of TAA that is appealing to the foreign policy community usually not interested in internal distributional questions. Although Richardson correctly points out the thorny internal equity issues raised by TAA, all categorical governmental assistance programs have efficiency and distributional consequences. The one distinguishing feature of the TAA program is that the international distribution of income is affected. TAA is an integral part of United States commercial policy, and to the extent it promotes expanded trade, other countries gain and we increase our links to the rest of the world.

Returning to Richardson's paper, several key research issues for the future are suggested by his analysis. They include: (1) What are the costs and benefits of alternative ways of reducing the costs of worker dislocation while minimizing employment disincentives following such dislocations due to trade? (2) How can the current empirical measures of adjustment costs be improved to reflect all aspects of costs including uncertainty and secondary consequences for other workers in the industry or community? (3) What can we learn from studying adjustment processes and policies in other countries and in different institutional settings? and (4) How and at what cost can we encourage workers to take positive adjustment actions, and what is the best method of delivering adjustment services?

The last question may prove to be the most crucial in the 1980s. It has become trite to point out that the United States is rapidly becoming more internationalized, but this internationalization is causing structural changes for United States industry. In order to respond to this structural change, the United States needs policies and programs which promote rather than impede the adjustment of dislocated workers. Alteration of the existing TAA program to emphasize adjustment, if successful, could enhance the flexibility and adaptability of the economy. The basic policy challenges are to develop a compensation scheme that will not serve as a disincentive for adjustment and to design a delivery system for the adjustment services.

However, all programs raise difficult efficiency and equity questions, and they must be examined closely in order to design an improved adjustment assistance program which minimizes distortions. When ideal lump-sum transfers are not possible but compensation is still desired, the objective should be to compensate while minimizing distortions. And when the price system is used to aid displaced workers, some distortion is inevitable. Although we recognize that in the absence of market imperfections (imperfect mobility, uncertainty, etc.) the price system would allocate resources most efficiently, we are in a second-best world.

Whenever a price is altered, it influences market behavior and it distributes income. If we object to the allocations and distributions that result from government intervention, we must ask ourselves what the alternative is. In a real-world setting where political and distributional questions often dominate efficiency considerations, a second-best compensation policy may indeed be superior to a world in which government interference is minimized, and the incentives for special interest-group lobbying are increased. If the lobbying were not effective, then the case for a special trade-related program would be much weaker. But the market for political influence is not perfectly competitive, and it is very likely that impacted workers (firms, communities, regions) can lobby successfully for import relief. By reducing dislocations costs the TAA program helps to reduce the incentives to lobby.

After reading Richardson's paper some of you may be asking, Whither TAA? In my opinion, the principle of a special program for trade-impacted workers is worth keeping because it can have desirable effects nationally and internationally by promoting expanded trade opportunities and more efficient adjustment to changes in trade. Further, because individuals and interest groups made concessions and altered their own economic and political decisions in exchange for a liberalized TAA program, it is unlikely that the TAA program will be eliminated. Granted, some may wish to alter certain features of the program to minimize disincentives or to rectify perceived distributional inequities; but those are essentially political decisions.

From that perspective, the question now becomes, How can the program be improved? This is where Richardson's study and the Mathematica survey can play an important role by providing objective analysis to the policymakers who ultimately must decide.

Notes

1. The MTN passed in the United States Congress by overwhelming votes: 395 to 7 in the House of Representatives and 90 to 4 in the Senate. However, the fragility of that political support was aptly demonstrated by a quote from Representative Vanik from Ohio, the chairman of the House Subcommittee on Trade. In arguing for the need for an expanded TAA program, Representative Vanik noted that "trade support on the Hill is fragile—there are 100 members of Congress who don't believe in trading with anybody. A majority in opposition to free trade can be achieved if labor is alienated." Cited in *Barrons* (5 May 1980).

References

Aho, C. M., and T. Bayard. 1980. American trade adjustment assistance after five years. *World Economy*, vol. 3, no. 3, November.

Corson, W.; W. Nicholson; D. Richardson; and A. Vayda. 1979. *Final report: Survey of trade adjustment assistance recipients.* A final contract (J9K70010) report by Mathematica Policy Research, Inc. (Princeton, New Jersey), to the United States Department of Labor, Bureau of International Labor Affairs, Office of Foreign Economic Research, December.

Jacobson, L. 1978. Earnings losses of workers displaced in manufacturing industries. In W. Dewald, ed., *The impact of international trade and investment on employment*, a conference on United States Department of Labor research results (Washington: Government Printing Office).

Comment   Martin Wolf

These comments comprise, first, a brief discussion of the paper; second, a critique of the United States trade adjustment assistance (TAA) program for workers; third, a cursory review of the parallel program for firms; and, finally, an assessment of the relevance of this program to experience in other developed countries, especially in Europe.

The Paper

Professor Richardson's paper provides a lucid and convincing account of the origin of, and justification for, the United States trade adjustment assistance program for workers. He also offers a description of the characteristics of workers helped by the program both in simple tables and in the form of regressions. There are a few surprises. Thus the tables show that the workers tended to be better paid than the average of recipients of unemployment insurance and that almost 60 percent were only temporarily laid off as against 40 percent for recipients of unemployment insurance. The regressions indicate that benefits were actually positively associated with number of weeks worked between separation and interview, while the latter was—perhaps less surprisingly—negatively associated with educational attainment. Other observed characteristics of the workers are more or less what would be expected. The interpretation of these results is made difficult, however, by the wealth of independent variables and the lack of information on the extent to which they are correlated with one another.

It should be noted that the two characteristics of the assisted workers that are most surprising, namely, their high average wage and the large number of temporary layoffs, are probably explained by the substantial presence of steel and auto workers among those helped in 1976. Indeed, the role of the program in providing countercyclical aid to workers in these industries is one of its more controversial aspects.

An Evaluation of United States Trade Adjustment Assistance for Workers

Five questions can usefully be asked: What are the implications of the program for economic efficiency? Does the program have a positive impact on the distribution of income? Is adequate compensation provided for losses borne by workers when deprived of a job? Is the program an effective bribe from the point of view of reducing protectionist pressure? Does it have a satisfactory philosophical basis?

At the time of writing this comment Martin Wolf was a senior economist at the World Bank. He is currently director of studies at the Trade Policy Research Centre in London. He has recently authored *Textile Quotas against Developing Countries* with Donald Keesing, which was published by the Trade Policy Research Centre.

What are the efficiency implications of TAA? The program provides
assistance to workers for job search, relocation, and training. The theory
is that such support will directly improve the efficiency of adjustment,
perhaps because of capital market constraints that would otherwise deter
workers. In practice, these provisions have hardly been used. Thus, out
of 335,000 workers helped under the post-1974 program by May 1978,
only 1,075 were approved for job-search allowances, 557 were approved
for relocation allowances, and 9,843 were trained. The same justification
might, however, be given for the income support payments themselves,
since they may make it easier to finance efficient job search, retraining,
and relocation, if workers lack savings or recourse to credit. Finally, to
the extent that the existence of the program encourages workers to accept
layoffs, efficiency may be promoted or retarded depending on whether,
on balance, adjustment would otherwise tend to occur too slowly or too
rapidly.

In its current form the present program is as likely to impair efficiency
as to improve it. For those who enjoyed relatively well paid jobs the
payments may encourage them to wait in the hope of getting the old job
back. This tendency will be increased by the knowledge that there is a
permanently higher likelihood of what is, in effect, greater unemployment compensation in import-affected industries than in others. This is,
indeed, a general moral hazard created by TAA, since entry into industries subject to import competition is encouraged. It should also be noted
that, as with any scheme to provide periodic payments for the unemployed, there is a reduced incentive to seek work. Whether these various
potential problems are significant in practice is unclear. Richardson
indicates that there is no tendency for those who receive higher benefits
to remain unemployed for longer periods (if anything the contrary).
Furthermore, since certification is by no means a foregone conclusion,
uncertainty about eligibility will reduce the temptation to get in the way
of a potential "accident." A reasonable assessment has to be that it is
unclear whether the program is beneficial, harmful, or neutral from the
point of view of efficiency.

Does TAA improve the distribution of income? It is not obvious that the
program is even designed to improve the distribution of income. One
obvious point is that many of the recipients have been relatively well paid
in the past and can expect to be so again in the future. Furthermore, those
worst hit, who are likely to be those who have little possibility of obtaining work again, get nothing after the eligibility period of one year.

Does TAA provide adequate compensation for losses? Even if income is
not transferred to the relatively poor, the program may be justified as
compensation for undeserved losses on the lines of Corden's (1974)

conservative social welfare function argument. TAA is, in fact, far from ideal compensation, since it is certainly nŏt generous enough (as Bale 1976 has shown, for example). Furthermore, compensation is provided only for loss of income while unemployed. There is no compensation for permanently lost quasi rents to owners of sector-specific human capital.

Is TAA an effective bribe? By providing compensation to those injured by a change that benefits the public as a whole, it is expected that, in the first place, the political resistance of those directly affected will be reduced and, in the second place, the more altruistic members of the public will have their consciences mollified and will consequently regard liberalization as more acceptable. The first part of the argument does not seem to work since compensation is insufficient for most of those who move and provides nothing for those who do not (whose prospects are also likely to be worsened). Furthermore, because the assistance is usually uncertain at the time of the job loss (since the certification process takes time and is usually *post hoc*), it is likely to be discounted (thus reducing both the moral hazard and the effectiveness of the bribe at the same time). It is also worth noting that some of the most influential lobbyists—industrialists and trade union leaders, for example—fall entirely outside the net. It is therefore not surprising that the program has been dismissed as "burial insurance."

The second point seems to be more persuasive. It has been argued that without adjustment assistance for workers neither the 1962 Trade Expansion Act nor the Trade Act of 1974 could have passed. Furthermore, the existence of the program may perhaps make it easier to avoid granting protection in individual injury cases.

What is the ethical basis for the program? It is important to note the change pointed out by Richardson between TAA under the 1962 act, which was triggered by a finding that a government policy decision, namely, Kennedy Round liberalization, was a "major" cause of injury, and TAA under the 1974 act, which could be triggered by any injury to which imports contributed "importantly." In the former case transitional equity considerations (Hochman 1974) may justify compensation since citizens can reasonably expect to make decisions on the assumption that announced government policy is stable. Compensation for change in general, however, is more difficult to justify and can hardly be restricted to that created by one particular source, namely, imports. This blurring of the rationale was the heavy price for making the program more effective. The ethical problem is still greater if those assisted are obviously not among the least well off in society. Finally, if "political reality" justifies such a supernormal bribe, a very clear reward is given to politically obstructive behavior.

One quasi-philosophical issue raised by the program is frequently overlooked. By its nature TAA involves the grant of substantial amounts of money by the bureaucracy on an essentially arbitrary basis. The criteria for determining whether imports contribute "importantly" can never be watertight, and, in addition, some discretion must be allowed in applying them. This creates problems both for the bureaucrats themselves and, still more, for the public, who can come increasingly to see the former as essentially a source of arbitrary and therefore unfairly distributed benefits.

Conclusion. It is clear that TAA is open to a number of strong objections which result in part from the multiplicity of objectives, in part from difficulties in justifying any program restricted to a particular source of injury, and in part from specific features of its operation. Possible improvements could include the provision of some benefits to those who stay on in an industry; the offer of an unconditional lump sum rather than periodic payments; relating the sum to age, length of service, and other factors that determine adjustment costs to workers; and making all benefits available as of a certain (unique) date to those then in the industry (or firm) with no subsequent repetition. The date could be that of a policy change (e.g., liberalization) or an injury finding. While there is no program that will satisfy all objections, improvements can certainly be made in such ways.

What Is the Effect of TAA for Firms?

Industrialists are hurt by import competition and form powerful lobbies. They may also not know how to improve their operations. Thus there is some sort of case for assistance to them. Interestingly, United States assistance to firms, by rewarding attempted survival rather than exit, is the inverse of that to workers. Thus the program provides loans and loan guarantees, as well as assistance in obtaining consultants, to firms that intend to stay in business, usually in the same industry. If imports are really a key source of problems (which is the rationale for TAA), the assistance is unlikely to work, strong comparative disadvantage being difficult to reverse. If imports are not the cause, the case for special assistance is more difficult to make. In practice, failure by assisted firms seems to have been common. As politics the program has the major disadvantage that the protectionist lobby is preserved in being. These features of assistance to firms facing problems with imports are common to most programs around the world.

Is the United States Program Generalizable?

As it now exists, United States TAA is essentially unique. In Europe, in particular, no equivalent exists. Why? The reasons are relatively straightforward. In the first place, trade is so large in relation to most countries' GNP that trade-related change could never be separated out. The only answer would be to focus on extra–EEC trade or a component of it (such as trade with developing countries). While the Dutch do have an (unsuccessful) program for firms which does the latter, the political resistance to favoring extra–EEC trade specially would be great. In the second place, social security benefits are already higher in most European countries than the United States even after the TAA supplement. Any additional benefits could raise the levels to almost ridiculous heights. Finally, the entire approach to adjustment tends to be more active and dirigiste. Thus European governments pursue "active labor market policies" (especially in Sweden), as well as strong regional policies (aimed at moving investment rather than labor), and even get directly involved in decision making by industries and firms. The approach consists therefore not of bribery to allow the market to work (which is essentially the United States approach), but of actively managing and redirecting the adjustment process itself. The polar case of this approach among the developed countries is Japan's. Thus the United States programs consist of a response to import competition that is uniquely suited to its own economic and political circumstances but that is, unfortunately, flawed in a number of respects even within that framework.

References

Bale, M. D. 1976. Estimates of trade-displacement costs of U.S. workers. *Journal of International Economics* 6, no. 3 (August): 245–50.

Corden, W. M. 1974. *Trade policy and economic welfare*. Oxford: Oxford University Press.

Hochman, H. M. 1974. Rule change and transitional equity. In H. M. Hochman and G. E. Peterson, eds., *Redistribution through public choice*, pp. 320–41. New York and London: Columbia University Press.

13　　European Community Protection against Manufactured Imports from Developing Countries: A Case Study in the Political Economy of Protection

Eric Verreydt and Jean Waelbroeck

In recent years the European Community (EC) has been torn between its natural mandate as an institution set up to promote free movement of goods and production factors, and the strong pressures for protection resulting from the recession and from the sharp difficulties experienced by a number of industries. Through agreeing to the Tokyo Round package, the EC committed itself to participate in a unprecedentedly wide ranging package of multilateral trade liberalization, the precise significance of which still remains to be hammered out in the GATT committees which will implement the newly agreed to codes of behavior. The Lome agreement has been renegotiated, and the Generalized Scheme of Preferences will be renewed soon. Both are basically bilateral agreements concluded before the recession. On the other hand, there have been sharp turns of the protection screw for textiles and clothing and for steel especially, whereas the EC has found itself involved in trying to moderate a subsidy war in shipbuilding.

The aim of the present paper is to review these developments from the point of view of the political economy of protection. This approach, developed by a number of recent authors, focuses on the political motivations of protection and leads to conjectures many of which have been verified econometrically. In this paper we take a noneconometric approach. It appears worthwhile to look at the recent history of protec-

Eric Verreydt is presently a staff member of the Research Department of the National Bank of Belgium. He was at the Center for Mathematical Economics and Econometrics of the University of Brussels, working on import penetration. He has published several articles on this subject with Jean Waelbroeck. Jean Waelbroeck is professor of econometrics at the Free University of Brussels. His main work has been devoted to the modeling of world trade.

tion in the EC in the spirit of a case study and try to explain recent events using this new approach to international trade theory. This may also be a useful way of verifying its validity and may help to put flesh on abstract ideas. Finally, the case study approach may point out aspects of the problem that have been underresearched.

Throughout this paper, we will assume that the reader has read the excellent survey of this theory by Baldwin (chapter 10 of the present volume). This will relieve us from the task of restating the theory and the main concepts.

The paper is organized as follows. We first discuss the institutional aspects of decision making in the market for protection. The instruments available are presented (tariffs and import quotas, trade adjustment assistance subsidies, and control of cartels). This is complemented by a description of the interrelations between the four decision levels involved in the formulation of trade policies. The paper then turns to the general goals of these policies: efficiency, income distribution, avoidance of retaliation, and provision of public goods, in particular creating a stable political and economic framework for future growth of the EC. The last section describes the objectives of interest groups and the EC's policy responses to their demands.

13.1 Decision Making in the Market for Protection

It is useful to organize the discussion of EC protection policies around the concept of a political market for protection, where special interest groups seek to pressure policy makers to supply desired measures. The description should recognize the way in which national interests perceived by voters may through the "adding machine" of democratic decision making block the measures sought by interest groups.

The usual presentations of the political economy of protection are quite vague about the institutions through which the political market operates, because of the concern for generality of their authors. This is no reason to be so vague in a case study. Accordingly, we shall discuss at length institutional aspects of trade policy making in the EC.

13.2 The Institutional Framework

Under the Rome Treaty, the EC is responsible for the establishment of trade policies. To an academic economist used to considering trade theory as a separate subject, this looks like a clear mandate. In practice, the range of government policies which have an impact on trade is extremely wide, including for instance social legislation, safety and health regulations, and other policy areas which at first sight would not seem to be relevant.

13.3 Tariffs and Import Quotas

Even for decisions which are clearly related to trade, governments of member countries retain significant residual powers. Tariffs are firmly under control of the EC but not customs regulation—which is important in enabling countries to resort to outward processing to carry out labor-intensive stages of fabrication in low-wage countries. The transfer of import quotas to EC control is not complete: France and Italy in particular continue to impose drastic quotas on imports of automobiles and electronic goods from Japan, for example. There is a broad penumbra of quotas run via market-sharing arrangements at the business level (e.g., imports of Japanese cars into the United Kingdom), backed by governments and carefully designed not to run afoul of EC anticartel regulations. Finally, a third country (usually a developing country) may get a sharp warning that it should restrict exports of a good to an EC country "voluntarily" for the sake of good commercial relations, and (usually) decides to obey; no visible measure is taken by a public authority in the EC, but imports are clearly restricted. Even quotas which are formally established by the EC may be allocated between member countries, and the reshipment of the imported goods across frontiers within the Community is then controlled as provided for under Article 115 of the treaty. Such quotas are formally initiated by the EC, but it is clear that the country affected has a good deal to say about their management.

There has been a slow, and in principle irreversible, process under which the residual import quotas of member countries have been gradually transferred to Brussels. Progress in this direction is embodied in a "liberalized list" of goods over which member countries have given up the right to impose import quotas. It is important not to lose sight of the fact that Community institutions have no enforcement power on national governments. Under the "I am your leader, I must follow you" philosophy their actions may be dictated by the concern to forestall or to take over illegal trade restrictions by member governments. This was quite obvious at the time of the 1977 renewal of the MFA, when the very tough negotiating stance of the EC was in part motivated by France's introduction of quotas on textiles and clothing in violation of Community rules, and clear indications that other member countries might introduce illegal restrictions if the EC did not act to restrict imports sharply.

The EC itself is subject to the rules of the GATT, and thus does not control fully the trade policy instruments which are in principle available to it. Governments do (fairly rarely) violate EC rules and (much more frequently) fail to observe or implement them; but the Community, whose only power resides in respect of the legal superstructure created on the basis of the Rome Treaty, has to be narrowly legalistic in respecting GATT treaties.

372 Eric Verreydt/Jean Waelbroeck

This essentially deprives it of control over normal tariffs (imposition of antidumping and other temporary tariffs is of course possible). As the implementation of the Tokyo Round leads to the establishment of agreed codes of behavior, the freedom of action of the Community is becoming further restricted (conceivably implementation of the Tokyo Round may be so successful that GATT rules might regulate aspects of national policies such as public procurement over which the EC has not succeeded in establishing effective control).

13.4 Trade Adjustment Assistance, Subsidies

Economic theory has tended to regard adjustment assistance more and more as a trade policy instrument which is as important as tariffs and other measures of restriction. The pressures of interest groups, to the extent that they cannot be controlled, can lead to market-distorting measures of import restriction—and hence to a waste of resources—or the interest groups can be bribed by offers of assistance which reduce their losses and give them time to find other profitable employment. These two ways of dealing with protectionist pressures are sometimes termed "negative" and "positive" adjustment.

The concept of trade adjustment assistance is clear in the academic way of looking at problems, in which trade theory is a sharply defined and distinct area of investigation. The idea is much more difficult to apply to the real world, in which agents are continually subjected to shocks of all types and origin. Trade adjustment assistance is a workable policy concept only if a way is formed of "tagging" agents whose problems are caused by trade, but such tagging is extremely difficult to carry out fairly and accurately. To the extent that agents whose misfortune is due to trade are better treated than agents whose misfortune has other causes, a problem of equity arises; inevitably there is pressure to extend the scale of trade assistance benefits across the board, and this can prove very costly.

It is finally very hard to distinguish trade adjustment assistance from subsidies. The difference between these two is that at some point in the future the beneficiary of the first will shift his production resources to a new type of activity which does not require public aid to be viable. If he does not, he is relying on a subsidy to continue an inefficient productive activity as wastefully as if he were protected by a tariff.[1] Indeed, economists have sometimes used the term "domestic protection" to describe the economic impact of subsidies. The gift of prophecy is needed to distinguish between the two types of aid, and this is a second reason to doubt that the theoretician's concept of "trade adjustment assistance" is useful for analysis of the real world.

So it is probably not unfortunate that lack of funds prevents the EC from engaging in a big way in the dubious business of allocating trade adjustment assistance. Two special funds were set up initially: the European Social Fund, and the ECSC reconversion and readaptation fund, set up under the Rome Treaty and the ECSC Treaty, respectively. In 1975, a European Regional Fund was created to provide resources for regional reconversion; this fund is a good deal smaller than initially envisaged. The European Investment Bank and the Ortoli Facility could also be useful to create jobs in regions affected by trade adjustment. Existing studies, however, suggest that these various funds are not very effective. The sums they can distribute are not large; more important, it seems difficult to bring potential users to make effective use of the system.

What this means is that the EC has little ability to compensate individuals in member countries for losses suffered from changes in international trade; this is probably as it should be, as the Brussels Eurocrats have enough to do without also getting heavily involved in compensating individuals, industries, or regions in every member country. It might perhaps be thought desirable that they should have funds to compensate countries for trade losses—to shift funds to France if French wine producers are suffering from the entry of Spain into the Community, subject to the French government's redistributing the money as it sees fit. In practice, EC negotiating sessions haggle over so many issues that there is ample scope to buy off one country's objections to a measure by offering it satisfaction on another issue.

In practice, adjustment assistance is therefore a national responsibility, and adjustment to trade is carried out under the same schemes as adjustment to other disturbances.[2] The operation of this assistance in member countries has been bewilderingly complex, and subject to much grassroots improvisation as politicians and bureaucrats at all levels have sought to reduce the social and economic costs of the recession. Bureaucrats and politicians have used instruments ranging from delays in payment of taxes and social security contributions to permission to violate pollution regulations, from interest rebates to wage subsidies, from tax relief and preferential access to outward processing licenses to subsidies and nationalization, from government purchases of the products of an enterprise to pressures on other producers to inject capital into ailing firms and to encouraging cartels. These instruments can in turn take a wide range of legal forms, be justified by a great diversity of pretexts, and be decided at any level or in any part of the administration. The Ministry of Foreign Affairs has directed aid projects to help particular enterprises, the Ministry of Health has tried to save others by ignoring antipollution regulations, the Ministry of Education has pushed schools to purchase equipment from enterprises in difficulty. Most of these interventions have required lengthy efforts and numerous contacts on the part of those concerned—a vast expenditure of efforts inspired by a laudable sense of public duty, the result of which has, however, mostly been the pushing around of unemployment: destroying jobs in the enterprises which compete with those getting assistance.

From this point of view, the treaty provisions which empower it to eliminate market distortions have been one of the most important policy instruments the EC wields. The directorate general for competition monitors inter alia government aids and subsidies; controversies are put before the Court of Justice if agreement cannot otherwise be reached. It is of course not possible to monitor all schemes (there are more than 1,200 laws in force in the nine member countries), but the EC can control the larger, more visible ones. As the Rome Treaty binds governments, individuals can challenge before the courts aids which have been granted to their competitors. Of course, civil servants like to forget to notify the commission of aids which they have proudly contrived to help countrymen to beat foreign competitors; these foreign (and sometimes national) competitors often lack the firm evidence required to bring a case before the courts. Many trade-distorting interventions therefore escape the watchful eye of Community institutions. But there is no doubt that the EC's control of government interventions has been an important element of trade policy, and has been useful to firms outside the EC as much as to EC firms in making markets more accessible and transparent than they would otherwise be.

13.5   Regulation of Cartels

The Rome Treaty antitrust provisions have likewise developed into an important instrument of trade policy. Forming a "recession cartel" is a classic reaction to the recession of enterprises in concentrated industries. These cartels may have as large an effect in restricting trade as import quotas; they may cause price distortions through dumping and other means. In Europe, governments have generally been inclined to support these cartels as a way of safeguarding production resources they fear might otherwise be destroyed.

In fact the ECSC Treaty explicitly grants to the EC the power to regulate in time of crisis production and prices of coal and steel, i.e., to run a recession cartel. This power has not formally been invoked, but it provides the background for the Davignon Plan for the steel industry.

13.6   Levels of Trade Policy Decision Making

Decision making with respect to trade policy making is obviously not concentrated in the hands of one "government" or even of a group of "politicians" as envisaged by presentations of the political economy of protection. Reality is a good deal more complex. In practice, it is useful to think of a four-tier apparatus of decision making, where each tier is subject to a different degree of control by interest groups and voters.

a) At the bottom, an enormous number of decisions which are individually small but important in the aggregate are taken at the level of the bureaucracy. The decision level is here what Messerlin (1979) has called the *bureaus*; it is decisions at this level which are alluded to when economists try to explain why Japan has such low imports, or claim rightly or wrongly that Germany's liberal trade policy stance does not correspond to its real behavior. These decisions are almost invisible, and thus represent an ideal area for exertion of pressures by special interest groups. Indeed, because complaints are bad for the careers of bureaucrats and because bureaucrats come to be sympathetic to the people they administer, it is frequent to find agencies within the administration which have become as devoted to the interests of special interest groups as the lobbies financed by these groups.[3]

b) What *elected politicians* do is more visible than what is done at the level of the bureaus, and the influence of the general voters is correspondingly larger. This is the decision level that advocates of the political economy of protection have in mind in their analysis of decision making in the market for protection. Perhaps the theory would become more realistic if a way were found to recognize that governments are only one echelon of a ladder of decision makers; that they have only a dim understanding and cognizance of what is decided by the bureaus and do on the whole respect the restraints on their freedom which are imposed by treaties to which they have subscribed.

c) The views of interest groups and voters filter up to government via a complex system of parties, lobbies, and institutions for the concerted action of socioeconomic groups, which in Europe sometimes have significant influence. Distortions may take place, and it is often clear that (sometimes to their detriment) governments have misread the strength of the political forces which are affected by a particular decision. The accuracy of what filters up to the *European Community level* is even more questionable, and indeed most of the activity of the Brussels bureaucracy is concerned with remaining in contact with the politico-administrative base in member countries, in order to strike compromises which balance interests nationally and internationally. Because the only source of its influence is legitimacy, the Community must be even more careful than governments in respecting the treaties under which it was established and the GATT agreements it helped to negotiate.

d) *The GATT* is the top tier of the system, its operation has tended to be rigidly formalistic. Initiatives at that level have been dominated by the United States, Japan, and the EC. Developing countries in particular have tended to feel that the GATT forum was not one in which they could get their views across effectively.

A key property of this edifice is the changing balance between special and general interests as one moves up from one tier to the next. As pointed out by the "theory of the core," there are good reasons to believe that a completely open and general negotiation between economic agents will lead to a "point in the core of the economy" which coincides with a situation of free trade; and indeed, this idea appears to be more than a theoretical construct. As international contacts have become closer, the role of negotiating forums such as the GATT and the European Community has grown, the operation of which has visibly operated in favor of a free exchange of goods and services across countries.

Another property of this edifice is the extent to which the discretionary decision making which is so important at the level of the bureaus gives way to the operation of formal rules at higher levels. Economists have been very interested[4] in analysis of the advantages of stable decision rules as a framework for the operation of a market economy, freeing agents from the need to outguess or influence government decisions and allowing them to concentrate on using resources efficiently. From this point of view also, the postwar tendency to shift decisions from lower to higher decision levels has probably contributed to efficiency.

13.7 European Institutions and Their Relations to Lobbies and General Voters

Theoretical analysis glosses over the practical difficulties of reconciling conflicting interests or of obtaining agreement on stable formal decision rules. In practice, achieving these goals is far from a trivial task, and this leads us finally to a brief sketch of how Community institutions have evolved to deal with this problem.

The core of the system of European institutions is the Commission, which directs the work of the Secretariat and is controlled by the Council of Ministers. The function of these bodies is to implement the treaties forming the EC. The Court of Justice in Luxemburg decides on cases bearing on the interpretation of the treaties; it has turned out to be an important component of the system, tending quite systematically to give a broad interpretation of the authority granted to the Community by the treaties. The court can hear cases submitted to it by governments and individuals as well as by the EC, so that it provides one link with the political base of the EC.

The European Council brings together heads of states, and its agenda is not restricted to items which fall under the scope of the treaties. This is a new organ which has not as yet found a stable role—if it has to have one. Its meetings have sometimes sounded as shrill as an opera performance where several prima donnas compete for the role of Carmen, a common feature of summit meetings. Hopefully, creation of the council will broaden the sphere of European cooperation (the European Monetary System is a first result).

The European Parliament—500 kilometers away from Brussels in Strasbourg—is now elected, but has limited powers. It can reject the budget and revoke the EC—and then what? Its main function appears to be to act as a sounding board for the views of political parties, which are one of the main political forces the Community must understand to orient its decisions correctly. The Economic and Social Council, also a weak body, brings together representatives of economic and social groups; to speak in the language of the political economy of protection, it represents lobbies. In spite of their sometimes sizable staff, the Brussels lobbies have little power: they serve mainly as yet another (two-way) channel of information between the Community and political forces in member countries; on key issues they are often bypassed by members of national lobbies or of large firms.

The main channel through which both lobbies and general voters influence the Economic Community is the governments of member countries, via the Council of Ministers. The commissioners are usually themselves politicians. And it is perhaps not sufficiently recognized by outsiders to what extent the Secretariat is a political intelligence agency, the function of which is not to get to the bottom of problems and map solutions, but to run a complex and often apparently pointless system of committees and working groups (in six languages with simultaneous interpretation), the basic function of which is to keep the EC in close contact with government thinking in member countries. Nor is it recognized to what extent important decisions are influenced by personal contacts between the commissioners or members of their staff, and influential politicians, civil servants, businessmen, and trade union leaders (in nine countries).

13.8   The Genesis of Trade Policy

The formulation of trade policy by politicians strikes a balance between the pressures exerted by lobbies and more general objectives accepted by voters. The role of lobbies can on occasion be extremely crude—e.g., the lengths to which France went to sustain the import ban on British lamb, widely understood to be directly related to the importance of sheep raising in the constituency of the leader of one of the majority parties; or the connection between the slide of the Labour Party to a protectionist stance and the frantic canvassing for support in the Callaghan/Tony Benn rivalry.

As in the United States, this juggling for the support of interest groups is tempered by the need of politicians to convince voters that they are dealing effectively and responsibly with the country's general problems.

How voters form their judgment is something that even politicians do not know very well. Voters know little about trade policies: there is an astonishing contrast between the accuracy and timeliness of the lobbies' knowledge of measures even before they are announced and the vague information about these measures which can be gathered even from serious newspapers. The diffusion of decisions between four interdependent levels of decision making also makes it easy for politicians to claim credit for popular measures and to shift to others the onus for unpopular ones.

Though Eurocrats do not confront voters directly, there is no reason to believe that their keenness to satisfy public opinion differs in a fundamental way from that of politicians and civil servants in national governments. Oversimplifying things a bit, we shall first describe their perception of the EC's general interest as they may sense it to be understood by voters. We shall then describe the concerns of interest groups which have played a key role recently and the EC's response to their demands. We shall finally describe how the Community has sought to use its trade policy to achieve a number of more general objectives.

13.9 Efficiency

Efficient use of resources, the basic goal of trade, is the first of these general objectives. At present there is a marked inconsistency in EC policymaking between the remarkable scaling down of most external trade barriers, which was not interrupted by the recession (cf. the conclusion of the Tokyo Round), and the parallel consolidation of extremely restrictive import policies for agriculture and for textiles and clothing. It is too early to say how other recently erected barriers will evolve (for shoes, steel, and synthetic fibers, for example).

The high barriers on textiles (and agriculture) affect large sectors and accordingly generate considerable waste. The extent of this is not widely appreciated. The growing criticism of the Common Agricultural Policy has focused on its budget implications, and has largely disregarded the invisible transfers implied by price distortions; it has furthermore hardly even dealt with the resource misallocation it causes. The Multifiber Agreement has largely escaped such public criticism because it does not have a budget impact.

An important aspect of debates in Europe about the impact of protection on efficiency is the widely accepted view that the free play of competition may lead to a wasteful destruction of resources in a situation of unemployment. It is argued that keeping enterprises afloat by government intervention is better that leaving the resources they employ unused: in effect what is argued is that there is a special type of market failure. As usual, of course, the enterprises and groups which ask for protection or other types of assistance claim that the light is at the end of the tunnel, so that all that is needed is a temporary boost.

Public opinion has, however, moved perceptibly to a more realistic view of things. "I am not a naive believer in perfect competition" remains the standard way to start a statement on market intervention. But there is growing realization that the assistance given out since the beginning of the recession has been costly and ineffective; that much of it has gone to firms which did not really need it, and in particular to a few large groups which have enough skilled staff to understand how the system works; and that milking the assistance and subsidy system has become so profitable that it is absorbing valuable productive resources, a type of rent seeking associated with significant deadweight costs.

"But I don't think that lame ducks should be coddled" has accordingly become the quasi-automatic follow-up of expressions of disbelief in the efficiency of competition, reflecting a growing understanding that there are considerable dynamic economies to be reaped by letting workers and employers understand that they have to confront competition through greater efficiency rather than by securing subsidies, or even by allowing bankruptcy to detach workers and capital goods from inefficient managers. Recent elections and the evolution of the stock language of politicians have provided clear indications that the shift in attitude has a broad base in public opinion.

13.10   Income Distribution

As indicated above, the EC's concern for income distribution within countries is essentially symbolic: the activity of such bodies as the European Social Fund is not a major component of the Community's trade policy. Distribution of income between countries is another matter: negotiators understand well the costs and benefits of trade diversion.

Trade diversion is the Achilles heel of customs unions, as it is acceptable to losers only if external protection is low; this is the basic reason why customs unions between developing countries have failed up to now. The sharp tensions about the Common Agricultural Policy illustrate this danger. As discussed below, similar disputes may arise in the not so distant future over textiles and clothing protection. Hopefully, the EC will understand the risk which maintenance of the present very high barriers to this trade poses for the future cohesion of the Community.

13.11   Fear of Retaliation

The fear of retaliation has been one of the main reasons why interest groups have found it difficult to get support for protective measures from the general public. One of the main achievements of the Rome Treaty has been the constitution of a trading block with enough power to persuade United States officials and the United States public that protectionist measures will bring forth meaningful retaliation. Japan's inability to obtain normal treatment of its exports by the EC is to a significant extent due to the fact that its trade with the Community is so unbalanced.

From this point of view a striking aspect of the trade of developing countries with the EC (and other developed countries) is their inability or unwillingness to retaliate against the strongly discriminatory protection to which they have been subjected. The reasons for this are many.

a) A very large fraction of their exports comes from a few countries which have very little bargaining power. Hong Kong is a colony of an EC member; a trade war would be disastrous both to its and to Singapore's trade. Taiwan's international situation also argues for cautiousness, as does South Korea's need for United States military support.

b) The VER system which is the main means of protection against developing countries generates significant rents, which are appropriated to an overwhelming extent by exporting firms in those countries. The effortless profits yielded by this rent farming in effect bribe exporters not to press their governments too strongly to complain about protection.

c) Despite very low wages, most developing countries are not capable of meeting the competition of the large developing manufactured goods exporters, as shown by the fact that a surprising number of them do not reach the low textile and clothing quotas allocated to them by the EC. They have a deep and probably exaggerated fear of what they perceive to be China's enormous competitive potential. Why should they press for the suppression of a system of complex and detailed import controls which protects them against their competitors? Likewise why should the present large exporters desire the abolition of a system which grants them the lion's share of exports of sensitive goods from developing to developed countries, the existence of which has in past years deterred so effectively potential exporters like India from daring to undertake the transition to an export-oriented strategy?

d) The strongly protectionist policies pursued by almost all developing countries have excluded inessential goods from their imports. They therefore cannot afford the import cuts required to implement policies of retaliation.

e) The developing countries have been unable to constitute effective bargaining units. The Group of 77 is an instrument for the dramatized expression of dreams; apart from OPEC, developing countries have not been able to form groups with enough interests in common and a large enough size to extract trade concessions from the EC, the United States, or Japan.

13.12 The EC as a Producer of Public Goods

The function of governments is not only to create conditions conducive to maximum production of market goods, but also to produce a number of "public goods" valued by voters, such as national security, access to culture, and national prestige, which the market cannot provide. The EC has sought to fashion its trade relations with developing countries to create a number of such goods.

13.12.1 Maintenance of Good Regional Relations

The EC maintains a four-tier system of agreements with developing countries, granting them different degrees of preferential treatment. The strongest preference is granted to new entrants, under agreements preparing for entry to the Community. A complex system of regional and national treaties regulates relations with Mediterranean countries; the most important concession is that these countries' exports to the EC are not regulated by the Multifiber Agreement (MFA), but by informal agreements which have turned out to be more favorable than the MFA. The Lome countries, mostly African colonies, benefit under the Lome Convention from a slightly better treatment of manufactured exports than that provided for by the EC's Generalized System of Preferences (GSP). (Their exports were exempted from quantitative controls by the Lome I Convention, but this important advantage did not survive in Lome II.) Other developing countries benefit from the tariff quota system defined by the GSP.

This system is intended to promote stability in the region to which the EC belongs, and to promote the enlargement of the Community. It also maintains cultural and other ties which are valued by member countries, such as consolidating the "community of francophone countries."

13.12.2 Stabilizing Future Markets and
Supplies of Raw Materials

This system of agreements has also a more directly practical value in helping businessmen to retain the commercial advantages acquired when Western Europe dominated the Mediterranean and black Africa politically. The EC has tried to go further by having developing countries agree to guarantee its access to their raw materials, and to undertake not to nationalize its investments. This policy has been unsuccessful.

Finally (also unsuccessfully up to now) the EC has sought to promote via the "graduation principle" a process of integration of the more advanced developing countries into the constitutional framework of world trade by having them accept gradually the obligations imposed on the developed signatories of the GATT.

13.12.3 Diversification of Developing Countries' Exports of Manufactured Goods

The exports of developing countries have been distributed over an extremely narrow range of goods. A greater diversification would make it easier for producers in developed countries to adjust to the expected large growth of these exports. Promotion of such diversification is a "public good" to which public opinion in developed countries attributes a good deal of value.

This goal is pursued by both a very weak and a very strong instrument. The weak one works in favor of developing countries; the strong one is probably quite costly to them.

The weak instrument is the Generalized System of Preferences (GSP), which establishes duty-free quotas for manufactured goods exported by developing countries. The scheme distinguishes three categories: highly sensitive, sensitive, and nonsensitive goods, which are offered preferences scaled according to the degree of sensitivity.[5] The scheme, like the analogous schemes enforced by the United States, Japan, Sweden, and other countries seems in principle to be an ingenious way of fostering "infant exports" in developing countries while safeguarding the interests of the weaker sectors in the EC. For several reasons the scheme has made only a small contribution to achievement of its stated goal. Its provisions are complex and subject to yearly revisions, leading to an uncertainty and opaqueness which reduce its impact on investment in developing countries. Most of the easily produced goods which are the mainstay of the early phase of developing countries' export drives are "highly sensitive goods," poorly treated under the scheme and subject to the threat of MFA discrimination. Tariffs in developed countries are low anyway and have been getting lower. The evidence, econometric and otherwise, is that the EC GSP scheme, like the schemes designed by other trading nations, has had little impact on exports of manufactured goods from developing countries.

The negative instrument is the sword of Damocles hung over export-oriented investments of developing countries by the threat of discriminatory import quotas imposed as selective safeguards. Imposition of such quotas is possible under the EC MFA regulations, authorized as an exception to Article XIX of the GATT. The Community has pressed strongly in the Tokyo Round and subsequently for extending this exception to other goods under an appropriate code, and has threatened to impose selective safeguards even if agreement on such a code is not possible.

This ill-defined threat to future exports represents a powerful instrument of preventive protection, by discouraging investments which are hardly profitable, or even by discouraging timid (prudent?) developing countries from undertaking the sweeping and politically costly policy changes required by a switch from an import-substituting to an export-oriented trade strategy. It is likely that this threat has a considerable impact on the level and pattern of exports of developing countries in the direction sought by the EC.[6] To the extent that—as is highly probable—developing countries have felt driven to promote the export of goods for which their comparative advantage is less than for their traditional exports, the result is a (probably large) waste of resources.

13.13   Interest Groups, Their Objectives and Achievements

13.13.1   Producers of Textiles, Clothing, and Shoes

From the point of view of the political economy of protection, it is not immediately clear why lobbying for protection plays so large a role in the industrial strategy of the textiles and clothing sector. This industry has a very elastic long-run supply curve, so that protection has less impact on unit earnings of capital and labor than in most other industries. Entry is relatively easy; because of the sharp separation between the textile machinery producers and the textiles and clothing sector, and because of well-developed training programs for workers and staff, technology is available to anyone willing to enter the industry. Exit is easy too. A large number of firms obtain a very low return on assets even when the latter are valued at liquidation prices (textile machinery has a market, and much capital is tied up in inventories). The owners of such firms must be tempted to invest their money elsewhere, and indeed government-administered schemes, in the United Kingdom in particular, designed to bring about a shrinkage of productive capacity have identified readily enough producers who were willing to be bribed to cease production.

It is debatable how mobile labor is. To a significant extent the industry recruits its labor force in "pockets" of the labor market containing workers with low mobility who are willing to accept low wages: women in regions where female employment is low, young girls between high school and marriage, illegal immigrant workers sheltered from the police by the anonymity of big cities. On the other hand, labor turnover is typically high, so that the work force can be reduced by attrition with less social tension than in most other industries. Wages are very low, so that if other jobs can be created by market forces or "adjustment policies" or by widening job opportunities through better education, the workers who shift out of textiles will gain significantly. The industry finally requires few skills: little human capital is lost by workers who move to other sectors.

Yet it is elasticity of supply which from a deeper point of view accounts for the strong unity of the industry in support of protection. Textiles and clothing producers are deeply afraid of the competition of low-wage countries with their huge labor reserves and proven ability to expand output very quickly; their only hope for survival is to deny low-wage countries entry into markets in developed countries. This explains the paradox that an industry with an elastic supply curve, where the large number of producers and their diversity make it difficult to reach a common view, should have lobbied so hard for protection. What has welded the industry together is the feeling that producers in low-wage countries can destroy most of the textiles and clothing industry in the EC: not only is it marginal producers who feel threatened; even prosperous firms are afraid of going out of business.

This fear is excessive, because it does not allow for the great diversity of the industry. Large subsectors would indeed disappear—mostly those producing the "highly sensitive goods" of the EC MFA agreement regulations. But the fact that EC exports and imports are in rough balance shows that there are subsectors which can meet open competition. Clothing is competitively much weaker than textiles, but it should be remembered that effective tariffs on clothing are of the order of 20 percent in the EC, so that domestic producers would retain substantial protection even if MFA quantitative controls were relaxed. Technology is becoming more and more capital-intensive, reducing the impact of wage costs on output: for certain types of weaving one worker can tend some one hundred looms, and microelectronics is beginning to make possible automation of key operations in the clothing industry. Specialization is often an asset: German industrial textiles and carpet making on the "carpet freeway" in Flanders are strong and expanding subsectors. That adjustment to competition from low-wage countries is possible finally is shown by the example of the Swiss textiles industry. Despite very high wages, specialization has enabled this industry to survive, although Switzerland has not introduced quotas on imports from developing countries.

However exaggerated the fears of the industry, it is what it believes that has led it to wield its considerable power to force policymakers to supply the protection it believes to be needed. This power results to a significant extent from its size: the textile and clothing vote is very worthwhile competing for by any party—and the regional concentration of the industry provides it with the assured and loyal support in parliament of a number of members.

The weakness of trade unions does not handicap lobbying, to the extent that it reflects close personal contacts between owners and workers in the typically fairly small plants which characterize the industry. The resulting climate of cooperation has facilitated the formulation of common demands to government.

This lobbying proved decisive when in 1977, at a time of recession when developing countries were expanding rapidly their market shares in the Community, the EC drastically reinforced controls on textiles and clothing imports from low-wage countries through a set of voluntary export restraint (VER) agreements imposed under the second Multifiber Agreement (MFA II). The new system proved very effective, curbing import growth from 25 percent per year in volume in 1973–76 to 4 percent in 1976–79 for MFA countries. Rates of growth of imports from preferential countries have been marginally higher.

As similar measures were taken at the time by other developed countries, what happened was the establishment of a worldwide system of strongly discriminatory import controls against developing and Eastern bloc countries: developed countries have formed a kind of textiles and clothing common market to which the Third World has only limited access.[7] In equivalent tariff terms the external barriers are highly variable (and hence unnecessarily wasteful):[8] of the order of 100 percent for some articles of clothing, a few percent only for many textiles. Some German textiles firms have been able to export to Hong Kong, and for their products the equivalent tariff is zero. The welfare cost to consumers of these barriers is obviously high, particularly for low-income groups, as the comparative advantage of developing countries is greatest for the cheaper types of clothing.

A striking consequence of this system of worldwide discrimination was the trade diversion it has caused. In the EC, Italy has improved its net exports rapidly, at the expense of its northern neighbors. United States producers have likewise registered sharp gains, reflecting an edge in technology and marketing techniques, the fall of the dollar, and the availability of pockets of low-wage black and Hispanic labor.[9] Northern EC countries have gained a respite for their producers, who would have had to contract output more rapidly if protection had not been tightened. But as production and employment shrinks, this gain is diminishing; in fact, two such countries, Germany and the Netherlands, seem to have been achieving to a significant exent the purported goal of the MFA of shifting output to products which do not need protection. For these countries the advantage of continuing protection are shrinking, but the extra cost to the consumer of buying from high-cost sources is a permanent loss.

One of the sources of strength of the textiles lobby in the EC has been that the net exports of different countries were not too different. As Italy continues to gain—and as Greece, Spain, and Portugal join it to form a low-wage EC sunbelt—producers in the North will have to concentrate more and more on special articles and capital-intensive products which can meet competition from developing countries. Their interest in protection will decrease. At the same time the shift to export-oriented policies by a number of developing countries, in particular the influential countries of South Asia, will strengthen the hostility of the Group of 77 to the MFA. There are therefore hopes that the balance of negotiating forces which has generated the present system of protection will shift in favor of freer trade.

The synthetic fibers sector is undergoing a severe crisis in EC countries and has resorted to a cartel to deal with the situation. The Community at one time was inclined to give its blessing to this cartel, but decided to avoid so blatant a violation of the Rome Treaty. The cartel came into being anyway, and the Commission, with obviously ambiguous feelings, is watching and trying to moderate its action.

There was no "external component" to the original Davignon proposal of support to the cartel. As always trade distortions generate demands for government intervention, and synthetic fibers producers have recently been fighting hard for the external protection required to stabilize their cartel, arguing that energy price distortions in the United States give producers in that country an unfair competitive advantage; these demands benefit from a favorable political climate, because of EC resentment over the threatened imposition of antidumping duties on steel. We will not discuss further the details of this story of incipient escalation of distortions, intervention, and retaliation, as developing countries are not likely to become large exporters of synthetic fibers and yarn (those which have cheap energy, e.g., natural gas, may someday become exporters). The most interesting lesson from their point of view is the contrast between the interplay of effective threats and counterthreats between the United States and the EC, and their own inability to put up a fight in 1977 for fair treatment under the MFA.

Of greater immediate relevance is the leading role played by producers of synthetic and artificial fibers in support of protection of the textiles and and clothing industry. These producers have played a key role in the relevant lobby, providing it with a good deal of the basic analysis and data required to present a convincing case to policymakers. To some extent therefore producers in the higher stages of the industry, where output is not concentrated, have been free-riding on the lobbying effectiveness of a few highly concentrated primary producers who wish to help the downstream producers who absorb their output.

The EC shoe industry includes Italy, a low-cost producer, and will probably include Spain, which can be expected to recover a competitive strength sharply reduced by the social problems which have accompanied the move to democracy. Special quota protection is therefore not necessary. The shoe lobby is also much weaker than the textiles and clothing lobby. In the wake of the 1977 MFA negotiations, some European governments have, however, moved to impose VER agreements on the world's main shoe exporters.

13.13.2 Steel

The steel industry is almost a textbook illustration of the forces which bring about demands for protection. The elasticity of supply is low except in the long run, so that the industry can easily hold on to gains secured as a result of protection. The supply of capital is unresponsive to prices; almost none of the capital stock can be retrieved once production stops, as there is little variable capital and as most equipment cannot be moved. Prices would have to be a good deal higher to justify construction of new mills.

Labor is also not mobile. Much of the employment is in practice for life, so that it is hard to reduce the work force by attrition; work practices are rigid, for technical reasons and because of union resistance. Steelworkers are well paid, and often owe part of their income to special skills and seniority which would be lost if they changed jobs.

As in the textiles and clothing sector, the industry is welded together in its lobbying by realization that the adjustment effort which is required is large and unpleasant. Production fell by 20 percent from 1974 to 1975, and has hardly recovered since; EC countries, like the United States in earlier years, seem to have reached a stage of development where growth has little impact on the demand for steel. At the same time, technological progress is strongly biased toward equipment with a very large unit capacity. As a result, modernization tends to increase capacity; this tendency is reinforced by the efforts of trade unions and regional politicians to maintain employment, which leads them to press for plans which increase capacity. It is therefore very difficult to close the gap between a slowly increasing demand and a capacity growth which is hard to curb.

The prospect for closing this gap is worsened by the fact that in the long run the EC will probably not be able to maintain the level of its net exports. Japan's steel industry has obviously lower costs than do EC producers. In the last decades there has also been a marked shift in comparative advantage in favor of developing countries, because technical progress has reduced the need for special skills, key on door plants can now be acquired quite readily, and a number of developing countries have cheap energy (e.g., natural gas) and iron ore. Production in these countries is growing very fast, and a few are now exporters.

Rationalization of the EC steel industry finally requires a major geographical shift. This industry consists in reality of two very different parts. The older and larger component was built up close to sources of coal and iron ore which now have vanished or are more costly than imported materials. These factories, which were built at a time when the optimal scale of output was far smaller than today, have crowded plants which are not as conveniently laid out as in factories built on greenfield sites. Productivity is in many instances held back by work practices to which trade unions have been clinging in spite of the evolution of technology. During the long postwar years of prosperity they were well placed to resist technical changes which would have eliminated jobs. Opposition to rationalization has continued in the recession, with less success.

Costs are lower in the modern and efficient plants built on the seacoast. These embody the latest technology and process low-cost imported materials.[10] These producers seem to have weathered the recession successfully. A broad long-term shift of the industry to the coast would, however, cause considerable political resistance in the older steel-making areas, except of course in countries like Holland or Italy, where the industry is already there.

This brings us finally to a discussion of the strength of the steel lobby, which has a remarkable record of achievement in milking governments for special benefits. Steel making is a highly concentrated industry, with very strong unions and a concentration of employment in limited areas. It enjoys a peculiar prestige as a symbol of industrialization. These advantages have enabled the industry in postwar years to enjoy privileged access to low-interest loans and grants to nationalized companies. When the recession started, some governments, e.g., Belgium and France, virtually opened their pockets to steel makers to enable them to cover their losses (leading after a few years to nationalization, the ultimate subsidy). The confidence of the industry in its power to extract money from the government was illustrated in 1980 by the United Kingdom steel strike, in which workers quite rightly never doubted that the government would pay up their wage claims.

The main limit to the drive for protection of the steel lobby is that its interests are opposed to those of the much larger metal-working industry. It obviously makes no sense to shelter steel from a needed adjustment at the expense of losses of jobs and exports in the automobile, shipbuilding, and other large steel-using sectors which also have difficulty in meeting outside competition. Steel users understand their need for access to low-price raw materials and have enough lobbying power to moderate protection of their supplies of steel.[11] It is not surprising, for example, to find that Germany, the largest exporter of metal products, has been insisting firmly on a strong link between the renewal of the current steel protection scheme and continuing progress in rationalizing output.

The EC's response to these pressures has been to back a recession cartel. Under the Davignon Plan and later through the imposition of production controls under Article 58 of the ECSC Treaty, producers have been pressed to respect minimum price and production guidelines; the plan, which is supported by VER agreements with other steel producers (including some developing countries), is in practice part of a worldwide recession cartel. As for the MFA II agreement, the EC scheme is a component of a scheme enforced by the cooperation and joint power of developed countries.

Whether this protection will become permanent is uncertain at present. The EC, which runs highly protectionist Common Agricultural and (via the MFA) Common Textile Policies, may find that it has fathered a third highly restrictive system, holding up domestic prices and dumping surpluses on world markets. This would be disadvantageous to developing countries, whose steel expansion would be thwarted by EC dumping, and to the EC metal-using industry.

Ending this steel protection hinges on successful rationalization of the industry. And in fact rationalization has made creditable progress. Governments and employers have in the last two years not hesitated to confront trade unions on the issue of productivity and production cutbacks, forcing through employment cuts in spite of major strikes in the Federal Republic of Germany, France, and the United Kingdom. It appears that there is a definite possibility that the Common Market steel industry will not follow the pattern of gradual permanent isolation from world markets which seems to be establishing itself in the United States. The main uncertainty lies in the EC's ability to force through the cuts in production capacity which are required to reestablish balance between supply and demand, as is needed to make it possible to abolish the plan.

Marked progress can be expected in the next few years from scrapping uneconomic plants, increasing productivity in others through rationalization, eliminating excess capacity, and reducing energy costs by continuous casting and other means. In the longer run a change in the regional balance of the industry is required, with a shift of basic steelmaking processes to the coast and perhaps even to countries with cheap energy (Australia? the Middle East?). This will be difficult to achieve in a declining and politically powerful industry.

13.13.3 Shipbuilding

Shipbuilding like steel is an excellent example of an industry which can gain significantly from protection and has natural advantages in pressing the government for favors.

The industry is not capital-intensive. Unlike steel there is appreciable freedom of entry. The inelasticity of supply results rather from the need to keep production going to keep together a crucial core of engineers and skilled workers.

Some shipyards are in large harbor cities like Hamburg, Rotterdam, and Antwerp, where alternative employment opportunities are numerous, but a large fraction of the capacity is in depressed areas of Scotland and Brittany.

Demand for ships fell sharply after 1973, as it is geared to the rate of increase of world trade, and in particular of shipments of oil. For a time activity was sustained by order backlogs; but the ships which were launched thus added to the excess supply which had to be absorbed before recovery became possible.

The industry confronts the most unpleasant adjustment of all: extinction. Apart from a few specialized yards, notably those building warships, it appears that shipbuilding will die out. In spite of generous subsidies and of creditable efforts to overcome the rigid work practice rules which prevented modernization of the industry, especially in the United Kingdom, EC shipbuilders could take only a small fraction of the increased orders generated by the 1978–79 recovery in demand. Japan is by an overwhelming margin the dominant builder today, but a number of developing countries such as Korea, Brazil, and India have shown themselves capable of exporting ships at competitive prices. Developing countries have a comparative advantage in a sector where the capital output ratio is low and where the need for skilled labor can be reduced through prefabrication. To the extent that Japan loses part of the market it will be to the benefit of the Third World, not of Europe.

The shipbuilding industry has organized very effectively to win favors from governments. Like steel it is endowed with a mysterious prestige, which has helped in persuading the authorities to set up intricate schemes to promote construction of merchant ships in home shipyards. The strength of the powerful unions has been helpful from this point of view.

Like steel, the action of the shipbuilding lobbyists has to take account of the countervailing demands of their client, the shipping industry. In fact the structure of the shipping industry makes it almost impossible to promote shipbuilding by tariffs or quotas, prohibiting the use of these classical tools of trade policy. Shipping is par excellence a world market activity. There is little point in protecting domestic shipbuilders by tariffs, as national shipping firms would simply buy elsewhere. Forcing them to buy at home would be pointless, given the ease with which capital can emigrate and escape governmental control by the flags of convenience device. It is for this reason that protection of shipbuilding has been extended almost always through subsidies rather than through tariffs and quotas. The subsidies were sometimes quite indirect, such as the obligation to carry United States aid on ships flying the American flag, which channeled to national shipping and shipbuilding firms a part of the aid intended for developing counries.

Protection of shipbuilding has therefore been the responsibility of governments. The Community's role has depended on its power to regulate aids and subsidies and to approve mergers; its efforts have curbed somewhat the absurdly generous aids granted by member countries. The EC has nevertheless proposed a Community scrap and build scheme to bring about a resurgence of demand. The response of governments to this plan has not been enthusiastic, and it is doubtful that it will get off the ground.

Discussions of that plan illustrate the difficulty of getting support for protection in the EC when the costs and benefits are not balanced between countries. In this instance the proposal was killed by the objections of Germany—where the shipbuilding industry has shrunk very sharply—and Denmark.

13.14   Conclusions

We embarked on this case study as a way of verifying the empirical validity and usefulness of the political economy of protection approach to the study of trade policy. Our feeling is that the experiment was successful. The approach enabled us to classify facts and events in an interesting and suggestive way, and to illuminate reality convincingly. Its main weaknesses appear to be as follows:

a) It neglects complications resulting from the fact that trade policy decisions are taken at several levels, that many decisions may be taken jointly, rather than *one* tariff being set by *the* government. In fact it would be worthwhile to analyze rigorously from a theoretical point of view why decisions taken simultaneously at higher decision levels tend to be more liberal than the blow-by-blow decisions of the government bureaus.

b) Trade adjustment assistance is not a useful concept empirically, because of the difficulty in determining whether agents' problems are due to trade or to other forces, and because it is so easy to use adjustment schemes to grant subsidies.

c) It may be worth stressing even more than is done by the political economy of protection the enormous difference in accuracy and timeliness of the information on protection which is available to lobbies as opposed to general voters. The EC has made laudable efforts to explain the reasons for its decisions; the performance of the United States government in this respect is, however, markedly better. The information distributed by governments on subsidies and protection is abysmally poor. Even members of the administration find it well nigh impossible to keep track of what is decided.

d) We have been surprised to realize to what extent, from the Davignon Plan to the Tokyo Round, from the GSP to the MFA, trade policy is made today at the world rather than at the national or EC level. This also is a fact that the political economy of protection has overlooked.

The most important policy conclusions are not unexpected:

a) Study of the record confirms the fear that—with MFA II and the Davignon Plan—the EC is sliding into permanent support of an increasing number of "Common Restrictive Policies." Experience with the

Common Agricultural Policy illustrates the way in which distortions lead to remedial measures and thence to further distortions, leading to disputes which undermine European unity. Hopefully, the danger will be perceived in time.

b) Under MFA II a "Common Textile Policy" embraces the developed world; developing countries rightly perceive that the EC insistence on selective safeguards aims at legalizing this way of organizing world trade under the GATT. De facto the selective safeguards discrimination against developing countries is of course already widely applied, without significant resistance from the Group of 77.

c) There are, however, hopeful signs that public opinion is getting less receptive to proposals for intervention in favor of particular industries. It has seen that the measures adopted in recent years did not lead to the hoped for results and that not adopting other proposals did not lead to the announced catastrophes. In a nutshell, voters are in effect becoming reassured about the flexibility of the economic system. If this evolution of thinking continues—and if the business cycle situation does not deteriorate catastrophically—there may be hope of easing MFA controls and discarding the Davignon Plan.

Notes

1. Adjustment assistance will of course also cause some waste, except if it takes the form of lump-sum transfers. But this waste is likely to be small and is temporary.

2. The brave scheme introduced by the Dutch government to help adjustment by enterprises affected by import competition from developing countries was a failure. The scheme was little used and has in practice been abandoned.

3. By the same token, the Ministry of Foreign Affairs is commonly the most free-trade-oriented body within the administration, because of its unique exposure to the points of view of other countries.

4. In particular, in the recent spate of work on rational expectations.

5. For nonsensitive goods, there is no quota; however, if exports grow substantially, these goods are transferred to the "sensitive" or "highly sensitive" categories for which the amounts which can be sold free of duty are limited.

6. And other industrial countries which have pursued similar policies.

7. The system has roots in looser import control schemes going back to 1962.

8. Assuming linear supply and demand curves, the welfare cost is proportional to the square of the rate of protection. It is therefore desirable to avoid sharp tariff disparities in policies of trade restriction.

9. And, for synthetic fibers, low energy costs.

10. The price of which has, however, been distorted by input levies designed to protect domestic coal against foreign competition.

11. Naturally, they have no reason to object to subsidies.

References

Blancus, P. 1978. The common agricultural policy and the balance of payments of the EEC member countries. Banca Nazionale di Lavoro, December.

Caves, R. E. 1976. Economic models of political choice, Canada's tariff structure. *Canadian Journal of Economics*, May.

Helleiner, G. K. 1977. The political economy of Canada's tariff structure, an alternative model. *Canadian Journal of Economics*, May.

Keesing, D. B., and M. Wolf. 1980. Textile quotas against developing countries. Trade Policy Research Center.

Kohler, B. 1980. Decision making and the enlargement of the EC. Paper presented to the Conference on Southern Europe and the Enlargement of the EC. Lisbon, May.

Messerlin, P. 1979. The market for protection: A tentative study of the French case. Université de Paris Working Paper 7. Forthcoming in *Weltwirtschaftliches Archiv*.

Peacock, A., and associates. 1980. Structural economic policies in West Germany and the UK. Anglo German Foundation.

Pincus, J. P. 1975. Pressure groups and the structure of tariffs. *Journal of Political Economy*, August.

Noelke, M., and R. Taylor. 1981. EEC protection: Present practice and future trends. European Research Associates.

Strasser, D. 1980. The Finances of Europe. European Steel and Coal Community.

Tovias, A. 1977. *Tariff preferences and Mediterranean diplomacy*. Macmillan.

Walter, I. 1979. Protection of industries in trouble, the case of steel. *World Economy*, May.

Yeats, A. J. 1979. Trade barriers facing developing countries. Working Paper of the Institute for International Economy, Stockholm. To be published by UNCTAD.

Comment William R. Cline

Verreydt and Waelbroeck have prepared an excellent summary assessment of current European protection against manufactured imports from developing countries. They have found the same pattern that exists in the

William R. Cline is a Senior Fellow at the Institute for International Economics, Washington, D.C. His publications on international and development economics include *Trade Negotiations in the Tokyo Round* (1978, coauthor), *International Monetary Reform and the Developing Countries* (1976), and *Potential Effects of Income Redistribution on Economic Growth* (1972).

United States: these imports are highly concentrated in a few product sectors, causing problems of domestic adjustment even though their aggregate level is minor. The sectors are generally the same as in the United States: textiles and clothing, shoes, and television sets, although for Europe (but not for the United States) LDC competition is also a conspicuous problem in shipbuilding.

The authors believe they can identify a slowdown in protectionism in Europe. They cite the public's fatigue with costly industrial subsidy programs and the pressure from Germany for a free trade policy. The optimist might reach the same conclusion for the United States, but for a different reason: anti-inflationary concern. In the past two years the administration has resisted demands for automobile protection, rejected International Trade Commission recommendations to protect leather wearing apparel and extend shoe quotas to Italy, and abolished the trigger price mechanism for steel. The President has repeatedly cited the need to reduce inflation in these and other actions resisting protection. Nevertheless, it may be premature to declare even interim victory for open trade. The atmosphere is heavy with protectionist pressures, and recession will make matters worse. The renewal of the Multifiber Agreement in 1980 will be a major test of the force of protectionism.

Verreydt and Waelbroeck offer several perceptive thoughts on the political economy of protection. They remind us that the more advanced developing countries may have a vested interest in quota regimes that insulate them from newcomer competition; that the inattention of LDCs to trade in the North-South dialogue reflects the high concentration of manufactured exports among a few LDCs; and that Europe is embarking on an integration of the Mediterranean countries that will by itself be a large adjustment, making the prospects dimmer for digesting still further growth in manufactured imports from the Third World. They also discourage any illusions that meaningful planning for adjustment exists on an EC–wide basis, suggesting that Europe is not as far ahead of the United States in this area as one might think.

I have some doubts about the paper's statement that manufactured exports from developing countries have approximately equal penetration in the EC and United States markets but lower penetration in Japan. Estimates in a current Brookings project using United Nations trade and output data for 1976 show average penetration ratios of 2.24 percent for the United States, 2.43 percent for Japan, and a range from 1.89 percent for France to 2.88 percent for the United Kingdom. These and other measures suggest that penetration is no lower in Japan than in the United States and Europe, and that the range of variation among individual European countries is relatively high. Except perhaps within Europe, no individual nation appears holier than any other.

On textiles, the authors make the interesting point that the sector's low-wage, unskilled labor is easier to shift than would be high-wage, specially trained workers in other sectors such as automobiles and steel. The reverse argument is usually made in the United States; there is a tendency to assume, as Baldwin does in chapter 10 of this volume, that labor adjustment is more difficult for the low-wage, unskilled workers. In the American case it is usually added that textile workers tend to be aged, female, black, and located in rural towns, reducing flexibility. But it is an interesting theoretical question whether labor mobility in general is positively or negatively related to skill and wage level, as the influences of skill specificity and worker expectations play off against different unemployment rates by skill level.

The paper's discussion of textiles would be improved by a more direct separation of textiles from apparel. The textile industry tries to keep the two sectors together in order to evoke sympathy for protection, but in fact imports are a problem only for apparel. The EC has a substantial trade surplus in textiles, but is has had a rapidly growing deficit in apparel; for the United States, trade is roughly in balance for textiles but shows a large deficit in apparel. Moreover, technological change has been able to strengthen United States competitiveness in textiles, but the same solution is unlikely to be feasible in labor-intensive apparel.

The paper's discussion of footwear leaves out an important point: most of Europe's import problems appear to come from Italy and other Mediterranean nations, not developing countries. The Brookings estimates find LDC penetration ratios of 10 percent in the American market for nonrubber footwear but approximately 3 percent in Germany and the United Kindgom and less than half a percent in Italy.

The discussion of steel raises another important issue: much of recent protectionist conflict has been among the industrial countries, not between North and South. The paper gives the impression of a cozy cartel within the North against steel from the South, but the real conflict in steel has been among the United States, Europe, and Japan. LDC exports in steel remain marginal, although their import substitution has affected exports from the North. Another issue raised by the case of steel is that of distortions from state firms in trade. With state ownership of steel in much of Europe, already complicated issues in dumping and countervailing duties become all the more complex and subject to charges of unfair trade practices on both sides of the Atlantic.

For policy purposes, the study could have given much more emphasis to the Safeguards Code. Inability to reach agreement on this code was the largest failure of the Tokyo Round from the standpoint of the developing countries. The authors suggest the EC should not be so reluctant to agree because they can impose voluntary export restraints in any case, but a major United States objective in the code was to place international discipline on VERs. Verreydt and Waelbroeck do leave some room for hope, as they note that the EC is prepared to give up some of its present protective flexibility in exchange for international legitimacy now lacking under the restrictions imposed largely outside the GATT.

The paper's somewhat cynical view of adjustment assistance does not follow even if it does not move workers out of industries or retrain them, because, at a minimum, adjustment assistance is an income transfer to workers in industries affected by imports, and such a transfer is socially efficient when it enables politicians to adopt trade liberalization that provides larger benefits to the rest of the community. Quite apart from politics, adjustment assistance viewed as a transfer follows the welfare economics principle that compensation must actually be paid to the losers if we are to say that actual welfare has improved from efficiency gains through freer trade. In the United States, changes in the 1974 act made this transfer much larger (and indeed opened it to nongermane use for unemployment due to recession largely unrelated to trade, as in the case of autoworkers in 1980), although hopefully there is still room to make adjustment assistance play an adjustment as well as a transfer role. Finally, the assertion that exchange rates are used for protection sounds outdated. We are no longer in the interwar period of competitive devaluation but in an environment where in the fight against inflation, industrial countries often seek to avoid devaluation rather than promote it for mercantile reasons. To be sure, there are signs that Germany and especially Japan tried to moderate appreciation in 1977–78, but they intervened massively to avert devaluation against the dollar in 1979–80.

Overall, the state of protection in Europe and the United States raises two broad questions of trade strategy. For the North, the question is whether we are going to create more and more pockets of industries insulated from LDC competition and sustain them more or less indefinitely despite their inefficiency, as we have done for textiles and apparel and are on the road to doing for footwear and television sets. For the South, the question is whether to rely on traditional comparative advantage and as a result confront stiff protection in labor-intensive industries, or instead follow a second-best strategy, pursuing a whole range of other products with much less product concentration, but also less comparative advantage, than in the past.

Comment   Gene M. Grossman

The interesting paper by Verreydt and Waelbroeck raises the question of how much of the adjustment in various industries in the EC has been necessitated by competition from imports from non–EC, and particularly

Gene M. Grossman is assistant professor of economics and international affairs at Princeton University.

less developed, countries. In any dynamic, open economy resource allocations between sectors have many proximate causes, including differences in the rates of accumulation of alternative factors of production, which may effect changes in relative factor prices, and therefore in relative costs of production; differences in the income elasticities of demand across goods; differences in the rates of technological progress across sectors; and differences in the extent of trade competition that arise from changes in the structure of world production and demand. As a microeconomic phenomenon, import competition becomes potentially problematic if the short-run dislocations of labor that are associated with shifts in the foreign supply curve are large relative to those caused by other economic factors.

Much recent research has been devoted to assessing the effect of import competition on employment. The overriding conclusion of investigations of many countries (many of them nicely reviewed in Martin 1979) is that historically the changes in employment that have been "caused" by import competition have been miniscule in comparison to those associated with the other causes mentioned above, and in particular technological progress. Indeed, Verreydt and Waelbroeck subscribe to this view in their discussion of the textile and clothing industry in the EC. Often the inference is then drawn, and has been disseminated by influential organizations (e.g., IBRD President McNamara's recent speeches), that the costs of structural adjustment to changes in comparative advantage are small—absolutely, and in relation to other dynamic adjustment costs that must be borne in a growing economy. This leads to the conclusion that protection from import competition is *not* justified if it is to be based on adjustment cost calculations. While this may in fact be correct, I believe that the methodology used by many previous researchers to allocate changes in sectoral employment to their various causes is inappropriate and does not allow these writers to draw their strong conclusions.

Most writers have employed an accounting framework that has been developed, apparently by Karsten Laursen, to examine the extent to which imports have been responsible for adverse trends in employment in particular industries. Recent studies using this approach by Krueger (1980) and Frank (1977) on the United States, Cable (1977, 1978) on the United Kingdom, and Wolter (1977) on West Germany have been unanimous in their findings that "technological progress" has been a much more important determinant of employment shifts than has import competition. I base my criticism of this approach obviously not on the validity of the identity on which it is based, but rather on its interpretation.

The authors (see, for instance, Krueger 1980) define $a = Y/L$, the average productivity of labor, and $S = Y/C$, the share of domestic output in apparent consumption. They then write the identity $L \equiv CS/a$, and log differentiate to obtain

(1) $\hat{L} = \hat{C} + \hat{S} - \hat{a}.$

Finally, they collect data for two observations on each variable and attribute changes in employment to consumption growth, import competition, and technological progress, respectively. In almost all cases in which employment has been observed to fall, they find that $\hat{C}$ is relatively large and positive, $\hat{S}$ is negative, but small, and $\hat{a}$ does all the work in "explaining" the change in employment. The authors qualify their findings slightly by suggesting that consumption growth and technical progress may not be exogenous to import competition, if for example a shift in the foreign supply curve allows increased consumption of the good or spurs technical progress domestically.

My objection concerns the interpretation of changes in the average product of labor as reflecting "technological progress." Consider a competitive industry that produces according to a CES production function that is augmented by Hicks-neutral technological progress (labor-saving technological progress would alter the detail, but not the thrust of the argument),

(2) $$Y = e^{\pi t}(\alpha L^{-\rho} + (1 - \alpha)K^{-\rho})^{-1/\rho}.$$

Profit maximization implies

(3) $$\frac{w}{p} = \frac{\alpha}{e^{\pi(1-\sigma)t/\sigma}}(\frac{Y}{L})^{1/\sigma}.$$

Note that equation (3) holds as a first-order approximation for any production function, and nothing in the discussion hinges on the use of a CES production function. Finally, log differentiation of (3) gives

(4) $$\hat{a} = \frac{\hat{Y}}{L} = \sigma(\frac{\hat{w}}{p}) + \pi(1 - \sigma).$$

Only if $\sigma = 0$ (fixed-coefficient technology) can we associate changes in the average product of labor exclusively with technological progress. In fact, for a Cobb-Douglas production function ($\sigma = 1$), the average product is *independent* of the technology parameter (π).

Now, consider a small industry for which the product price is determined on the international market (i.e., $p = Ep^*$, where p^* is the foreign currency price of the imported good and E is the exchange rate). If a shift in the foreign supply curve (or the exchange rate) causes Ep^* to fall, this will cause an increase in the average product of labor in the domestic industry, provided that a fall in w does not completely offset the fall in p. It is therefore impossible to attribute changes in the average product of labor to technical progress rather than to import competition, once we admit the possibility of movements along isoquants in addition to shifts in isoquants.

How then can we measure the effect of import competition on sectoral employment? Unfortunately, there is no short cut that satisfactorily averts the need for specification and estimation of an econometric model that simultaneously determines employment and imports. If all one is interested in is the ultimate effect of various variables on employment, it may be possible to resort to reduced-form estimation, thereby sidetracking some of the difficult data problems that plague empirical trade research. However, methodologies that promise answers while avoiding estimation completely must ultimately be based on the assumption of the exogeneity of important economic variables.

References

Cable, V. 1977. British protectionism and LDC imports. *ODI Review*, no. 2, pp. 29–48.

————. 1978. Sources of employment displacement in U.K. industries competing with LDC imports. Overseas Development Institute, mimeographed, April.

Frank, C. R., Jr. 1977. *Foreign trade and domestic aid*. Washington: Brookings Institution.

Krueger, A. O. 1980. Protectionist pressures, imports, and employment in the United States. NBER Working Paper no. 461, March.

Martin, J. P. 1979. Measuring the employment effects of changes in trade flows: A survey of recent research. In OECD Secretariat, *The impact of the newly industrializing countries on production and trade in manufactures*. Paris: OECD.

Wolter, F. 1977. Adjusting to imports from developing countries: The evidence from a human capital rich–natural resource poor country. In H. Giersch, ed., *Reshaping the world economic order*. Tubingen: Mohr.

Contributors

C. Michael Aho
Office of Financial Economic
  Research
Department of Labor
Washington, D.C. 20210

Robert E. Baldwin
Department of Economics
University of Wisconsin
Madison, Wisconsin 53706

Jagdish N. Bhagwati
Department of Economics
Columbia University
New York, New York 10027

Richard A. Brecher
Department of Economics
Carleton University
Ottawa, Ontario
Canada

Michael Bruno
Department of Economics
Hebrew University
Jerusalem
Israel

John S. Chipman
Department of Economics
University of Minnesota
Minneapolis, Minnesota 55455

William R. Cline
Brookings Institution
Washington, D.C. 20036

Peter A. Diamond
Department of Economics
MIT
Cambridge, Massachusetts 02139

Avinash Dixit
Woodrow Wilson School of Public
  and International Affairs
Princeton University
Princeton, New Jersey 08544

Ronald P. Dore
Center for European Studies
University of Sussex
Brighton, Sussex BN1 9RE
England

Robert C. Feenstra
Department of Economics
Columbia University
New York, New York 10027

Ronald Findlay
Department of Economics
Columbia University
New York, New York 10027

Gene M. Grossman
Woodrow Wilson School of Public
    and International Affairs
Princeton University
Princeton, New Jersey 08544

Paul Krugman
Department of Economics
MIT
Cambridge, Massachusetts 02139

Kelvin Lancaster
Department of Economics
Columbia University
New York, New York 10027

Stephen P. Magee
Department of Finance
Business School
University of Texas
Austin, Texas 78712

Michael Mussa
Graduate School of Business
University of Chicago
Chicago, Illinois 60637

J. Peter Neary
Department of Political Economy
University College
Belfield, Dublin 4
Ireland

J. David Richardson
Department of Economics
University of Wisconsin
Madison, Wisconsin 53706

Carlos Alfredo Rodríguez
C.E.M.A.
Virrey del Pino 3210
Buenos Aires 1426
Argentina

Alasdair Smith
Department of Economics
Sussex University
Brighton, Sussex BN1 9RE
England

Eric Verreydt
c/o Jean Waelbroeck
CORE
C.P. 135
Avenue F.-D. Roosevelt, 50
1050 Brussels
Belgium

Jean Waelbroeck
CORE
C.P. 135
Avenue F.-D. Roosevelt, 50
1050 Brussels
Belgium

Stanislaw Wellisz
Department of Economics
Columbia University
New York, New York 10027

Martin Wolf
Trade Policy Research Centre
1, Gough Square
London EC4A 3DE
England

Leslie Young
Department of Finance
Business School
University of Texas
Austin, Texas 78712

Author Index

403

Subject Index